SACRED SPRING

SACRED SPRING

God and the Birth of Modernism
in Fin de Siècle Vienna

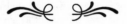

ROBERT WELDON WHALEN

William B. Eerdmans Publishing Company

Grand Rapids, Michigan / Cambridge, U.K.

Published 2007 by
Wm. B. Eerdmans Publishing Co.
2140 Oak Industrial Drive N.E., Grand Rapids, Michigan 49505 /
P.O. Box 163, Cambridge CB3 9PU U.K.

Printed in the United States of America

12 11 10 09 08 07   7 6 5 4 3 2 1

Library of Congress Cataloging-in-Publication Data

Whalen, Robert Weldon, 1950-
Sacred spring: God and the birth of modernism in fin de siècle Vienna /
Robert Weldon Whalen.
p.   cm.
Includes bibliographical references.
ISBN 978-0-8028-3216-0 (cloth: alk. paper)
1. Modernism (Christian theology) 2. Vienna (Austria) —
Intellectual life — 19th century.   I. Title

BT82.W53   2007
943.6'130441 — dc22

2006103518

www.eerdmans.com

For Meg,
My best friend and soulmate,
A souvenir from our Vienna

CONTENTS

THANKS   ix

Overture   1

1. *Fairy Tale City*   21

2. *Necropolis*   58

3. *Resurrection*   94

4. *Dreams and Visions*   124

5. *Hieroglyphs*   149

6. *The Feminine Divine*   187

7. *The Uncanny*   218

8. *The Artists' Hour*   245

9. *Song of the Earth*   277

Finale   304

BIBLIOGRAPHY   316

INDEX   325

THANKS

I owe many people many thanks.

As the notes and bibliography demonstrate, I have benefited from the work of several generations of scholars, and I am in their debt. If somehow I have failed to give credit where credit is due, the fault is entirely mine; I apologize in advance, and will make every effort to correct any oversights.

Many archivists and librarians have cheerfully given me invaluable help. I want to thank in particular the staff of the Wienbibliothek im Rathaus, the Vienna City Library, where much of the research for this book was done, and the librarians of my own Everett Library, here at Queens University of Charlotte.

My Queens colleagues deserve many thanks too, especially my fellow historians: Suzanne Cooper Guasco; Mollie Davis; Henry Kamerling; Norris Preyer; Charles Reed; and William Thompson. Carolyn G. and Sam H. McMahon generously endowed the professorship which provided much of the financial support for this book's research. I also want to thank Queens President Pamela Lewis Davies; Vice-President J. Norris Frederick; Dean Betty Powell; and Chairman F. William Vandiver Jr. and the Queens Board of Trustees for providing me with the time I needed to finish this project.

I would like to thank the Eerdmans team who brought this book along from manuscript to monograph, especially Jon Pott, vice-president and editor-in-chief; Linda Bieze, managing editor; my editor, David Bratt; Klaas Wolterstorff, who designed the book's layout, and Willem Mineur, who designed the cover. I want to thank them all heartily for their great patience and professional skill.

I began this book long before our three children, James, Julia, and Cecilia were born; now that they're big and this book is finished, I hope they can find in it a little of the magic their mom and dad found in Vienna.

This book is for Meg. Many years ago, when we were first married, Meg and I had our own "moveable feast" in Vienna. Meg studied music; I studied the fin de siècle; we were very poor but very happy. We've been with the characters in this book so long that they've become our great friends. Lots has changed since those days, but one of the miracles about mysterious Vienna is that it never fades away. And so this book, a souvenir of our Vienna, is for Meg, with my thanks and my love.

OVERTURE

There are no people however primitive without religion and magic.

Bronislaw Malinowski[1]

We are the stuff of Viennese dreams, we moderns. To be sure, we sometimes delude ourselves by calling ourselves "postmoderns," but as Philippa Berry writes, "our thinking is still positioned as it was at the very beginning of the twentieth century." "Much intellectual activity," Berry argues, "continues to occupy the disturbing twilight zone which was evoked by Nietzsche in 1888 in *The Twilight of the Idols*; that indeterminate moment which ostensibly marks the limit of the bright day of the Enlightenment."[2] The modernist experiment, launched at the end of the nineteenth century and the beginning of the twentieth century, and postponed by the catastrophes of the latter, has only just begun. What we label "postmodern" — uncertainty, bricolage, fluidity, iconoclasm, a frightening strain of nihilism, crass materialism, a yearning for the spirit — is better thought of as "modern," as part of that vast experiment from the last fin de siècle only now returning to life.

1. Bronislaw Malinowski, *Magic, Science, and Religion* (New York: Doubleday, 1954), 17.
2. Philippa Berry, in *Shadow of the Spirit: Postmodernism and Religion*, ed. Philippa Berry and Andrew Wernick (New York: Routledge, 1992), 1.

The turn of the last century was, as Stephen Kern has written, a time when "a cultural revolution of the broadest scope was taking place, one that involved essential structures of human experience and basic forms of human expression."[3] The work of the Viennese avant-garde was central to this cultural revolution; one hardly need argue that Freud, Mahler, Schoenberg, Klimt, Schiele, Kokoschka, Loos, and Otto Wagner were central figures in the creation of "modernism." A symbol perhaps of Vienna's role: in 1898, a Viennese doctor made a film of a "surgically exposed, pulsating human heart."[4] It was in the brilliant and dying Habsburg Empire that one could, more than anywhere else, feel two of the great issues of early modernism, "the disintegration of the self and the temporality of tradition."[5] Peter Berner and his colleagues, in their survey of Vienna in 1900, argue that the "20th century was created in Vienna."[6] In Vienna around 1900, Otto Breicha and Gerhard Fritsch write, "twentieth century consciousness first evolved and was first expressed, a consciousness cryptic; dependent, not autonomous; and alone in the face of the absurd."[7] Again, Gerhard Fritsch:

> The glimmering twilight; the flashes from an outwardly intact but actually fracturing social hierarchy; the morbid fascination of a dying world; the unreal pomp of the last act of old Europe, symbolized in the Habsburg Empire, through whose crooked alleys, beneath gas lanterns, crept Kafka-like figures pursued by their nightmares — all this exerted a remarkable attraction on the sensibilities of the latter half of the century.[8]

3. Stephen Kern, *The Culture of Time and Space* (Cambridge: Harvard University Press, 1983), 1.

4. Kern, *The Culture of Time and Space*, 143.

5. Giuliano Baioni, "Zionism, Literature, and the Yiddish Theater," in Mark Anderson, ed., *Reading Kafka* (New York: Schocken, 1989), 101.

6. Peter Berner, Emil Brix, and Wolfgang Mantl, eds., *Wien um 1900. Aufbruch in die Moderne* (Vienna: Verlag für Geschichte und Politik, 1986), 11.

7. Otto Breicha and Gerhard Fritsch, *Finale und Auftakt. Wien 1898-1914* (Salzburg: Otto Müller, 1964), 5.

8. Gerhard Fritsch, "Die Wirbel der Sprache führen ins Bodenlose," in Breicha and Fritsch, *Finale*, 9.

But wasn't modernism invented in Paris? Yes indeed, and in Berlin, London, and New York too. But Vienna must be considered, if not the only birthplace of modernism, one of the birthplaces. Wolfgang Fischer, writing about Gustav Klimt, remarks that, with Paris and Berlin, Vienna is something of a "third Athens" of the twentieth century; and maybe, Fischer speculates, at the turn of the twenty-first century, "Kafkaesque Vienna" will finally be recognized as the "true diamond" of the last century.[9] Historian Norman Stone writes that it was in Vienna "that most of the twentieth century intellectual world was invented. Practically in every field, from music to nuclear physics, Austro-Hungarian subjects were leaders." Michale Pollack agrees that Vienna was one of the "cradles of the modern" in almost every area,[10] and Jean Améry speaks of turn-of-the-century Vienna as the "world capital of the spirit."[11] Martin Swales, writing about Arthur Schnitzler, comments that "it is remarkable how many corner-stones of modernity were laid in Austria around the turn of the century."[12] The modern century of Freud was born in Freud's Vienna. Among modernism's primal creators was the fin de siècle Viennese avant-garde, and we moderns are their children. In this sense we moderns are the stuff of Viennese dreams.

But, as Allan Janik and Stephen Toulmin ask, "is it simply an accident that the beginnings of twelve-tone music, 'modern' architecture . . . abstract painting, and psychoanalysis all had their beginnings at the same time, and that all of them arose in Vienna?"[13] They certainly don't think so. Like other historians, they argue that Vienna's distinctive culture, its specific moment in time, its oddities and failings, gave rise to "modernism." All of which is true, of course, but one more point is needed.

Classic modernism is the product of Viennese dreams. And these Viennese dreams were sacred dreams.

9. Wolfgang Georg Fischer, *Gustav Klimt und Emilie Flöge* (Vienna: Christian Brandstätter, 1987) 11.

10. Cited in Wolfgang Mantl, "Wien um 1900 — ein goldener Stachel," in Berner, *Wien,* 249.

11. Welan, "Hauptstadt," in Berner, *Wien,* 39.

12. Martin Swales, *Arthur Schnitzler: A Critical Study* (Oxford: Clarendon, 1971), 21.

13. Allan Janik and Stephen Toulmin, *Wittgensteins Wien,* trans. Reinhard Merkel (Munich: Carl Hanser, 1984), 21.

Viennese modernism, I want to argue, was at root a religious phenomenon. It witnessed to what Paul Tillich would call a moment of "kairos," a "fulfilled time" in which the "Other" intruded into human space and time. Modernism arose because God visited Vienna.

"There are no people however primitive without religion and magic," Bronislaw Malinowski wrote,[14] and one might add, neither are people, no matter how modern, without religion and magic.

But isn't it true that an insistent secularism was the very engine of modern times?

In the fall of 1894, in Vienna, at St. Peter's Church in the very heart of the old city, as part of a conference on Christian apologetics, Albert Wiesinger delivered an ominous warning to his fellow believers. Everything we think of as "civilized," he began, comes from Christianity. And yet, in our day, Christianity is under fearsome attack. Who is attacking Christianity? A vast, sinister, destructive, secular conspiracy. In literature, in science, in politics, in journalism — yes, even in theology — wherever we look, the "evangelists of anti-Christianity" are at work. Wiesinger was troubled. Secularism was rampant, pervasive, and implacable. "Let me close," he told his audience, "with the words of Moses: 'Look, I set before you today life and death, blessing and curse. Put your hand out. What you choose you will be given.' And now I ask you, gentlemen, shall our 'Fin de Siècle' choose only death and curse?" Alas, Wiesinger warned, it might well be that death and curse would be all that Europe's tidal wave of secularization would bring.[15]

Now if there is one thing we know, or think we know, about the modern, it is that Albert Wiesinger had a point. It is clear, isn't it, that "modernization," that long cultural trend beginning in the sixteenth century, and "modernism," that burst of cultural efflorescence around the last fin de siècle, were profoundly secular? Certainly a vast literature insists on this. "God is dead," Nietzsche famously proclaimed, and Thomas Hardy thought of the nineteenth century as "God's funeral." An inexhaustible literature supports Hardy and Nietzsche.[16]

14. Malinowski, *Magic, Science, and Religion,* 17.
15. Albert Wiesinger, *Das Anti-Christentum* (Vienna: Doll, 1895), 57.
16. On Hardy, see A. N. Wilson, *God's Funeral* (New York: Norton, 1999). Literary critic J. Hillis Miller argued a generation ago that Victorian writers like Matthew Arnold

True, some of the old religious battles continued and demonstrated a certain vitality. Ludwig Wahrmund, for instance, an indefatigable hammer of the Papists, in a series of fiery books, grimly warned fellow Protestants of Romanish tricks; a former Jesuit, Paul Hoensbroech, jumped to the Protestants and vowed to expose all the jesuitical secrets.[17] Various species of Protestants also squabbled among each other. In Prussia, for instance, Lutherans in 1912 got into an angry battle concerning the autonomy of local churches. When one pastor refused to include the Apostles' Creed in worship services because it wasn't scriptural, the Lutheran authorities declared him out of communion with the Lutheran church. Even the great theologian Adolf von Harnack wrote a pamphlet about the fuss (he said "bully for the local pastor!").[18] A Catholic champion, Albert

---

and even Gerard Manley Hopkins were haunted by the absence of God; see J. Hillis Miller, *The Disappearance of God: Five Nineteenth-Century Writers* (Cambridge: Harvard University Press, 1963). Peter Gay points out that Victorian Europeans, from elites to the peasants, were increasingly secular; Peter Gay, *Schnitzler's Century* (New York: Norton, 2002). According to theologian David Wells, "the truth is that the public dimension of our chrome and plastic world . . . admits to no interest in the divine presence, seeks no grace, and asks for no forgiveness." The effort to be "both modern and Christian produces," Wells insists, "deep and perhaps insoluble problems." David Wells, *God in the Wasteland* (Grand Rapids: Eerdmans, 1994), 16. John Thornhill, another theologian, writes that the "modern" was born in the sixteenth century precisely as a repudiation of the "sacralized" culture of the Middle Ages; John Thornhill, *Modernity: Christianity's Estranged Child Reconstructed* (Grand Rapids: Eerdmans, 2000), 7. Peter Berger argues that "secularization has posited an altogether novel situation" for modern people. He continues: "probably for the first time in history, the religious legitimations of the world have lost their plausibility not only for a few intellectuals and other marginal individuals but for broad masses of entire societies. This opened up 'an acute crisis' both for social institutions and individual psyches." Peter Berger, *The Sacred Canopy* (Garden City, N.J.: Doubleday, 1967), 124. As a nervous Edmund Wilson remarked to fellow American critic Alfred Kazin in the 1920s, "we must simply live without religion"; Alfred Kazin, *God and the American Writer* (New York: Knopf, 1997), 5.

17. Ludwig Wahrmund, *Religion und Klerikalismus* (Innsbruck: A. Edlinger, undated); *Das Deutsche Reich und die kommenden Papstwahlen* (Frankfurt: Neuer Frankfurter Verlag, 1903); Paul Hoensbroech, *Ultramontane Leistungen* (Berlin: Walther, 1895); Paul Hoensbroech, *Des Jesuiten von Nostitz-Reineck Schrift: Graf Hoensbroechs Flucht aus Kirche und Orden* (Leipzig: Breitkopf und Härtel, 1913).

18. Adolf von Harnack, *Die Dienstentlassung des Pfarrers Lic. G. Traub* (Leipzig: Hinrich, 1912); for more on these intra-Protestant fights, see Emil Felden, *Protestantische Kirchen in Deutschland* (Frankfurt: Neuer Frankfurter Verlag, 1902).

Ehrhard, thought that this unceasing ill will among Christians was getting worse; he ascribed it to the "nervousness of our times."[19]

But to other observers of Central European religious life, these echoes of seventeenth-century polemics seemed increasingly irrelevant. What struck them was not religious energy but lassitude and indifference. Rudolf Seydel, pleading for a truce between Christians and Darwinists, wearily remarked, "no one can call church life at the moment exactly encouraging."[20] Paul Göhre agreed. More and more people simply find the churches irrelevant, Göhre wrote in 1909, and millions are drifting away from organized religion. In Prussia, for example, Göhre showed that all bad numbers were going up — between 1906 and 1908, some 30,000 Prussians officially left their churches — and all the good numbers were going down — the percentage of church weddings dropped (among Lutherans, from 88.6 percent in 1905 to 84 percent in 1906, among Catholics from 71.6 percent in 1905 to 69 percent in 1906), the percentage of funerals that took place in church dropped (among Lutherans, from 53 percent in 1905 to 51 percent in 1906; among Catholics, from 49 percent in 1905 to 45 percent in 1906), and so on. Why? According to Göhre,

> The first and decisive reason for this new movement away from the churches is . . . the massive spiritual upheaval which is underway in our time, a massive spiritual upheaval which affects millions of people of all classes and opinions. What is at the root of this spiritual upheaval? At the root is the conversion of more and more people to "modern" and "scientific" ways of thinking.[21]

Ludwig Mies van der Rohe, the great apostle of "modern" architecture, argued that

> The whole trend of our time is toward the secular. The endeavors of the mystics will be remembered as mere episodes. Despite our greater understanding of life, we shall build no cathedrals. Nor do

19. Albert Ehrhard, *Der Katholizismus und das zwanzigste Jahrhundert* (Vienna: Roth'sche Verlag, 1902), 15-16.

20. Rudolf Seydel, *Religion und Wissenschaft* (Breslau: Schottlaender, 1887), 397.

21. Paul Göhre, *Die neueste Kirchenaustrittsbewegung aus den Landeskirchen in Deutschland* (Jena: Diederich, 1909), 22.

the brave gestures of the Romantics mean anything to us, for behind them we detect their empty forms. Ours is not an age of pathos; we do not respect flights of the spirit as much as we value reason and realism.[22]

Sylvain De Bleeckere speaks for many in writing that the distinctive quality of "modernism" was a "self-assured atheism."[23] As the members of the controversial "Jesus Seminar" insist, "the Christ of creed and dogma . . . can no longer command the assent of those who have seen the heavens through Galileo's telescope. The old deities and demons were swept from the skies by that remarkable glass."[24]

It would seem beyond question, then, that "modernism" in its many guises — Viennese modernism included — had little if anything to do with the "sacred." The point of this book, though, is to question that which seems beyond question. My claim is not simply that one *can* do a religious reading of the *Wiener Moderne;* one can do a religious reading of anything. My point is that one *must.*

In 1909, August Heinrich Braasch, in his *Die religiösen Strömungen der Gegenwart,* made a similar argument. A Protestant, Braasch attempted to defend Protestantism from the twin hazards of Catholicism and "modernism." To Protestants, the wickedness of Catholicism was well known; therefore Braasch focused on modernism. What struck him about modernism at the birth of the twentieth century was precisely how "religious" it was. To be sure, older, established churches were losing both members and social influence. But on the other hand, there was an immense increase in para-religions, alternative religions, and religious yearning. Central Europe, Braasch argued, was alive with "nature-religions," "neo-paganism," "Eastern religions," and so on. Political revolutionaries' promises of "The Revolution" were clearly eschatological and deeply religious; Nietzsche's

---

22. Ludwig Mies van der Rohe, in Richard Francis, ed., *Negotiating Rapture: The Power of Art to Transform Lives* (Chicago: Museum of Contemporary Art, 1996), 162.

23. Sylvain De Bleeckere, "The Religious Dimensions of Cinematic Consciousness in Postmodern Culture," in John May, ed., *New Image of Religious Film* (Kansas City: Sheed and Ward, 1997), 97.

24. Cited in Paul Minear, "Wanted: An Exegetical Realism," *Theology Today* 59:2 (July 2002): 181.

struggle to define the *Übermensch* and construct a New Morality "beyond good and evil" was, Braasch thought, fundamentally a religious effort to understand conversion and transcendence.

Braasch made a crucial distinction between "religion" and "church." Obviously the two are related, but they are not identical. Religious movements often live outside churches — and for that matter, churchly life is not always religious.[25] If you accept the notion that "religious" phenomena exist outside the "church," Braasch continues, then you are struck by the fact that "secular life, social and political life, philosophy . . . literature, art, all reflect religious movements."[26]

If we must attempt a religious reading of fin de siècle Vienna, we quickly find ourselves in a thicket of definitions. "Fin de siècle Vienna" is by far the easiest term to define. Vienna's fin de siècle lasted from roughly the heartbreaking suicide of the heir to the Habsburg throne, Crown Prince Rudolf, in 1889, to the outbreak of the Great War in 1914. Fin de siècle Vienna was the birthplace of the cultural flowering called the *Wiener Moderne* and the home of one of the most scintillating of Europe's many avant-gardes.

Defining that avant-garde is a bit trickier. Most Viennese were not part of it; in fact, neither were many of Vienna's artists and scholars and intellectuals. Ludwig von Mises would later comment on the "unbridgeable chasm between a minuscule group of Viennese intellectuals and the mass of the so-called educated people."[27] Vienna was home to vitally important scholarship and research around the turn of the last century, but most of these scholars were not really part of the cultural avant-garde. Much of Vienna's academic establishment was hostile to it. Like all avant-gardes, Vienna's was self-appointed, cliquish, and self-absorbed. In fact, the Viennese avant-garde was an amazingly tiny group. Among musicians, it included Mahler, Schoenberg, Berg, and Webern, and their various friends and students. Among visual artists, the avant-garde included Klimt, Schiele, and Kokoschka, and among architects, Hofmann, Olbricht, Loos, and Wagner. Among writers, the central figures were Schnitzler, Hofmannsthal, and Altenberg. Satirist Karl Kraus spent years mocking the

25. August Heinrich Braasch, *Die religiösen Strömungen der Gegenwart* (Leipzig: B. G. Teubner, 1909), 2.

26. Braasch, *Strömungen*, 3.

27. Hofmann, *The Viennese: Splendor, Twilight, and Exile* (New York: Anchor, 1988), 281.

avant-garde, yet he too needs to be included with it. Hermann Bahr was the dramatist and critic who became the avant-garde's impresario extraordinaire. Sigmund Freud was never really part of Vienna's artistic circles, yet his concerns clearly echo theirs. There were important predecessors, like Bruckner, and heirs, like Wittgenstein. There were other talented people who played important roles in the avant-garde, though their share of its fame was small: writers like Felix Salten and Richard Beer-Hofmann and painters like Richard Gerstl, for example. But even a generous count would produce a remarkably small number, and all were connected to each other. Allan Janik, for instance, notes that composer Anton Bruckner gave piano lessons to physicist Ludwig Boltzmann; Bruckner's disciple Gustav Mahler consulted Freud; Freud was intrigued by Arthur Schnitzler's stories; Freud's colleague Josef Breuer was the physician of philosopher Franz Brentano; socialist Viktor Adler attended the same *gymnasium* as the future Emperor Karl I; Adler, Freud, and Schnitzler all went to medical school and all interned at the Meynert Clinic. One might add that the painter Gustav Klimt was the mentor of both Oskar Kokoschka and Egon Schiele; that Mahler was a patron of both Arnold Schoenberg and Anton Webern; that as a young man, Mahler's roommate was art-song composer Hugo Wolf; that Mahler almost got into a fistfight defending Schoenberg's music at a riotous concert; that Schoenberg was a writer and painter as well as a composer and was intimately connected to networks of writers and painters; that expressionist poet Georg Trakl was a close friend of painter Oskar Kokoschka; that Kokoschka had a tumultuous affair with Gustav Mahler's widow, Alma, who may (or may not) have had an affair with Klimt; that artist Richard Gerstl was infatuated with Schoenberg's wife; that social critic Karl Kraus went to school with poet Hugo von Hofmannsthal; that when Kraus had his premiere as an actor in 1893, playwright Arthur Schnitzler was in the audience; that architect Adolf Loos, writer Peter Altenberg, and Karl Kraus were very close friends. One could pursue such connections almost indefinitely. The Viennese avant-garde was a very tight, incestuous, intimate circle.[28]

They were in most ways representative of no one. They were all male (though they were obsessed with women), they were from the middling

---

28. Janik, *Wittgensteins Wien*, 119.

classes mostly, and they were well enough off financially so that they could devote their leisure to their art. They were young, and many had serious conflicts with their parents, especially with their fathers. They were very smart and very talented. They were obnoxiously narcissistic. They were riddled with contradictions. For example, on the one hand, they yearned to be popular and to produce a genuinely popular art, while simultaneously thinking of themselves as a tiny, suffering, misunderstood, prophetic elite. Or another contradiction: many of the avant-garde artists were Jews, who had come to associate Judaism with poverty and discrimination, and who therefore rejected any explicit Jewish identity; and yet at the very same time, whether they practiced a militant atheism (like Freud) or converted to Christianity (like Mahler), they could not escape a continuing obsession with the puzzles of Jewish identity, if only because their society, infected with a virulent anti-Semitism, insisted that the "Jewish Question" was decisive for the fate of humanity.

Heaven knows no one would ever accuse them of piety. Several, to be sure, would find their way to Christianity and Judaism, but most were not religious by any conventional standard, and though not all were as hostile to religion as Freud, most had little use for Vienna's formal religions. Kraus — born Jewish, a convert to Christianity, and then a convert back to Judaism — laughed that "when a culture feels that its end has come, it sends for a priest,"[29] and Arthur Schnitzler remarked to believers that "if there is a God, then the way you worship Him is a sacrilege."[30]

Representative of no one, these artists were confident that they were representative of everyone, that their terrors and loves reflected the terrors and loves of their world.

If defining the avant-garde is a trick, defining religion is even trickier. One might begin defining religion by considering the work of the Victorian anthropologists who created the discipline of comparative religion around the very time that the Viennese avant-garde were creating modernism. The anthropologists of most use here were the great fin de siècle cultural explorers, people like Tyler, Durkheim, Frazier, and their heirs. Of course, their

---

29. In Harry Zohn, *Karl Kraus* (New York: Twayne, 1971), 31.
30. Timothy Farley, "Arthur Schnitzler's Sociopolitical *Märchen*," in Petrus Tax and Richard Lawson, eds., *Arthur Schnitzler and His Age* (Bonn: Bouvier, 1984), 107.

work is limited, fallible, culturally biased, and sometimes simply wrong. Their comments about "savages" can be condescending and insulting. Nevertheless, for all their faults, these founders of modern anthropology provide us with an especially rich understanding of religion.

Religion, they insisted first of all, is everywhere. Certainly no "primitive" society has ever been discovered that was free of religion. Edward Tyler thought that at root, religion was the conviction that reality consists of at least two dimensions; that our human dimension is only one, and not the most important, of these dimensions; that the other dimension, the dimension of spirits, ghosts, angels and demons, is by far the more powerful dimension; and that these two dimensions, the human world and the spirit world, interact and intersect in multiple ways. "Animism," the belief in the reality of the "spirit world," Tyler argued, was the root of religious belief and practice.

Just where and when the human world and spirit world intersected was thus a vital issue. Those places of intersection were special, but also dangerous. Those places, and the things in those places, became multivalent, charged with meaning and power. They became very special and dangerous — "taboo." They could become power sources for the clan — "totems." Networks of "totems" and "taboos," then, became integral to "savage religion."

Death and life were the foundational themes of "savage religion." What happened after death, where life came from, how to combat death by instilling life — these were the fundamental issues in "savage religion." James Frazier famously identified fertility cults as central to religious experience; fertility cults were powerful, though, because of the terrifying experience of death. The more intense the awareness of death, the greater the longing for rebirth, and the more intense the phenomena of religion.

Religion, the anthropologists quickly learned, is a social, not an individual, experience. True, religion is experienced individually, and its power can be drastically transformative, but religion itself is collective and social. Emile Durkheim argued that religion is in some ways a symbol of the "clan" or "people" itself. Should the clan face a crisis, that crisis is experienced as a religious crisis. Should the clan experience a triumph, that triumph is experienced as a religious triumph.

Among the "savages," religion does not arise from within; it explodes from without. It may well be true, as Romantic theologians like Schleier-macher famously argued, that human beings have some sort of "religious sensibility" or "religious instinct." But it appears that persons involved in the religious event experience that event as a kind of intrusion, invasion, and eruption. Of course there is a psychological dimension to this, but the psychic experience is one of what Tillich describes as "kairos," as a "ful-filled time," as a moment when "external reality" assumes an overpower-ing thickness, density, and electricity. However much of "me" may be en-gaged in the religious experience, that which the "me" experiences is something — or someone — that most decidedly is "not-me." As Abra-ham Joshua Heschel writes,

> Ever since Schliermacher it has been customary in considering the nature of religion to start with the human self and to characterize religion as a feeling of dependence, reverence, etc. What is over-looked is the unique aspect of religious consciousness of being a re-cipient, of being exposed, overwhelmed by a presence which sur-passes our ability to feel.[31]

What the "me" experiences is what Rudolf Otto would describe as the "Totally Other." Indeed for Otto the essence of the religious experience was the encounter with the "mysterium tremendum fascinans." This encounter was with something deeply mysterious — dangerous, frightening, tremen-dous, and awesome. Yet as terrible as this mysterious other is, it is also fas-cinating, amazing, and life-changing. Otto attempted a phenomenology of the holy, a careful description of the experience that would link the cultural occurrence to philosophical reflection. Otto's groundbreaking work influ-enced a host of other writers who, like Otto, take the experience of the holy as the starting point for reflection — writers like Louis Dupré, Gerardus Van der Leeuw, Mircea Eliade, and Paul Ricoeur.[32]

31. Abraham Joshua Heschel, *Who Is Man?* (Stanford: Stanford University Press, 1965), 75.

32. Rudolf Otto, *The Idea of the Holy*, trans. John Harvey (New York: Oxford Univer-sity Press, 1969). See G. Van der Leeuw, *Religion in Essence and Manifestation*, trans. J. E. Turner (New York: Harper and Row, 1963); Louis Dupré, *The Other Dimension* (New York: Doubleday, 1972); Mircea Eliade, *Patterns in Comparative Religion* (New York: Meridian, 1958); Paul Ricoeur, *Figuring the Sacred* (Minneapolis: Fortress Press, 1995).

To be sure, the "totally other" may become manifest in some dramatic event; just as often it may be experienced as the odd, the bizarre, the uncanny and weird. Among the "savages," the weird and uncanny was experienced as a kind of "force," something the Victorian anthropologists called "mana." But "mana" is more than just "force"; it is not natural but supernatural or even unnatural; while superhuman, it is neither blind nor arbitrary but in some way conscious, alert, and intent.

Such phenomena really do occur, and certain persons — "shamans" — are those skilled in encountering and interpreting the weird. Their ecstasies and trances are moments when the weird and the human intersect. The shaman's task is both to interpret the human to the divine and to interpret the divine to the human.

Their interpretations become "myths" and "rituals," the narrative and dramatic stuff of religion. Myths and rituals relate human time to "that time," that is, divine time, or eternity. Myths and rituals narrate and enact the matter of religion — spirits, totems and taboos, death and life, the life of the tribe and the life of the individual, the career of the weird — in ways such that those who are not directly touched by the divine can nevertheless feel something of its breath.

Finally, it is important to note that this religious experience is coextensive neither with religious ethics nor with organized religion. Religious ethics, to be sure, follows from the divine encounter, and, for example within the Jewish tradition, becomes central to religious self-consciousness. But ethics is a response to a prior event, the revelatory intrusion of the divine. In the years after World War I, Karl Barth and Dietrich Bonhoeffer, for example, would insist on this. Religious ethics arises not from human initiative, not even simultaneously with divine revelation, but in response to a prior divine revelation. Revelation is in this sense much more primal, primitive, even savage, than ethics. Both Barth and Bonhoeffer insist as well that the encounter with the divine, while it of course gives birth to the sociological phenomenon of organized religion, is not identical with organized religion. Karl Barth would castigate the Christian churches for failing to live up to the duties imposed by revelation. Bonhoeffer would speculate on the possibility of "religionless Christianity," that is, religious faith independent of organized churches. Barth insisted that religious faith is not simply one realm of human experience among others; religious faith deals with "real life in its totality." Paul Tillich writes, "Religion is the aspect of depth in the totality of the human spirit":

> The religious aspect points to that which is ultimate, infinite, unconditional in man's spiritual life. Religion, in the largest and most basic sense of the word, is ultimate concern. . . . Ultimate concern is manifest in the realm of knowledge as the passionate longing for ultimate reality. . . . Ultimate concern is manifest in the aesthetic function of the human spirit as the infinite desire to express ultimate meaning. . . . You cannot reject religion with ultimate seriousness, because ultimate seriousness, or the state of being ultimately concerned, is itself religion. Religion is the substance, the ground, and the depth of man's spiritual life.[33]

Religion is the spark that leaps between "is" and "ought." The world we inhabit "is" a certain way, and maybe that is all there is to it. Yet again and again humans have been haunted by an "ought," by a sense that "is" is not all there is, that "is" needs to be judged by standards that stand outside and beneath and beyond, by a mythic past (a sense of "in those days," "in illo tempore"), and an impending future (the "eschaton"). "Ought," though embedded in the human experience, is experienced as something much more than merely human aspiration. "Ought" is intrusive and judgmental, and the moments when "ought" reveals itself, "hierophanies," are moments when the very foundations of reality awesomely if only momentarily shatter. These hierophanies generate a sense of the metaphysically "true" ("here is how reality really is"), and the morally "good" ("and so we ought to live this way and not that way because this is how reality is"). Hierophanies also generate a sense of the beautiful ("this experience is deeply satisfying and profoundly moving because it is an experience both true and good").

But what has all this to do with fin de siècle Vienna?

It is not news that religion and art were somehow tied together in fin de siècle Vienna. There, Carl Schorske writes, "art almost became a reli-

---

33. Karl Barth, *Dogmatics in Outline* (New York: Harper and Row, 1959), 21; Paul Tillich, *Theology of Culture* (New York: Oxford University Press, 1978), 7-8.

gion."[34] This might be thought of as a secularization of religion; to say that "art replaces religion" might mean something like "religion is replaced by human art." This book will argue the contrary. Rather than religion becoming secularized, I think what occurred was that art was sacralized. Religious experience occurred within the context of art, meaning not that religion took on the form of the human, but that art took on the echo of the divine.

This is the point Austrian novelist Hermann Broch, for example, made in a note to his publishers concerning his 1931 novel, *Der Schlafwandler*. Part of that "silver generation" of artists who succeeded the fin de siècle "golden age," Broch was convinced that neither science nor philosophy could illuminate the spirits that haunted him, and so Broch turned to art. The novel, he wrote, has taken over responsibility for those issues that other disciplines dismiss as "unscientific," "or as Wittgenstein says, 'mystical.'" Broch's self-appointed task then became, as critic Theodore Ziolkowski writes, "to raise life to myth."[35]

Central to this "mystical task," to raising life to myth, was not simply recording human encounters with reality, but even more important, recounting reality's impingement on humans. "I feel the air from other planets," sings the soprano in Arnold Schoenberg's Second String Quartet, while the musical setting of the text brings to the listener an eerie new world of atonality. To cite Broch again, the artist's task is not to reduce the metaphysical to the psychological, but to raise the psychological to the metaphysical.[36]

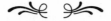

Fin de siècle Vienna is a protean beast. Just when you think you have it by the throat you discover you have it by the tail, if at all. No doubt, much of

34. Carl Schorske, *Fin-de-Siècle Vienna* (New York: Knopf, 1980), 9.

35. Theodore Ziolkowski, *Dimensions of the Modern Novel: German Texts and European Contexts* (Princeton: Princeton University Press, 1969), 141, 143.

36. Ziolkowski, *Modern Novel*, 144.

what follows needs qualification, refinement, and polish. If it is anywhere near true, though, its consequences are startling.

It implies, for instance, that what we have known about modernization and modernism for generations — that both were incarnations of a relentless secularism — is suspect. If all this is anywhere near true, then Viennese modernism was born not out of secularism, but out of a renewed encounter with the *mysterium tremendum fascinans*. But the *Wiener Moderne* was integral to the entire modernist enterprise. Could it be, then, that modernism itself is profoundly religious?

And yet, if it is true that modernism is religious, what does that mean? Does it mean that modernism expressed some unchanging, eternally fixed, religious quintessence? Jürgen Habermas has referred to the "modernization of faith itself" as a crucial dimension of the entire modernization process.[37] Could it be that religion was itself modernized? Could it be that the religion modernism expresses takes on, at least in part, the particular accents, tones, fears, and hopes distinctive to modernism's era?

Is, then, modernism religious? Is, then, religion modern?

Yes, deeply so. This book will try to show how. It is structured thematically. The first chapter sets the stage by introducing fin de siècle Vienna, the "fairy tale city." Chapter Two examines the Viennese artists' obsession with decline, decay, and death. Chapter Three next considers the artists' fascination with rebirth and resurrection. Chapter Four studies the dreams, visions, and voices that guided the avant-garde. Chapter Five investigates the religious implications of the "crisis of language" so characteristic of late Habsburg Vienna. Chapter Six sketches the ways in which Vienna's artists not only attempted to express the divine, but also the ways in which they encountered the divine as feminine. Chapter Seven's focus is the uncanny, perhaps the single most important concept in turn-of-the-century Vienna. Chapter Eight concentrates on the artists themselves and their role as cultural priests and prophets. Finally, Chapter Nine examines the artists' ultimate response to their encounter with the sacred.

There is certainly no shortage of attention paid to fin de siècle Vienna.

---

37. Jürgen Habermas, *Religion and Rationality*, ed. and intro. by Eduardo Mendieta (Cambridge: MIT Press, 2002), 150.

The stunning artistic experiments of the era are often thought of as responses to the changes sweeping through Europe at the end of the nineteenth century: the jolting shift from agriculture to industry, from village to big city, from low tech to high tech, from face-to-face relationships to relationships mediated by bureaucracy, the media, and popular culture; from "tradition" to "progress"; from static, hierarchical societies to fluid, experimental societies; from ethnic homogeneity to ethnic plurality — all these changes roaring along in but a generation or two. Vienna's artistic experiments were efforts to comprehend, articulate, and direct this "outbreak of the modern." Peter Gay locates this struggle particularly in the trials of the middling classes. Hermann Broch interprets Viennese modernism as an art of the "irrational" that arose because all these sweeping changes exploded stable structures and habits but left behind a "moral vacuum," out of which arose all sorts of terrors. David Luft sees Viennese modernism, particularly the work of novelist Robert Musil, as a response to and expression of a pervasive moral and spiritual crisis in European culture.

Carl Schorske has offered the single most influential explanation of the *Wiener Moderne*. His interpretation is fundamentally political. For a brief period, in the 1860s, it looked as though Vienna might make the transition from an aristocratic, monarchical conservatism to middle-class liberalism. Viennese merchants, lawyers, and journalists, like their cousins across Europe, believed in science, technology, education, and reason; they argued for greater personal freedom in both politics and economics; they wanted a parliamentary monarchy and a free market economy. Liberalism, strongly embedded if hardly completed in Britain, the United States, and to a lesser extent in France and the low countries, flowered but then died in Austria-Hungary. The free market crashed, hurtling central Europe into a long depression. Parliamentary politics were paralyzed by ethnic hatred. Rapid cultural change produced not confidence in progress but dizziness and terror. Reason seemed unable to comprehend, let alone leash, the psychic forces suddenly loose in Vienna. It is this collapse of the liberal project, Schorske argues, that triggered the distinctive art of the *Wiener Moderne*.[38] Obviously all these interpretations have great merit, and

38. Shearer West, *Fin de Siècle: Art and Society in an Age of Uncertainty* (Woodstock, N.Y.:

since Schorske's is the dominant view, it will appear frequently in these pages. But none of these interpretations sees the *Wiener Moderne* as a fundamentally religious phenomenon. This book, then, draws on existing and original resarch to show that in fact fin de siècle Vienna was comprehensively and inescapably religious.

Eduardo Mendieta, introducing Jürgen Habermas's writings on religion, argues that

> the question of religion is once again at the forefront of critical thought precisely because it crystallizes some of the most serious and pressing questions of contemporary social thought: the relationship between social structure and rationality; between reason as a universal standard and the inescapable fact that reason is embodied only historically and in contingent social practices; that reason as universality was, if not discovered, at least enunciated as a teleological standard by religions; that in an age of secularization and scientization, religion remains a major factor in the moral education and motivation of individuals uprooted from other traditions; and at the very least, in an age of accelerating homogenization and simultaneous manufacturing of difference, what sociologists of globalization call globalization, religions are articulated as the last refuge of unadulterated difference, the last reservoir of cultural autonomy.[39]

The mythologist Joseph Campbell noted in conversation that Nietzsche's famous aphorism about god's demise is both true and false. It is certainly true, Campbell thought, that religious expression underwent profound change in the nineteenth century; the "gods" Nietzsche grew up with did indeed die. But, citing the mystic Meister Eckhart (and echoing the theology of Paul Tillich), Campbell noted that there are "gods beyond god." Our sense of the divine tends to become rigid; symbols for the divine are reified and become idols; the idols collapse; and in the twilight of the

---

Overlook Press, 1993); Hermann Broch, *Hugo von Hofmannsthal and His Time* (Chicago: University of Chicago Press, 1984); David Luft, *Robert Musil and the Crisis of European Culture, 1880-1942* (Berkeley: University of California Press, 1980); Gay, *Schnitzler's Century;* Schorske, *Fin de Siècle Vienna.*

39. Habermas, *Religion and Rationality,* 1.

idols, new gods are born. "As soon as you smash the local, provincial god-form, God comes back," Campbell remarked.[40] Yes indeed, provincial god-forms were smashed in the nineteenth century, but God came back. God came back to fin de siècle Vienna.

40. Joseph Campbell, *An Open Life* (New York: Harper, 1989), 56.

Chapter 1

FAIRY TALE CITY

It is like a vision of fairyland.

Maria Landsdale[1]

Sometime between nightfall on January 29 and sunrise on January 30, 1889, Crown Prince Rudolf, heir to the Austro-Hungarian throne, shot his mistress, Mary Vetsera, to death, and then put the pistol to his own head and killed himself. They were staying at the royal hunting lodge at Mayerling, outside Vienna. Rudolf and Mary had arrived on January 28, a bitterly cold day. A small group of the crown prince's intimates had joined them. The next day, January 29, they had seemed normal enough. That night, Rudolf and Mary retired to their bedroom after what had seemed to be a pleasant evening.

But the next day they didn't return from their bedroom.

At first, the crown prince's servants assumed that the couple had simply slept late. But as the minutes, then hours, ticked by, the servants began to worry. They tapped respectfully on the bedroom door. No response. They tapped again. Nothing.

1. Maria Horner Landsdale, *Vienna and the Viennese* (Philadelphia: Henry T. Coates, 1902), 282.

They hurried outside, propped a ladder up to the bedroom window, and a servant peeked in. There they were, together, side by side. Neither one was moving.

Panicked, the servants broke the window and tumbled into the bedroom. The bed was covered with blood. The crown prince and Mary Vetsera were quite dead.

A messenger rushed to the royal palace, the Hofburg, in the center of Vienna, with the ghastly news. Officials frantically hurried out to Mayerling.[2]

The morning edition of Vienna's *Neue Freie Presse* had reported an odd turn of events in German politics. It seemed that Berlin's archconservative, vehemently monarchical, fiercely anti-democratic newspaper, *Die Kreuzzeitung*, had, astoundingly enough, criticized the Kaiser. The *Neue Freie Presse* remarked, "it's a peculiar time in which we live. All concepts, all traditions, all social inheritances seem to have been turned on their heads, and again and again one has to ask whether what we see is really true."[3] Of course the editors didn't realize that something far more astounding than the political fight they reported had already occurred.

By midday that frozen January, rumors about some dreadful catastrophe swept the city. Rumors raced through the mazes of the old Inner City, past the elegant shops on Kärtnerstrasse, along the Ringstrasse (where the recently demolished city walls had once stood guard), and out from the Ring, into the city's proletarian suburbs, out Mariahilfe and the other new boulevards, out into the workers' tenements at the sprawling city's edge. Inside coffee houses and government ministries, outside shops, bundled against the January cold, the Viennese stared mutely at the stunning newspaper reports:

2. The Mayerling suicides have inspired a vast and inexhaustible industry. Though the royal family did its best to censor all reports of the suicides, printed accounts began to circulate only weeks after they occurred. A century later, interest in Mayerling seemed unwavering. In 1992, a grave robber opened Mary Vetsera's grave, exhumed her remains, and turned them over to a pathologist, who confirmed that the remains were indeed those of a young woman who had died by gunshot wound. After a suitably outrageous scandal hungrily followed by the press, Mary's remains were reburied. Television specials, films, and Internet sites have now joined books in telling and retelling the Mayerling story. Mayerling is the central event in Frederic Morton's recreation of the early years of fin de siècle Vienna; see Frederic Morton, *A Nervous Splendor: Vienna, 1888-1889* (New York: Penguin, 1979).

3. "Die Kreuzzeitung im Anklagestand," *Neue Freie Presse*, January 30, 1889, 2.

Crown Prince Rudolf

A horrible, shocking, crushing accident has happened. Crown Prince Rudolf, heir to the throne, the hope of the dynasty and the empire, is dead!

In the full bloom of maturity, in the midst of his life's energies, his young mind filled with plans for his future reign, for expanding the power of the Empire, for encouraging art and science, a sinister, deadly accident, the kind of accident the jealous gods hurl against mortals, has mysteriously struck him down, and torn him away from his imperial father, away from his lovely wife, away from his child, his land, his people.

The pain which has struck Austria-Hungry is too intense to overcome, too enormous even to express. The loss we have suffered is so immense that now, in the very midst of it, we are not even fully aware of it. This horror has fallen like a thunderbolt, which destroys the very moment it appears. Thrones themselves are overcome by the enormity of such pain.

Only this much is clear so far — today, the Empire has been transformed into a land of weeping and wailing. A hope millions had looked to has been destroyed. A life which expressed only love, courage, spirit, and nobility, has ended. The incomprehensible hand of fate has hanged a dark cloud over the future, which had seemed so golden and promising. . . .

He had hoped that Vienna would be a sea of light in the world. Today it is a sea of tears. The only pain he has ever brought to his imperial father or his land is the greatest pain that could ever be imagined.

God comfort the Emperor, the Empire, and us all, for we have all lost him.[4]

Rudolf von Habsburg, the crown prince and heir to the Austro-Hungarian imperial throne, was thirty-one years old. He had been one of Europe's most eligible bachelors. He was handsome, witty, and charming. His marriage to Stephanie, a Belgian princess, had been one of the empire's great social events. Any day, his ancient father, Emperor Franz

---

4. "Kronprinz Rudolf," *Neue Freie Presse*, January 30, 1889, 1.

Josef, might go to his reward, and Rudolf, young and energetic, would succeed to the throne, and the long-awaited change in generations would symbolize not just simply dynastic continuity but the replacement of age and tradition with youth and promise.

But now Rudolf lay dead.

"The unbelievable is true," the *Neue Freie Presse* continued the next morning, January 31, 1889:

> It is a hard, iron, incomprehensible reality, we must submit to. The young heir to the Habsburg throne, so noble, so filled with life, the promise of joy and hope to his House and to Austria, in a single night a storm struck him, and an impenetrable mystery has overcome the Danube monarchy, a mystery of pitiless fate. . . . Enormous, immeasurable grief flows through our land, grief for Rudolf, that extraordinary man in whom so many had placed their hopes . . . may heaven, which has sent such terrible pain, which has broken so many hearts, give the Empire and the Imperial house the strength to endure![5]

Oh, there had been rumors, of course, rumors of tension and trouble in the imperial house. The old emperor, Franz Josef, and his son Rudolf were estranged, people whispered. The emperor was very old and very set in his ways and very uninterested in the new-fangled ideas that his son found so interesting. There were policy differences too — the emperor, for example, was insistent on maintaining intimate ties with Germany, while the crown prince was deeply skeptical of Germany. But it went far beyond matters of policy. The emperor had no intention of sharing power with his son, no intention even of preparing his son to rule. So Rudolf spent year after grinding year attending Vienna's innumerable formal ceremonies, greeting foreign dignitaries, opening homes for orphans, and dedicating new bridges, all the while isolated from any real power. Both he and his father knew, of course, that only his father's death would free him from his glamorous prison, and it may well have been that the son wished his father's death, and that the father knew that his son wished his death, but the father lived on and on, fending off his son, keeping him away from any real power, any real influence.

5. "Wien, 30 Januar," *Neue Freie Presse*, January 31, 1889, 1.

Some said that relations between mother and son were distant and cold, too. The Empress Elizabeth — "Sisi," intimates called her — was one of the most remarkable women in Europe. She was beautiful, athletic, and smart; her marriage to Emperor Franz Josef had been a great public and political success. But if there had ever been any love between Franz Josef and Elizabeth, it quickly faded. The emperor was devoted to the tedious routines and rigid protocols of rule; the empress despised them all. She spent more and more of her time away from Vienna, traveling all over Europe, traveling through the Mediterranean — traveling anywhere, it seemed, just so she could be away from her husband, away from the chilly stone mass of the Hofburg, away from Viennese gossip and intrigue. Away from her family as well.

Rudolf's marriage to Crown Princess Stephanie had been a political marriage, of course. Stephanie was a Belgian princess. They had married in May 1881, in Vienna's Augustinerkirche. The guest list was impressive. As Alan Palmer, biographer of the last Habsburgs, notes, celebrating with the Habsburgs that spring were the British Prince of Wales (and eventually King Edward VII) and his nephew, who would become Germany's Kaiser Wilhelm II. Johann Strauss dedicated his *Myrthenblütenwälzer* to Stephanie, while Eduard Strauss composed another waltz, *Schleier und Krone* (Veil and Crown). The newly wedded couple spent their honeymoon at the Laxenburg palace. Stephanie would write later that the weather was strange that early spring; there was unexpected snow, and stepping out of the coach, she was met "by a breath of air as cold as ice in a cellar," while the place smelled above all of "mould."[6]

The marriage was happy enough on the surface at least; Rudolf and Stephanie had one child, Elizabeth. But Rudolf, as the years went by, became more and more melancholy. His life was punctuated by a series of romantic liaisons. On gaslight evenings, incognito, he would ride through the streets in his coach to one rendezvous or another. But none brought him any peace; each began with passionate intensity and ended in boredom and frustration. Yearning for love, he seemed incapable of love; yearning for power, for a role in the world, he was isolated from power, all the while obsessed no doubt with the guilt-ridden wish for the liberating

6. Alan Palmer, *Twilight of the Habsburgs* (New York: Grove Press, 1994), 222.

death of his own father. He could not stay in Vienna, but he could not leave. He desperately needed love, but none came from father or mother or spouse or lovers; his role in life was fundamentally a facade; he was an ornament, a prop in a sterile drama that ranged from farce to tragicomedy. Toward the end, Rudolf seemed fascinated by death. He spoke of it often, not in fear but wistfully, as if death would finally provide him with an escape from a trivial life. He kept a skull on his desk. He once remarked, "I am . . . the most nervous man in the most nervous century."[7]

The *Neue Freie Presse* was jittery too. In December 1888, the paper's editor, Moritz Szeps, wrote to Rudolf about the strange year just ending. Up north, in the muscular new German Empire, the morticians had been busy. First the old Emperor Wilhelm I had died. Then, shockingly, his son Friedrich III had died. By the end of the year, Friedrich's blustery son Wilhelm had become Emperor Wilhelm II — three German emperors in one year. Szeps wrote,

> The past year will figure in history as the Undertakers' Year . . . the undertakers of 1888 have, however, not rejuvenated or removed much, and uncanny indeed is the stillness which broods over Europe . . . the oppressiveness cannot last forever, surely the year of change will arrive.[8]

The paper's January 1, 1889, New Year's editorial was sullen:

> There is a general air of discontent . . . a breath of melancholy brushes through our society. The rich do not enjoy their surfeit. The poor can bear their misery less than ever. At our St. Stephen's Cathedral there is a strange and ancient tablet with the inscription, "Here I lie, Simon Paur, ambushed and killed in treachery and envy." The story of his death is not known. Nobody can tell who the unfortunate Simon Paur was; but his grave may become the emblem of our city. The envy that acted as his assassin has grown into the dominant passion fermenting the populace and jeopardizing the peace of our citizens.[9]

7. Morton, *Splendor*, 219.
8. Morton, *Splendor*, 188-89.
9. Morton, *Splendor*, 184.

By end of that bleak and cold January ("crisp and cold," the papers reported the day before Rudolf's death, "westerly winds, cloudy, tendency toward snow, temperature to hover around zero centigrade")[10] even grimmer stories circulated about Crown Prince Rudolf, stories that quickly found their way into the press. "It can no longer be doubted," reported the *Neue Freie Presse,*

> that unfortunately the Crown Prince did not die of a heart attack, but from a gun shot wound, and that in a moment of tragic confusion, he inflicted the wound on himself.... As proof that the Crown Prince had earlier thought of suicide, is that fact that he so often spoke of his own impending death.[11]

But there was more, much more, that the paper never reported. The imperial censors made it clear that none of the details of the suicide would ever be officially revealed, but they leaked out anyway, whispered in palace corridors and in coffee houses.

Rudolf had gone to the Imperial hunting lodge at Mayerling with his mistress, Mary Vetsera. She was 18 years old. She was from an aristocratic family, and her mother had groomed her to be a courtesan. Little did mother or daughter dream — or perhaps did they dream? — that Mary's greatest conquest would be Crown Prince Rudolf, the heir to the Imperial throne. The affair had begun the year before. Rudolf and Mary met secretly, their liaisons arranged by the Prince's trusty coachman. That January night, Rudolf killed her, then himself.

Court officials rushed to Mayerling. They hurriedly cordoned off the hunting lodge.

Scandal had to be avoided. Men, including Mary's own uncle, carried her corpse out of the lodge, pushed a broomstick up the back of her dress to prop her up, and hurried through the snowy fields to a nearby monastery. She was hurriedly buried to the accompaniment of mumbled prayers, and her family was convinced that they should never, ever, say

10. Weather report from Tuesday, January 29, 1889, in *Neue Freie Presse,* January 30, 1889, 7.

11. "Kronprinz Rudolf," *Neue Freie Presse,* February 1, 1889, 1. It appears that the rival *Wiener Zeitung* first broke the story.

anything about her again, that she should disappear as if she had never existed.

Rudolf's corpse, its head covered in bandages, was taken back to Vienna, and carried through the complex rituals of an imperial Habsburg funeral.

As it had been with all the Habsburgs before him, Rudolf's heart was removed, and placed in a small urn; the urn was taken to the Augustiner Church, built into the Imperial Hofburg complex. His viscera was removed, and placed in another urn that was deposited in St. Stephen's cathedral. And the mummified corpse was taken, in a long and elaborate procession, to the Habsburg resting place, the crypt of the Fransiskaner Church on the Neuer Market, a short walk away from the Hofburg.

It had been carnival time, but no more. All that February Vienna was grief-stricken. "The city's dark colors grow from hour to hour," the *Neue Freie Presse* reported, "in the main streets of the Inner City, especially along Kärntnerstrasse, the Graben and Kohlmarkt, black banners flutter in the wind from every rooftop,"[12] and

> the entire Monarchy is bowed deep by the burden of the frightful misfortune imposed by the death of the Crown Prince. The latest reports about the one we mourn so much, make the pain so much more bitter, so much more burning.[13]

The funeral was on Tuesday, the fifth of February. The weather had been miserable on Monday, with snow and rain, but Tuesday was clear and cold. The grand funeral procession carried Rudolf from the Hofburg, through the city gate at Michaelerplatz, down the short stretch of the Kohlmarkt, to the Capuchin Church on the Neuer Market. Huge crowds, stunned and grief-stricken, lined the way. According to police, some thirty-four people fainted or fell or were otherwise injured in the crowd.[14]

Since the 1600s, nearly all the Habsburgs had been placed in the Fransiskaner crypt. A strict formula governed their interment. The leader of the funeral procession would pound on the door of the crypt, and from

---

12. "Kronprinz Rudolf," *Neue Freie Presse*, February 1, 1889, 2.
13. "Politische Übersicht," *Neue Freie Presse*, February 1, 1889, 2.
14. "Kronprinz Rudolf," *Neue Freie Presse*, February 6, 1889, 1.

inside, a monk would ask "who's there?" The leader would respond with all the titles of the deceased, but the door would not be opened. Finally, the leader would say that a poor sinner sought burial, and only then would the monk open the door. That is how it had been with Rudolf.[15]

Ordinary people were let down into the crypt a few days later. They were frantic to get into the crypt and see the place where the corpse lay. "The crowds were so huge," the *Neue Freie Presse* reported,

> that the police had to take extraordinary measures to make sure no one was hurt. As usual, most of the visitors were women and young girls, many of whom had to be rescued from the pushing and shoving crowd by the police. One rather plump lady complained that in all the pushing, one of her ribs had been broken.[16]

Who were these mourners, these Viennese? And what sort of place was their Vienna?

Allan Janik, writing about Ludwig Wittgenstein's Vienna, explained that, "simply put, to understand Vienna means to understand Vienna as a city of contradictions."[17] Historian William Johnston agreed. What is distinctive about Viennese culture?

> A flair for fitting disparate elements into a harmonious whole characterizes Viennese culture from at least the seventeenth century onward. The Viennese accommodate and accumulate elements disparate in origin and nature to comprise a new pattern. They do not exclude like the Spanish, or streamline and stereotype like the French. They prefer elusive and subtle harmonies to harsh dichotomies or abrupt transitions. With their nostalgia they cultivate the residues of the past with a naturalness that is both disarming and intransigent.... The hallmark of Viennese culture in its Golden Age

---

15. For an account of the burial, see, for example, Morton, *Splendor*, 261-64.

16. "Localbericht — Der Einlass in die Kaisergruft," *Neue Freie Presse*, February 10, 1889, 5.

17. Allan Janik, "Kreative Milieus: Der Fall Wien," in Peter Berner, Emile Brix, and Wolfgang Mantl, eds., *Wien um 1900. Aufbruch in die Moderne* (Vienna: Verlag für Geschichte und Politik, 1986) 46; Harry Zohn, *Der farbenvolle Untergang: An Indefatigable Hammer of the Papists* (Englewood Cliffs, N.J.: Prentice-Hall, 1917), 4.

is conglomerates like the Ringstrasse, whose buildings range in style from a Greek Parliament to a Flemish City Hall to several neo-Renaissance museums. These buildings resemble the symphonies of Mahler, with their profusion of melodies . . . or the dream analyses of Freud, who discerned in dreams layer upon layer of accreted memories and associations.[18]

All these contradictions gave Vienna its charm — and Vienna's army of journalists their material. Journalist Alfred Polgar, for example, writing about Vienna's famed coffee houses, joked that

> Vienna's Café Central is a coffee house unlike any other coffee house. The Café Central is a world view, a world view whose deepest insight is that it's an awful waste of time to try to view the whole world.

Who went to places like the Café Central? Its denizens, Polgar continued, were "for the most part people, who want to be alone, but who need company for that . . . it's a great place for people who are trying to kill time — before time kills them." The "Centralist" enjoys "living the private lives of other people." Regulars at the Café Central, Polgar explained,

> are a bit like fish in an aquarium. They swim in tight circles around each other, round and round, without any destination. They use the odd beam of light that breaks into their world for amusement, but they're full of worry, yet full of expectation too, that one day something really new might fall into their glass bowl, into their artificial pond which they pretend is the great ocean.

This "riddle-filled coffee house," Polgar warned, "provokes in those disturbed people who visit it, something which I'd call a kind of 'cosmic unease.'"[19]

---

18. William M. Johnston, *Vienna, Vienna: The Golden Age, 1815-1914* (New York: Crown, 1980), 6.

19. Alfred Polgar, in Zohn, *Der farbenvolle Untergang*, 24-25.

Vienna in 1889, on the brink of that cosmic unease called "modernism," was a very old city. A Roman outpost on the Danube frontier — Emperor Marcus Aurelius lived in Vienna for a time — with a Celtic name, "Vienna" most likely comes from a Celtic expression for the Danube's rapids — Vienna was a medieval fortress which had evolved into the capital of a vast, multinational empire where one of Europe's oldest dynasties, the Habsburgs, reigned. The Habsburgs were old; the great aristocratic families, which uneasily shared power with them, were old; the deeply conservative Catholic Church that dominated Viennese life was very old. Habits were old, customs were old, and attitudes were old. In 1889, the emperor, Franz Josef, was very old indeed.

In age, Franz Josef was not unique. His contemporary, Queen Victoria, had actually come to power eleven years before he had, and she was still in power. What made Franz Josef so distinctive was not his age, but his disasters.

While Queen Victoria presided over the spectacular expansion of the British Empire, Franz Josef reigned over the melancholy decline of the Austro-Hungarian Empire. While he was monarch, Austria was driven out of northern Italy by Camillo Cavour and Piedmont; driven out of central Europe by Bismarck and the Prussians; and threatened on its southern borders by Serbia, backed by Russia. Franz Josef was no political genius, but he was diligent. He was the empire's bureaucrat-in-chief, and day after day, year after year, decade after decade, he grimly trudged through mountains of files and sat through thousands of meetings. At his best, he was kind-hearted (Austria's military defeats were in part a product of his distaste for blood), modest, and dutiful. At his worst, he was wooden, unimaginative, and rigidly set in his ways.

Franz Josef, like Victoria, seemed immortal. His reign began in 1848; a half-century later, in 1898, he was still on the throne, his mutton chop whiskers grayed, his shoulders a little bent, but still active, still in charge. Only Queen Victoria could claim greater longevity. She had come to power in 1837, eleven years before Franz Josef. But Victoria died in 1901, with Franz Josef, a little greyer, a little more bowed, still on the throne. He would rule, in fact, until his death in 1916.

Children grew to be parents, parents became grandparents, babies aged into old men and women, and still Franz Josef was there, up from his simple army iron bed well before dawn, poring over the empire's business. He was born when Andrew Jackson was the president of the United States; he came to power in 1848, when James K. Polk was president; he died, sixteen presidents later, during the administration of Woodrow Wilson.[20] He came to power in an age of horse-drawn carriages, cavalry charges, and candles in the evening, an age unchanged in essentials from the days of the Romans. He died in the time of automobiles, airplanes, telegraphs, and electric lights.

It was a comfort to think that Franz Josef would live forever. Hurrying home just after a winter dawn, after an all night party, and passing through the grounds of the Hofburg, you would inevitably see, against the frost, light in the emperor's window, and you would know that the old man was still there, still at work, as he had been when you were a child, when your parents and their parents were children.[21] But it was disturbing too. The older the emperor got, the more obvious his mortality, the more intense the realization became that someday he, who had been there forever, would be gone — and what would happen then? "Every look into the future," Otto Friedländer recalled,

> ended with the refrain, "as long as the Kaiser lives. . . ." Everyone complained, everyone said, "well, it can't go on like this much longer" and everyone was afraid of the future, which even the cleverest spirits couldn't and didn't even want to imagine.[22]

The emperor was ubiquitous, yet, peculiarly, never quite there. His portraits were everywhere, in every post office and bank and government building. The old face with the mutton chops and thinning hair looked

20. See Arthur May, *Vienna in the Age of Franz Josef* (Norman: University of Oklahoma Press, 1966), 4.

21. Otto Friedländer, *Letzter Glanz der Märchenstadt. Das war Wien um 1900* (Vienna: Molden-Taschenbuch-Verlag, 1969), 25.

22. Friedländer, *Glanz*, 21.

down on everyone from Alpine villages to Slovenian towns, and the vast army of bureaucrats dutifully mimicked his appearance, so that every postal carrier and sewer inspector seemed to be an imperial clone. Friedländer recalled that

> a magical power seemed to come from him, a quiet authority. He ruled by quiet suggestion, only seldom did one actually hear him speak, and then one only heard him say conventional things . . . or he would read a few phrases from a scrap of paper with a light, firm voice, with a hint of a Viennese dialect which came from some other time.[23]

All the bigger theaters had an imperial box, decorated with flags, the empire's double-headed eagle, and imperial photographs. The imperial palaces were among the most accessible in Europe. Every day, Viennese and tourists gathered inside the Hofburg to watch the elaborate changing of the guard; at night, people hurried through the grounds going here or there. Yet the old man, especially as he got older, was rarely seen. The web of court ritual grew tighter and tighter around him, his public appearances were fewer and fewer, he had little interest in plays or concerts, and the imperial boxes in the theaters were most often empty. At times the emperor seemed most present in his absence.

Yet by 1889, ancient, staid, set-in-its-ways Vienna had become the New York of Central Europe, a sprawling, booming, immigrant city, which had turned itself inside out and upside down.

Few cities in Europe — few cities in the world — presented as heterogeneous a face to the world as did turn-of-the-century Vienna (perhaps only immigrant New York City was a close competitor). By the 1890s, Vienna had become the Mecca for hundreds of thousands of Central and

23. Friedländer, *Glanz*, 21.

Eastern Europeans eager to leave farm and village and make their way in the big city. Strolling down the elegant Kärtnerstrasse, in the old part of town, one could overhear snatches of Yiddish and Hungarian, Polish and Slovenian, Czech and Slovak, even occasionally German. German was, to be sure, Vienna's traditional language, and the city had a majority of German-speakers. But colloquial Viennese German had what seemed to other Germans such a peculiar singsong rhythm, and was so peppered with catch-phrases and strange words, that it barely sounded German. Maria Horner Landsdale, a British visitor, noted with apparent irritation, and not a little ethnic prejudice: "Observe attentively the passersby on a Vienna Street. Out of a hundred of those whom you meet, twenty perhaps will have German features."[24] Wander up Kärtnerstrasse toward St. Stephen's, and just before the cathedral, turn left, on to the Graben (*Graben* means "trench," or "moat," or even "grave," and it traced the moat of the old Roman fort), the short, shop-lined street in the heart of the old town. "If," Landsdale continued, "on leaving the Graben, you will cross the Hoher Markt into the Jews' street, you will think that you have strayed into a Carpathian village."[25]

The Austro-Hungarian Empire was a great Noah's Ark of peoples, patiently gathered in by generation after generation of Habsburgs. By the late 1800s, the empire included at least twelve major languages, of which six were "official": German, Hungarian, Czech, Italian, Polish, and Serbo-Croatian; five major religions or major subsets of Christianity: Roman Catholicism, Protestantism, Greek Orthodoxy, Judaism, and Islam; and somewhere between fifteen and twenty quite distinct ethnic groups, at least ten of which (Czechs, Slovaks, Hungarians, Poles, Italians, Ukrainians, Rumanians, Serbs, Croats, and Slovenes) wanted some sort of independence from the dominant Germans.[26]

Vienna's statistics were astounding. Between 1857 and 1890, the city population grew at the remarkable rate of nearly 4 percent each year. In 1857, there were some 595,832 residents; in 1869, there were 824,519; by 1880, the population was up to 1,083,748, and in 1890, the city had ex-

24. Maria Horner Landsdale, *Vienna and the Viennese* (Philadelphia: Henry T. Coates, 1902), 11.

25. Landsdale, *Vienna*, 16.

26. William Johnston, *Vienna, Vienna*, 8-9.

34

panded to an amazing 1,341,897.[27] Some of this, to be sure, was the result of annexation; Vienna's geographic size grew rapidly as scores of little villages were incorporated into the city limits. In the 1850s, the city had an area of around 55 square kilometers; by the turn of the century, it had expanded to 178 square kilometers.[28] Most of the population growth, though, was the result of immigration. One official study of poverty in the city estimated that in 1900, probably no more than 35 percent of the city's population was native Viennese.[29] By 1910, the city had a population of around two million, of whom perhaps 46 percent were native to the city.[30]

Of all the immigrants who flooded into the city, somewhere between a quarter and a half were German-speakers from the Sudetenland, the mountainous crescent on the western edge of Czech-speaking Bohemia. In 1900, around 10 percent of the city spoke Czech.[31] Another 10 percent or so were Jewish (up from around 3 percent in 1857); by 1900, Vienna had some 42 synagogues.[32] Every day, trains rolled into the city's stations with enormous loads of immigrants, and whole sections of the sprawling city were filled with immigrants. Poor Jewish immigrants typically ended up in the northern sections; eastern Vienna was filled with Czechs and Hungarians and was avoided by proper Viennese. "The Viennese didn't much care for this part of town," Otto Friedländer recalled,

> where it still smelled of Turks, where the neighborhoods had such odd names . . . where the seemingly endless streets, all rigidly straight, passed between low hills, out to the wide-open Hungarian steppes.[33]

27. Maren Seliger and Karl Ucakar, *Wien. Politische Geschichte, 1740-1934*, two vols. (Vienna: Jugend and Volk, 1985), 2:437.

28. Seliger and Ucakar, *Wien. Politische Geschichte*, 2:414.

29. Wiener Magistrat, ed., *Kurzgefasster Führer durch die Wiener öffentliche Armenpflege* (Vienna: Gerlach and Wiedling, 1909), 2.

30. Manfred Welan, "Wien — 'eine Welthauptstadt des Geistes,'" in Berner, 40.

31. Waissenberger, "Metropole," in Robert Waissenberger, ed., *Wien 1870-1930. Traum und Wirklichkeit* (Vienna: Residenz Verlag, 1984), 15, 68.

32. May, *Franz Josef*, 63-67.

33. Otto Friedländer, *Glanz*, 10.

There were some rough neighborhoods. Emil Kläger, like turn-of-the-century New York City's Jacob Riis, was an explorer of Vienna's poverty-stricken underworld. Tudor Edwards, summarizing Kläger's discoveries, writes,

> A legion of people slept in the Prater, sheltering beneath the arches of the Rotunde when it rained, and on the mud banks of the canal, and some went down into a hole in the earth, into the city sewers. The entrances to the sewers were underground corridors closed (but easily opened) with iron doors, and a few advertisement kiosks also led to this underworld. These were the haunts of tramps and wanted criminals, sleeping, and even cooking, on wood fires, in dark, foul, slimy, rat-ridden tunnels in which in places a man could barely stand. Sometimes they were so crowded that one man would be nominated as Hausmeister, to select the best places for sleeping and cooking, to limit the number of "guests," to guard against possible flooding and to contrive the best routes of escape when the police raided them, as they frequently did. For those with, say, six heller . . . in their pockets, there were innumerable doss-houses, mainly in the tightly-packed alleys and courts of Leopoldstadt, where grasping tenants of bellying, decaying houses would sub-let several squalid, bug-ridden rooms each night.[34]

Yet Vienna was also, for all these thousands, the land of opportunity, an America in the very heart of Europe. Jews from all over Eastern Europe, for example, flocked to Vienna. By 1910, Jews would make up around 8.6 percent of Vienna's population. Yet already by the 1890s, Jews, though only a small minority, made up some 48 percent of medical students and 58 percent of lawyers.[35]

By 1857, Vienna had turned itself inside out. The Vienna of Mozart, Beethoven, and Schubert was a snug little medieval town nestled inside its enormous ring walls. In less than an hour one could hike through the

34. Tudor Edwards, *The Blue Danube: The Vienna of Franz Josef and Its Aftermath* (London: Robert Hale, 1975), 93. See also Emil Kläger, *Durch die Wiener Quartiere des Elends und Verbrechens* (Vienna: Karl Mitschke, 1908).

35. Monika Glettler, "Urbanisierung und Nationalitätenproblem," in Berner, *Wien*, 185-96.

winding alleys and narrow lanes from one side of the city to the other. It was these stout walls that had twice protected the city from the invading Turks. But by the mid-1800s, the walls had become more a nuisance than a comfort. Napoleon, who captured the city in 1808, demonstrated that they offered little protection, and his engineers blew big holes in them. For that matter, the Viennese themselves rarely spent money on their upkeep — what was the use of spending money on fortifications in peacetime anyway? Land just outside the walls, the *glacis*, was supposed to be kept completely open, so that an attacker would have no cover and defenders would have a completely open field of fire. But the *glacis* was typically littered with shops and sheds, and no sooner would the authorities tear them down than enterprising Viennese would build them up again. In fact, some of the city's finest buildings, including the splendid baroque Karlskirche, Prince Eugene's Belvedere Palace, and the grand Schönbrunn Palace, were built outside the walls, and the walls increasingly became an obstruction rather than a defense. As the city swelled in size in the mid-1800s, most of the construction occurred outside the walls — so that, oddly enough, the massive fortifications were actually inside the city. The Viennese, to be sure, loved their old walls, and on Sunday afternoons, after church and after lunch, families would hike around the walls and children would scramble up and down them.

But by the 1850s, soldiers and business people and government officials were convinced that the old walls had become a nuisance and an eyesore. In December 1857, Emperor Franz Josef decreed that they would come down. And where they had been, the magnificent Ringstrasse, lined with all new imperial buildings, would go up.

For the better part of a generation, from the 1860s well into the 1890s, Vienna was a beehive of construction. Down came the giant old wall (though not everywhere; here and there sections remained, embedded, often, in old buildings, and one of the old gates was preserved as part of the Hofburg). Battalions of construction workers paved the new Ringstrasse where the wall had been, and other battalions raised up the magnificent new buildings: the Opera, the City Hall, the Theater, the Parliament, the Art and Natural History Museums. They laid out the fine new parks: the Volksgarten, Hofgarten, and Stadtpark.

"A mysterious veil had come over the city," one Viennese recalled;

magic was at work. Overnight a fantastic, elegant street suddenly appeared. Palaces seemed to spring up, their gold and strange frescoes shimmering . . . the sun flashed in thousands of new windows. A world of balconies, cupolas, and roofs arose, supported by marble columns shaped like warriors and goddesses, and high overhead bronze figures in chariots glistened.[36]

The Ringstrasse, she continued, "seemed to be a theater of costumes and masks, an art of fassade."[37]

The results certainly were extraordinary. "Forty-six years ago," A. S. Levetus wrote in a 1905 guide to the city, "Vienna was a medieval city with fortifications and bastions surrounding her." But now, it was a dazzling city of wide boulevards and imperial splendor.[38]

Maria Landsdale explained in her guide to the city:

No capital in Europe . . . had undergone such startling architectural changes in so short a space of time. In 1858, this city, which has occupied the same site since the beginning of the Christian era, was still enclosed by walls and moats.[39]

But in the twinkling of an eye, everything had changed. The old Inner City, once the city's center, Landsdale continued, "is like a dark island, well-nigh engulfed in the white sea of the new suburbs . . . [it is a] labyrinth of dark streets . . . that turn and twist and cross and re-cross one another."[40] The old Inner City still had its attractions, of course. For example, the old "high market," the Hohermarkt, was still well worth a visit, especially when it was decorated for the annual Christmas fair, the "Christkindlmarkt":

The time to visit the Hoher Markt . . . is Christmas eve. A forest has suddenly grown up there in a single night — a forest as marvelous as that of a fairy-tale. . . . It looks as though a magician had waved

36. Ann Tizia Leitich, *Verklungenes Wien* (Vienna: Wilhelm Andermann, 1942), 9.
37. Leitich, *Wien*, 20.
38. A. S. Levetus, *Imperial Vienna* (London: John Lane, 1905), 149.
39. Landsdale, *Vienna*, 3.
40. Landsdale, *Vienna*, 6.

his hand over a rainbow and turned it into myriads of serpents. . . .
At night, when the whole square is lit up, the effect is still more fantastic. The ground, covered with snow, and the wooden booths arranged like streets underneath the dark fir branches, give the place
the character of a scene in the Black Forest.[41]

The university, once in the center of the historic district, had moved out to
the elaborate new campus on the Ring. The city hall and the old royal theater had once been inside the walls; they too moved out to new homes on
the Ring. The city's aristocrats, once inhabitants of the old baroque palaces crowded inside the walls, now preferred to live in the fine new apartments just outside the Ring, especially around the new square, the
Schwarzenbergplatz. And the city's thousands of immigrants lived not in
the old center, but in the sprawling tenements that radiated outward from
the Ring. Even the extensions of the massive Hofburg Palace reached not
back into the old city, but outward, toward the Ring.

The Vienna that tourists knew, or thought they knew, Baedeker Vienna,
was a city of balls and coffeehouses, chatty, gossipy, and gay.

No one in Europe had the celebrations, the mania for dances and parties and balls that Vienna had. Few cities had a greater reputation for
charm and gaiety than Vienna. It was the city of the waltz, the city of constant music, the home of Mozart and Haydn and Beethoven, the city of
splendid, glorious, mid-winter balls.

The ball season began after Christmas and stretched all through the
dead of winter to Ash Wednesday. From January to March, each year, Vienna danced and swayed to the music. The city government sponsored a
ball; so did the lawyers, the fire department, and the police department.
There were two royal balls, one more or less public, the other reserved for

41. Landsdale, *Vienna*, 24.

the closest members of the court. There were costume balls and charity balls, small balls and huge and elaborate balls. Newspapers from January to March were filled with reports about balls, and in the cold winter nights, the gas-lit streets were filled with well-bundled figures in coaches on their way to the balls.

There were balls of all sorts — exclusive balls for the royalty, civil servants and policemen's balls, even balls for the patients in mental hospitals. All the guides to Vienna commented on them. An anonymous "English Officer" wrote that "one of the most amusing balls is given at the Drei Engel Saale . . . to the corps de ballet of the . . . Hofoper. Gentlemen receive invitations, otherwise they are not allowed to enter the room. The gentlemen are mostly from the nobility."[42]

No city in Europe had coffeehouses like Vienna's coffeehouses. It was the Turks who most likely brought coffee to Vienna, and probably a Pole living in Vienna who opened the first coffee house in the 1600s. Behind St. Stephen's Cathedral, not far from Mozart's "Figaro House" on Domgasse, a small wall plaque, presented to Vienna by Polish coffeehouse operators, informs passersby that here a Pole opened Vienna's first coffeehouse. By the late 1800s there were scores of them.

A coffeehouse was an unusual place. It was a public place, like a restaurant, but Vienna's coffeehouses were highly specialized. Journalists could be found at one café, artists at others. While artists frequented the Scheidl, and the Fenstergucker, actors tended to congregate at the Dobner or perhaps Café Stadtpark. Café Gabesam was a good general place for middle-class people.[43] Business people preferred one café, government officials another. Each had its distinct ambience, its own mood and feel, its

42. An English Officer, *Society Recollections in Paris and Vienna, 1879-1904* (London: John Long, 1907), 188.
43. See Robert Waissenberger, "Eine Metropole der Jahrhundertwende," in Waissenberger, *Wien*, 19-20.

distinct clientele, and its remarkably sophisticated waiters, who silently brought their regular customers their regular orders.

Coffee came in hundreds of varieties (black, lightly creamed, half-coffee/half-cream, with sugar, without sugar) and was normally served in a small cup and saucer carried on a silver platter. A small glass of water came with each cup. Coffeehouses always carried the latest newspapers; by the 1890s Vienna had scores of newspapers, and coffeehouses were where one went to sip coffee, catch up on the news, and — not least important — catch up on city gossip. Public places with a strong sense of privacy, open businesses with intimate charm, they were the Viennese equivalent to public squares. Landsdale, in her turn-of-the-century guide to the city, noted that "the café is the center of social life; there business is discussed and bargains concluded . . . it corresponds to the Forum of the ancients."[44] Every place in central Europe influenced by Vienna — from Prague and Budapest to Zagreb and Belgrade — had its own coffeehouses modeled after those of Vienna.

Vienna was a marvelous place in those days — at least for those with money. Landsdale provides a panorama of fin de siècle Vienna in her guide book:

> The Viennese streets are full of life and movement. . . . On a fine spring or autumn day, court equipages file by, the drivers wearing yellow breeches and laced three-corner hats; private carriages tear by like the wind; horsemen prance up and down, bowing to the ladies who promenade on the side-walks under full sail; here and there one sees picturesque groups of Hungarian officers, in boots and skin-tight pantaloons. . . . Austrian officers lounge by in pairs, charming — curled and scented like the gallant militarires of light

44. Landsdale, *Vienna*, 146.

opera, bodies swaying, chests inflated, a glass stuck in one eye. . . .
They are usually tall and thin, poised on top of their long legs like
herons. . . . Long-haired students, artists in peaked caps, child-
nurses in striking costumes — scarlet shirts, embroidered bodices
and caps of gold cloth — turbaned Turks . . . scholars of the
Theresianische Ritter-Academie, in the natty and becoming military uniform, small flower-girls.[45]

Luxury shopping was best along the Graben and the Kohlmarkt, in
the historic Inner City, an anonymous "English Officer" wrote in 1907.[46] In
the early evenings, from around 6:00 p.m. to around 8:00 p.m., when the
weather was fine, the better classes of the city make a kind of "corso"
through the old town, strolling up the Kärtnerstrasse toward St. Stephen's
Cathedral, then left on the Graben, then left again onto the short
Kohlmarkt, past the elegant shops and coffeehouses (including the world-
famous Dehmels), toward Michaelerplatz and the city gate of the Hofburg
Imperial Palace. "The people who walk there at this hour are mostly of the
well-to-do middle class, some officers of the line regiments, and a great
many of the demi-monde."[47] In the Inner City, grand old baroque palaces
still stood cheek to cheek, and there the leading families, the Esterházys
and Kinskys and Auerspergs and Lichtensteins and Metternichs, dined
and intrigued — not all year long, of course, but only in the winter — "the
season is in the winter, and all the fashionable world leaves Vienna in June
and returns in October."[48]

The principal club in Vienna is the Jockey Club, which is in the
Augustinerstrasse, opposite the Albrechtsplatz, where the palace of
the Archduke Frederick is situated . . . the subscription to the Jockey
Club is two hundred florins a year, and the requirements for admission are that the members be of noble family and have money; the
second requirement is much more insisted upon than the first.[49]

---

45. Landsdale, *Vienna*, 107.
46. An English Officer, *Recollections*, 141.
47. An English Officer, *Recollections*, 142.
48. An English Officer, *Recollections*, 305.
49. An English Officer, *Recollections*, 167.

In the northern part of the city was the great Prater amusement park. It had everything: a huge Ferris wheel (the "Risenrad"), puppet shows, beer tents, dancers, and singers. The Prater was a magical, unreal world. The "English Officer" explained the odd social mix in the Prater:

> The men among the audience are for the most part of the aristocracy, and the ladies are of all sorts and kinds. A great many of the demi-monde are present and a good number of actresses besides ladies in high society; but few of the middle class are seen.

The overall atmosphere was, he concluded, "fast."[50]

But Theodor Herzl wrote that, especially in the summer, everyone from every social class went to the Prater, leaving the city strangely abandoned. In 1899, Herzl, writing for the *Neue Freie Presse*, described Vienna during July this way:

> The connoisseurs of odd sensations will be especially attracted to the abandoned city. Everything is so strangely dead. You see for the first time, in the stony stillness, houses that you'd passed by dozens of times; it's a bit like looking at the face of a corpse of a good friend, and feeling that odd sensation that you'd never seen that face before. The homeowners are gone; disappeared. Who knows for how long? Their loves and hates are gone. Through gates, oddly opened now as if there were nothing left to protect, you can gaze into odd, silent courtyards. Here, in this old courtyard, a well with a crooked pump handle; grass grows between the flagstones; there, a hole in the ground, maybe it was a cistern. If you look down into these holes in the ground, you'd see terrifying, or maybe lovely secrets of the great silence. Now and again, one of the smaller doors around the courtyard swings open. Some unexpected, or maybe mythical, animal creeps out and reveals the magic behind this enchantment.

In the Prater, Herzl explained, dancers danced wildly until they were unconscious; children stared in awe at Punch and Judy shows and strongmen; young men and women flirted; fugitives from unhappy marriages looked for love. But that distinctive Viennese melancholy was never far

---

50. An English Officer, *Recollections*, 161.

away. Sooner or later, you'd have to leave the Prater, and Herzl concluded, "the passion of the dancers and all the noise and finally the kisses died away, and a kind of sadness fell on your heart, mixed with regret."[51]

But beyond and behind tourist Vienna was something very odd. To some people it seemed like everything in Vienna was just a little off, a little out of whack. You can't even figure out what time it is in this city, the *Neue Freie Presse* complained. By the late nineteenth century, the railroads had adopted standard Central European Time, but Vienna itself kept to its own city time, different from Central European Time. So Vienna operated according to two quite different times. Meantime, none of the public clocks along the Ringstrasse told either the one time or the other, because more often than not they were broken, or fast, or slow, or just plain wrong.

> So, everyone's supposed to be punctual … but … there are no public clocks anywhere that show the correct time! Vienna is the only major central European city that has yet to introduce Central European Standard Time … even though, of course, the trains, the telegraph office, the mail service and so on all operate on Central European Standard Time.[52]

The elegant Ringstrasse too was just a little peculiar. It was, to be sure, a magnificent boulevard, lined with fine chestnut trees. The thing was, though, most magnificent boulevards in most European capitals went somewhere, they led to or from some grand square. But the Ring simply went in a circle (or rather a horseshoe), from the Danube canal, south, then east, then north, following the lines of the old city fortifications, back to the canal. It was a fine place for walking in circles — Sigmund Freud often took his midday exercise by walking around the Ring — but it went nowhere.

51. Theodor Herzl, "Juli Sommer im Prater" (1899), in Zohn, *Untergang*, 110.
52. "Wien," *Neue Freie Presse*, January 3, 1897, 1.

And the buildings around the Ring were odd. They were grand structures, to be sure, and troops of tourists and immigrants wandered around the Ring, and craned their necks at the gigantic shapes that slowly seemed to float past them, the Opera (at the corner of Kärtnerstrasse and the Ring), the huge museums for art and natural history (westward along the Ring), the magnificent new Greek-style Parliament, with its colossal statue of Athena, and next to it, the medieval-style City Hall, and across from it, the new Theater, and down a ways, the gothic Votiv Church. The odd thing was that they all looked very old, and yet, of course, they were all brand new, all constructed after the 1860s. Vienna did have very old buildings, to be sure, but they were all nestled in the historic center of the city. The old-looking buildings along the Ring were, by the 1890s, no more than thirty years old.

Their very juxtaposition was strange too — the gothic City Hall sat next to the faux-Greek Parliament, which sat next to the massive neo-renaissance natural history and art museums. Their immense size, their Wagnerian scale, was impressive but also overblown. Even their structure was peculiar. The Parliament, for example, had no stairs in front; one entered via ramps sweeping on either side of the main entrance. The Opera, the Hofoper, seemed to squat elephant-like. That's what Kaiser Franz Josef disliked about it, and when he mentioned it, the horrified architect, Eduard van der Null, committed suicide. (Ever afterward, the Viennese said, the emperor refused to comment on anything. The only public remark he made about anything was "es hat mich sehr gefreut," "it pleased me very much.")

St. Stephen's, the medieval cathedral that was the city's landmark, was just a little off. Its medieval designers had planned for it to have two great towers, one on the north side, one on the south. The south tower was built, but for various reasons, the north tower was never completed; in the 1500s, it was simply capped off. The Viennese joked that the undone tower actually reflected the real Vienna perfectly: everything half-done, put-off, and covered-up.

The "blue" Danube, of course, was not blue at all, but like most great rivers, a murky green-brown. And for that matter, the city wasn't even on the Danube. The great river swept down from the Alps in a dozen different channels, and Vienna was built in ancient times on the south bank of one of these channels. Generations of Viennese worked to control these multiple Danubes and keep them from flooding; it was only in the late nineteenth century that the work was completed and the main course of the Danube was channeled away from the city, leaving the more modest Danube Canal on the city's north side. And for that matter, the "Vienna River," which flows through the city to the Danube, is no river at all, but is a rather innocuous creek.

Some thought it was the weather that made Vienna so strange. Vienna is perched on low hills on the far eastern extension of the Alps. The famous Wienerwald, the Vienna Woods, on the city's western edge, are the last reaches of the Alps. Winds periodically rush down from the Alps — the *Föhn,* they're called — and dramatically change the barometric pressure. Viennese are convinced that the *Föhn* gives some people headaches and make others act very strangely. Vienna's winters can be harsh and cold, but what distinguishes them are not the lovely snows of the Alps (though there can be heavy snowfalls), but the dull, unrelenting, leaden grey skies that obscure the sun for weeks on end.

Or perhaps it is the fact that Vienna had always been a city straddling several worlds, always a city delicately perched at the intersection of multiple borders.

Vienna, the far eastern bastion of German-speaking Central Europe, was bordered on the north by the Czechs, on the east by the Hungarians, on the south by Slovenes and Croatians. For years, it marked the far frontier of German-speaking Christian Europe, and twice was besieged by the panoplied armies of the Muslim Turks. Vienna's great prime minister of the Napoleonic era, Klemens von Metternich, pointing to the highway on the city's eastern edge, supposedly remarked that "Vienna still belongs to Europe, but Asia begins on the Landstrasse."[53] Here at Vienna's gates, according to Otto Friedländer,

> begin the strange and wild expanses of the east, the far east of the Kaiser's empire, which only soldiers and traders know. The Viennese clung to the friendly spirits of their mountains, they feared the melancholy of the steppes, on whose edges they buried their dead,

53. When and where Metternich supposedly said this is a matter of some debate, but the phrase quickly became part of Vienna's identity; see, for instance, Friedländer, *Glanz,* 10.

as if the poor souls were there to protect them from the evils spirits of the east . . . the Viennese were frightened by the spooky, wide-open spaces outside their gates, and even though they turned their backs to them, they were always there, dark and distant and scary.[54]

In 1888, emissaries from God visited Vienna.

Marie Meyer and her husband ran a milk and egg shop in the city. On the last day of 1888, two women came into the shop and asked Frau Meyer to make change. They chatted with her for a few moments. "Business isn't very good, is it?" they asked. "How in the world do you know that?" Frau Meyer, amazed, replied. "We're Gypsies, from Egypt," the visitors whispered, "we're not like normal people, we've been sent to you from God." One picked up an egg, hid it under a handkerchief, pulled the handkerchief away, and showed the egg to Frau Meyer.

There was a face on the egg.

"My God, what's that?" Frau Meyer exclaimed.

"That," the visitors grimly remarked, "that is the poor soul who haunts your house, who brings you so much grief."

Poor Frau Meyer was horrified. Whatever could she do? There was only one thing to do, the visitors exclaimed. The spirit had to be propitiated, a handful of coins would do it.

Frau Meyer and her frightened husband agreed, and handed the visitors some money.

The gypsies returned the next day. They had been in contact with the spirit, they excitedly explained, they had driven it away, but it had told them that there was treasure buried somewhere in the milk and egg shop! If only the Meyers would make another monetary sacrifice to the spirit, it would surely tell the gypsies where to find the treasure.

Alas for the gypsies. Suspicious, Herr Meyer went to his parish priest

54. Friedländer, *Glanz*, 10-11.

for advice. The priest called the police. The two gypsies were arrested (it turned out that only one really was a gypsy; the other was an Austrian), and were sentenced to three months in prison.

"It's scarcely to be believed," the *Neue Freie Presse* reported, that in an age of science and progress, "so much superstition can be found among the inhabitants of Vienna."[55]

Turn of the century Vienna was the capital of illusion. Nothing was quite what it seemed to be. Things had a strange way of turning into their opposites, not so much dramatically and openly as imperceptibly and subtly. It was as if everything were make-believe and masked.

Vienna's cityscape had changed so much that parents' Vienna was not their children's Vienna; habits and values of a decade earlier had become gauche a decade later. But the changes were not at all neat and precise; there was no clear demarcation between "then" and "now," in part because "then" lived well into "now," in part because no sooner had "now" been established than it faded into "then."

Paul Hofmann describes Vienna as a kind of "two room apartment." In one room is tourist Vienna: gay, frivolous, flirting, lovely, elusive; this is the room of Viennese *Schmäh*, that is, "blarney," and hand-kissing, and *Schlamperei*, that hopeless but jovial disorganization that seemed to affect everything in Vienna. But in the other room, hidden from the tourists' view, is another Vienna: bitter, resentful, frustrated, xenophobic, and violent. In Vienna, Hofmann writes, one always has the odd sensation that multiple realities flow past each other, that nothing is quite what it seems, that beneath official reality there is another, secret, shadowy reality, a world of nods and winks and illusions.[56]

---

55. "Die beiden Zigeunerinnen," *Neue Freie Presse*, February 10, 1889, morning edition, 6.

56. Paul Hofmann, *The Viennese* (New York: Doubleday, 1988), 1ff.

Vienna was an imperial city filled with self-important bureaucrats and stern soldiers. But nothing seemed to work quite right. By the 1890s, there hadn't been a military victory or a diplomatic triumph in generations. Austere Prussians in Berlin mocked Vienna's chronic *schlamperei*, the "sloppiness" with which Viennese seemed to do everything. To be sure there was something endearingly humane about this *schlamperei*. But there was also something frustrating about it, something maddening in the bureaucratic maze that made up official life, in the byzantine intrigues that characterized high society, in the insouciant attitude expressed by a Viennese saying: "It's disastrous but not serious."

The anonymous "English Officer" explained that costume was very important in Vienna. Outer dress immediately put you in your social category, and thereby made the vast anonymous urban population intelligible to each other — though, of course, the reliance on costume increased the possibility and significance of disguise. "Officers of the nobility," the "English Officer" wrote, "wear a brown overcoat instead of a black one, which is worn by other officers not belonging to the nobility. Then those officers who have fifteen ancestors on their father's and mother's sides wear a small gold band on the right side between two gold buttons, which means that they are the chamberlains of the Emperor."[57] He added that caste distinctions were extremely rigid and bewilderingly complex. The royals were at the top of society, of course, but were subdivided into a host of bickering factions. Then came the great nobles and beneath them the lesser nobles, divided as well into factions and cliques. The wealthy middling classes merged with the great nobles, but imperfectly. The more middling middle classes, on the other hand, were decidedly separate from the nobility. Below them were the lower orders, ranging downward from respectable artisans to proletarians to the criminal classes. The whole system was then cross-cut by religion and ethnicity: Hungarians, Czechs, Slovaks, Croatians, Poles, Italians, Jews, and all the others had their own class structures, which ran roughly parallel to the German-Viennese system. Aristocrats stayed in the Hotel Bristol or Hotel Imperial; middle-class people would never dream of staying in those places even if they could afford it. Cavalry officers, all sons of the aristocratic elite, almost never socialized

---

57. An English Officer, *Recollections*, 214-15.

with officers from other branches of the military. True, sometimes classes actually mixed, the "English Officer" explained:

> Of late years all these classes meet at certain balls, but they rarely marry out of their class, and if they do the Vienna world is always shocked, and they talk about it for weeks and sometimes for months afterward. The lady who marries into a higher class very rarely if ever enters into the society of that class.[58]

Everyone was acutely conscious of both class difference and class rank:

> It is astonishing what a great deal the people of the rich middle class think of the "aristokraten," as they call them; they look upon them as belonging altogether to a different sphere from themselves, and it is amusing sometimes to see how they cringe to them.[59]

Oddest of all, thought the "English Officer," was that peculiarly Viennese elusiveness, that fluidity between public and private, open and secret. The Viennese, he wrote, had an absolute mania for intrigue, gossip, whispers, private dinners and secret assignations.

> The people of all classes in Vienna are very free and easy and they seem to think that "péché caché est à demi pardonné," but anything done openly is very wrong indeed. I have known several instances of young girls of the nobility taking dinner or supper with an officer on the sly in a "chambre separée," whereas they would think twice before they would be seen with him in any public place, or walking in the streets, for they consider that in this case they could lose their reputation entirely, and in the former one it might pass by unperceived.[60]

The "personals" in the back pages of the newspapers revealed something of this peculiar and mysterious Vienna. Often the personals, even

---

58. An English Officer, *Recollections*, 220.
59. An English Officer, *Recollections*, 221.
60. An English Officer, *Recollections*, 299.

the back pages of the ultra-respectable *Neue Freie Presse,* were filled with secret messages:

> I cannot escape these bitter feelings. Do not expect a letter. (Sunday, December 1, 1889)

> The last time I saw you, you were coming from the theater. Look in the post office box (you know which one); there'll be a letter from me; I've signed it with the name of the play you were attending. (Wednesday, December 4, 1889)

> Dear Rosa! Please come home! Mother is deathly ill. Father deeply regrets his harshness. You can continue with your studies. Everything will be all right. (Friday, December 6, 1889)

> D.Z. I was there yesterday, but why didn't you come? I've got to speak with you. Please, please, send me a note. Address it to me, "poste restante," Mariahilf. (Friday, December 6, 1889)

> I'm beginning to be afraid of you. I can't write to you anymore. (Tuesday, December 17, 1889)

> Petersburg. Impossible this week. Next Tuesday, after 5 is best. Please answer yes or no. (Wednesday, December 25, 1889)

> Geometry. I can't stop thinking of you. Please let me see you again. (Wednesday, December 25, 1889)

> To Karoline. Have you read notice #1? Still with Mama. How I miss you! A million kisses. Therese. (January 5, 1890)

> The anonymous letter writer G.K. is requested to evidence proof for his claims. The recipient of this evidence, S.F., promises to pay 1000 Gulden. (Sunday, February 2, 1890)

> 4 3 2 1. Please don't come! We can never meet again! It's for the best! (Wednesday, February 5, 1890)[61]

---

61. All are from the "personals" in the back pages of the *Neue Freie Presse.*

Vienna was a city of stern family virtues, a patriarchal, hierarchical society in which children obeyed their parents and especially sons their fathers. And yet Vienna was a city of disintegrating families, of families laced with bitterness and intrigue. Vienna's first family, the Habsburgs, was a facade family. Publicly, they were the very model of the ideal Christian, aristocratic family. Privately, the family was filled with resentment. The marriage between Emperor Franz Josef and Empress Elizabeth was loveless. The relationship between the emperor and his son and heir, Rudolf, was cold and rancorous; that between empress and son was distant at best. Crown Prince Rudolf's marriage with Princess Stephanie was a marriage in name only; Rudolf's search for love in innumerable illicit relationships was pitiful. The Habsburgs could be amazingly cruel to each other. When the emperor's nephew (and later heir), Franz Ferdinand, announced his marriage to Countess Sophie Chotek, the Habsburg clan was outraged. Sophie Chotek was an aristocrat to be sure, but of the minor, Bohemian, aristocracy, and the clan angrily struggled to dissuade Franz Ferdinand from marriage. When he insisted on the marriage and won the emperor's grudging approval, he and Sophie were forced through a series of lifelong humiliations. He had to publicly declare the marriage "morganic" — that is, he had to agree that any offspring would have no claim to the Imperial throne; Sophie was forbidden entry to the royal palaces unless accompanied by her husband; in processions, Sophie could not walk beside her husband, but had to follow far in the rear; at dinners, she sat with the "lesser nobility," not with the Habsburg royals. The entire clan buzzed with misunderstandings and bruised feelings, frustrations and resentments, betrayals and deceits.

Vienna itself was a new city, with scores of new buildings both great and small, cross-hatched with new boulevards, graced with a new university rapidly becoming famous for its scientific research, and yet Vienna's ruler was an ancient old man addicted to wooden old ways (Franz Josef despised electricity and motor cars and all the confusing new ways), who was absorbed in court ritual and bureaucratic routine.

Vienna was a bustling metropolis, with one of Europe's most brilliant avant-gardes. But Vienna was also a closed, remarkably provincial city. Everyone in the elite knew everyone else. The better families married only into the better families. Social rules were strict; prohibitions were endless.

Among the better sort, one dressed this way for dinner, that way for theater, used these words at home and those words in company. The stifling turn of the century parlors of the proper middle classes symbolized, for frustrated young artists, the stodgy rigidity of Vienna. Egon Friedell, who would become an important social critic, remembered the parlors of his youth:

> Those weren't "living rooms." They were pawn shops, antique stores. There was a passion for everything satin, for silk . . . for patent leather, and gold frames, gold trinkets . . . ivory and pearl . . . for every kind of trinket, none related to the other: rococo mirrors with multiple pieces, windows with multi-color Venetian glass, thick and heavy old German cutlery. On the floors were thick rugs of animal skins . . . in the foyer, a life-size wooden Moor. Every sort of style was mixed together . . . there was every imaginable kind of ornament and ornamentation . . . there was no interest at all in utility, in purpose, everything was only a kind of parade . . . the biggest, airiest room of the whole house, the so-called "best room," was not a living room at all, but only a kind of show room for visitors.[62]

Otto Friedländer considered the city itself to be an enormous museum:

> Vienna is the gate to the orient, but Vienna is more than that. It is the gate to a hundred pasts. Innumerable relics, living and dead, are gathered and cared for here — exiled monarchs, worthies with extinguished titles, ancient orders of knights, none of which have any purpose beyond preserving themselves.[63]

Newspapers around the world live for sensation, so Vienna's papers were hardly unique in highlighting the weird. That said, the fact remains that hardly an issue of any of Vienna's papers appeared without at least some small feature like this:

---

62. Egon Friedell, cited in Allan Janik and Stephen Toulmin, *Wittgensteins Wien*, trans. Reinhard Merkel (Munich: Carl Hanser, 1984), 125.

63. Friedländer, *Glanz*, 12.

Scene at a Funeral
(Tuesday, January 19, 1897, *Neue Freie Presse*)

Yesterday, around 4:00 p.m., a funeral procession, led by a funeral band, was winding through Simmeringerstrasse, when Joseph Bauer, 24, a day laborer, suddenly rushed into the middle of the funeral band and began to dance. His antics naturally provoked outrage, and he was immediately arrested. At the precinct house he continued with his wild behavior, and cursed the police officers who tried to restrain him. He was charged with interfering with the legitimate functions of a legally recognized church, and with resisting arrest.

Or this:

Conflict in a Coffeehouse
(Tuesday, May 18, 1897, *Neue Freie Presse*)

In an unnamed coffeehouse, filled with officers and their ladies and miscellaneous civilians, one officer suddenly sprang to his feet, ran to one of the civilian men and shouted: "I will not permit you to molest these ladies with your looks!" The officer pulled his sword, the civilian pulled his umbrella, and only the intervention of others prevented blood being shed.

Not every encounter with the strange was so grim. Everyone in Vienna loved parades, for example — the more spectacular, the better. The greatest parade of all was the summer Corpus Christi procession. "It is like a vision of fairyland," Maria Landsdale told her readers,

All this Imperial and sacerdotal pomp, the robes of crimson and violet, the glowing tunic and chasubles, the floating albs, the gold-laced uniforms, the plumbed head-pieces, the theatrical liveries, the cloud of lace, the flaming mass of gold braid, church ornaments of gold and jewels, sweep before one's dazzled eyes like a celestial vision.[64]

---

64. Landsdale, *Vienna*, 282.

The Viennese, Landsdale added, were fascinated by omens and occult signs. It was vital to say "God bless you" when someone sneezed, to ward off disease. Everyone had some secret technique for calculating the lottery's winning numbers; "mention to your landlady that you have lost your pocket-book," Landsdale writes, "and she will eagerly inquire the exact date and hour when it was lost, in order to purchase a lottery ticket with the corresponding numbers."[65]

By the 1880s in Vienna, writes Bruno Bettelheim, "it was as if the city could not decide which way to turn: toward the glorious (though receding) past, or toward a new and modern future."[66] The city's mood became darker, and words like "fate" and "doom" became increasingly common. The Empress Elizabeth, "hysterical, narcissistic, and anorexic," according to Bettelheim, seemed to reflect Vienna's, and the empire's, increasing nervousness. Indeed, even before the economic crash of 1873, Elizabeth had become stranger and stranger, ever more frantic. "In 1871," Bettelheim writes,

> when the emperor wrote to Elizabeth, who, as always, was not in Vienna, asking her what gift she would like best to receive on her name day, she wrote back, probably in a spirit of self-mocking, "what I would really like best would be a completely equipped insane asylum."[67]

As early as the 1880s, Vienna had begun to acquire those distinct qualities associated with the ends of centuries. According to historian Tudor Edwards:

> Vienna ... had ... acquired the peculiar perfume associated with fin de siècle qualities. It was a heady perfume that was wafted along the Ringstrasse and the Kärntnerstrasse and blew through the city parks and gardens, where not even the chestnut and lilac could dispel it. It smacked of abandon and risqué pleasures, of purple patches and strange quests, of love and melancholy. It spoke for a

65. Landsdale, *Vienna*, 293.
66. Bruno Bettelheim, *Freud's Vienna and Other Essays* (New York: Knopf, 1990), 3.
67. Bettelheim, *Freud's Vienna*, 9.

world of rarefied culture, refinement, lassitude and decadence, symbolized in the work of Hofmannsthal and Rilke, as its physical love and spiritual malaise were expressed in the novels of Schnitzler and Bahr. It was suggested by the tobacco kiosks, little pagodas of ornamental cast-iron, that were now appearing at street corners and other strategic points. It was reflected in the art nouveau costumes of the women, with their velvet facings and cascades of lace, their hats trimmed with feathers and artificial fruits and flowers, and their shoes starred with silver buckles.[68]

"Beautiful thou art," Grillparzer, one of Vienna's greatest writers, wrote of the city, "yet dangerous too."[69]

In 1897, newspaper reports of a grisly murder attracted *Neue Freie Presse* journalist (and future founder of Zionism) Theodor Herzl's attention. Herzl's specialties were feuilletons, human interest stories that were part editorial, part poetic evocation. A man, it seems — a stupid and vulgar man — was accused of poisoning his wife. A disgusting but simple story. But, Herzl wondered, was it really so simple? It reminded him of the medieval "Bluebeard" legends, those legends about horrific murderers of women and children, legends reworked in the modern stories of Offenbach and Huysmann. Such terrors belong in fiction or in some other epoch, don't they? Herzl rhetorically asked. Certainly they don't belong in our modern times. But then, alas, Herzl worried, maybe they do. Maybe the moral of the murder story is that even in our day, the monstrous waits restlessly just below the civilized surface, ready to explode at the least provocation.[70]

Later that year, on Halloween, in another feuilleton, Herzl reviewed a ghost story play by Ernst Raupach, "The Miller and His Child." Why, Herzl asked, are we all so fascinated by ghosts?

That we, who so love sunshine and blue sky, will someday cease to exist, that one day it will be as if we had never even existed, we sim-

---

68. Edwards, *Danube*, 81.

69. Hofmann, *The Viennese*, 330.

70. "Scene bei einem Leichenbegräbniss," *Neue Freie Presse*, January 19, 1897, 7; "Conflict in einem Kaffeehaus," *Neue Freie Presse*, May 18, 1897, 7; "Der neue Blaubart," *Neue Freie Presse*, March 21, 1897, 1.

ply cannot endure that thought. And so we manufacture ghosts. It's sort of a comfort to have them around; they are far less terrifying than Nothingness. And so they haunt us in all sorts of guises, and the drive that compels us to conjure them up is the drive to defend ourselves against extinction, against Nothingness.[71]

71. "Vom Grusseln," *Neue Freie Presse,* October 31, 1897, 5.

Chapter 2

NECROPOLIS

Horror at the corpse and . . . fear of the ghost . . . [is] the very nucleus of all religious belief and practice.

Wilhelm Wundt[1]

On January 1, 1900, on the first day of the first month of the brand new twentieth century, the lions in the Vienna Zoo ate the zoo's snake-handler.

The victim's name was Carl Rudowsky, he was forty years old, and according to the *Neues Wiener Tagblatt* he was an "industrious, good-hearted, and intelligent man." Rudowsky was a snake-handler who always wanted to be a lion-tamer. He had spent that special New Year's Eve, which inaugurated not only a whole new year but a whole new century, drinking with friends. That perhaps explains why, early on the morning of January 1, he decided to climb into the lions' cage and tame them.

But they were not to be tamed, and they attacked Rudowsky fiercely. He fought back bravely and screamed for help and frantically fended the lions off, and within a few minutes a half-dozen zoo workers had run to

---

1. Wilhelm Wundt, cited in Bronislaw Malinowski, *Magic, Science, and Religion* (New York: Doubleday, 1954), 17.

his rescue, but what could they do? It took a good ten minutes for the workers, using poles and water hoses and finally flaming straw to drive the lions away. By then, poor Rudowsky was quite dead.

According to the reporters, "Rudowsky lay there, bleeding from a score of wounds. Sarah the Lion had gnawed his head so awfully that he was scarcely recognizable . . . his nose and his ear had been entirely torn away." The doctor who performed the autopsy on Rudowsky told the papers that Rudowsky had died not of his terrible wounds, but rather of sheer terror. The zoo's management attempted to comfort Rudowsky's widow, who also worked at the zoo, by assuring her that the zoo would always have a job for her.[2]

Vienna at the turn of the last century was the capital of death. Perhaps no city in Europe, no city in the world for that matter, had cultivated such a refined, and morbid, fascination with death. As Peter Hanák writes, "hardly anywhere else in Europe can one find a place so permeated by a death-aesthetic and a death-erotic as Vienna."[3] This death-aesthetic does not mean that the Viennese were all pious. But if Malinowski and Wundt are right that "horror at the corpse and . . . fear of the ghost . . . [is] the very nucleus of all religious belief and practice,"[4] then turn-of-the-century Vienna was a very religious place indeed.

A delicate whiff of nostalgia and melancholy was everywhere in the Viennese air around the turn of the century. In a sweetly maudlin piece called "Trudy's Tears," Theodor Herzl wrote about a little girl who burst into tears when she couldn't learn to read fast enough. Her tear stained her little book. One day, when Trudy's grown up, Herzl concluded, she might

2. "Im Löwenkäfig zerfleischt," *Neues Wiener Tagblatt,* January 2, 1900.

3. Peter Hanák, "Lebensgefühl oder Weltanschauung?" in Peter Berner, Emil Brix, and Wolfgang Mantl, eds., *Wien um 1900. Aufbruch in die Moderne* (Vienna: Verlag für Geschichte und Politik, 1986), 158.

4. Malinowski, *Religion,* 48.

come across that little book and that small tear stain. "And then, maybe a second tear will fall next to the first. 'Life's going too slowly!' said the first tear.' 'No, no,' says the second tear, 'life's passing by so fast!'"[5]

"Vienna," Frederic Morton writes, "had not only more suicides per capita than most European cities, but a particularly high incidence among the upper bourgeoisie."[6] Suicide, to be sure, was never exactly condoned by the Viennese, and it was rigorously condemned by religious Viennese. And yet, oddly enough, suicide seemed, if not exactly epidemic, then certainly frequent enough to be no stranger. Eduard van der Null was one of the architects of Vienna's grand Hofoper, constructed on the Ring; when Emperor Franz Josef made a disparaging remark about it, Null committed suicide. General Baron Franz von Uchatius invented a new gun; when it failed in its tests, he shot himself. Ludwig Boltzmann, one of the founders of statistical thermodynamics, killed himself. So did Otto Mahler, the brother of composer Gustav Mahler; artist Richard Gerstl; poet Georg Trakl; Otto Weininger, the controversial author of *Sexuality and Character;* and several members of philosopher Ludwig Wittgenstein's family. Franz Strauss, the progenitor of the famous composers, drowned himself in the Danube. Hofmannsthal's son and Schnitzler's daughter would both commit suicide.[7]

The press regularly printed suicide reports. For example:

Officer commits suicide (Sunday, January 10, 1897)

Last Sunday, First lieutenant Friedrich Neumann went to the Franciscan Church in Gran then returned to his apartment, sat down at his desk, and took out his pistol, and shot himself in the chest. Just before, he had sent his man out on an errand; when he returned, he discovered the lieutenant's body. Lieutenant Neumann was described as a quiet, introverted young man. He avoided parties, took long walks alone, and lived only for his profession. His only reading consisted of military books. He spent every evening alone,

5. Theodor Herzl, "Trudel's Träne," *Neue Freie Presse,* April 2, 1899, 7.

6. Frederic Morton, *A Nervous Splendor: Vienna 1888-1889* (New York: Penguin, 1979), 67.

7. See Allan Janik and Stephen Toulmin, *Wittgensteins Wien,* trans. Reinhard Merkel (Munich: Carl Hanser, 1984), 79; Peter Gay, *Freud: A Life for Our Time* (New York: Norton, 1988), 40; Paul Hofmann, *The Viennese* (New York: Doubleday, 1988), 172.

studying. He was so shy among women that he was described as a misogynist.

"Tired of living" (Sunday, January 17, 1897)

Attorney Franz E., who resided on Mariahilfe, 42 years old and single, committed suicide yesterday by shooting himself in the head. In a suicide note sent to his work supervisor, E. cited a long, exhausting, and very painful nervous disorder as the motive for his deed.

The *Neue Freie Presse* reported in 1897 that between 1888 and 1896, some 3,164 Viennese had committed suicide, averaging 352 per year. In 1896, 318 men and 78 women killed themselves. Hanging was the preferred suicide method, followed by gunshot. Suicides were rarest, in 1896, in December (only 15); they were most common in May (56). According to the paper, May had long been Vienna's preferred month for suicide.[8]

No one, it seemed — indeed, still seems — is as fond of a "handsome corpse," a *schöne Leich*, as the Viennese say. Some say the Viennese morbidity is a strange product of the weather. The city is on the easternmost spur of the Alps; the Alps drift down into a network of rolling hills, the famous Vienna Woods, the Wienerwald, and just farther east is Vienna proper. Farther east, the land flattens out into the Hungarian plains and Eastern Europe. Odd winds — the Viennese call them the *Föhn* — blow down from the hills and out into the plains, and when the air pressure suddenly shifts, people's moods seem to change inexplicably. Still others think it the winter. From early fall well into late spring each year, Vienna is inevitably overcast: leaden clouds hang over the city, light ranges from daylight grey to nighttime black, and while snow sometimes adds light and color, most of winter Vienna is grey and bleak.[9] But if the winters explained the morbidity, why would May be the month for suicides?

The more historically minded point to the enormous impact of the Baroque, and especially the Spanish Baroque, on Vienna. Vienna was one

8. "Selbstmord eines Offiziers," *Neue Freie Presse*, January 10, 1897, 7; "Lebensmüde," *Neue Freie Presse*, January 17, 1897, 7; "Selbstmordstatistik," *Neue Freie Presse*, January 15, 1897, 6.

9. Hofmann, *The Viennese*, 213.

of the capitals of the Catholic Reformation in the 1500s and 1600s. The Baroque imagination that fueled the Catholic Reformation was drunk with the spiritual, the mysterious, the otherworldly. The Viennese Habsburgs, moreover, were influenced powerfully by their Spanish Habsburg cousins; the Viennese imported not only the Spanish riding school and the intensely formal and rigid Spanish court etiquette, but also a certain Spanish fascination with the horizons of life. The Habsburg custom of burial — removal of the heart, removal of the viscera, mummification of the corpse — most likely came from the Spanish (who most likely learned the technique from the Arabs).

Wherever this phenomenon came from, Vienna was a city haunted by death and fascinated by the macabre.[10] The late 1800s redesign of the city's main cemetery, the Zentralfriedhof, became a major civic issue.[11] Describing a museum display recounting the city's siege by the Turks in the 1600s, Maria Landsdale wrote in her guide:

> Under glass it preserved a ghastly trophy, the skull of the Turkish general Kara Mustapha, together with his shirt — the one in which he died — and the silken cord pointedly sent him by the Sultan after his defeat. . . . [T]he copper-colored skull, stuck on a peg, with the strangler's cord lying by it, has a really horrible effect. It seems to grimace still, as though in the last convulsions.[12]

"It would seem as though the Viennese were desirous of imparting something cheerful even to the idea of death itself," Landsdale noted. "[T]heir coffins are of the finest workmanship." The Viennese celebrated All Souls Day, in early November, she continued, with "reverent piety":

> The graves are decorated with wreathes and flowers, and lit up with lanterns, tapers, and small lamps. Among the lower classes it is firmly believed that, should one have the courage to walk through a cemetery at midnight of that day, he would meet a long procession

10. Hofmann, *The Viennese*, 3-5.

11. William Johnston, *Vienna, Vienna: The Golden Age, 1815-1914* (New York: Crown, 1980), 188-89.

12. Maria Horner Landsdale, *Vienna and the Viennese* (Philadelphia: Henry T. Coates, 1902), 52.

of phantoms, following after whom would be seen the spirits of all those who were destined to die in the course of the ensuing year.[13]

Europeans in general, at least European intellectuals, seemed obsessed with death as the fin de siècle approached. Historian Shearer West suggests that the end of every century brings with it an inescapable sense of endings and deaths. While the term "fin de siècle" was popularized in 1888 by two Parisian writers, a fin de siècle tone, a mood of decline, doom, and impending disaster, seems to be a recurring phenomenon, typically bound up with millenarian prophecies, warnings of Christ's Second Coming, omens of the end of the world, and a pervasive cultural pessimism. These fears took on a decidedly Darwinian tone in the late nineteenth century in Max Nordau's immensely influential book, *Degeneration* (1892).

Modern times, Nordau insisted — including such things as industrialization, city life, immigration, changes in sexual behavior — all triggered an undeniable "racial degeneration." Its symptoms? Crime, illness, suicide, sexual perversions of all sorts, rebellious youth, psychiatric disease. Conservatives throughout Europe, fearful of losing their fragile hold on power, quickly picked up Nordau's refrain. As trade unions and Socialist parties grew rapidly, corporate executives began to echo aristocrats' fears of future chaos. Christian leaders, notably the pope, warned of the awful dangers of "modernism." Women's demands for equal rights triggered a pervasive fear of "sexual anarchy." What all this produced was the "cultural pessimism" distinctive of the late nineteenth century.[14]

Viennese pessimism, then, was obviously part of a much wider European phenomenon. But pan-European fin de siècle cultural pessimism had, in Vienna, a distinctive Viennese accent. Partly this came from the bizarre experience of the Habsburgs. They were, it seemed, cursed.

Franz Josef came to power in 1848, in a tide of violence and blood.

13. Landsdale, *Vienna,* 292.

14. Shearer West, *Fin de Siècle: Art and Society in an Age of Uncertainty* (Woodstock, N.Y.: Overlook Press, 1994), especially Chapter 1, "The Fin de Siècle Phenonenon," and Chapter 2, "Degeneration." For more on cultural pessimism, see Fritz Stern's classic account, *The Politics of Cultural Despair: A Study in the Rise of the German Ideology* (Berkeley: University of California Press, 1974); on sexual anarchy, see Mary Louise Roberts, *Disruptive Acts: The New Woman in Fin-de-Siècle France* (Chicago: University of Chicago Press, 2002).

That year, across Europe, liberals and nationalists had united to overthrow Europe's old monarchical and aristocratic order, which had been terribly shaken by the French Revolution and Napoleon, though it was propped back up largely by Austria's Klemens von Metternich. But by 1848, explosives like "human rights," "democracy," and "national self-determination" detonated under the old order's pillars of command, obedience, hierarchy, and privilege. Viennese democrats and Hungarian and Czech nationalists poured into the streets; troops loyal to the dynasty fired on them; chaos wracked the empire for months. In the end, as part of the settlement, the befuddled emperor Ferdinand I abdicated, and was succeeded by his eighteen-year-old nephew, Franz Josef. Franz Josef promised reform but vowed simultaneously to defend the status quo, and though the violence subsided, everyone recalled that he came to the throne with guns cracking in the distance and blood in the streets.

Death followed him every step of his seemingly endless reign.

In 1853, an assassin almost killed him. The twenty-three-year-old emperor was standing atop the massive old wall on the southern side of the city, very near an apartment building where Beethoven had once lived. The assassin slashed at the emperor with a knife, but the blade caught in the emperor's thick leather collar. In thanksgiving for the emperor's survival, the Viennese built the neo-gothic Votiv Kirche just outside the old city walls.

In the 1860s, France's slippery Emperor Napoleon III hatched a scheme to seize power in Mexico. (Mexico was in chaos; the United States was distracted by its civil war; France had no New World colonies to speak of but dearly wanted some; and Napoleon III, in any case, counted a day without a conspiracy to be a lost day.) He needed a cat's-paw and found one in Franz Josef's brother, Maximilian. Max was only two years younger than his big brother Franz Josef, but had no hopes for inheriting the throne, especially after the birth of Crown Prince Rudolf in 1858. Napoleon III's offer to make Max "Emperor of Mexico" was appealing. And so Max and his wife, Carlotta, daughter of the king of the Belgians, set off for Mexico City. They had no idea what they were getting into. Benito Juarez led a fierce struggle against the invaders, and in 1867 the French were defeated — and, while Carlotta frantically traveled Europe looking for help, Maximilian was captured. On June 19, 1867, Archduke Maximilian was shot to death by firing squad. His bullet-riddled corpse was sent home and buried in the Capuchin Church on the Neuer Markt. Carlotta returned to Belgium, where she would live another sixty years, mad and ghost-ridden. (Max and Carlotta had no children together, but apparently Maximilian had a son by his Mexican mistress. And it appears that Carlotta had a son by a Belgian officer; the boy grew up in France, and became famous in 1940, as General Maxime Weygand, who surrendered the French army to the invading Germans.)

Crown Prince Rudolf, Emperor Franz Josef's son, committed suicide in 1889.

In 1896, Franz Josef's brother, Archduke Charles Ludwig, died of typhoid fever after becoming infected during a pilgrimage to the Holy Land.[15]

Then, in 1898, while Vienna was gaily celebrating Franz Josef's fiftieth year as emperor, Empress Elizabeth was assassinated while on holiday in Switzerland. She was stabbed to death by an anarchist. Her funeral, like all the other royal funerals, left an indelible mark on the souls of those who saw it. A. S. Levetus, who later wrote a history of the city called *Imperial Vienna*, wrote,

> Never can I forget that night when they brought the murdered Empress back to Vienna . . . it was a warm September night, a dead silence reigned over all, the very air seemed motionless, and a deep and solemn hush fell over the stricken city.

Levetus remembered that the street lights had been turned off and replaced by thousands of torches, "lighted torches which shed an uncertain, lurid, light on the faces of the expectant and silent crowd."[16] When he heard the report, for a moment, Franz Josef's dogged stoicism failed him, and he exclaimed, "Mir bliebt doch gar nichts erspart auf dieser Welt?" ("Am I to be spared nothing in this world?").

---

15. For a report on the funeral, see "Erzherzog Karl Ludwig," *Neue Freie Presse*, May 19, 1896.

16. A. S. Levetus, *Imperial Vienna* (London: John Lane, 1905), 164. For news coverage of the murder and funeral, see, for example, "Kaiserin Elizabeth," *Neue Freie Presse*, September 11, 1898, and reports on the subsequent several days.

He was spared nothing. In 1914, the new heir to the throne, Archduke Franz Ferdinand, the son of Charles Ludwig who had died of typhoid, was shot to death together with his wife in Sarajevo, in the terrorist action that would trigger the Great War. In 1916, Franz Josef himself would die, after some sixty-eight years as Austro-Hungary's emperor. Two years later, the vast empire he had spent a lifetime trying to preserve collapsed and shattered into pieces.

The chronology of Franz Josef's reign is scarred by one disaster after another:

1848: The reign begins with blood. The Revolutions of 1848 nearly topple the House of Habsburg, and fighting in the empire kills some 6,000 people. Franz Josef comes to power promising reform, but is determined to keep the Habsburgs in power.[17]

1859: Piedmont's cunning prime minister, Camillo Cavour, plots with French emperor Napoleon III to expel Austria from northern Italy. In the brief but bloody war of 1859, Austria is defeated at Solferino; Austria is expelled from northern Italy, and Cavour and Garibaldi proceed to unify Italy under Piedmont's House of Savoy.

1866: To the north, Prussia's Otto von Bismarck plots to expel Austria from Central Europe. Austria and Prussia join forces in 1864 to defeat Denmark, but two years later Prussia turns against Austria. Austria is defeated and expelled from Central Europe. Bismarck proceeds to unite German-speaking Central Europe under Prussia's House of Hohenzollern.

1867: Franz Josef and the Hungarians reinvent the empire. Hungary becomes a separate kingdom, but its king would be Franz Josef, thus uniting Hungary with Austria to form the Austro-Hungarian Empire. But now the Czechs begin to demand autonomy too. The German-speaking western half of the empire, incidentally, is not really named "Austria" at all; in fact,

17. There are many accounts of 1848 in the Austrian Empire; see, for example, Tudor Edwards, *The Blue Danube: The Vienna of Franz Josef and Its Aftermath* (London: Robert Hale, 1973), 19.

in official documents, it has no name. The official designation of the empire as "royal" and "imperial," "königlich und kaiserlich," or "kk," sounds like "kaka," a child's name for excrement.

1873: Vienna hosts a World Exposition. Theodore Roosevelt Sr. visits, representing the United States, and brings his bustling family, including his son, Theodore Roosevelt Jr., the future president. But disaster strikes: on May 9, 1873, financial markets around the world collapse, plunging the world economy deep into depression. Vienna's liberals, who have advocated free markets as the road to prosperity, fall back into panicky retreat. Many of Vienna's Jews have embraced the liberal ideals of both free market and open society; bankrupt Viennese begin to denounce Jewish financiers for the crash, and anti-liberalism turns anti-Semitic.

1884: Politics takes an increasingly tribal and demagogic turn. Among German-speaking Viennese, a mean-spirited, paranoid, anti-immigrant, anti-foreigner mood evolves; its spokesman is Georg von Schönerer, fanatic and racist. While Schönerer is generous with his hate, his focus is especially on Jews. At the height of his power in 1884-85, Schönerer adds a vicious "new tone" to Viennese politics, a tone of threat, hysteria, and violence.[18] Jewish Viennese, the targets of Schönerer's attacks, find themselves in an odd No-Man's Land, no longer at home in the ultra-Orthodox ghettoes of eastern Europe, but neither fully accepted by non-Jews in the metropolis. As Peter Pulzer writes, "the Jews of Vienna drifted somewhere between integration and segregation," and this eerie and painful condition shapes much of fin de siècle Vienna's distinctive art.[19]

1897: A doubly disastrous year. First, after endless struggles and intrigues, and despite Emperor Franz Josef's protests, Karl Lueger becomes Vienna's mayor. Lueger is one of the founders of the Christian Social Party. Folksy

---

18. See Carl Schorske's comments on Schönerer in Carl Schorske, *Fin de Siècle Vienna: Politics and Culture* (New York: Vintage, 1980), 120-33. Nazis, of course, rightly saw Schönerer as a forebear; for a Nazi-era biography, see Wilhelm Bauer, *Georg Ritter von Schönerer* (Klagenfurt: Das deutsche Volksbildungswerk, 1941).

19. Peter Pulzer, "Liberalismus, Antisemitismus, und Juden in Wien der Jahrhundertwende," in Berner, *Wien*, 32.

and shrewd, Lueger combines populism with anti-Semitic demagoguery. Two years earlier, after Lueger and his allies scored a big win in city elections, the *Neue Freie Presse* mourned:

> Well, the election is over. Vienna has been handed over to its arch-enemy, the arch-enemy of freedom, intelligence, progress, the arch-enemy of Vienna's whole effort to become a major city. Or rather, the Viennese have themselves, all on their own, decided to plunge themselves into slavery.[20]

And two years after that, after yet another big electoral win by Lueger and his followers, the *Neue Freie Presse* expresses its shock this way: "Our constitution is radically changed, our party system has suffered an earthquake, our whole political physiognomy has been totally altered."[21]

Then riots erupt in Prague. Vienna has decreed that bureaucrats in Prague have to speak Czech, since, after all, the majority of people in the city are Czech-speaking. But the German minority, which is also the political and social elite, is furious, and terrified at being overwhelmed by the "foreign" Czechs. College students take up arms on both sides, and violence sweeps the city. Back in Vienna, in Parliament (that is, in the Parliament for the non-Hungarian side of the empire), Czech and German members shriek at each other, and when fistfights break out, police have to rush inside to restore order.

By 1900, it appeared to nearly everyone that the empire was on the verge of disaster.

Politics had turned very sour. The number of people who would openly advocate the old liberal values of open minds, open societies, open markets, and open politics had shrunk drastically. Meanwhile, ethnic animosity and race-baiting had given politics a vicious and violent tone. Most worrying, this violent, racist authoritarianism wasn't simply a fringe mentality; more and more respectable people began expressing these attitudes, and mass organizations like the Christian Social Party openly advocated them. As the great historian of late Habsburg politics, John Boyer, wrote on Karl Lueger's becoming mayor of Vienna: "Nowhere else in Cen-

20. "Wien," *Neue Freie Presse*, September 17, 1895.
21. "Wien," *Neue Freie Presse*, January 1, 1897.

tral Europe in the nineteenth century did an explicit non-liberal political movement with a powerful command of bourgeois loyalties take control of a major urban administration."[22]

The old empire was dying a very strange death. "On the surface," as Edward Crankshaw writes, "this beautiful city had never seemed more vital than when it was dying."[23] One didn't know whether to laugh or cry. On the one hand, the preposterous old empire had to die. For one thing, quite literally, no one knew quite what to call it. Sometimes, as novelist Robert Musil wrote, it was called "kaiserlich-königlich" (Imperial-Royal), and other times it was "kaiserlich und königlich" (Imperial and Royal).

> Everyone and everything was marked either "k.k." or "k.u.k.," but it took a secret science to figure out which was properly "k.k." or "k.u.k." In writing, it was officially the Austro-Hungarian Empire, but most people just called it Austria, a name it had officially dropped, but nevertheless emotionally retained, proving that emotions are as important as laws, and that regulations aren't really all that serious. According to its constitution it was officially liberal, but it was run by clericals. That is, it was run by clericals who lived like free-thinkers. All citizens equal before the law, but not everybody, of course, was a citizen. There was a Parliament, which made such great use of its freedoms that it normally was closed. There were emergency laws according to which the government could rule when Parliament was closed, but just when people rejoiced at the return to Absolutism, the crown would order that things should be ruled by parliament.[24]

Historian Robert Musil dubbed the monarchy "kakania."

There were threats everywhere. To the north, the empire's muscular and ambitious cousin, the German Empire, quickly became the dominant partner in their relationship. To the east, the Russian Empire threatened to expand into the Balkans. In the Balkans, Serbs schemed to expel the Aus-

22. John W. Boyer, *Political Radicalism in Late Imperial Vienna* (Chicago: University of Chicago Press, 1981), ix-x.

23. Edward Crankshaw, *The Fall of the House of Habsburg* (New York: Viking, 1963), 317.

24. Robert Musil, *Mann ohne Eigenschaften,* cited in Janik and Toulmin, *Wittgensteins Wien,* 44-45.

trians, just as the Italians and Prussians had done. And inside the empire, the multiple ethnic groups plotted bloody murder. As early as December 1873, Crown Prince Rudolf wrote:

> The kingdom still stands, a mighty ruin, continuing from one day to the next, but doomed finally to fall. For centuries it has endured, and so long as the people allowed themselves to be led blindly, it was good; but now its task is at an end, all men are free, and the next storm will sweep away this ruin.[25]

But as long as the Kaiser lived, everything would be fine. Year after year, decade after decade, generation after generation, no matter what catastrophe stunned the empire, the Emperor Franz Josef was still there.

As the years went by, Franz Josef lived as if nothing ever changed. He refused to have indoor plumbing or electric lights in the Hofburg Palace; he insisted on traveling by horse-drawn coach long after automobiles had invaded the city (by 1910, there were some 3,284 cars and 2,665 motorcycles in Vienna[26]); centuries-old court ceremonies ground on, oblivious to the calendar. There was nothing friendly or democratic about the royal court; it remained as aloof and detached from daily events as it had been generations before. An air of mystery and secrecy surrounded the court, Otto Friedländer remembered: "The secrets of the Austrian royal court were like the secrets of the Great Beyond; the more you heard about them, the more mysterious they seemed."

25. Cited in Crankshaw, *Fall*, 285.

26. Bundespolizeidirektion Wien, ed., *80 Jahre Wiener Sicherheitswache* (Vienna: Jugend und Volk, 1949), 44.

Conservatives worried that what was dying in Vienna was a whole way of life built around the ancient aristocratic elite. An anonymous 1878 anthology, entitled *Der Adel und der Conservatismus in Österreich (The Nobility and Conservatism in Austria)*, insisted that the landed elite had built the empire, and that therefore the empire owed the aristocratic elite privileges and subsidies, but that, alas, the old elite families were under constant political, economic, and social assault. Soon Austria would no longer have an aristocracy, and then, woe to Austria![27]

Carl Schorske argues, on the other hand, that the decisive death in Vienna was the death of liberalism. To be sure, the powers-that-be in fin de siècle Vienna — the House of Habsburg, the aristocratic clans, the military leadership, the Catholic Church — were deeply entrenched and fiercely resistant to change. But there were liberals in Vienna, believers in free minds, free markets, and a free society. Many, though not all, were from the commercial middle classes, and they advocated the classic nineteenth-century liberal agenda: individual rights, democratic rule, and a market economy. They, like fellow liberals across the continent, were optimists, rationalists, convinced that science and technology could free people from malevolent Tradition and propel them in the direction of a beneficent Progress. But the crushing blows the empire suffered shattered liberalism. The crash of 1873 seemed to show that free markets didn't work; the rise of racist demagoguery demonstrated that a parliamentary system would never work; ethnic tribalism killed any commitment to individualism. More than anything else, Schorske writes, it was the death of liberalism that gave birth to Viennese Modernism.[28]

What died with liberalism, as Schorske notes, was a distinct understanding of the human person. Liberalism argued that persons were free individuals, and that free individuals could be trusted to act well because they were rational. Within each of us is, or ought to be, a coherent center of action, a stable "I" that has a past, a present, and an agenda for the future. Each liberal "I" is of immense importance; each "I" has unlimited potential. The death of liberalism meant the death of the liberal "I."

Scientist Ernst Mach had begun to speculate that there really was no

---

27. *Der Adel und der Conservatismus in Österreich* (Vienna: Lechner, 1878).
28. Schorske, "Introduction," in *Fin de Siècle Vienna*.

such thing as an "I" anyway. We think that "I" is a constituent part of reality. According to Mach, it is not. While we may indeed believe that "I" is real, what in fact is "real" is simply a flow of impressions and energy. Our "I" is but a temporary, indeed momentary, construct, that, even while it exists, is fluid, and, in any case, will not exist for long. "I" is thus not part of reality; "I" is not real.

Historian William Johnston describes the whole avant-garde phenomenon in Vienna as "Viennese Impressionism," linking it to those cultural shockwaves emanating from Paris. Impressionism began when artists began to experience the outer world as unstable, uncertain, and unpredictable; as they did so, they began to feel as well that their inner world was every bit as uncertain and unstable as the outer world; "the self dissolved into a succession of discrete moments, which remain unconnected to any unifying ego." All this was exciting and dizzying, but it was frightening too. If it generated emotions of childlike excitement and delight, it also generated feelings of fear, apprehension, and melancholy. This whole mood, Johnston thought, is "typical of the heirs of a defeated liberalism who grew up with a sense of decay," and historian Richard Laurence agreed with Johnston and Schorske that the political defeat of an optimistic, scientific, rationalist liberalism generated among liberalism's children this peculiar spiritual "malaise," this "obsession with decay, decline, powerlessness, passivity, and death."[29]

What struck Hermann Broch about turn-of-the-century Vienna was the simultaneous collapse of values, what he called Vienna's "value-vacuum," and the rise of the "irrational." Like Schorske, Broch was struck by Vienna's systemic failures. The political system, ethnic relationships, the economy, all seemed to hover on the brink of catastrophic failure. It was this that generated Vienna's famous nervousness, which itself bred a kind of pervasive irrationalism — all this covered up by a kind of hectic frivolousness, jittery decoration, and sentimental kitsch.[30]

Sigmund Freud argued that the "I" — that is, the "ego" — is besieged in each of us by self-destructive urges, by a "death wish." According to

29. William Johnston, in Erika Nielsen, ed., *Focus on Vienna 1900* (Munich: Wilhelm Fink, 1982), 9; Richard Laurence, in Nielsen, *Focus*, 12.

30. Hermann Broch, *Hofmannsthal und seine Zeit* (Frankfurt: Suhrkamp, 1974), 45-47.

Freud, within each of us, the "I" is not a coherent, assertive, rational center of personality. To the contrary, the "I" is fragile, uncertain, and weak, assaulted by a "superego" with its set of ethical and social demands, and even more by an "id," a bundle of primitive urges and instincts, driven by hungers for sex and violence, which desires, more than anything else, to destroy the "I" that restrains it. The ravenous "id" within us yearns to devour the delicate "I." Death, then, is not something that befalls us; death is, rather, something within us. We are death.

Death was a recurring theme in Viennese visual arts long before the fin de siècle.[31] But during the fin de siècle, death became an obsession among Vienna's avant-garde artists. Consider, for example, Gustav Klimt's notorious "university paintings."

In 1900, Gustav Klimt decided to show the first of his three "university paintings." As he no doubt knew it would, the show triggered an uproar. Seven years earlier, the Austro-Hungarian Ministry of Education had decided to redecorate the Great Hall of the University of Vienna. The university's old campus had been wedged into the medieval labyrinth of the historic center, but the new campus was along the Ring, and the Great Hall, sitting prominently on the Ring just steps away from the new Parliament building and the vast new museums, was a proud witness not only to Vienna's prosperity but to the triumph of scholarship and rationality. The Ministry wanted three immense works for the ceiling: one on philosophy, one on medicine, and one on law. In 1893, the Ministry awarded the commission to Klimt and his partner, Franz Matsch. But things did not go smoothly. Indeed, the seven years between the award and the completion of "Philosophy" were tumultuous years for Gustav Klimt.

Gustav Klimt was born in Baumgarten, a Vienna suburb. His father was a goldsmith, and Gustav, one of seven children, inherited from his fa-

---

31. See Werner Hofmann, "La mort dans la peinture autrichiene," in *Vienne*, 82-97.

ther not only a love of gold as artistic medium, but a pride in artisanship. Even after he became famous as *the* fin-de-siècle Viennese artist, Klimt always spoke of himself as a simple craftsman. In notes called "commentary on a non-existent self-portrait," made when he was a successful artist, Klimt wrote,

> I can paint and draw. I believe as much myself and others also say they believe it. But I am not sure that it is true. Only two things are certain:
>
> 1. I have never painted a self-portrait. I am less interested in myself as a subject for a painting than I am in other people, above all, women. But other subjects interest me even more. I am convinced that I am not particularly interesting as a person. There is nothing special about me. I am a painter who paints day after day from morning until night. Figures and landscapes, portraits less often.
>
> 2. I have the gift of neither the spoken nor the written word, especially if I have to say something about myself or my work. Even when I have a simple letter to write I am filled with fear and trembling as though on the verge of being sea-sick. For this reason people must do without an artistic or literary self-portrait. And this should not be regretted. Whoever wants to know something about me — as an artist, the only notable thing — ought to look carefully at my pictures and try to see in them what I am, what I want to do.[32]

When he became famous he was riddled with contradictions and surrounded by rumors. Fascinated by love, he was fascinated also by women, and relationships, and sexuality. Since he was an artist he made images of everything that passed through his mind, including explicit sexual images (which he discovered, as other artists did, sold very nicely indeed) — even his non-explicit images are often intensely erotic. People said that he had to be a virtual satyr; Alma Mahler, herself the storm center of gossip in gossipy Vienna, vowed that Klimt had pursued her when she was little more than a naïve teenage girl (indeed, Alma Mahler was once a teenager, though it's hard to imagine her ever naïve); when Klimt died, there were any number of women who claimed to be mothers of his illegitimate chil-

32. Frank Whitford, *Klimt* (London: Thames and Hudson, 1990), 18.

dren. And yet, he lived modestly with his mother and two maiden sisters, and his one great romance, with his beloved Emilie Flöge, was entirely monogamous, long-lived, and committed.

Klimt preferred to work wearing sandals and a long, flowing blue robe. He spoke with a marked Viennese accent, made it a point to be direct to the point of gruffness, and was the center of Vienna's artistic bohemia. Yet he was no bohemian celebrity — his tastes were simple (he liked to go bowling, and he loved long dinners of rich food), he was indifferent to money and status, and his work habits were as steady and predictable as a banker. Every morning, he had a brief breakfast at the Tivoli Café near the Schönbrunn Palace, then took a horse-drawn taxi to his studio, where he worked the day through, painting, drawing, and sketching.

He was shockingly talented. Even as a boy, he had the uncanny ability to reproduce almost photographically anything his eye could see. He never attended a gymnasium, the university-preparatory schools which served especially Vienna's elite; he did attend the craft school in Vienna, the Kunstgewerbeschule. There were two art schools in Vienna in Klimt's day: the craft-oriented Kunstgewerbeschule, which was connected to the Museum of Art and Industry, and the Akademie der bildenden Künste, the Academy of Fine Arts, which trained future artists in the visual high arts. From the beginning, then, Klimt thought of himself more as a worker, an artisan, and a picture-maker than as an "artist." Even before he graduated, Klimt had joined with his brother Ernst, and their friend Franz Matsch, to form what they called the *Künstlercompagnie,* the "Artists' Company."

Very simple young men, Gustav Klimt, Ernst Klimt, and Franz Matsch wanted nothing more than to make a good living using the talents they had. They were neither aesthetes nor rebels. They knew full well what sorts of images wealthy Viennese wanted — it was the wealthy Viennese who could afford to buy paintings and grant commissions — and they were quite happy to provide the products demanded by their market.

When they were young, the king of the arts in Vienna was Hans Makart. Makart painted pictures for Vienna's newly rich. Vienna's newly rich desperately wanted to flaunt their wealth by having very big things; Makart painted for them very big pictures. They stuffed their homes with the objects they possessed; Makart stuffed his paintings with hundreds of objects. Vienna's newly rich ensconced in the vast Victorian piles around the new Ring liked gaudy objects; Makart's paintings glimmered and flashed. The newly rich thought of themselves as the new barons and captains of Austrian life, and they wanted pictures of people and events as important as themselves; Makart obliged with vast canvasses portraying kings and heroes and operatic battles. Makart's patrons were not especially interested in imaginative multi-dimensionality; they preferred images that were unambiguous, one-dimensional, uncontroversial. Makart obliged with pictures of kings, queens, and battle scenes that were more vast illustrations than artistic challenges. Perhaps Makart's greatest moment occurred in 1879, when Klimt was a young boy; that year, Makart designed all the costumes and floats for the vast parade around the Ring celebrating the emperor and empress's silver wedding anniversary. Some 14,000 Viennese, dressed in luxurious folk, historical, and fantasy costumes, marched around town that April. The celebration was one vast moving illustration of Makart's mission to entertain and divert the very rich.

Later critics might dismiss Markart's immense works as Victorian entertainment for the nouveaux riche, but not the young men in the *Künstlercompagnie*. Young Gustav Klimt worked on some of Makart's floats. Klimt and his friends would have been delighted to earn the sorts of commissions Makart earned, and when they all finally began their careers, in 1883, they determinately set out to out-Makart Makart.

They succeeded nicely at first. They did paintings for the Bucharest National Theater; they did the frescoes in the Kunsthistorisches Museum on the Ring; they did illustrations for a guidebook to "allegories and emblems," including images illustrating tragedy, youth, and love.

Gustav Klimt certainly knew how to touch a haute bourgeois heart. Here is critic Frank Whitford's description of Klimt's illustration of love:

> It is a piece of pure kitsch. The girl, eyes closed, head expectantly cocked, is about to be kissed by a handsome man, more gigolo than suitor, with a well-groomed mustache. In the background, a series of faces hover, perhaps symbolizing the three ages of woman. The gilded panels decorated with white roses to each side of the central scene push the sentimentality of the painting still further towards

bathos and the knowledge that white roses are traditionally the attributes of Venus and of the Blessed Virgin Mary do nothing to rescue it.[33]

There were signs, though, that Klimt could produce more than clichés. In 1888-89, for example, Klimt did a painting commemorating the demolition of the Old Burgtheater in Vienna. The Old Burgtheater, built into the Hofburg Palace complex on Michaelerplatz, had been the scene of many a lively theatrical night, but a whole new theater had been built on the Ring and the Old Burgtheater had to go. Klimt received the commission to immortalize the theater. He might have painted a routine exterior image but he didn't. He might have painted actors on the stage, but he didn't do that, either. Instead, he painted the audience, seen from the stage. Some are sitting, some rising, all staring at the stage, at the painting's viewer. It was a gimmick of course, and as word spread of Klimt's plan, Vienna's *tout le monde* pleaded with Klimt to be included in the picture. (The mayor is in it; so are the musicians Brahms and Goldmark; the emperor's mistress, actress Katherina Schratt, is in it too.) But the painting was more than just a gimmick. It reflected a curious turn of Klimt's mind, a turn that suggested that perhaps the real "play" in Vienna, the real "theater," was not acted on stage but lived out in people's lives.

The *Künstlercompagnie* was a hit. In 1893, they would receive their biggest commission yet, the university pictures.

Gustav Klimt, by his late twenties, was well poised to crank out high-class kitsch for great amounts of money. That after all had been his ambition all along. Artists are paid entertainers who sell their audiences what their audiences want — aren't they?

But something very odd happened to Gustav Klimt. In 1892, just turned thirty, Klimt moved into a big studio in Josefstadt, the Vienna theatrical neighborhood just south of the Ring. That year, his father died unexpectedly. Klimt succeeded his father as head of the family, and assumed financial responsibility for his mother and two unmarried sisters. Then, shockingly, his partner and younger brother Ernst died of sudden heart failure after an unusually heavy cold. Gustav took responsibility for look-

---

33. Whitford, *Klimt*, 41.

ing after Ernst's horrified young widow, Helene Flöge, and her infant daughter. The *Künstlercompagnie* died with Ernst too. Klimt somehow no longer had the heart to do the kind of work he had thought he had wanted to do. Within the next couple of years, he and Franz Matsch had gone their separate ways.

Yet that year of death was also the year of Klimt's great love. Caring for his widowed sister-in-law, Helene, Klimt fell in love with Helene's little sister, Emilie. He was a young artist; she was still in school. He helped her with her French lessons. They talked endlessly about art. They would become a couple, and though they would never marry, they would remain loyal to each other until death.

Frank Whitford thinks that this emotional turmoil was part of a "creative crisis" in Klimt's life.[34] Suddenly, Klimt's work stalled. Though he (and Matsch) received the university commission in 1893, he worked little on it. He produced very little for months. When he emerged from this crisis, though, he emerged transformed.

He finally had a concept, for example, for the university pictures, and in 1900, he agreed to show the first of the three, *Philosophy*.

Again, Frank Whitford:

> "Philosophy" consists of a towering column of naked figures who writhe and embrace against a background of limitless space from which emerges, like some gaseous nebula, a sleeping or meditating head, whose vaguely defined luxuriant hair tumbles down to form a twinkling galaxy of stars. At the bottom of the painting is a female head, its hypnotic gaze directly confronting the spectator; the hair obscures the lower half of the face like a cloak. In the exhibition catalog she is described as "Knowledge."[35]

Critic Ludwig Hevesi, who deeply admired Klimt, described the painting this way:

> One thinks of cosmic dust and whirling atoms, of elemental forces which first seek things out in order to become tangible through

34. Whitford, *Klimt*, 45.
35. Whitford, *Klimt*, 53.

them. Swarms of sparks fly about, each spark a red, blue, green, orange-yellow or flashing gold star. . . . The artist conjures up for us a colour harmony in whose peculiar nuances the eye loses itself, dreaming. At one point of this rolling wave of colour a green fog accumulates. . . . A stony, motionless visage emerges, as dark as that of a basalt Egyptian sphinx. . . . It is the riddle, the image of the cosmic riddle, an allusion to it. And flowing from top to bottom past this silent, veiled visage is a bright stream of life. . . . Shining children, bodies in the full bloom of youth which embrace experience, desire and misery, work, conflict, struggle, the suffering of human life and finally its passing. The lonely old man who, with his head in his hands, sinks down to the depths like an impotent shell. . . . Klimt . . . had to paint an allegory of the most mysterious branch of knowledge and found this truly painterly solution to his problem.[36]

This surreal explosion was not quite the Makart kitsch that the Ministry of Education had expected. What had come over Klimt?

Death had come over Klimt. To claim that Klimt is death-haunted is an obvious exaggeration. Like all great artists, Klimt is haunted by a multitude of spirits. Yet it would also be a mistake to overlook the immense presence of death in Klimt's imagination. Death, to be sure, is only implicit in *Philosophy*. The swirling column of entwined naked figures (an image Klimt would use again), the naked old man holding his face in his hands, suggest, perhaps, spirits spinning off into eternity (the stars in the background), perhaps toward God (that expressionless face in the stars, in the viewer's upper right). Death would be even more dominant in the next university painting, *Medicine*.

Medicine's structure and mood is much like *Philosophy*'s. *Medicine* too is a surreal image, a hallucinatory vision. On the viewer's left, floating in space, is a female nude, her left arm languorously extended to the viewer's right. There, another entwined column of humanity, floating, all entangled, young and old, and in their midst, at the top, a skeleton, death. And oddly, at the center foreground, a Greek-looking priestess figure, holding a serpent. The priestess is "Hygeia," the goddess of healing, who, in the

36. Ludwig Hevesi, in Whitford, *Klimt*, 55-57.

myth, is also the goddess of snakes. *Medicine* is a hallucination linking "mythic healing" with death.

The third university picture, *Justice,* would be terrifying. The justice Klimt has in mind is not that administered by Vienna's solemn bureaucrats. It is a kind of awful cosmic justice. A nude old man stands slightly off center in the foreground, arms behind his back as if he is a prisoner. Some terrible octopus-like thing grasps him. Before him, in the center of the image, three female nudes, spirits of some sort, the figure on the left sleeping, on the right waking, and in the center staring frightenly. In the far background, at the top of the image, glittering, a tribunal: last judgment as terror. Critic Werner Hofmann notes that perhaps the most striking quality of the university paintings is the abrupt break with secular liberal optimism, and a return to grimmer Christian and even pagan motifs. According to Hoffman, "in denying to the established sciences in the universities a liberating and saving force, Klimt broke with the humanist tradition of pictorial representation and returned to the Christian motif of the 'danse macabre.'"[37]

Death, in the university pictures, is the cause of terror, but also, oddly, the cause of healing. But death, for Klimt, was entangled with a host of other emotions.

Like many of his contemporaries, for instance, Klimt was fascinated by the story of Judith, and her archetypal sister, Salome. Both are biblical figures. Judith is the hero who saves the Jewish people by decapitating the Persian official, Holofernes, who plans to slaughter the Jews. Salome (according to the ancient historian Josephus) is King Herod's daughter; she dances for her father and his friends, and asks for her reward — John the Baptist's head.

Klimt completed his first *Judith* in 1901. Golden, sensual, a young woman with parted lips and open shirt looks dreamily out of the image — holding, to the viewer's lower left, Holofernes's head. *Judith II,* completed in 1909, is much more terrifying. Here the young woman looks off to the viewer's left. Though more explicitly nude than *Judith, Judith II* seems less erotic and more frightening. Her curved torso, and her claw-like hands, clutching the head below, give her a vengeful, not a sexual, quality; such

37. Hoffmann, "La mort," in *Vienne,* 87.

vengeful, frightening, emasculating mythic women appear periodically in Klimt's other fantasies, as in *Justice*.

Death, in the Judith images, is tied to eroticism, to women, to women's threats to men. In *Judith*, the heroic woman who saved her people and who conquered the male aggressor is transformed into an erotic creature, whose dreadful act of violence occurs in the midst of her orgasmic moment. She and *Judith II* suggest a "crisis of the male ego," fears and violent fantasies all entangled with an eroticized death, which women and sexuality aroused in at least some men around the turn of the century.

But death, for Klimt, was not only violently erotic. Only a short time after he completed *Judith*, Klimt painted *Hope I* (1903). It is yet another fantasy figure. To the right, standing sideways but looking directly at the viewer, is a lovely, nude, very young, and very pregnant woman. Hovering over her is a skull, and lining the top of the image are frightening faces of death. Life and hope, expressed in the image of the pregnant young woman, dominate the image; here death and life are juxtaposed, but the juxtaposition is unresolved. But four years later, in *Hope II* (1907-08), Klimt returned to the subject and rendered it quite differently. The background here is Klimt's signature Byzantine gold. In the center is a partly nude, presumably (though not explicitly) pregnant woman, the look on her face (and on those of the female figures at the bottom of the image) one of peace and repose. The woman is gowned in a brilliant explosion of patterned color. Death, suggested perhaps by a skull-like object the woman holds, has been absorbed in hope.

One of Klimt's last works is *Death and Life*, a large canvas completed in 1916. In it, Klimt returns to the allegorical style and the compositional features of the university pictures.

In *Death and Life*, a skeletal figure stands on the left. Its skull and bony fingers are visible, but the rest is clothed in a gown flashing with abstract design. To the right is the familiar mass of humans, all entangled with each other, all in a mass of brilliant abstract color. Once again, death and life are simply juxtaposed; they simply confront each other. Yet death, for all the scary qualities of the skull, really does have on a fine costume. And the mass of life to the viewer's right glitters in bright colors, and at the top of the mass, a sleepily smiling woman holds up a fine, plump baby boy.

Gustav Klimt died two years later, one more victim of the influenza that slaughtered millions in the aftermath of World War I.

Gustav Klimt met Egon Schiele in 1907. Klimt was forty-five, successful, the center of Vienna's avant-garde. Schiele was seventeen, awkward, troubled, and shockingly talented. Klimt helped Schiele's career, the way Klimt helped everyone, but he was never Schiele's mentor, and Schiele was never Klimt's disciple.

Schiele and Klimt were profoundly different people and different artists. Schiele was nervous, clumsy, in many ways very insecure and immature; Klimt was hard-working, genial, and reliable. Klimt was very much the art nouveau artist, with a lifelong love of brilliant color and flamboyant line. Schiele was the expressionist; his images were jagged and unsettling; his line vibrated with nervous energy.

Yet for all their differences, they shared a deep concern with death.

Death was not Schiele's only theme, or even his dominant theme. Identity perhaps came first for Schiele (Klimt never did a self-portrait; Schiele did scores of them, and in most of them he looks frightened, emaciated, and uncertain). Eroticism no doubt comes second. Like Klimt, Schiele was obsessed with all the emotions and terrors bound up with intimacy, and like Klimt, Schiele rendered them visible in images ranging from raw pornography to scores of nudes, to touching, loving, family portraits. But if eroticism is sometimes gaudily and flamboyantly frightening in Klimt, eroticism is almost always scary in Schiele — there are few erotic, sensual images, as there are with Klimt; instead, with Schiele, bodies are most often starved, awkward, even tortured.

If death was not necessarily Schiele's dominant theme, it was, as it was with Klimt, a constantly recurring theme.

In 1911, for instance, twenty-one-year-old Schiele completed a very Klimt-like image, *Pregnant Woman and Death*. Like Klimt did in *Hope*, Schiele juxtaposes a pregnant woman on the left with death on the right. If the theme and composition echo Klimt, the execution is distinctly Schiele. Even at such a young age, Schiele had already developed a unique mode of expression. Schiele's images, for example, are dark, fluid, and blocky, unlike Klimt's glowing images. Their faces are oddly mask-like and expressionless; they seem to express not horror, nor Klimt's Buddhist-like slumber and serenity, but rather a kind of numbness. Four years later, in 1915, Schiele completed the infinitely more poignant *Death and the Girl (Self-Portrait with Walli)*. The images are again blocky and collage-like, as if fractured blocks of color had been fitted together. Death is on the viewer's left, a dark black arc, the face not a skull, but Schiele's own emaciated, darkened face, hair close-cropped like a prisoner's, eyes staring, horrified. He embraces his love, Walli, who leans into him, her left arm bizarrely extenuated around him, his tentacle-like fingers gently on her head.

Schiele shared with Klimt a final tie to death. On January 11, 1918, Klimt suffered a stroke; he was fifty-six years old. A month later he died in the influenza epidemic. When Egon Schiele heard the shocking news, he rushed to the morgue, and there he sketched Klimt's face, in death. By the end of that awful year, influenza would kill Schiele too; he would die at twenty-eight.

Arthur Schnitzler was Gustav Klimt's exact contemporary. Like Klimt, Schnitzler was born in 1862; like Klimt, Schnitzler lived his entire life in Vienna. Just as Klimt was the center of Vienna's artistic avant-garde, Schnitzler was the center of Vienna's literary avant-garde. Both might be described as "impressionist" artists, representatives of the first wave of artistic ferment to strike Austria.

There were notable differences, to be sure. Klimt was of Christian heritage (though he was hardly pious). Neither was Schnitzler pious, but he was Jewish, and in fin de siècle Vienna, that was important. Klimt was proud of his artisan discipline; Schnitzler was equally proud of his aesthete, bohemian image. Klimt would die in mid-life; Schnitzler would live a longer life, dying in 1931, at age sixty-nine. Klimt worked in images, Schnitzler in narratives.

Yet for all their obvious differences, Gustav Klimt and Arthur Schnitzler shared a common obsession: an obsession with love and death.

Whether in his short stories, or in his plays, or in his novels, Schnitzler is concerned above all with the intimate life, the life of relationships and misunderstandings, the life, in his world at least, of deceptions and disappointments. Schnitzler writes about love; most often, he writes sad stories of failed and deluded love. He writes about young men like himself, well-off, self-absorbed, pleasure-seeking, directionless, who fall in love (or at least think they do) with "sweet young things" (Schnitzler made the "sweet girl" or *süsses Mädel* famous) from the dark working-class suburbs, who then discover that the relationship is impossible, that it is too full of masks and misunderstandings and deceptions ever to work. The men and women in Schnitzler's stories inhabit unhappy marriages, yet yearn for joyful intimacy; they try to find that joyful intimacy in affairs and liaisons, but fail.

Schnitzler burst into controversy in 1891 with his play *Das Märchen* (*A Fairytale*). Feodor is an open-minded, progressive, modern young man who falls in love with young Fanny, an actress. Fanny, alas, is a "fallen woman" who has had at least two previous affairs. Despite the tremendous weight of convention, Feodor defends Fanny and rejects the hypocrisy and judgmentalism of conventional Vienna.

A sweet melodrama? Yes, but only for a moment. The social pressure on Feodor is intense. He cannot resist it. He informs Fanny that her sexual history had left her with an "ineradicable shame." Fanny angrily repudiates Feodor and announces that she has just signed a lucrative contract that will carry her to Russia and make her famous. The lovers break up; their love, if it was love, is dead.

Schnitzler's *Anatol* dramas, a series of seven one-act plays, examine similar themes. In each, the main character is Anatol, a young Viennese man-about-town, an aesthete and narcissist, a Viennese Oscar Wilde, who is looking for love in all the wrong places. Anatol is not so much a person as a type, a type instantly recognizable in Schnitzler's Vienna. In each play, we see poor Anatol breaking up with yet another lover. Death is not an explicit element of the plays — the characters themselves don't die —

but they are death plays nevertheless, for what dies in them is love. Love, indeed, is stillborn in each. Anatol, in fact, seems entirely incapable of giving birth to love. He is, in that psychological sense, sterile; love does not so much die with him as it remains unborn.

In the play *Liebelei* (1895), a wealthy young man, Fritz, falls in love with a poor girl, Christine. Their love seems pure and genuine. But Fritz is challenged to a duel and shot to death. Alas, Christine learns that he was killed not by one of her former lovers, but by the enraged husband of yet another mistress. By the play's end, Christine has been widowed both by Fritz's death and by his infidelity. Their love is doubly dead.

Schnitzler was an enormously productive writer, and of course each of his creations is unique. Each, though, is also a version of *Liebelei*; each is yet another variation on the fundamental theme of love and death.

Karl Kraus was the lonely prophet of the city of the dead. For almost his entire life, from his first newspaper reviews, published in 1892, when he was eighteen, almost until the day of his death, in 1936, at the age of sixty-two, Kraus was Vienna's intellectual pest, its mocking Socrates, its self-appointed, often hated, and much admired conscience.

Kraus was, if there was such a thing, an archetypal Viennese. He was born in a small town in Bohemia, the son of a hard-working entrepreneur, into a non-observant Jewish family. Like so many eastern European Jews, the Kraus family worked hard to stop being Jewish — to be a Jew meant to be poor and despised, it meant to be the target of ceaseless harassment, so who in his or her right mind would consciously choose such a life? — and the road to not being Jewish was marked by hard work, business, education, and moving upward and into the German-speaking respectable classes. It meant moving to the big city, to Vienna. It did not necessarily mean conversion to Christianity though, and like so many Jews, Kraus would both ferociously identify with a cosmopolitan, central European, German culture, and simultaneously remain outside that culture. At one point, to be sure, Kraus would convert to Christianity, but he would leave the church a few years later. Freud, Schnitzler, Beer-Hofmann, Schoenberg, Mahler, and a host of other Viennese Jews would all share something of Kraus's experience.

He had wanted to be an actor, but his real talent was satire. He was clever; a born mocker, he had the gift of a kind of multiple sight, so that no matter the situation, he could see the oddities, contradictions, and juxtapositions in it. He had a nose for hypocrisy and deceit, for poses and facades, for absurdity, and it was as if he couldn't help himself, he simply had to point his finger and bark in laughter.

Kraus wasn't rich, but he was well-off. He attended the Akademisches Gymnasium in Vienna. He was one of those teenage boys who is simply too smart for school. He fussed with his religion teacher, he was bored by his other classes, his grades were mediocre.

He was obsessed with art, with literature especially. In 1892, even before graduating from the gymnasium, he had begun to publish book reviews in Viennese newspapers. He began hanging around the Café Griensteidl, on Michaelerplatz, the home of Young Vienna: Arthur Schnitzler, Felix Salten, Hermann Bahr, and others. Kraus should have fit right in — like the other café intellectuals, he was very bright, very young, very bookish, and very ambitious. But he couldn't do it. He would listen while Hermann Bahr, fresh from Paris, waxed effusively about the latest literary trends. Bahr was the self-appointed guru of the Griensteidl bohemians. Paris writers dressed like dandies, and so did Bahr; Paris writers talked endlessly about the newest new things, and so did Bahr.

It was as if Kraus couldn't help himself. When Bahr in 1893 published an earnest essay called "Overcoming Naturalism," which tried to explain why writers ought to abandon literary naturalism with its quasi-scientific aspirations, Kraus responded with an essay he called "Overcoming Hermann Bahr," which mocked Bahr's pretentiousness and self-importance.

In 1897, city planners decided to rebuild the Michaelerplatz, and Café Griensteidl had to go. For its resident artists, the demolition of the old Griensteidl was a traumatic event. For Kraus it was a moment for raucous comedy. He published a long essay called "Die Demolierte Literatur," "Demolished Literature," which was a tour of the doomed café. In his tour, Kraus pointed out all the writers, Bahr, Schnitzler, Salten, and all the others, and in an amazing tour de force, sketched brilliantly satiric portraits of each. He concluded:

> Yes here, all the literary machinery is on display: lack of talent . . . immature intuitions, poses, megalomania, poor girls from the suburbs, cravats, mannerisms, false datives, monocles, and secret nerves, it's all there. Timid poets are gently led out. Coming out from their dark corners, they're frightened of the daylight, which blinds them, they're frightened of life, which will overwhelm them . . . life, which will shatter their crutches of affectation.[38]

No wonder that one of his targets, Felix Salten, author of the children's story *Bambi* and successful pornographer, would punch him in the nose.

In April 1, 1899, the first issue of Kraus's life's work appeared, *Die Fackel (The Torch)*, a newspaper devoted to social commentary and cultural criticism. Kraus was founder, editor, and principal reporter. *Die Fackel* would appear, with rare interruptions, for the next thirty-seven years, almost until the very day of Kraus's death. It was funny and outrageous, mocking and earnest. Satire, of course, is more than simple mocking. Mockers can be nihilists; if nothing is valuable, nothing is true, then everything becomes a target for mockery. Satirists are more than mockers and are definitely not nihilists. Satirists poke fun by comparing the "is" to the "ought," the "actual" to the "ideal." The whole point of the satirist's work is to prod the "is" closer to the "ought"; satirists are idealists. "It's not a question of what we're bringing," *Die Fackel* announced in its first issue, "it's what we're bringing down" (not "was wir bringen," but rather "was wir umbringen"). The aim of the paper, Kraus wrote, was to "dry up the vast swamp of rhetoric" ("die Trockenlegung des weiten Phrasensumpfes").

Die Fackel instantly became required reading for anyone interested in politics or culture. Kraus would win many admirers, and become the center of a small circle of his own — the eccentric writer Peter Altenberg, the architect Adolf Loos, and the wild young painter Oskar Kokoschka would all become friends — but he would provoke legions of enemies as well. Kraus proved to be a genius at multiple meanings, in-jokes, double enten-

38. Paul Schick, *Karl Kraus* (Hamburg: Rowohlt, 1989), 34.

dres, and complicated references. One of his favorite techniques was to flash a glaring spotlight on blunders by other newspapers simply by highlighting, often with little comment, the language in question. This "I'm not making this up" style, hilarious as it was to readers, infuriated other writers; shortly after *Die Fackel* appeared, Kraus was beaten up again, this time by outraged reporters.

Die Fackel went after everyone: Hermann Bahr and his circle of young dandies, Zionists, politicians, the police, the media, and the empire in general.

Austria-Hungary was headed for the abyss, and no one seemed to care. Politicians were idiots, artists were frauds, the newspapers were filled with cant and hypocrisy, the police were on the take, the bureaucracy was a lunatic labyrinth, demagogues and fools had hijacked politics — yet the Viennese partied and looked the other way.

In an upside-down world, Kraus would write, I've learned to lead an upside-down lifestyle. He would sleep during the day, get up late — "When stupidity finally goes to sleep, I get up"[39] — head for the cafes, then work all night on getting out *Die Fackel.* His mission in life was to watch for the apocalypse. Anyone could detect a full-blown plague or an earthquake once they hit; it took great skill to watch for the signs of their coming, in small infections, in the shivering of the surface of the water.[40] What was Austria-Hungary? Well, Kraus would remark that while Prussia was a place where one was free to move but was gagged, Austria was an isolation cell — but one in which one was permitted to scream.[41] Vienna was "an experimental station for the end of the world."[42]

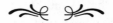

39. Schick, *Kraus,* 44.

40. Schick, *Kraus,* 58.

41. In Frank Field, *The Last Days of Mankind: Karl Kraus and His Vienna* (New York: St. Martin's, 1967), 31.

42. Johnston, *Vienna,* 197.

No one, not even Karl Kraus, was as familiar with necropolis Vienna as Gustav Mahler.

Mahler was two years older than Klimt and Schnitzler. He was the second of fourteen children born to a loveless marriage. His father, Bernard, was gruff, grasping, and sometimes violent. A coachman, he eventually became a shop owner. His wife, Marie Hermann, married him just after breaking up with someone else. It was her life's greatest mistake. Marie was the daughter of a prosperous businessman, and all her life she felt that she had married beneath her, an attitude that no doubt enraged Bernard.

Everyone recognized that young Gustav was a prodigy. He was also a little odd. He had a peculiar tic, a habit of twitching his right leg, even when he walked, which gave him a peculiar, jerking kind of gait. His mother had a limp, and Mahler's tic may perhaps have been a kind of physical identification with her. He was a dreamy sort of boy, and his wife Alma would write much later that Gustav "dreamed his way through family life and childhood"; perhaps that was his way to avoid what Alma referred to as the "unending tortures" his mother endured at the hands of his "brutal" father.[43]

The Mahlers were Jews, and as Gustav grew up, he inherited all the complexities of being a Jew in Central Europe. It was only in his childhood that the ancient laws segregating and punishing Jews — restrictions on property ownership and travel and limitations on civil rights — were slowly dismantled. But as legal segregation was dismantled, social segregation, if anything, worsened. Mahler learned that in his world Jews were unwelcome, mistrusted, mocked, even threatened. Being Jewish created the kind of "double-mindedness" that W. E. B. DuBois identified in African Americans in the United States. Being Jewish was a source of pride for Mahler; though he would later convert to Catholicism, Mahler never repudiated his Jewish ancestry. But being Jewish was very hard. It bred the self-doubt that comes from always being looked down on, nervousness, and suspicion. Being Jewish, Mahler remarked to his friend Alfred Roller, was like being born "with one arm shorter than the other";[44] it was a kind of handicap that made you constantly feel self-conscious and caused others

43. Michael Kennedy, *Mahler* (New York: Schirmer, 1990), 3.
44. Kennedy, *Mahler*, 5.

to act just a little oddly around you. It was something you always had to explain, defensively, aggressively, or exhaustedly.

Like so many other Viennese, the Mahlers were a family from a village in Bohemia who eventually moved to the big city. Like many immigrants to the big city, Mahler always felt a little odd in Vienna. He never felt entirely at home; it was as if his real home were back somewhere in the villages of Bohemia. He once remarked, "I am thrice homeless, as a native of Bohemia in Austria, as an Austrian among Germans, and as a Jew throughout all the world. Everywhere an intruder, never welcomed."[45]

Mahler's astonishing musical abilities were a great gift, but they were also a burden. His head was filled with sounds and echoes and tones, and somehow he had to find a way to express them. A dreamy boy, he would grow up to be a driven young man, nervous, demanding, always in a hurry, impatient.

In most ways, to be sure, he was an entirely normal human being. He was fully capable of love — he loved his siblings dearly, and he fell in and out of love several times before marrying the love of his life, Alma. For all his earnestness, his friend Alfred Roller remembered, Mahler "laughed readily and heartily, like a child, tears streaming from his eyes. He would then take off his glasses to wipe the lenses dry, and give a little dance of joy on the spot where he stood."[46]

Yet Mahler was haunted by death.

He was the second of fourteen children. The first child, Isidor, died as a baby. Of the twelve who were born after Gustav, six died as children. Mahler's childhood and adolescence were filled with grief for yet another little brother or sister who died. The last of the fourteen, little Konrad, born when Gustav was nineteen, died at twenty-one months. Of the fourteen, only six survived childhood.

Gustav was particularly close to his brother Ernst, a year younger. In 1874, when Gustav was fourteen and Ernst thirteen, Ernst was diagnosed with what would be a fatal heart disease. Ernst lay dying for weeks, with Gustav by his side, telling him stories, trying to comfort him.

In 1889, when he was twenty-one, the year his Symphony No. 1 pre-

---

45. Kennedy, *Mahler*, 2.
46. Kennedy, *Mahler*, 3.

miered, his father, his mother, and his younger sister Leopoldine all unexpectedly died. Gustav, as the eldest surviving child, was now responsible for the family. In 1895, his younger brother Otto, twenty-two, plunged into a deep depression and shot himself to death.

It did not stop there. In 1907, when he was forty-seven, Mahler was diagnosed with a fatal heart disease. That same year, his daughter Maria, his oldest, died at age four of scarlet fever and diphtheria. Mahler himself died four years later at the age of fifty.

When he was eighteen, in 1878, he began to write what would be his first major work, a cantata, which he called *Das klagende Lied (A Sorrowful Song)* (he completed it in 1880). He began with the words, not with the music. One of the many oddities about Mahler was that deep inside him, all through his life, was a dreamy little boy who refused to grow up, who lived in a world of fairytales and make-believe. It was that inner little boy that was at least in part the source of Mahler's amazing creativity, and he returned to his inner child repeatedly. Though Mahler read widely, his favorite book of all time was *Des Knaben Wunderhorn (The Boy's Magic Horn)*, a fairytale storybook he had loved as a child. He would return to it again and again for inspiration for his music. In composing *Das klagende Lied* he turned to a collection of folktales published by Ludwig Bechstein, *Neues deutsches Märchenbuch*. Mahler's text is taken from the third story, "The singing bone." Mahler reworked the tale and told it in *Wunderhorn* style.[47]

Mahler's fairytale tells a very strange story. A queen promises to marry whoever can find a certain red flower. Two brothers hunt for the red flower. The younger brother finds it, sticks it in his hat, and lies down to sleep. The older brother finds him, snatches the flower, then kills him and buries him under a willow tree. The murderous older brother triumphantly presents the red flower to the queen and marries her.

Later, a minstrel, the "Spielmann," appears. The musician finds a bone under a willow tree. The musician carves the bone into a flute. When he plays it, the bone-flute tells the terrible story of the murder.

The minstrel arrives at the queen's castle on the wedding day. The murderous older brother has just married the queen and become king.

---

47. This summary follows Michael Kennedy's in Kennedy, *Mahler*, 112. See also Egon Gartenberg, *Mahler: The Man and His Music* (New York: Schirmer Books, 1978), 232-42.

The minstrel plays the flute and it tells the awful story. The king snatches the flute and tries to play it; when he does, it accuses him of murder: "O brother! You murdered me!" The queen collapses, the horrified guests run off, and the castle crashes to the ground.

Das klagende Lied's music is, Michael Kennedy writes, "no masterpiece."[48] And yet it is pure Mahler; many of its technical qualities recur in his later work. Just as important, its moods of mystery, eeriness, and tension — all structured around death — will become Mahler's signature.

In 1884, while working on his first symphony, Mahler completed another song cycle, this time unquestionably a great work. He called it *Lieder eines fahrenden Gesellen* ("Songs of a Wayfarer"). Again, he worked with folk material — "wayfarer" songs and poems had been around for generations. And again, the obsessive theme is death — this time, the death of love.

The first song introduces the wanderer. It is his beloved's wedding day — but she is to marry another. The broken-hearted wanderer turns to nature and is stunned by the contrasts between nature's loveliness and his own grief. In the second song, nature, in the form of birds and flowers, tries to speak to him, but his sadness deafens him to it. In the third song, his beloved's blue eyes haunt him so terribly that he wishes he were dead. In the fourth song, the wayfarer continues his journey alone, to a funeral march. At last, though, he finds a lime tree and rests, and forgets his sorrow in sleep — in a moment not unlike the death of the younger brother in *Das klagende Lied.* In both cases death is associated not so much with annihilation as with release, with dreams, with entry into some other, better dimension of reality.

The music of the Gesellen songs is compelling, according to Michael Kennedy:

> The Gesellen songs constitute a masterpiece because they still sound original, fresh, and evolutionary. . . . Mahler perfectly reconciles the simple folk-like lilt of his vocal tunes with the sophisticated tone-painting of the accompaniment. The use of tonality is startlingly unorthodox, as it was always to be. Keys are roughly and illogically contrasted. The cycle begins in D minor, and ends in F

48. Kennedy, *Mahler,* 113.

minor after experiencing F sharp minor, B major and E minor. The music, for all its attractive tunefulness, has a sharp edge, verging on bitter irony, which is far more characteristic of Mahler than sentimentality.[49]

Irony, not sentimentality, but still a double hope: these sad songs were expressions of imagination and creativity; as acts of creation, they were the very opposite of death. In content, these songs raised what would become for Mahler a set of inescapable and profoundly religious questions: could death somehow be transcended? Could somewhere in death be the promise of life?

Ancient Christians made a distinction between a "necropolis" and a "cemetery." A necropolis was literally a city of the dead. The dead there were indeed dead, annihilated and destroyed, though perhaps here and there a shade survived. The early Christians refused to think of their burial sites as cities of the dead. They insisted on the word "cemetery," from the Greek *koimētērion*, "an abode for the sleeping." A Christian "cemetery," then, was not a city of the dead, but a place of rest where the dead slept, to be sure, but would one glorious day awake. Could it be that necropolis Vienna was not a city of the dead, but rather a city of the sleeping, the sleeping who were awaiting a call to awake?

49. Kennedy, *Mahler*, 114.

Chapter 3

RESURRECTION

~⊙ ⊙~

They have gathered under the banner of Ver Sacrum, *feeling not that their own personal interests but that the sacred cause of art itself was in danger. Thus, without wanting to achieve anything but their own aims by their own efforts, they were and always have been solemnly and enthusiastically prepared to make any sacrifice for the sake of art. The spirit that united them was the spirit of youth, the spirit of spring which makes the present ever modern.*

Max Burckhardt, *Ver Sacrum* (1898)[1]

When Gustav Klimt graduated from the School of Applied Art in Vienna in 1883, at the age of twenty-one, when he and his brother Ernst and their friend Franz Matsch formed the *Künstlercompagnie* and began trying to drum up work, he was hired by a publisher to provide illustrations for a luxurious tabletop book. The book was to be a guide to symbols and allegories. Klimt's commission was to create images to express things like "organist" (part of the "allegories of music" section), "youth," "folktale," and "love." Artistically, this was at best high illustra-

---

1. Max Burckhardt, *Ver Sacrum*, January 1, 1898, cited in Gottfried Friedl, *Gustav Klimt*, trans. Hugh Beyer (Cologne: Benedikt Taschen, 1991), 69.

tion, but it was work. Klimt submitted pictures off and on for the next decade.

Early illustrations, like "Youth" (1882) and "Organist" (1885) are indeed painfully cliché-ridden. "Youth" for instance consists of an arch, infested with putti. Standing in the middle of the arch, to the viewer's left, is a lovely young woman holding a lovely young baby. To the right is a young man, dressed in stylized Renaissance costume (billowing sleeves, short skirt, long white hose), and strumming a lute. Young love.

But later, the illustrations become entirely different. To be sure, they are clearly illustrations for a luscious book. But clichés they have ceased to be.

Consider "Sculpture" (1896), for example. At the top of the image, crowded along a shelf, is a miscellany of portrait busts. In the center top is a huge Greek portrait bust of a woman, staring, Buddha-like, at the viewer. But in the very center of the image is a female nude — no frozen Greek sculpture, but a lovely young woman, in the picture very much alive, Eve perhaps (she's holding an apple) or a goddess. And, oddest of all, the head of another young woman, laurel-wreathed, pops up from the very bottom of the illustration.

"Sculpture" reverses the sculpture process; instead of a live model being transformed into cold marble, Klimt sees cold marble being transformed into beautiful young women. Frozen art comes alive. "Sculpture" conveys many messages, but the most insistent message is life and youth, eroticism and energy. Klimt would often use the technique of vivifying classical images — he did so in an earlier and very similar "Sculpture" (1889). His "Pallas Athene" (1898) takes the ancient image of the goddess Athena, and inserts into the helmet and armor a living, beautiful, and mysterious young woman. The routine Athena image becomes alive, contemporary, enticing; long-dead mythology visually springs back to life.

Death indeed haunted fin de siècle Vienna, but it was a peculiar death, a death infused with life, and energy, and love, and youth, and rebirth. The writers of Young Vienna like Hofmannsthal, the artists of the Secession, and musicians like Mahler were driven not only to explore the night world of death, but to proclaim the dawn of resurrection.

A traveler to Vienna in the 1890s would arrive on one of the scores of long swaying trains that pulled into the city every hour. The train, like the city itself, would be a Noah's Ark of humanity, filled with, perhaps, Germans or Czechs from the north, or maybe Hungarians from the east, or Croats and Slovenes from the south, or perhaps Jews from some shtetl in Poland or Western Russia; all of them peasants or maybe artisans, young people most likely, fresh from a thousand villages and small towns, off wide-eyed to the big city to make their fortune. In the first-class compartments might be business people in dark and stiff high Victorian dress, or diplomats, or soldiers in gaudy uniforms, or sober imperial bureaucrats clutching briefcases, reporting to the capital on some very important business.

The long trains would slowly glide through the seemingly endless tenements of Vienna's outer districts, and then squeal to a halt at the station. There was, oddly enough, no central station in Vienna, so the train might pull into the South Station, or the West Station, or Franz Josef Station, each a pandemonium of shouting parents chasing screeching children and friends calling to each other, the shouts and calls echoing in the vast railroad caverns.

For the poor, the next stage was a long hike, pulling and dragging whatever belongings they had stuffed into cardboard suitcases. For the slightly better off, it might mean a tram ride; for the wealthy, there would be coaches waiting.

But at some point, maybe after settling in and washing up, maybe right away, there would be the pilgrimage to the magical Ring, to the magnificent fairytale buildings that seemed to float by dreamlike as the visitor strolled or rode along the Ring under the chestnuts, past the parks, through the crowds.

"The best time of all to see the Ring," Maria Landsdale advised tourists,

> is in the afternoon, between the hours of three and five, especially on a Sunday toward the end of autumn or in the beginning of spring. . . . It is like being on the Prado at Madrid. There is nothing

that quite corresponds to it in Paris, for the Ring is a place where all classes are to be seen — the great world, the 'demi-monde,' the middle class, even the exclusive Court and diplomatic set.[2]

The Ring, she excitedly explained, "is a mass of visual coloring."[3]

It is a famous place, moreover, for flirtations; in that moving, shifting crowd eye seeks eye, and many things are said in that mute language that lovers understand. It is the hunting-ground for what has been called the "eye-chase," while every spoken language can be heard there, much as on the Tower of Babel. The number of idlers, loungers, dandies, first and second secretaries of legations, is incalculable, all armed with sticks and eye-glasses.[4]

Everyone seems to be walking a dog; all the better-dressed men have flowers in their lapels. "There is no better place," she concluded, "than the Ring in which to study the many and various types of the Monarchy. Take your seat at the window of one of the cafés and look. The spectacle is quite unique."[5]

Perhaps visitors would have friends to meet. If so, they would all inevitably gather at the "Sirk," the intersection of the Ring and Kärtnerstrasse, across from the Hofoper, once one of the city gates, but now, in the 1890s, the place where everyone met everyone else. On the Sirk would be wasp-waisted young officers and elegant women with cartwheel hats, vendors of a thousand oddities and eastern European Jews in long black caftans, Italian diplomats and foppish students, everyone talking and lounging and milling about. Karl Kraus would imagine the Sirk, in his extraordinary fantasy, *Die Letzten Tagen der Menschheit (Humanity's Last Days)*, as the cosmic omphalos.

And perhaps a native Viennese would lead a visitor into the old city center, up Kärtnerstrasse toward St. Stephen's, then left, onto the Graben, pointing out the baroque St. Peter's, a smaller version of Rome's St. Peter's,

---

2. Maria Horner Landsdale, *Vienna and the Viennese* (Philadelphia: Henry T. Coates, 1902), 114.

3. Landsdale, *Vienna,* 113.

4. Landsdale, *Vienna,* 115.

5. Landsdale, *Vienna,* 116.

then left again, down the Kohlmarkt, past Dehmel's famous pastry shop, to Michaelerplatz. Directly in front would be the city gate of the massive Hofburg Imperial Palace, next to it the site of the old theater, demolished now and replaced by the elegant new theater located on the Ring. And to the right, across the square from where the old theater had been, the Viennese guide might point out to the visitor a stuffy little building with the name "Griensteidl" over it, one of the most famous coffeehouses in the city.

This was "Café Megalomania," and it was the breeding ground for the avant-garde who would usher in the twentieth century.

By the fall of 1891, Hermann Bahr had settled back in Vienna (though given his wandering habits, it was hard to tell just when he was back to stay). He had a message, and in the Café Griensteidl, he found his pulpit.

The Griensteidl was in the heart of old Vienna. In ancient times, when "Vindabona" was a Roman fort, there were officers' quarters and merchants' stalls here. In the Middle Ages, St. Michael's Church was the Habsburg's court church (though as they expanded their royal palace, the Habsburgs eventually built their own chapel inside the palace). For years, the area around the square was a graveyard, but in the 1700s, Emperor Joseph II had closed the cemetery and the church's crypt (twenty-first-century tourists can tour the crypt and peek at mummies propped up in open caskets). The elegant Kohlmarkt, filled with shops that catered to the royal family, led to the square. And the Herrengasse — "Lord's Lane" — lined with grand palaces inhabited by the city's first families, ran off from the square. The royal palace's city gate was on one side of the square, catty-corner from St. Michael's, and next to the gate was the old Court Theater.

In the early 1840s, the Griensteidl family opened their little coffeehouse on the square, opposite the theater, and it quickly became the city's gathering place for artists and actors and writers and all those who wished they were one or the other. By the 1890s, the Griensteidl was the place where sensitive young men went to sit around small, marble-topped tables, sip their coffee, skim through the day's newspapers, and share their dreams for stories and plays and novels. They would eventually become known as "Young Vienna."

Young Vienna was not so much a formal organization as it was a clique (as critics complained) or a circle of friends (as they themselves insisted). It was a fluid group of some twenty to thirty people at most: young men, well-educated sons of Vienna's bourgeoisie, many Jewish, all of whom were passionately dedicated to the arts. They were acutely aware of themselves as young people with a profound mission, though it was never easy to explain quite what that mission was — other than to transform the world. E. M. Kafka wrote in 1892: "From day to day it became more and more obvious what separated the young from the old. It wasn't simply a new aesthetic, but it was above all a new worldview, a new understanding of the development of the world, of truth, of morality, of society."[6] The one commandment that shaped their ethic, Hermann Bahr explained, "was above all, to be modern. But not just to be modern, but rather to remain modern. And since the modern was constantly changing, that meant, at each moment, to be a revolutionary."[7]

"What brought them together," according to critic Richard Specht,

> was the sense that they lived in a kind of springtime, the sense of something new and alive breaking through, a new will to be truthful, to be simple and open to experience. They felt they needed the company of people who thought and felt the way they did (or at least people they assumed thought and felt the way they did), and through this association, to arrive at a kind of self-consciousness, to discuss the problems of life and art, to measure their own limits and abilities, to share their pains and sorrows.[8]

It was never quite clear to themselves or to others just what name should be applied to them. Hugo von Hofmannsthal, one of the stars of the group, noted in 1893 that they struggled unsuccessfully to find a name for the concerns of the epoch: "decadence, synasthetics, dilletantism, neuroticism, symbolism, renaissance, impressionism, fin de siècle, satan-

6. E. M. Kafka, "Beiträge zur Charakteristik der zeitgenössischen Literatur sowie zur Verständigung über den modernen Realismus" (1892), cited by Denscher, "Literature," in Robert Waissenberger, ed., *Wien 1870-1930. Traum und Wirklichkeit* (Vienna: Residenz Verlag, 1984), 45.

7. Hermann Bahr, "Zur Kritik der Moderne," 1890, cited by Denscher, "Literature," in Waissenberger, *Wien*, 45.

8. Richard Specht, cited by Denscher, "Literatur," in Waissenberter, *Wien*, 47.

ism, modernism, life-and-death."[9] Some, like Hofmannsthal and Arthur Schnitzler, became famous. Others, like Richard Beer-Hofmann, were admired by smaller circles. But all of these sensitive, passionate, self-absorbed young men were fascinated by Hermann Bahr. And it was from the Café Griensteidl that Hermann Bahr launched his revolution.

Every day, or almost every day, they found their way from the university, or from offices or from their plush middle-class homes, young men from good families, some barely beyond adolescence and some into their thirties — they found their way to Café Griensteidl. There they talked and talked, endlessly, animatedly, about everything, about love and intimacy, about parents and children, about music and books and plays (rarely about politics). They were exquisite and catlike in their movements; they emitted a scent of subtle cologne and great (if affected) sensitivity. And of them all, the most perfect, the most exquisite, was Loris.

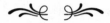

It was the spring of 1891. Vienna's long grey winter had passed; the chestnuts along the Ring were finally in bloom; young men flirted with young women in the flower-filled Hofgarten and the Volksgarten along the Ring. The early spring air filled the shops and offices and coffeehouses.

In the Griensteidl, Hermann Bahr looked up from his newspaper and asked again whether anyone knew who this "Loris" was. For weeks now, Bahr had been reading book reviews and essays signed mysteriously with the single name "Loris." Whoever this Loris was, he was a remarkable person. He seemed to know everything there was to know about the latest trends in French literature. He had a powerful sense of the terrors and

9. Hugo von Hofmannsthal, cited by Denscher, "Literatur," in Waissenberger, *Wien*, 45. Modern critics have been no more successful in coming up for a name for the obsessions of Young Vienna. "Impressionism" has long been the typical category applied to them, but there are major problems with this category; see William A. Johnston, "Viennese Impressionism: A Reappraisal of a Once Fashionable Category," in Erika Nielsen, ed., *Focus on Vienna 1900* (Munich: Wilhelm Fink, 1982), 1-11.

hopes modern artists faced. And his prose style was astounding; it was passionate but gentle, lyrical but absolutely clear. Who was this "Loris"?

Hermann Bahr found out that April of 1891, and he was astounded. A high school student came up to him, a strikingly handsome boy barely seventeen, and introduced himself as Hugo von Hofmannsthal. He was Loris.

Hugo von Hofmannsthal was the very incarnation of Young Vienna's ideal. Handsome — one might even say beautiful — and shy but strikingly articulate; a genius.

He was born in Vienna, in 1874, in a solid upper-class home complete with classical facade, on Salesianergasse, a few blocks south of the Ring, near the Belvedere Palace, the magnificent baroque residence designed in the 1700s for Prince Eugene. The Hofmannsthals were among "the" families in Vienna. Their fortune dated back to Hugo's great grandfather, Isaak Löw Hofmann, a Jewish silk merchant. Great-grandfather Isaak had come to Vienna from Prague, made a fortune, and established himself not only as a successful businessman but as a philanthropist as well. In 1835, great-grandfather Isaak had been named to the hereditary nobility, and took the name "von Hofmannsthal." His son, Hugo's grandfather, Augustin Emil von Hofmannsthal, preserved and expanded his father's fortune, married a wealthy young Italian woman, and converted to Catholicism. And in turn his son, Hugo August Peter von Hofmannsthal, made the final and typical transition from commerce to law, and worked as an official in one of Vienna's major banks. His wife, Anna Maria Josefa Fohleutner, was the daughter of a judge. Their son would be "Loris."

Hugo von Hofmannsthal grew up in what Stefan Zweig called "the world of yesterday," that upper-bourgeois world of stability and respectability, of overstuffed furniture and stiff collars, of certainty and security, a world represented especially by Hugo's father. Hugo himself, though, took after his mother. She was, he remembered, a nervous woman, inclined to melancholy and illness. 1873, the year before Hugo was born, was the year of the terrible economic crash, the "Krach" as the Viennese said, and though the Hofmannsthal family fortune survived, Hugo's mother never quite recovered from the shock.

Young Hugo had private tutors as a child, and as a boy he attended one of Vienna's most exclusive schools, the Akademische Gymnasium.

The Akademische was housed in a grand neo-Gothic building south of the Ring, and it would count among its alumni some people who would be very famous in Vienna, including Arthur Schnitzler, Peter Altenberg, and Richard Beer-Hofmann.

Hofmannsthal flourished in the Akademisches Gymnasium. He had a remarkable memory, an insatiable curiosity, a great capacity for work, and above all a passion for language. He studied, of course, German, Latin, and Greek, but he fell in love with French. As a teenager he easily read Homer, Virgil, Dante, and Shakespeare in the original languages; as a kind of game, he and his friends wrote to each other in Latin.

But he was an odd boy in many ways. With his extraordinary intellectual gifts, he didn't quite fit in with his teenage friends; he lived much of the time in a dreamy world of stories and fantasies. "Those were the days," he recalled,

> when the eyes of pictures of Our Lady sometimes threatened, sometimes smiled; days when he was sure that the way things would turn out depended entirely on signs and omens, for example, everything depended on whether the fourth house on the street had three stories, or whether a raindrop hit just in the center of a cobble stone. . . . This period didn't last all that long though . . . and then came a time of nervous thinking about dying.[10]

The young boy needed to explore everything; he seemed to crave sensations, even sensations like fear and pain. Writing of himself later, Hofmannsthal explained,

> he played even with his fear of the dark, and seemed to find a kind of pleasure in frightening, even hurting, himself. For that he used the sharp points of needles and hot wax and melted lead soldiers and the barking and howling of animals. . . . Sometimes he would give himself some hard task or some ascetic exercise. At first he would do these things without any clear purpose, out of a vague kind of pleasure he found in being able to overcome himself, out of a pleasure he

10. Hugo von Hofmannsthal, *Loris. Die Prosa des jungen Hugo von Hofmannsthal* (Berlin: Fischer, 1930), 7.

found in the taste of his sensations; it was a bit like when one tastes a grape... to taste simultaneously the sweetness and the bitterness.[11]

Above all, he loved make-believe. One of his favorite books as a boy was a collection of historical romances, and he dreamed of exotic costumes and wild adventures. He would run through the streets until exhausted. His parents were bewildered by all this, and Hofmannsthal wrote that as a boy "he hated their inability to understand. He lied, he lied in order to cover himself with a kind of cloak, he lied so he could keep his secrets, he lied out of shame and nervousness."[12] What made all the difference, though, is that young Hofmannsthal possessed the ability to translate his dreams, dreams about magic and nervousness and death, into poems and stories of astounding beauty.

Even as a teenager, Hofsmannthal was thoroughly familiar with the French "decadent" writers, as well as the essays of Hermann Bahr. Of the decadents, Bahr had written:

> Theirs is a nervous romanticism. That is what is new about them, that is their chief characteristic. It is not emotions that they seek, but rather impressions and sensations.

Like the romantics, Bahr explained, the decadents yearned for the "inner person,"

> but it's not the spirit they seek, not emotions exactly, no, what they want to express are nerves. They have created a nervous art, which their fathers are unable to comprehend.

And there was another characteristic distinctive of the Parisian decadents:

> a feverish search for the mystical. "Exprimer l'inexprimable, saisir l'insaisissable" — that is everywhere in their work. They are fascinated by allegories, by dank, dark images ... they are fascinated by the magic of the middle ages, the riddles of hallucinations; the miracles of old legends from the birth of humanity utterly absorb them.

11. Hofmannsthal, *Loris*, 8.
12. Hofmannsthal, *Loris*, 10.

Finally, Bahr wrote,

> there is among them an insatiable attraction to the monstrous, the
> unlimited.... They reject the ordinary, the routine, the everyday ...
> and passionately search out the exceptions.[13]

To nervous young Hugo von Hofmannsthal, all this sounded like
himself. Still in gymnasium, Hofmannsthal was producing great reams
of poems and stories and notes for plays and outlines for novels. Like his
French and Italian models, they were an attempt to capture in delicate
and sensual language those fleeting sensations evoked by a spring breeze,
by the rustle of autumn leaves, by the play of light on Vienna's golden baroque palaces.

When he was sixteen, in 1890, he had begun sending his work off to
Vienna's multitude of small presses and literary journals. Since no one
would publish a teenager's work, he borrowed the name of the Russian
general he had read of in the news, Loris-Melikow. He wrote to E. M.
Kafka, the editor of *Moderne Dichtung:*

> Dear Sir,
> Your magazine is the meeting place for a great number of the
> representatives of Young Germany, people of struggle, people
> struggling to create new, living forms of expression, who want un-
> adorned Truth, who want liberation from conventional lies in all
> their thousand deadly manifestations. Perhaps the enclosed bits of
> poetry, written by an unknown like I am ... will be of interest.[14]

Kafka was interested, and so were many others.

Teenage Hofmannsthal grasped the cultural issues of the day with
stunning clarity. The new French and Italian writers he read were struggling to comprehend the crises of the moment; "they are the few," he
wrote, "who suffer the sufferings and think the thoughts of their times."[15]

---

13. Hermann Bahr, "Die Dékadence," 1891, in Gotthart Wunberg, ed., *Das junge Wien*
(Tübingen: Max Niemeyer, 1976), I:423-27.
14. Cited in Werner Volke, *Hofmannsthal* (Hamburg: Rowohlt, 1967), 21.
15. Hugo von Hofmannsthal, review of Henri-Frederic Smiel, *Fragments d'un journal
intime*, in Hugo von Hofmannsthal, *Loris*, 36.

In 1891, commenting on the work of Maurice Barrès, he wrote, echoing Bahr's concerns:

> We have no center, we have no form, no style. Life for us is a puzzle of appearances without contexts. Happy to fulfill some lifeless career, we ask no questions. We speak with frozen formulas; the stream of things inherited carries us onward. We feed on chance, we learn from chance, thankfully we enjoy what chance brings us, without complaint we give up what chance takes away. We quietly think the thoughts of others, and don't even recognize that the best parts of ourselves are slowly dying. We live a dead life. We strangle our own selves . . . we are shadows. . . . The holy fathers called this a "life without grace," a harsh, deaf, rigid existence, a living death. This is the kind of being [Barrès] portrayed earlier . . . this is the system of modern life, this is the ethic of modern nerves.[16]

And in 1893, commenting on Gabriele D'Annunzio, young Hofmannsthal wrote, "One has the impression that our fathers . . . left us only two things: over-stuffed furniture and over-refined nerves. This furniture is the past; the play of these nerves is the present."[17]

Hofmannsthal had actually first visited the Griensteidl in the fall of 1890; by the spring of 1891, he was not only a regular, but in some ways the star of Young Vienna. "A remarkable talent," Arthur Schnitzler wrote in his diary in April 1891, "a 17 year old, Loris (v. Hofmannsthal). Knowledge, clarity, and it seems genuine artistic ability, amazing for his age."[18]

By that summer, Hofmannsthal, Schnitzler, and Felix Salten planned their own literary magazine, a magazine for "modern" literature. In the Griensteidl, or more often in Schnitzler's bachelor apartment, they passionately read their work to each other late into the evenings and dreamed not only of revolutionizing Viennese literature, but of transforming the world's imagination.

In the early 1890s, Hofmannsthal himself returned again and again to the themes of decadence, decline, decay, and death, and to the tasks of the

16. Hofmannsthal, "Maurice Barrès," in Hofmannsthal, *Loris,* 50.
17. Hofmannsthal, "Gabriele D'Annunzio," in Hofmannsthal, *Loris,* 85.
18. Volke, *Hofmannsthal,* 23-24.

artist who confronts these themes. It was in 1891 that Hofmannsthal read to his friends his first major work, a one-act play in rhyme which he called *Gestern (Yesterday)*. Within the next couple of years he produced, among other things, two more verse plays that explored the obsessions of the decadents, *Der Tod des Tizian (Titian's Death)* (1892) and *Der Tor und der Tod (Death and the Fool)* (1893).

All three were little plays, or play fragments, and had far more words than actions — but such words! When Hofmannsthal, still not yet twenty, read his works to his friends, on long, languorous evenings filled with wine and talk, they were astounded above all by the sounds, the images, the sensuous texture of his language. His works were filled with what he referred to in a poem called "Leben" ("Life"), as "heavy, rich, and purple-colored thoughts." If the hearer's imagination cooperates, the hearer is plunged into a rich, kaleidoscopic world bathed with sight and sound. *Der Tor und der Tod*, for example, begins with the main character, Claudio, brooding by a window on a summer evening. The play begins:

Die letzten Bergen liegen nun im Glanz,
In feuchten Schmelz durchsonnter Luft gewandet.
Es schwebt ein Alabasterwolkenkranz
Zuhöchst, mit grauen Schatten, goldumrandet:
So malen Meister von den frühen Tagen
Die Wolken, welche die Madonna tragen.
Am Abhang liegen blaue Wolkenschatten,
Der Bergesschatten füllt das weite Tal
Und dämpft zu grauem Grün den Glanz der Matten;
Der Gipfel glänzt im vollen letzten Strahl.

(Now the last mountains lie in gleaming shrouds,
Clothed in the moistened glow of sun-steeped air.
There hangs a wreath of alabaster clouds
Above, here rimmed with gold, grey shadows there:
So once did Masters of past centuries
Paint clouds which bear Our Lady through the skies.
Down on the slope some blue cloud-shadows lie,
The shadows of high mountains fill the valley,

Matting the meadows to a greenish grey;
The summit glistens in the last full ray.)[19]

To be sure, later generations might find "moistened glow of sun-steeped air" and "alabaster clouds" a bit too rich. But to Hofmannsthal's young friends in the 1890s, to Arthur Schnitzler and Felix Salten and Richard Beer-Hofmann and Hermann Bahr, and all the other elegant young men of Café Griensteidl, these were intoxicating words.

The form of the works was equally intriguing. All three were plays in verse. They were plays, but they were all brief, one-act plays, more like play fragments than formal plays; they were dramatic episodes, moments, sudden impressions that glow brilliantly and then fade quickly. They were poems too, rimed and cadenced and filled with arresting images. It was as if for young Hofmannsthal, neither drama nor poetry was quite what he needed. It was as if for him the borders between the genres were fluid and open.

The theme of all three was death, but also the life concealed in death.

Gestern was the earliest of the three, and the work that established Hofmannsthal as a young man who could write more than sweet lyrics. Its plot, if it can be called that, is simple: a young man, Andrea, is betrayed by his mistress. But *Gestern* is not about action. More music than story, it evokes a mood, a mood of bitter regret and unnamed misgiving. Commenting about women, Andrea really comments about himself: "Ich seh ihr Lächeln und die törichten, die Tränen/Das rätselhafte Suchen, das ruhelose Sehnen . . ." ("I see their smiles and the foolish tears/the mysterious searching, the restless yearning . . .").

Young Andrea, like Hofmannsthal and his friends, angrily rejects both past and present. Only the moment, only the immediate sensuous impression, only the intensely personal sensation is true. But by the end of the little play, Andrea experiences a sudden insight. Yesterday, memory, the past, the dead — none of these is really gone. Andrea recognizes that time is not linear at all — not a simple progression beyond past, through present, and off into future. Andrea realizes that the past is actually a dimension of the present, the past is somehow the foundation, the core, of

19. Hugo von Hofmannsthal, *Hugo von Hofmannsthal, Poems and Verse Plays*, 2 vols., ed. and trans. Michael Hamburger (New York: Bollingen, 1961), 1:91-137.

the present; the past acts and shapes and molds the present whether the present realizes it or not. The past is alive, not dead. The past haunts the present, accompanies the present, directs the present. As Andrea says,

> Dies Gestern ist so eins mit deinem Sein,
> Du kannst es nicht verwischen, nicht vergessen:
> Es ist, so lang wir wissen dass es war . . .
> Was einmal war, das lebt auch ewig fort.

> (Yesterday is one with your very being,
> You cannot wipe it away, cannot forget it:
> It is, so long as we know that it was . . .
> What once was, lives on eternally.)[20]

Der Tod des Tizian is also about death. It is set in Venice, in the dying Renaissance, in the midst of plague. The old master, Titian, is dying. His pupils gather outside the death chamber and wait. They struggle to reconcile the inevitability of death with the promise of art, the brute fact of mortality with the yearning for immortality.

Hofmannsthal would later talk about his desire for *Zusammenschauen*, literally "seeing together." Like the French writers of his day, he longed for some sort of "synaesthesia," some bringing together of sight and sound and scent into a single moment, some reconciliation of opposites and contradictions. Like Richard Wagner, he hungered for a total work of art, a *Gesamtkunstwerk* that would compress reality and fantasy into a single act of the imagination.

Titian's pupils achieve no such grand unity. But they do learn from their dying master that they must prize each day available to them. They must understand the beauty of form. They must learn to look on life itself as something not separate from art, but rather as a kind of artwork in process, a kind of beautiful make-believe.

Der Tor und der Tod is yet another meditation on death. Again, an exquisite young man, Claudio, confronts decay. Claudio has practiced looking on life as a bemused aesthete, sensitive but insistently unattached, finished

---

20. Hofmannsthal, *Gestern*, in Hugo von Hofmannsthal, *Gesammelte Werke*, Bd. I, *Gedichte und Dramen* (Frankfurt: Fischer, 1979), 242.

and polished but utterly cold. And now death wants him. Claudio franti-cally insists that he is not yet ready to die, that he has not fully lived. But death brings forward witnesses who prove that Claudio did have an op-portunity for life and for love, but that in his self-absorption he had failed to live when he could. Ironically, it is only at the moment of death that Claudio realizes something of the potential richness of life.

Hofmannsthal was no systematic philosopher. His meditations on death (continued in a variety of other works, for instance, in *Alkestis*, which formed a trilogy with *Tizian* and *Tor*) are contradictory and para-doxical. But Hofmannsthal wasn't especially interested in tidy logic, in stringing thoughts along like beads on a string. Our lives are not so tidy. Events in our lives jump out at us. They collide with each other; the fantas-tic and the mundane rub against each other. What he wanted to recreate in his art was that mix of "normal" and "fantastic," predictable and surpris-ing, that one found, for example, in fairy tales and dreams. In 1892, Hofmannsthal illustrated his notion of *Zusammenschauen* when he re-corded his impressions traveling through southern France:

> Once I saw a Chinese picture book. On each page were pictures of the most extraordinary things, the pictures followed each other all mixed together, all with the energy that real life has. For the epi-sodes of our life follow one after each other with no context, no ob-vious system. . . . One thing especially I remember from the picture book. Beautiful flying dogs, mixed with red grape leaves, beneath them, gracious enamel vases, and next to them was a green garden with white geese and orchids, spiders . . . monkeys . . . and a small stream. On the bank of the stream was a young girl, and above the stream floated demons, light blue giants covered with hair, with grinning birds' heads and red-green tails. The whole thing had the strange, senseless excitement of a dream. Travel reports should be like this, because that's how one experiences travel, because be-tween sensation and sensation there is no obvious link, no more than there were between the vases and demons and monkeys. And our memories of travel are like this too; they are so strangely dream-like, so odd, as if they weren't real.[21]

21. Hofmannsthal, "Südfranzösische Eindrücke," in Hofmannsthal, *Loris*, 68.

It was this stream of sensations that young Hofmannsthal, just graduated from gymnasium, not yet a freshman in college, brought to Young Vienna, a stream of luxurious and vibrant sensations.

In the evenings, in their endless talks, Young Vienna talked too about those desperate adolescent themes, identity and intimacy — both, it seemed to Young Vienna, painfully unresolved as the old century died and the new century was born. "With us," Hofmannsthal wrote,

> nothing is left but a kind of frozen life, a blank, dull reality, lame farewells. We have a sentimental memory, a lamed will, and the strange gift of disengaging from our own lives. We watch ourselves. We look for the cup and yet remain thirsty . . . we experience loss at the moment of possession, failure in the moment of experience. We have no roots in life, we drift, clear-sighted yet light-blinded, like shadows. . . . We! We! Yes, I know that I cannot speak of my entire generation. I can only speak of a few thousand people, scattered through the great European cities . . . they are neither the heart nor the head of their generation, only its consciousness.[22]

They knew they were profoundly and suddenly different from their parents; they knew that a gulf, an abyss, had suddenly ruptured their present from their fathers' pasts. They knew they were "modern," and the word became for them an incantation, but what in the world it meant no one could quite say.

"Just what 'modern' means," Hofmannsthal wrote,

> is easier felt than defined. . . . Two things do seem modern, the analysis of life, and the flight from life. . . . One examines the anatomy of one's own life, or one dreams. Reflection or fantasy, mirror images or dream images. 'Modern' means old furnishings and young nervousness. 'Modern' means somehow hearing the grass growing, the murmuring of a fantasy world of wonders . . . 'modern' means the instinctive, almost somnambulist self-giving to every revelation of beauty, to blendings of colors, to sparkling metaphors, to wondrous allegories.[23]

22. Hofmannsthal, "Gabriele D'Annunzio" (1893), in *Loris*, 86.
23. Hofmannsthal, "Gabriele D'Annunzio" (1893), in *Loris*, 87.

What struck Hermann Bahr especially was "nervousness," the sudden and acute sensitivity born from the disintegration of old verities and assumptions. When nothing could any longer simply be taken for granted, when the old order was disintegrating, when everything changed at dizzying speed, everything, even the simplest things, became strange, odd, new; even the trivial promised a kind of revelation. Rigid old distinctions became fluid; the neat frontiers between good and bad, reality and dream, fact and illusion, became porous and obscure. Some revelation was at hand.

In 1897, Vienna's very intimate art world was all abuzz.

Professional visual artists all belonged to the artists' professional association, the *Künstlerhaus*. Like any professional association, the *Künstlerhaus* was many things. It was a fraternal association (all its members were male); it was a means of networking and sharing information; it was a club, membership in which was a mark of professional acceptance and status. The *Künstlerhaus* performed mundane but necessary tasks such as arranging commissions. Implicitly, and sometimes explicitly, the *Künstlerhaus* set the tone for what sort of art was acceptable and what wasn't.

In the 1890s, the *Künstlerhaus* was very self-conscious about this last point. Acceptable art, "real" art, was historicist art, the triumphal images of Hans Makart, the massive faux-Greek, faux-medieval, faux-Renaissance buildings along the Ring. What was not acceptable art — what was not, for that matter, "real" art — was the bizarre stuff the French were up to, "impressionism" and all that. The *Künstlerhaus* decided, for all practical purposes, what art could be seen in Vienna and what couldn't. French experimental art, for example, was decidedly not welcome in the museums and galleries of Vienna.

The *Künstlerhaus* artists not only had a rather narrow vision of what art was and could be. They also increasingly viewed art not as an expression of spirit and experiment but as a commodity to be peddled. Art was a thing, an object; the object of that object was to divert, entertain, and convert viewers to conformity. Artistic creation meant finding out what potential buyers wanted (only a small circle of Vienna's upper classes could afford to buy art), and give it to them.

Gustav Klimt had joined the *Künstlerhaus* in 1893 as a matter of course. By 1897, he couldn't stand it any longer. Klimt had come a long way from the Makart echoes of a decade earlier; his art had been transformed, not totally but unmistakably, and he was simply no longer at home in the world of Vienna's official art. And he wasn't alone.

By 1897, a whole band of artists, mostly younger artists but some very experienced and older, had gathered around Gustav Klimt: people like Carl Moll, Koloman Moser, and Alfred Roller. They bitterly objected to the majority's narrowness and provincialism. They fundamentally disagreed with the commercial definition of art. Of course, art is a commodity, they agreed, but it has to be something more. True, artists needed to please their audiences, but artists, if they were to be great artists and not simply court jesters, needed also to educate, challenge, and even provoke their audiences.

The *Künstlerhaus* was riven into factions — "conservatives" and "progressives," "traditionalists" and "radicals." In 1896, the "progressives" around Klimt tried to get one of their own elected chair, but they failed.

In April 1897, they walked out.

They cast their walkout in classical terms. Just as the "people" in ancient Rome had expressed their fury with the patricians by a "secessio," a secession from the city, so too Vienna's artists were expressing their frustration with the artistic establishment by striking out on their own.

To be sure, this "secession" was hardly unprecedented. Similar artistic secessions had already occurred in Paris, of course, and in Munich (1892) and Dresden (1893), and would soon occur in Berlin (1898), and the Viennese artists were in a way simply enacting what by now had become something of a ritual among artists. Nor was it simply a clash between "progressives" and "traditionalists." Not all those remaining loyal to the *Künstlerhaus* were hidebound philistines, and not all the secessionists were inspired idealists. The secession was not simply a clash of young and old; the secessionists' first honorary chair was the respected artistic elder statesman Rudolf von Alt. And the secessionists were hardly radicals; one of the first visitors to their shows was the old emperor himself.

Resurrection

Still, the 1897 secession was a dramatic turning point in Vienna's cultural life. Like the writers of Young Vienna, the secessionists were determined to break with the old and give birth to the new. The secessionists were absorbed by the future, not the past; they were cosmopolitan, not provincial; internationalist, not nationalist; they admired experiment and innovation and hated mere repetition. All this they bundled under the magic word they loved so well: "modernism."

For Vienna's visual artists, 1897 and 1898 were years trembling with expectation: the expectation of revival, rebirth, and resurrection.

Once they got themselves organized, they pronounced themselves the Vereinigung Bildender Künstler Osterreichs (the Association of Austrian Artists), and they began raising money to construct their own gallery. The money came in quickly (at least some members of the upper classes were stimulated by all the sudden excitement), and Josef Maria Olbricht, with some suggestions from Klimt and others, designed the extraordinary Secession Building as a temple to art. It would open in November 1898. Inscribed above its main entrance would be the motto, "Der Zeit, ihre Kunst. Der Kunst, ihre Freiheit." ("To each time, its art, to art, freedom.") Critic Ludwig Hevesi was credited with the motto, with its stress not only on artistic freedom in the abstract, but on the need for artists to create art relevant to their own time.

Hevesi would be a tireless promoter of the Secession and the avantgarde. "Art," Hevesi wrote in February 1897, "constantly renews itself in spring-time struggles, which inevitably occur. To live in such a time of rebirth is perhaps lovelier than to live in peace and quiet at the height of a given epoch . . . there can be no doubt that today a new art is being born."[24] In a March 1897 column, he wrote, "well, Vienna, capital of the arts, this monstrous small town, finally will become a greater-Vienna, a genuinely New Vienna."[25]

Meantime, Koloman Moser, Alfred Roller, and Baron Felician von Myrbach (the head of the School of Applied Art) created the Secession's own magazine, Ver Sacrum, which premiered in January 1898.

The title was important. Yet again, the secessionists expropriated a

24. Ludwig Hevesi, *Acht Jahre Sezession* (Vienna: Carl Konegen, 1906), 7.
25. Hevesi, *Sezession*, 1.

classical symbol, a marker of the staid, traditional, and unmovable establishment, and made it their own. Max Burckhardt explained where the
name came from in the introduction to the first edition:

> Whenever the tensions caused by economic antagonism had
> reached a climax in Ancient Rome, part of the people would leave
> the city and move onto the Mons Sacer, the Aventinus, or the
> Janiculum, threatening to found a second Rome right there, out-
> side the ancient mother city and before the very noses of its digni-
> fied fathers, unless their wishes were fulfilled. This was known as
> the secession of the plebes. . . . However, when the country was
> threatened by great danger, every living thing brought forth during
> the next spring was offered to the gods as a Sacred Spring offering
> — a ver sacrum. And when those born during a Sacred Spring
> reached adolescence . . . they would move out of their home town
> to found a new community elsewhere, a community built by their
> own hands and geared to their own aims.[26]

The images associated with *Ver Sacrum* and with the Secession and its
multiple exhibits were images of struggle, yes, but even more, images of
rejuvenation and rebirth. Klimt's famous poster for the very first secession
show, in 1898, highlighted the struggle between Theseus and the Mino-
taur, suggesting, of course, a multitude of struggles: progressives versus
conservatives, young versus old, sons versus fathers. Far more typical,
though, were, for instance, Alfred Roller's lithograph on the first cover of
Ver Sacrum, a blooming potted tree bursting out of its pot, its roots stretch-
ing everywhere, or Koloman Moser's later cover lithograph, also from
1898, showing a delightful pixie-like figure emerging from a bundle of
flowers. Moser's poster for the 1902 Secession show has the same theme,
expressed more abstractly. Three circular, stylized female heads form a tri-
angle at the top of the image; below them, the title *Ver Sacrum* and information about the exhibition. The colors are red and white and blue; the bold
capital letters are sinuous and vibrating.

The Secession's favorite images were art nouveau/*jugendstil* images of
young men and especially young women, incarnating youth and energy

26. Hevesi, *Sezession,* 7.

and vitality and rebirth. This, though, was more than a celebration of youth. The Secessionists were convinced that they were on a prophetic mission to Vienna and to the world, a mission expressed in a Klimt drawing from 1898. A nude young woman faces the viewer and holds a mirror toward the viewer. The bottom of the image helpfully identifies the figure as "Nuda Veritas," the Naked Truth. The epigraph at the top ominously warns: "Truth is Fire and To Tell the Truth means to Glow and to Burn." Klimt again takes the prophetic tone in an 1899 oil-on-canvas version of the same image. This time, the nude is more strikingly erotic, but her immense, fiery orange hair (dotted with daisies) and her cold, dangerous stare give her a weird, otherworldly feeling. The swirling blue and the stylized floral patterns behind her, at the top, locate her in some entirely other space. To the bottom of the image Klimt adds a snake curling around the woman's ankles; the title, "Nuda Veritas," stays the same. At the top, though, there is a new epigraph, from the eighteenth-century poet Friedrich Schiller: "If You Cannot Please the Many with Your Deeds and Your Art, at least Please the Few. It is Bad to Please the Many."

Writing in *Ver Sacrum*'s first edition, Hermann Bahr enthusiastically explained that the Secession was not about death but about life, and creativity, and the very meaning of art itself:

> I learnt to understand at that time what the duty of our young Viennese painters is and that their Secessio must be something quite different from the one in Munich or Paris. In Munich and Paris the Secession aimed at establishing a "new" art alongside the "old" . . . it is different with us. We are not fighting for or against a tradition, because we have none anyway. It is not a struggle between the old art . . . and a new one . . . but for art itself . . . and for the right to be artistically creative.[27]

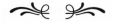

27. Hermann Bahr, in Friedl, *Klimt*, 68.

The year 1888 had been a tumultuous one for Gustav Mahler. Only twenty-eight years old, he was the second conductor of the Leipzig symphony. Restless and combative, Mahler quit his Leipzig post that year and moved to the Prague symphony, but left that job almost immediately after a quarrel. His talent was so amazing, though, that no matter how difficult he could be, he was in demand across the musical world. He left Prague and went to Budapest as the musical director of the Budapest opera. Writing of Mahler some years later, after Mahler had moved to Vienna, Young Vienna's Felix Salten said, "the intensity of his being seemed to fill the whole city."[28] Salten continued,

> His eyes seemed somehow illuminated from within, illuminated by shimmering, flickering, beckoning lights . . . he was as a man as small as a boy, and every movement was still filled with stormy youth . . . that there were people watching him, for that matter, that there were other people at all, he seemed to forget. Pleading, cursing, laughing and crying, plunging from the extremes of joy to the depths of sorrow, beside himself, outside himself, he struggled with the complexities of life to create the works of spirit.[29]

In 1888, Mahler completed his first symphony; it would premiere in 1889, in Budapest. Technically, there was much in Mahler's First Symphony that struck listeners as odd and disconcerting, such as its eerie and ominous (or promising?) opening with the soft violin vibrato, its juxtaposition of solemn music with hurdy-gurdy street tunes, and its sometimes jarring orchestration. The symphony, like the early song cycles, *Das klagende Lied* and *Lieder eines fahrenden Gesellen,* is all about love; Michael Kennedy writes that the symphony is a kind of "love story," though, as Kennedy notes, Mahler himself would disagree. Mahler insisted on a distinction between the *reason for* a musical work and the *content of* the work itself. Some life event, such as a musician's experience of love, might well be the reason for a composition; but if the composition is a genuine work of art, it must transcend the idiosyncrasies of the composer's biography. If it doesn't, or if all the music does is illustrate some

28. Felix Salten, *Das Osterreichische Antlitz* (Berlin: Fischer, 1990), 125.
29. Salten, *Antlitz,* 127.

generic feeling, it is no more than "programme" music, musical cliché. Mahler wrote,

> I should like to see it emphasized that the symphony begins at a point beyond the love affair; it forms the basis, i.e. it dates from earlier in the composer's emotional life. But the real life experience was the reason for the work, not its content. . . . The need to express myself musically — in symphonic terms — begins only on the plane of obscure feelings, at the gate that opens into the "other world," the world in which things no longer fall apart in time and space. Just as I find it banal to compose programme-music, I regard it as unsatisfactory and unfruitful to try to make programme notes for a piece of music. This remains so despite the fact that the reason why a composition comes into being at all is bound to be something the composer has experienced, something real.[30]

In 1888, living and working in Budapest, Mahler began struggling with what would be his Second Symphony. It would take him some six years to complete. He would finish it in 1894, and premiere it in 1895, at the time when the tension was building in the *Künstlerhaus* which would explode in the Secession. In the Second Symphony, Mahler would try to penetrate that "gate that opens into the 'other world.'"[31]

Technically, the Second Symphony is an extraordinary creation. It runs eighty-five minutes, markedly longer than a "normal" symphony, and has five movements instead of the typical four. Mahler expanded the orchestra to include eight trumpets, ten horns, and much more percussion. A chorus is included, and even an off-stage miniature orchestra.

Most striking of all is Mahler's conception of the work. Movement I, "Allegro maestoso," Mahler nicknamed "Todtenfeier" or "funeral." It lasts

---

30. Michael Kennedy, *Mahler* (New York: Oxford University Press, 2001), 116.

31. The description of the Second Symphony that follows is based especially on that provided in Kennedy, *Mahler*, 119-24. For other interpretations of the Second Symphony, see Deryck Cooke, *Gustav Mahler* (New York: Cambridge, 1988), 52-60; Constantin Floros, *Gustav Mahler. The Symphonies*, trans. Vernon Wicker (Portland, Ore.: Amadeus Press, 1993), 51-82; Egon Gartenberg, *Mahler* (New York: Schirmer Books, 1978), 265-76; Henry-Louis de La Grange, *Gustav Mahler. Vienna: The Year of Challenge* (New York: Oxford, 1985), 240, 365, 521-23.

some twenty-one minutes. Constructed in the familiar sonata format, it surprises by moving from exposition to a development, then, oddly, to a second development, and only then to the recapitulation.

Movement I introduces the problem of the symphony — the problem of death. It introduces the theme of death musically by means of a funeral march. The funeral march conjures up the expected mood of grief and loss, but several different and conflicting emotions as well. For example, Mahler contrasts the funeral march with a kind of lyrical "pastorale," music that is vaguely yearning (suggested by his use of the English horn) and nostalgic, and filled with memory. Somehow, for Mahler, the pain and shock of death are also bound up with an intense experience of nostalgia and memory. Mixed into this is the ominous "Dies Irae" theme, which will haunt the piece. "Dies Irae" ("Day of Wrath") was the hymn sung at Catholic funerals in Mahler's day. The hymn not only evokes grief and nostalgia, but above all, fear. Death is a time of final reckoning and ultimate judgment; the moment of death is "that day" of wrath when we will have to pay for every lie, every crime, every secret vice. Yet mixed in with all this terror are other, hopeful themes, "Resurrection" and "Eternity" themes, which Mahler will develop later in the symphony. Death and life, then, terror and hope, are not opposites but twins, intimately and inexorably bound together emotionally.

But all this is no mere detached brooding. Stunning crashes, invasions, interruptions, and eruptions punctuate the movement.

Movement II, "andante moderato," radically shifts the emotional tone of the work. Short, less than ten minutes long, the second movement seems radically different from the first movement. It is song-like and pleasant and is based on an Austrian folk dance, called a "Ländler." For Mahler, this short, sweet section is enormously important. It is as if the listener, or perhaps the composer, shocked by the intrusion of death, withdraws into a dreamy, fantasy, nostalgic world of happiness and innocence. But behind the simple happiness of the dance is an inescapable sense of loss, of yearning and longing, of homesickness and melancholy, expressed now in instruments like the oboe and English horn, now in minor keys.

Movement III, the "scherzo," Mahler calls "Die Welt im Hohlspiegel," the "world in a fun-house mirror." The scherzo lasts ten and a half minutes. As a "scherzo" it is, in musical terms, a "light," even "funny" sort of section. Mahler bases part of it on a song he wrote called "Des Antonius von Padua Fischpredigt" ("St. Anthony Preaches to the Fishes"). But there is an ominous tone here too. Happy and lyrical passages (echoing Movement II) are transformed into and interrupted by much grimmer, angrier, even sinister sounds. Things don't quite fit in the movement; sounds are somehow off, instruments clash with each other. All this doesn't so much state an idea as create an emotion, an emotion of dissonance, of disharmony, of things being wrong, going badly. The happy, cheery music that begins the movement changes into something strange, distorted, and frightening. All this leads to a sudden crash, a kind of orchestral shriek.

Movement IV, "Urlicht" ("Primal Light"), is very brief — just over five minutes. But in some ways it is one of the most moving parts of the entire symphony. It is written for voice (a solo alto), not just for instruments — a single woman's voice singing a simple little child's prayer. Mahler, in the Second Symphony, is trying to explore all the emotions connected with death. Terror, shrieks, longing, yearning, memory of past times, fears that all this might mean nothing, all of them are part of what rushes through his heart. But there is something else too — the simple child's faith that somehow there is salvation.

Mahler's child's prayer (borrowed from his favorite collection of children's stories, *Des Knaben Wunderhorn*) is immensely touching. The child speaks to a "little red rose." The child says that we all suffer, that we all want heaven, that a "little angel" tried to keep me away but I won't stay away, that "I will not let myself be sent away," that "I am from God, I want to return to God," that "God will grant me a little light." In the background tones the simple chime of a Glockenspiel.

Symphonies normally have four parts; Mahler's Second has five, and Movement V, the "finale," is tremendous. Mahler called it "Apocalyptic Vision," and musically it transforms brooding on death into a stunning cosmic vision. The final movement is huge — over thirty-four minutes in length. Musically it is vast — the orchestra is accompanied by a choir, which itself is accompanied by a smaller orchestra off stage. It is also vast thematically — Mahler takes up all the musical themes he has introduced, rushes them against each other, develops them one after another, and tries to force the entire emotional mass toward resolution.

Movement V is, like Movement I, in a sonata form, with an exposition, a development, and finally a recapitulation. It begins with an introduction to the exposition — a rapid introduction to the entire enterprise. And the very beginning is a terrifying musical crash, the "terror fanfare," a veritable explosion of sound. Interwoven with it are Mahler's "eternity" and "ascension" themes.

The exposition itself begins with "horns offstage" — as if something or someone "out there" is now suddenly involved in this entire experience. The horns play the "Call Theme." For Mahler, the cosmos is anything but empty or inert. The cosmos is alive, intelligent, active, and insistently intrusive. There is, in this symphony, "something out there."

And then, in the exposition begins a wild struggle of the emotions. All the themes Mahler had introduced already rush on stage and grapple with each other. The ominous "Dies Irae" theme comes first, but it is immediately followed by the "Resurrection" theme and the "Eternity" theme. Then comes the "Terror" theme and the "Faith" theme. All through the exposition these themes struggle with each other in an emotional explosion.

In the development, the themes are gathered up and transformed. Mahler begins with yet more "Terror" accompanied by "Dies Irae." And then something odd; "Dies Irae" turns into a kind of jaunty march — absurd perhaps, but almost in a triumphant kind of absurdity. Even more intriguing, Mahler turns the "Dies Irae" theme into the "Resurrection" theme, as if the one had been transformed into the other.

There is still ominous material. Toward the middle of the development, Mahler introduces the sinister "tritone," that weird combination of sound which medieval musicians had considered too evil to play. But this sinister tritone is quickly absorbed by the increasingly triumphant "Faith," "Eternity," and "Ascension" themes. And this ends the development.

The recapitulation is a surprise. Normally, a recapitulation is simply a summary of what went on before; typically it is really not much different from the exposition. But the recapitulation of Movement V is stunning.

First — off stage — sounds the "Call" theme. It is accompanied by a woodwind "Nightingale Call." The mood is still, quiet, but also filled with expectation. And then — without standing, beginning almost as a hum, the immense choir begins singing. The singing swells and builds, eventually the choir arises, and its music incorporates and embraces all the themes from before.

Friedrich Nietzsche, that great prophet of the "Modern" and the inspiration of the Viennese avant-garde, had announced that "god is dead." His point was not, as armies of commentators have noted, theological or metaphysical. His point was that *to us and for us,* god is dead; we humans act in such a way that we have, in effect, killed the divine. And in our homicidal ignorance, we have killed all frame of reference, all orientation, all horizons.

> Who gave us the sponge to wipe away the entire horizon? What were we doing when we unchained this earth from its sun? Where is it orbiting? Where are we orbiting? Away from all suns? Are we hurtling straight downward? And backwards, sideways, forwards, in all directions? Is there still an up and a down? Aren't we drifting through infinite nothing? Isn't empty space breathing on us? Hasn't it grown colder? Isn't night after night closing in on us? Don't we need lanterns in the morning? Are we still deaf to the noise of the gravediggers digging God's grave? Has the smell of divine putrefaction not reached our nostrils? . . . The holiest and mightiest being in the world bled to death under our knives.[32]

If "god is dead" as Nietzsche had warned, then Mahler's "Resurrection" proclaims the "rebirth of God."

"Resurrection" is, of course, an exercise in "wish fulfillment." Little wonder that a man so haunted by death would wish intensely for something beyond death, some cosmic inversion of death. Yet "Resurrection" is more than wish, it is an expression of hope. Now "wish" and "hope" are not synonyms. "To wish" is passive; "to hope" is active. "To wish" is to yearn for what cannot be; "to hope" is to imagine, to create spiritually what could be, or rather, to connect spiritually with what is. Wishing is a sort of escapism. Hope is a form of transcendence, an assertion that reality is greater than the here and now, the way things are, and the powers that be. To wish means to imagine, with a sigh, the way things are not; to hope means to insist that things can be different because reality, in its deepest meanings, is different. Wishing is a weary but futile escape from the inexorable quotidian; hope is the determination to transform the quo-

---

32. This famous and much commented on passage is from *Die Fröhliche Wissenschaft* (*The Happy Science*), p. 125. For a good interpretation of the passage, see Ronald Hayman, *Nietzsche, A Critical Life* (New York: Penguin, 1980), 238ff.

tidian in light of the eschatological. Mahler's "Resurrection" is an expression not primarily of wishing but of hope; it insists that as real as death and annihilation are, so too are life and creation, and that in fact, in the end, creation will transform annihilation itself. The symphony's created universe of sound is itself a promise and sign of that transforming hope.[33]

When he had finished the work, despite his detestation of "program notes," Mahler wrote a brief "program note" for it. The "program" caused instant controversy; critics charged that it narrowed the symphony far too much, and Mahler himself later refused to distribute the program at presentations of the symphony. This is what the program said:

Program of the Second Symphony

We are standing beside the coffin of a man beloved. For the last time, his battles, his suffering, and his purpose pass before the mind's eye. And now, at this solemn and deeply stirring moment, when we are released from the paltry distractions of everyday life, our hearts are gripped by a voice of awe-inspiring solemnity, which we seldom or never hear above the deafening traffic of mundane affairs. What next? it says. What is life — and what is death?

Have we any continuing existence?

Is it all an empty dream, or has this life of ours, and our death, a meaning?

If we are to go on living, we must answer this question.

The next three movements are conceived of as intermezzi.

Second Movement (Andante)

A blissful moment in his life and a mournful memory of youth and lost innocence.

Third Movement (Scherzo)

The spirit of unbelief and negation has taken possession of him. Looking into the turmoil of appearances, he loses together with the clear eyes of childhood the sure foothold which love alone gives.

---

33. Feuerbach, of course, was among the first modern philosophers to argue that religious themes are essentially "projections" of human aspirations; Freud would take up this theme and argue that religion is the product of neurotic wish fulfillment and fantasy.

He despairs of himself and God. The world and life become a witches' brew; disgust of existence in every form strikes him with iron fist and drives him to an outburst of despair.

Fourth Movement: the Primal Dawn (Alto Solo)

The morning voice of ingenuous belief sounds in our ears.

"I am from God and will return to God! God will give me a candle to light me to the bliss of eternal life."

Fifth Movement

We are again confronted by terrifying questions.

A voice is heard crying aloud: "The end of all living beings is come — the Last Judgment is at hand and the horror of the day of days has broken forth."

The earth quakes, the graves burst open, and the dead arise and stream on in endless procession. The great and the little ones of the earth — kings and beggars, righteous and godless — all press on; the cry for mercy and forgiveness strikes fearfully on our ears. The wailing rises higher — our senses desert us; consciousness dies at the approach of the eternal spirit. The

"Last Trump"

is heard — the trumpets of the apocalypse ring out; in the eerie silence that follows, we can just catch the distant, barely audible song of the nightingale, a last tremulous echo of earthly life! A chorus of saints and heavenly beings softly breaks forth:

"Thou shalt arise, surely thou shalt rise!" Then appears the glory of God! A wondrous, soft light penetrates us to the heart — all is holy calm!

And behold — it is no judgment. There are no sinners, no just. None is great, none is small. There is no punishment and no reward.

An overwhelming love enlightens our being. We know and are.[34]

---

34. Cited in Gartenberg, *Gustav Mahler*, 265-66.

Chapter 4

DREAMS AND VISIONS

O Mensch! Gib Acht!
Was spricht die tiefe Mitternacht?

(O people, take heed!
What does deep midnight say?)

Friedrich Nietzsche;
sung in Mahler's Symphony No. 3

On Tuesday, January 2, 1900, on the second day of the first month of the first year of the new century, on a cold and foggy dawn, Juliane Hummel was hanged in Vienna's city prison.

Hummel, 29, was a poor girl from the city's working-class outer districts. She took in washing. Her husband, Joseph, was a servant. She and her husband had a little girl, Anna. Anna was born before her parents, Joseph and Juliane, were married, and Joseph probably was not Anna's father (Joseph and Juliane later had a child of their own). Neither mother nor father had any affection for little Anna; neighbors complained that the parents either neglected the child utterly, or beat her unmercifully. Finally, on March 9, 1899, at age five, Anna died. The doctor ruled that she had been starved and beaten to death.

Anna's mother, Juliane, police said, had struck the fatal blow, and Juliane was charged with homicide. Pregnant with a third child when she was arrested, Juliane gave birth to the child in prison. Her trial was in November 1899, and it attracted fervent media attention. Vienna's reporters packed the courthouse and breathlessly described every event, every speech, and every gesture. "It would take the moral power and psychological expertise . . . of a Tolstoy," a reporter for the *Neues Wiener Tagblatt* wrote, "to bring into harmony the horrible as well as the pitiful dimensions of this case." Juliane was a person riddled with contradictions; she was a monster toward little Anna, her illegitimate child, and yet she seemed to love her other children. It is astounding, the reporter concluded, that "we have such a person in our culture, and a woman no less."[1]

Joseph, in the meantime, had been tried and convicted of child abuse and negligent homicide; he was sentenced to life in prison.

Juliane was sentenced to death.

She would have been hanged on January 1, 1900, but that was a holiday, so the execution was postponed until January 2. Reporters swarmed to the execution site. "It was still twilight," the *Neue Freie Presse* reported in its evening edition that day, "and grey fog still cloaked the city, as the final preparations for the execution were completed in the prison's triangular courtyard."[2] The condemned had spent a quiet last night; doctors told the press that her pulse was normal. She spent her last night in a gas-lit cell, clutching a rosary, surrounded by burning candles and images of the Virgin. She repeated again and again that her husband was guilty and she was not. At 8:00 a.m., she attended a mass celebrated by the prison chaplain. The press noted that "she was a small, fragile looking woman, in dark clothing, her black hair unkempt, her head hanged over to one side."[3]

According to the *Neues Wiener Tagblatt,* the condemned wore

> a dark dress, over which was placed a green Loden coat. She wore dark stockings, and brown clogs; her dress was open at the neck. Her hair was in a loose braid. The chaplain and the warden had to hold her up and virtually carry her to the scaffold, she crying and

1. "Juliane Hummel vor der Hinrichtung," *Neues Wiener Tagblatt,* January 2, 1900, 4.
2. "Die Hinrichtung der Juliane Hummel," *Neue Freie Presse,* January 2, 1900, 3.
3. "Die Hinrichtung der Juliane Hummel," *Neue Freie Presse,* January 2, 1900, 3.

weeping the entire time. A kind of leather vest was placed over her shoulders; her arms and ankles were tied.

Some thirty to forty people had obtained admission tickets to the hanging, and as the condemned was readied for execution, an "almost fever-like tension gripped the observers." All the while a kind of whimpering could be heard: "it was the condemned, calling 'O my God,' 'O my God.'" Her countenance was pale. She lay her head on the shoulder of the warder to her left; "my God, I'm not guilty of starving Anna, I'm not guilty of killing her!" she screamed. But her final words couldn't be heard. The executioner had placed the noose around her neck and pulled it tight. He stepped backward and shouted: "Up!" and the warders raised the platform on which the condemned stood. "Now!" called the executioner, and the warders pulled away the platform. The executioner covered the head of the condemned and pushed it backwards. It took a half-minute. The condemned was dead.[4]

Doctors, the *Neue Freie Presse* reported, would conduct an autopsy. Juliane's skull in particular would be subjected to a "scientific examination."[5]

Once it was over, there was little rejoicing. Karl Kraus thought the whole episode disgusting, particularly the media's voyeuristic reports of Hummel's last hours and violent death. He wrote in *Die Fackel:* "So, a fine occasion to revel in a woman's dying moments . . . and sensationalist reports of the act of execution. . . . Monstrous. Years ago we banned public executions on market squares because they brutalized our values." But now, he continued, the media reports are even more brutalizing than those medieval executions.[6] The *Neue Freie Presse* mused,

> The new year has begun here in Austria with a frightful act of justice, an act the like of which can't be recalled, an act which has stirred up again all the debates about capital punishment, but above all, an act which strikes a blow against all the belief in progress, culture, and civilization: the new year has begun with the execution of a woman . . . a weak woman, who, given her womanly na-

4. "Hinrichtung der Juliane Hummel," *Neues Wiener Tagblatt,* January 2, 1900, 2.
5. "Die Hinrichtung der Juliane Hummel," *Neue Freie Presse,* January 2, 1900, 3.
6. "Sensationslust der Reporter," *Die Fackel,* Special New Year's issue, January 1900, 1.

ture, must be judged differently. . . . What an image! What an act with which we refined, civilized children of the nineteenth century, greet the twentieth! . . . One can only say: absit omen. And may this not be an evil omen for the coming century.[7]

The Viennese were obsessed with signs and omens, dreams and visions. Fin de siècle Vienna, one might say, was a bit like a painting. While a painting is simply a two-dimensional canvas covered with paint, at least since the Renaissance, the surface of the canvas is actually the first spatial plane of a complex image. Behind that foreground plane is a middle-ground plane, and behind that, more and more planes, all parallel to each other, all leading the viewer's eye deeper into the image, to the "vanishing point." By the late nineteenth century, French experimental painters had begun pushing those planes forward, and as the background and then the middle ground became opaque, it was as if the foreground images were being pushed entirely out of the frame of the image, into the space of the viewer. Cubists kept multiple planes in their images but rotated them at odd angles to each other, and pushed them all into the foreground. Thus, in a cubist painting, juxtaposed to each other might be several objects all seen simultaneously from quite different angles. Foreground, middle ground, and background all flow and fade and collide into each other. In Vienna, right around the turn of the century, for example, Gustav Klimt completed a series of portraits of society women, *Portrait of Sonja Knips* (1898), *Portrait of Serena Lederer* (1899), and *Portrait of Marie Henneberg* (1901-2), in which the women's faces emerge strongly and clearly, but their gowns and chairs seem to fade into the background. He would experiment with this technique until, in works like *Portrait of Adele Block-Bauer I* (1907), the abstract patterns on the gown and in the background absorb the human figure, even as the human figure simultaneously seems to emerge from the background. What in the image is moving where? Which part of the image is "real," and which part is "abstract"? And how do you tell?

Dream and reality were fluid in fin de siècle Vienna, and some Viennese had the strange sensation that in those dark corners where dream and reality flowed together, the sacred lurked.

---

7. "Die Hinrichtung der Juliane Hummel," *Neue Freie Presse*, January 2, 1900, 1.

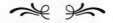

When reality seems confused, we often look for signs. In Vienna, around 1900, people saw signs everywhere. People debated, for instance, about just when the new century would begin. Calendar purists argued that 1900 was really the last year of the *nineteenth* century, and that the twentieth century really wouldn't begin until 1901, but for most people the dramatic shift in digits from 1899 to 1900 was proof enough that the new century really had begun, and sometime between Sunday evening, December 31, 1899, and Monday morning, January 1, 1900, the new year and new century arrived softly in Vienna.

But what would this new century mean? What did the signs say?

The signs were clouded.

Vienna's police reported that the city was quiet on Sunday night, December 31. Monday, January 1, was not much different from the 365 days just passed: the old Kaiser celebrated New Year's Day in the Hofburg; Germany's bombastic Wilhelm II gave a self-congratulatory New Year's address in which he compared himself to his grandfather, Wilhelm I, and promised that just as his grandfather had made a place for Germany in Europe, he would make a place for Germany in the world; there was news about the bitter war between the English and the Boers in South Africa; Crown Prince Franz Ferdinand entertained the Chinese ambassador in the Belvedere Palace. Austria's first twins of the new year (a boy and girl) were born at 12:05 a.m. in Tulln to Mrs. Maria Göbl; they were Mrs. Göbl's eleventh and twelfth children.

Nothing new here, but there were some odd signs. It snowed black snow in Mödling, up in the mountains to the west of Vienna, on December 31, and maybe that meant something, though skeptics argued that all that had happened was that a cloud of fleas had somehow gotten mixed up in the snowstorm. The New Year's Day papers (which appeared on January 2) reported that in Vienna, horses pulling a snowplow marched right off the Brigittabrücke into the Danube, and that a soldier named Chaim Abraham, of the 64th Infantry, shot himself to death ("unhappy with the service," the papers reported). Up in Bohemia, a teacher was "buried in two different centuries." It seemed that teacher Joseph Ponischil had died and was buried in December 1899. But rumors swept his hometown: some said that a look-alike had been buried, others that Ponischil had been poisoned. So the body was exhumed on January 3, 1900; yes, it really was teacher Ponischil; no, he had not been poisoned (his last meal consisted of fish and noodles). He was re-buried a few days later, and thus was buried in two different centuries. Maybe that meant something.

As for New Year's Day itself, the weather in Vienna was cloudy, the temperature hovered around zero degrees Celsius, and the city was cloaked in a dense fog.[8] Maybe the fog meant something. On Tuesday, January 2, 1900, the *Neue Freie Presse* described the "foggy New Year":

> The year 1900 introduced itself foggily, very foggily indeed! Viennese who want change haven't been disappointed. Since New Year's Eve, they no longer need to complain about the snow and slush, now they can complain about the fog. Here in Vienna we enjoy neither "English freedom," nor Hungary's "industrial boom," but our Viennese fog is every bit as dense as London's and the swamps of Mayor Lueger's administration are every bit as awesome as Hungary's prairies. Well, at least it's a beginning.[9]

Vienna's politics were unimproved by the new century, and more than ever before you had to watch carefully for secret signs and whispered messages.

In 1900, Kaiser Franz Josef, seventy years old now, began his fifty-second year on the throne. He was frail, bald, his once ramrod back now bent, his famous muttonchop whiskers long since gone gray. His son, Rudolf, had taken his own life eleven years before; his wife, Empress Elizabeth, had been assassinated. The older he got (and he would get very old), the deeper back in time the Kaiser drifted. He despised all these new modern gadgets — motor cars and electric lights and whatnot — and he still lived in a world of horse-drawn carriages and candlelight. He remained the empire's bureaucrat-in-chief, up at daybreak to wade through moun-

---

8. See "Wien," *Neue Freie Presse*, January 2, 1900; "Wien," *Neues Wiener Tagblatt*, January 4, 1900.

9. "Die Jahreswende im Nebel," *Neue Freie Presse*, January 2, 1900, 2.

tains of files and to chair innumerable meetings. Ever more taciturn, ever more addicted to strict, almost liturgical, court ritual, surrounded and supported by a clique of elderly and secretive men who were frantic to retain their power and privilege, Franz Josef was a living contradiction to the extraordinary changes underway in the turbulent metropolis.

His son Rudolf had been his successor, but Rudolf was dead. His brother Karl-Ludwig had been next in line, but Karl-Ludwig had died in agony from whatever disease it was (the doctors said it was typhoid fever) he had contracted in the Holy Land. Now it was Karl-Ludwig's saturnine son, Franz Ferdinand, who was heir to the throne.

Franz Josef could not stand his nephew Franz Ferdinand. The emperor would hear nothing about the succession, and the old men around him, and the senior members of the House of Habsburg, would not even consider the matter, at least openly. The court camarilla coldly excluded Franz Ferdinand from as much as they could, as they had Rudolf a dozen years before.

Franz Ferdinand, in response, had formed his own clique, a kind of shadow government in the Belvedere Palace, made up of younger men, loyal to him, who looked forward to their day in power. Relations between the old men around Franz Josef in the Hofburg and the younger men around Franz Ferdinand in the Belvedere were poisonous. And so, by 1900, the empire had two governments, the public one led by the emperor and the secret one led by the crown prince.

There were even more nods and winks and whispers.

Franz Ferdinand had been struck down by tuberculosis, but by 1900 he was almost fully recovered. And he had fallen in love. It was hard to imagine that he, of all men, could love. Grim, authoritarian, stiffly reserved, a perpetual anger just beneath the surface, he seemed to have clockwork for a heart. But while living among the Bohemian aristocracy, recovering from his illness, he had met a charming young countess named Sophie, and the two instantly realized that they were soul mates.

Their courtship had all the intrigue of a novel. Though an aristocrat, Sophie was several universes below the Habsburgs in the social hierarchy. For Franz Ferdinand and Sophie to be seen together would provoke a wave of gossip; the gossip would surely infuriate Franz Ferdinand's Habsburg relatives and only give ammunition to the Hofburg clique which despised him. And so, just before the turn of the century, Franz Ferdinand and Sophie played their Schnitzler-like game of secret rendezvous. At one point, Franz Ferdinand arranged for Sophie to be named a lady-in-waiting to a grand aristocratic lady. The lady assumed that the amorous object of Franz Ferdinand's frequent visits was her daughter; when she discovered that Franz Ferdinand was secretly courting her lady-in-waiting, she was outraged.

Franz Ferdinand told his friends that he was determined to marry Sophie. They were shocked. The Kaiser had to approve any marriage by a member of the House of Habsburg, and he would never approve this marriage. All the Kaiser's old advisors would use the marriage issue to disgrace Franz Ferdinand. If Franz Ferdinand had any imperial hopes, he had better find another fiancée.

But Franz Ferdinand was adamant. He would not bow to threats; he would not abandon Sophie, nor she him. All through 1899, Franz Ferdinand worked furiously and secretly to persuade the Kaiser to approve the marriage, and finally, Franz Josef agreed, but with the aforementioned devastating condition: It had to be a "morganic" marriage. Franz Ferdinand would have to acknowledge publicly that any children of the marriage would have no claim whatsoever on the imperial throne.

It was a cruel condition, but Franz Ferdinand agreed. In July 1900, before a formal gathering of the Habsburg clan at the Hofburg, Franz Ferdinand read aloud the conditions of the marriage; publicly and irrevocably he agreed that Sophie would never be empress, even should he become emperor, and that their children would never have any claim on the imperial throne.

That same month, Franz Ferdinand and Sophie were married. It would be a remarkably happy marriage, one of those rare aristocratic marriages in which husband and wife truly love one another. But it was marred by all those petty snubs and insults orchestrated by Franz Josef's court. They bear repeating: Sophie could not sit next to Franz Ferdinand at formal occasions; in formal processions she could not walk next to him, but would have to follow far back in the line; she was not welcome in the imperial palace unless accompanied by him.

Thus the crown prince to the throne was married, but not exactly married; someday he would be emperor, but she would never be empress; he was heir to the Habsburg throne but his children would never be heir to him.

No European city was as famous for hidden passageways as Vienna, so notorious for its subtle deceptions, deceitful half-truths, facades and false fronts, multiple languages and secret codes. Hans Weigel wrote that "in Vienna, everything is around the corner,"[10] nothing in Vienna was quite what it seemed. Vienna was the capital of an empire that wasn't really an empire; it was the home of a parliament that hardly functioned. The twentieth-century empire was ruled by an emperor who lived emotionally in the nineteenth century; the heir to the throne in 1900 wasn't fully heir to the throne; an immense bureaucracy ran the empire, but an invisible court clique in the Hofburg ruled the bureaucracy, threatened by a second invisible clique in the Belvedere. Vienna, the home to some of the world's leading scientists, was also filled with people, at least according to some contemporary observers, who believed in every imaginable monster and superstition: vampires, changelings, good luck charms, hexes, witches, all sorts of spirits, astrology, and magical cures. Franz Strunz wrote in 1905 that ancient gods and demons were, in a sense, still alive in "modern" Central Europe,[11] and in 1908 Albert Hellwig wrote that these beliefs were widespread, irrational, and very dangerous.[12]

Dreams, Sigmund Freud argued in 1900, were the seedbed of signs and omens. Freud, to be sure, was hardly the first Viennese to be fascinated by dreams. "The dream," Peter Hanák writes, "was the central experience and the key discovery of Viennese culture":

10. In Inge Lehne and Lonnie Johnson, *Vienna: The Past in the Present* (Vienna: Bundesverlag, 1985), 11.

11. Franz Strunz, *Über antiken Dämonenglauben* (Prague: Deutscher Verein zur Verbreitung gemeinnütziger Kenntnisse, 1905).

12. Albert Hellwig, *Verbrechen und Aberglaube* (Leipzig: Teubner, 1908).

The characteristic and crucial achievement of Viennese culture was the modern reinterpretation of "appearance" and "reality." What this culture accomplished was not simply to demonstrate the illusory quality of so-called reality, or the real quality of imaginative work, but rather the importance of the relationship between the two.[13]

The Viennese had always rather liked dreams. Perhaps it came from generations of Catholic Baroque and Spanish-Habsburg influences. At the turn of the century, the Catholic Church still insisted on the reality of saints, angels, miracles, and divine intervention — a whole parallel universe, in other words, which haunted everyday life. Vienna's archetypal play, Grillparzer's *Traum ein Leben (Life is a Dream)*, was a reinterpretation of Calderon's famous Spanish-Baroque dream play.

It was Vienna's Freud, though, who in 1900 brought dreams back to life.

Freud had eagerly looked forward to the new century. In 1899, he had completed what he hoped would be his great work. He called it *Traumdeutung (The Interpretation of Dreams)*. In it he revealed what he would call the "royal road to the knowledge of the unconscious in mental life."[14] His publisher thought such an important book should come out in the new century, and Freud agreed. The book would bear the publication date 1900, which was a really a sort of façade, since the book really was ready for publication in 1899.

Freud had by 1900 finally found a home midway up the Berggasse, at Berggasse 19. Halfway up (or was it halfway down?), Berggasse 19 seemed suspended between two very different realities:

The street's flat beginning was at the permanent Vienna flea market, the Tandelmarkt, a jumble of junk shops most of which in Freud's time were owned by poor Jewish shopkeepers. Close to Berggasse's other end, on top of the hill, were the University of Vi-

13. Peter Hanák, "Lebensgefühl oder Weltanschauung," in Peter Berner, Emil Brix, and Wolfgang Mantl, eds., *Wien um 1900. Aufbruch in die Moderne* (Vienna: Verlag für Geschichte und Politik, 1986), 158.

14. Cited in Peter Gay, *Freud: A Life for Our Time* (New York: Norton, 1988), 104.

enna . . . and some of the choicest upper-middle-class quarters around the city hall.[15]

Junk shop chaos here; the university there; Freud in the middle. A sign?

The Interpretation of Dreams, Freud would later say, went back to a strange dream he had had while staying in Vienna's Bellevue Hotel. It was July 1895. He often spent some of his summer vacation in the Bellevue, in the Vienna Woods. He had been upset that summer, and, sleeping in the Bellevue, disturbing dreams had worried him. He had tried to push the dreams away, but the more he thought about them, the more convinced he became that they revealed something strange and true.

He was already convinced of the psychic origins of some physical maladies; he already thought of the human personality not as a unity but rather as a field of conflicting forces; he was already sure that much of what drives us arises not from conscious choice but from primitive, sub-terranean, unconscious urges. He was already sure that the unconscious was the engine behind much human behavior. But how to get at the un-conscious? By definition, the unconscious was not conscious; how then could one ever see its operations? Freud had tried hypnosis with his pa-tients; but hypnosis hadn't worked very well, and Freud suspected that hypnosis distorted more than it revealed. But his dreams in the Bellevue in 1895 had sparked a psychic revolution.

In *The Interpretation of Dreams*, Freud systematically and exhaustively analyzed dream structure. Dreams, he argued, were a species of "wish fulfillment"; they work as escape valves, satisfying urges and solving problems that elude our rational minds. The images in dreams are masks. In fact, Freud argued, dream images are actually layers upon layers of masks. A kind of silent censorship, displacement, and transformation oc-curs in dreams: wishes are translated into images; images are linked, not rationally but associatively, with other images; multiple worries are con-densed into a single symbol, single worries are sorted into multiple im-ages; threatening things are disguised as friendly things; friendly things are disguised as frightening things. Different times in waking life become a single moment in dreams, while single moments in waking life are dis-

15. Bruno Bettelheim, *Freud's Vienna and Other Essays* (New York: Knopf, 1990), 15.

sected and divided in dreams. However, Freud insisted, with patience and skill one could untangle this mass of material and expose the primal forces at work in our psyches. Dreams, he believed, are the royal road to reality.

The Interpretation of Dreams was a commercial failure. Freud's hopes of fame and fortune failed, and he returned to the drudgery of his neurotics. But the work was also a fanfare: this way truth lies, and if we are to find truth, we must go by way of dreams.

Lots of other Europeans were already traveling along that royal road. Historian Shearer West argues that the jarring technological, economic, and social changes typical of the late nineteenth century had triggered a cultural "crisis of belief," something like what Hermann Broch has called a "crisis in values." Among Europe's intellectuals and bohemians, this crisis spawned a dazzling array of cults, philosophies, metaphysics, and imported religions ranging from Theosophy and Anthroposophy to Rosicrucianism, Satanism, Buddhism, Hinduism, and all-purpose mysticism. As institutional religion began to lose its grip on artists' imaginations, they began redefining the roles of artist and priest, and art and religion. Little books filled with vapory poetry about other realities, such as Siegfried Lipiner's *Buch der Freude (Book of Joy)*, or Gustav Fechner's *Das Buchlein vom Leben nach dem Tode (The Little Book of Life after Death)*, first printed in 1836, reprinted scores of times later, were bestsellers.[16] Some religious experimenters applauded the decline of organized religions, and called for what one of them, Franz Mach, called the "free church principle" — that is, religion based on personal insights and inspirations, unencumbered by theological criticism or church hierarchies. (Mach's "religion" consisted of a brutal anti-Catholicism and anti-Semitism, combined with an occult fascination with "Germanism."[17])

Richard Wagner, the great master of so many turn-of-the-century intellectuals, linked this hunger for religion with the mission of the artist. In an essay entitled "Religion and Art," Wagner argued:

16. Gustav Fechner, *Das Buchlein vom Leben nach dem Tode* (Hamburg: Voss, 1896); Siegfried Lipiner, *Buch der Freude* (Leipzig: Breitkopf and Härtel, 1880).

17. Franz Mach, *Die Krisis im Christentum und die Religion der Zukunft* (Dresden: E. Pierson, 1908).

One might say that where Religion becomes artificial, it is reserved for Art to save the spirit of religion by recognizing the figurative value of the mythic symbols which the former would have us believe in their literal sense, and revealing their deep and hidden truth through an ideal presentation.[18]

Not everyone plunged into the occult. There were plenty of Central European rationalists, deists, and religious moderates. Heinrich Seuse Denifle argued in his 1879 *Das Geistige Leben (The Spiritual Life)* that though there was clearly a hunger for religion in modern Europe, mysticism simply was out of place in an increasingly materialistic, scientific, and secular world.[19] Another religious commentator, Georg Schneider, wrote in 1884 that a kind of "noble morality" ought to be at the "heart of all religion"; in 1902, Rabbi Armand Kaminka identified religious sensibility with the cultivation of a taste for high culture, the culture associated in German-speaking Europe with the Enlightenment humanism of Schiller and Goethe.[20] Still others fretted that all this occult revival was a prelude to mass lunacy.[21]

But in Vienna, at the turn of the century, just about everyone was fascinated by dreams and visions, signs and omens. Hugo von Hofmannsthal's work, especially his early work, is uniformly dreamy and visionary; he not only composed fictions, but he composed fictions that were self-conscious fantasies. He remarked in an early poem:

Merkt auf, merkt auf! Die Zeit ist sonderbar,
Und sonderbare Kinder hat sie: Uns.

18. Shearer West, *Fin-de-Siècle: Art and Society in an Age of Uncertainty* (Woodstock, N.Y.: Overlook Press, 1994), 119. For more on this "crisis in values," see West, *Fin-de-Siècle*, Chapter 7, "The Inner Life"; also Hermann Broch, *Hofmannsthal und seine Zeit* (Frankfurt: Suhrkamp, 1974), 59ff.

19. Heinrich Seuse Denifle, *Das Geistliche Leben* (Graz: Moser, 1879), viii-ix.

20. Georg Schneider, *Zweck und Ziel des Deutschkatholicismus* (Wiesbaden: Limbarth, 1884), 12; Armand Kaminka, *Wird das Gute belohnt?* (Vienna: Moriz Waizner, 1902).

21. See Otto Pfleiderer, *Theorie des Aberglaubens* (Berlin: Carl Habel, 1872); Theodor Schultze, *Die Religion der Zukunft* (Frankfurt: Neuer Frankfurter Verlag, 1901); Arthur Pfungst, *Ein Deutscher Buddhist* (Stuttgart: Frommann, 1901); see also Albert Sichler, "Die Theosophie (Anthroposophie) in psychologischer Beurteilung," in *Grenzfragen des Nerven- und Seelenlebens* 112 (1921): 1-43.

(Take heed, take heed! The times are strange
and have strange children — us.)[22]

In Richard Beer-Hofmann's novella, *Der Tod Georgs (George's Death)*, which also was published in 1900, Paul, the friend of the main character, George, is plagued by unhappy and ominous dreams. Paul is vaguely discontented with his life. He has a hard time distinguishing between fantasy and reality; a moment in "real life" triggers a flow of associations. He sees, for example, a young woman;

> She wasn't pretty exactly, but something about her made me think of prettiness.... She was as thin as a young boy, dressed in a closely fitting dress, and when she stood quietly, her head slightly to one side, her hand before her holding the handle of her umbrella, the umbrella pressed to the ground before her, I couldn't help but think of pictures of archangels, in golden armor, standing erect, holding a sword before them, the sword piercing the ground before them, their hands resting on the sword's hilt.[23]

Paul broods about his dreams. Are they in any sense "real"? Omens? It is as if, Paul comes to think, that he has two lives, one he lives by day, the other by night. His nightly dream life, free of the chains of time and space, he comes to think of as freer, maybe even more real, than his mundane daily life.[24] In fact, as the narrative goes on, Paul learns that "dreams were more real than the real life he led."[25] Paul, in fact, inhabits two distinct worlds — the conventional, routine, and vaguely disappointing world of day, and the extraordinary, mysterious, sometimes terrifying world of night. And who was to say which was the more real?

---

22. Cited in W. E. Yates, *Schnitzler, Hofmannsthal, and the Austrian Theater* (New Haven: Yale University Press, 1992), 6.

23. From Richard Beer-Hofmann, *Der Tod Georgs*, in Esther Elstun, *Richard Beer-Hofmann* (University Park: Pennsylvania State University Press, 1983), 40.

24. From Richard Beer-Hofmann, *Der Tod Georgs*, in Elstun, *Beer-Hofmann*, 45.

25. Richard Beer-Hofmann, *Der Tod Georgs*; see also Elstun, *Beer-Hofmann*, 58ff., and Dorrit Cohn's fascinating article, "A Triad of Dream-Narratives: *Der Tod Georgs; Das Märchen der 672. Nacht; Traumnovelle*," in Erica Nielson, ed., *Focus on Vienna 1900* (Munich: Wilhelm Fink, 1982), 58-71.

Over his daily life hovered a second life, the life of the night. . . .
Whoever dreams creates a world, sets the boundaries of sky and
earth, and inhabits it . . . no longer enslaved by time and space,
dreams live freer than the life of the day.[26]

Dreams reveal that what appears to be accident is really fate, what is
odd and uncanny is precisely the intrusion of truth into false routine. Our
tiny everyday life is embraced by mystery of unimaginable depth and
breadth, active mystery that speaks to us in the words of night. One needs
to learn that, as Beer-Hofmann writes, "fate prepares itself in the earth . . .
out of the depths it rises up and wanders . . . along strange, labyrinthine,
unknown paths toward us."[27]

Gustav Mahler was chronically superstitious and obsessed with omens,
signs, voices, and wonders. His Third Symphony, composed in 1895-96,
was, for example, based on a bizarre midsummer's dream. Mahler deeply
loved nature. What he thought he found in nature was not simply nature,
not simply the stuff of botany, biology, geology, and meteorology. In his
hikes around Salzburg's hills, Mahler felt free; he felt touched by nature's
eternal cycles; he felt the gaze of the transcendent. But whose gaze was
that? Could it be the gaze not of a loving Father, but of some grotesque nature god? Could nature's god really be Pan, leering, violent, mocking?
Mahler was fascinated by the horizons so powerfully visible in his summer mountains. He was convinced that there was something, or someone,
just beyond that horizon. In the midst of working on the Third Symphony
he was horrified to think that maybe just over the horizon squatted Pan.
His wife, Alma, remembered that during the summer when he was working on the Third Symphony,

26. Elstun, *Beer-Hofmann*, 45.
27. Elstun, *Beer-Hofmann*, 58.

One day . . . he came running down from his hut in perspiration, scarcely able to breathe. At last he came out with it: it was the heat, the stillness, the Pan-icy horror. He was overcome by this feeling of the goat-god's frightful and vivid eye upon him in his solitude, and he had to take refuge in the house among human beings, and go on with his work there.[28]

Mahler's Third Symphony would prove to be one of the strangest things he ever composed. Critic Deryck Cooke writes of the symphony's first movement:

[It] is the most original and flabbergasting thing Mahler ever conceived. To express the primeval force of nature burgeoning out of winter into summer, he built an outsize, proliferating sonata structure out of a plethora of "primitive" material: a rugged F major–D minor march tune for unison horns, like a great summons to awake; deep soft brass chords, eloquent of hidden power; sullen D minor growls on trombones, like primordial inertia; bayings of horns, upsurgings of basses, shrieks on woodwind, subterranean rumblings of percussion, and gross, uncouth trombone themes, like monstrous prehistoric voices. In opposition appears murmurous pastoral music in D major (wind chords, trilling muted strings, solo violin) with shrill bird calls (piccolo "fanfares" out of tempo). The final basic element, most extraordinary of all, is Mahler's "popular" march style raised to a cosmic level: summer, approaching from afar, "marches in" gaudily with thumping military band music, clad in a stark, blaring polyphony of fanfares and counter-melodies.[29]

Mahler himself would write of this immense, hallucinatory work:

Just imagine a work of such magnitude that it actually mirrors the whole world — one is, so to speak, only an instrument, played on by the universe. . . . My symphony will be something the like of which the world has never yet heard! . . . In it the world of nature

28. Cited in Deryck Cooke, *Gustav Mahler: An Introduction to His Music* (New York: Cambridge University Press, 1988), 61.
29. Cooke, *Mahler*, 64.

finds a voice. . . . Some passages of it seem so uncanny to me that I can hardly recognize them as my own work.[30]

And Arnold Schoenberg would later write breathlessly to Mahler:

> I think I have experienced your symphony. I felt the struggle for illusions; I felt the pain of one disillusioned; I saw the forces of evil and good contending; I saw a man in a torment of emotion exerting himself to gain inner harmony. I sensed a human being, a drama, truth, the most ruthless truth![31]

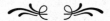

Gustav Klimt's "University" paintings, were, of course, paintings of visions, and that, in part, is what created the great uproar. *Philosophy*, the first of the three to be shown, triggered precisely the kind of scandal the Viennese loved so well. Vast crowds swarmed around the painting, newspapers were flooded with furious letters for and against it, and some eighty-seven university professors signed a petition demanding that the painting be rejected. Some critics were more or less reasonable. A professor Jödl, for example, insisted,

> It's not that I think the painting inappropriate for the university, it's that I simply think it a bad painting . . . it's not the nudity that offends, but the ugliness. Moreover, the dark, unclear symbolism, which no one can understand, contradicts the whole point of the work. . . . We're not opposed to nudity or artistic freedom, we're against ugly art.

Philosophy is a science, other academics insisted. Philosophy is a systematic, coherent, and logical enlightening of the mind; it has nothing whatsoever to do with mystery and darkness.

30. Cooke, *Mahler*, 61.
31. Cooke, *Mahler*, 62.

But most objections were far more heated. "Formless, incomprehensible, a dream-painting, the exact opposite of genuine philosophy," complained one critic; a "disgrace," exploded another, "it reminds one of Richard Strauss's outrageous musical piece, 'Also Sprach Zarathustra!'"; "ugly," a "joke," wrote another; "it's a freak, it belongs with Barnum and Bailey!" insisted yet another critic. One professor wrote, "I don't know Klimt. I haven't seen the picture. But I hate modern art so passionately that I avoid it whenever I can."[32]

Klimt's many friends immediately rushed to his defense. They organized a counter-petition demanding that the Ministry of Education accept the painting. Ludwig Hevesi, the art critic and champion of the Secession, thought *Philosophy* a brilliant work. "It is a great vision," Hevesi wrote, "a cosmic fantasy." The angry officials and professors, Hevesi continued, "were brought up in a time of anecdote-painting"; what they wanted was an illustration, not an artwork: "they simply can't imagine that one can experience a science not scientifically but artistically."[33]

Hermann Bahr weighed in on Klimt's side. (Bahr was a big man now both physically and socially; always stocky, he had put on weight, grown a wild beard and wore his hair long; he abandoned his Parisian dandy suit for a loose fitting smock and looked more like a "guru" than ever. But he was no bohemian innocent, Hermann Bahr. He worked Vienna's cultural networks shrewdly, he was a close friend with theater managers and editors, his reviews could make or break actors, and his own novels, essays, plays, flowed constantly. It made a difference that he defended Klimt.) Klimt, Bahr insisted, is a visual artist. He does not think in words. He sees in visions. Klimt is no mere illustrator — he is a seer. His task is to reproduce in colors and forms the vision he sees. One might not like the vision, but one can hardly deny its seriousness and grandeur. Later Bahr would write,

That this life is transitory is something every Austrian knows, (a profound truth within our misunderstood "gaiety"), and no one has brought this truth before our eyes with more grace than Klimt. To him the tiniest things are the portals of heaven. Every truth

32. All citations from Hermann Bahr, *Gegen Klimt* (Vienna: Eisenstein, 1903), 18-27.
33. Ludwig Hevesi, *Acht Jahre Sezession* (Vienna: Carl Konegen, 1906), 245-50.

fades into appearance. Whatever he touches eludes him, whatever he holds is transformed. Each thing is everything, everything is nothing, nothing is God, and anywhere God is, God is there fully and entirely; what God abandons is empty. Thus the inner blessedness which Klimt conveys in every image; he searches for God in everything . . . this inter-relatedness of everything, this sense that nothing exists on its own but everything shares in existence, this absorbs him.[34]

The very fact that Bahr would defend Klimt was enough to set off Karl Kraus. The university, Kraus insisted, had every right to reject the painting. Klimt's "cosmic fantasy" was, Kraus argued, "like everything in Austria, a mediocre compromise." He understood the painting at once, Kraus mocked — it was an allegory of the language situation in the empire, all confusion and chaos. Oh yes, Kraus said, by the way, he loved the Secessionists' shows — especially when they displayed paintings by people other than the Secessionists.[35]

The fight over *Medicine* and *Law* was every bit as furious as the fight over *Philosophy*. Critics accused Klimt of everything from incompetence to pornography. Klimt responded with a work he called *Goldfish*, yet another hallucinatory vision that included a nude female flashing her ample buttocks at the viewer while she smiles coyly over her shoulder. The Minister of Education moved to revoke Klimt's commission entirely; according to one perhaps apocryphal story, Klimt chased officials away from his studio with a shotgun. Opponents charged that Klimt was a madman. Hermann Bahr, for example, recalled that he was at a play in Josefstadt, just beyond the Ring, in March 1902, when reporters rushed up to him in the lobby.

> "It's Klimt!" they shrieked.
> "Klimt?" I asked, surprised.
> Now, all talking together, one said: "Haven't you heard? Klimt's gone insane!" and another said: "He's already in the madhouse . . ."

34. Cited in Eduard Castle, *Die Neue Generation um Hermann Bahr* (Vienna: Carl Fromme, n.d.), 169.
35. *Die Fackel* 36 (March 1900): 16-20.

and a third said: "It's rumored that he was so wild that he had to be carried away. . . ."

"Nonsense!" I replied. "His studio is only a few doors down the street, go and see for yourselves. But if you disturb him, you'll probably get a punch in the nose!"[36]

Gustav Klimt insisted that he was simply a working artisan, no different really from his goldsmith father. He routinely denied that he was any deep thinker, let alone religious prophet. And indeed, much of his art is entirely familiar.

Klimt was much in demand for portraits. His uncanny ability to produce almost photographically accurate images was, of course, the basis of his popularity, but his portraits were popular because they were much more than photographs. Klimt's portraits typically have a rich glow and often a mystery about them. Still, their content is quite recognizable. Klimt did many landscapes too, and they are comparable to contemporary impressionist landscapes — lovely, but not particularly radical. Yet by 1900 Klimt was utterly absorbed by visions, sometimes terrible, sometimes comic, visions occurring against the background of no known space and no known time.

Consider, for a moment, works like *Fishblood* (1898) and *Mermaids (Whitefish)* (1899). *Fishblood* is a pen and ink drawing of four female nudes floating, it would seem, in different positions, their amazingly long hair floating at various angles to their bodies. This image of female nudes, floating and drifting, eyes often shut but in some cases sleepily open, viewing the viewer, was a recurring motif — it can be seen in several *Recumbent Female Nude* sketches and the oil-on-canvas *Flowing Water* (1898). In *Fishblood*, to the viewer's left center, is the head of a very large fish (his head alone is at least twice the size of a human head). Strange images, more weird than frightening. But the same sorts of images could take on a threatening tone too, as in *Mermaids (Whitefish)* (1899), in which huge cobra-like creatures, with women's faces, spotted black with white and grey, stand erect against a green and gold background.

What in the world are these images? What space do they inhabit? The

---

36. Bahr, *Gegen Klimt*, 3.

paintings themselves have no spatial or temporal markers to locate the images, and so they can be anywhere and nowhere, out in space somewhere or deep inside our brains. Obviously they're on the canvas and paper, but they're there because they were first in Klimt's mind's eye. So, they're subjective to Klimt? Of course. Yet insofar as others can experience in them something which Klimt experienced too, something erotic and mysterious and frightening and yet alluring, the images are not simply idiosyncratic but, if not "objective," at least "inter-subjective." They are omens of realities that were at play in the gas-lit dreamscapes of fin de siècle Vienna.

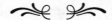

Arthur Schnitzler, that secular realist, out-Freuded Freud in his exploration of hypnosis, dreams, and their relation to sexuality. No wonder that Freud referred to Schnitzler as his "double." By the first year of the new century, Arthur Schnitzler had established himself as Vienna's premiere playwright. His work was translated into a number of languages, and increasingly foreign critics had come to respect his plays. The American Archibald Henderson became an admirer of Schnitzler's work. Henderson thought Schnitzler was the master, above all, of the one-act play. "The quintessence of the one-act play," Henderson wrote,

> is "Stimmung" — the creation of a certain mood or atmosphere. The author seeks, not to settle a problem and end a story, but to produce a certain effect. The effect is often pictorial, psychologically pictorial; we see the image of the states of mind of the individual characters wrought together into a certain complex. . . . The one-act play is truly suggestive in its nature, intimating a larger drama in the background, of which we have caught only a single revealing glimpse.[37]

37. Archibald Henderson, *European Dramatists* (New York: Stewart and Kidd, 1913), 415.

Schnitzler the dramatist was, in sense, a painter or even a musician, working not so much to develop a narrative but to evoke a mood. Behind the brief events of the play is the cosmic world of Klimt or Mahler or the hidden world of Freud — immense, unknown, threatening, inviting, a world that suddenly invades, intrudes, disrupts, what we think of as normal life. One bizarre one-act play, written just after the turn of the century, called *Zum grossen Wurstel,* is set in the Prater's "Punch and Judy" show. The play includes not only the characters, but the (fictional) author and a crude audience as well. But suddenly, an "Unknown" interrupts the show, and cuts the marionettes' strings with a sword. The "Unknown" says:

> just what I mean, that I don't know.
> Is it the truth that I bring, or night?
> Am I from heaven — or from hell?
> Am I God? . . . a fool . . . or one of you?
> Am I myself — or perhaps just a symbol?[38]

The years around 1900 were Schnitzler's most productive period. He was busy at century's end with a score of projects — each, it seemed, more experimental, more daring, than the other. A short story, *Lieutenant Gustl,* for example, managed to outrage the Austrian military. In the story, Schnitzler tried to paint a portrait of the archetypical Austrian officer, and it was not a pleasant picture. The story's officer is narrow-minded and woodenheaded; he believes in authority, in command and obedience, because that is all he knows; he has few genuine ideas but plenty of virulent prejudices. The army was furious, and Schnitzler was stripped of his lieutenant's rank in the army reserve.

The story is most famous for its stream-of-consciousness exploration of a single person's mind. The officer in the story does not seem to have a single consciousness; his mind, instead, is a flow of conflicting impressions and instincts, some of which he is aware of, most of which he only vaguely senses.

At a dinner party hosted by Bertha Zuckerkandl, Hermann Bahr once remarked:

38. Arthur Schnitzler, *Zum grossen Wurstel,* cited in Otto Breicha and Gerhard Fritsch, eds., *Finale und Auftakt. Wien 1898-1914* (Salzburg: Otto Müller, 1964), 70.

Yes, we want to provide some form to the dream "Austria," form, spirit, color and music. And precisely because Austria consists of a vast conglomeration of people, it is spiritually richer than any other state. . . . And so it's no accident, but rather a kind of fate, that it is above all Austrians . . . who peer down painful, dark, and primitive paths.[39]

These are the paths through dreams, paths littered with wonders and omens.

In the late 1890s, Schnitzler explored these painful, dark, and primitive paths in a grim play called *Reigen*. *Reigen* means a kind of round-dance, a dance-carrousel. The play is an interlocking set of ten dialogues. They focus on human relationships, especially love relationships. Schnitzler himself thought the play too blunt for a general audience, but in 1900, he agreed to have the manuscript printed for private circulation among friends. (It would not be known to the public until 1903, and not performed until 1920. It would be repeatedly banned, not only in Austria, but in many other countries, including the United States.)

A prostitute speaks with a soldier; the soldier with a maid; the maid with a young gentleman; the young gentleman with a young lady; the young lady with her husband; the husband with his mistress; and on and on the conversation goes, round and round through other characters, returning, finally, to the prostitute. They talk about love, and relationships, and sexual hunger. They talk about the spiritual rupture within people who hunger for physical intimacy but are refused spiritual intimacy. They talk about the games of love, the deceptions and deceits and confusions and frustrations of love. They talk about the confusion between love and sex, between sex and spirit, between mutual exploitation and real intimacy. They talk and talk, around the circle, from prostitute to soldier to wife and husband to aristocrat and back to the prostitute. Their words circle a dark and dangerous world of appetite and yearning, a world formless, hallucinatory, dreamlike, charged and immense, centered somehow on love.

39. Bertha Zuckerkandl, *Österreich Intim: Erinnerungen, 1892-1942* (Frankfurt: Propyläen, 1970), 80.

What are we to make of this Viennese obsession? Does all this going on about dreams, fantasies, hallucinations, and multiple realities mean that the Wiener Moderne was somehow a religion? Of course not. Freud, certainly, would insist that all these bizarre experiences are neurotic symptoms, not metaphysical revelations.

And yet, it is of the very essence of religion to insist on a multi-textured, multi-layered understanding of reality. Philosopher Louis Dupré, for instance, writes of religion:

> The religious act is not a simple experience, but a complex movement by which the mind discovers a new reality which, although lying beyond the phenomenal and contrasting with it, ultimately integrates all reality in a higher synthesis . . . any attempt to reduce the religious phenomenon to a purely subjective experience or a scientifically analyzable "object" is as misdirected in the present as it was in the past. It is essential to the religious experience to overcome the opposition between subject and object. The religious symbol and its mythical explication bring this subjective-objective unity to expression. To understand the distinct nature of this expression is necessary if one is to attain any insight into the uniquely religious category of revelation. Revelation is neither objective information nor subjective expression: its symbols unveil the transcendent dimension in which the real reaches its unification. Only after having fully understood the nature of religious expression and the concept of revelation can one attack the problem of God. For the concept of God originates exclusively in, and is developed solely by, the religious act. It never is a philosophical discovery and no philosophical argument can prove it to be true or false.[40]

40. Louis Dupré, *The Other Dimension: A Search for the Meaning of Religious Attitudes* (New York: Doubleday, 1971), 2.

The "religious act" is in fact this experience of "another dimension" that transcends what seems to be "normal" reality. This "other dimension" is experienced as a dimension of "depth," and is charged with a distinct "quality," and "meaning." It is both "subjective" — that is, I experience it as being intimately bound up with my life — and yet it is also "objective" in that I experience this other dimension as "not me," but rather as "out there" or "in here," but much more than simply an echo of me. In the process, my "old I" is annihilated even as a "new I" is born.

Clearly all this Viennese dreaminess is the sort of cultural stuff that John Dixon has identified as potentially a text not *of* theology — only rarely does this material speak about "God" directly — but rather a text *for* theology, that is, material that unquestionably shares some of theology's most fundamental concerns.[41]

And this dreaminess struck just about everyone who visited Vienna around 1900. Henry Wickham Steed, for instance, trying to describe the "quintessence of Austria" in 1915, wrote that "Austria is a country . . . more Eastern than Western in character," adding, to stress Austrian exoticism, that "the Austrian atmosphere is Asiatic." Steed remarked on the "baffling air of the Austrian capital" and continued:

> an anonymous diplomat writes . . . "what a strange place this is! On the inside it is quite different from what it seems to be from the outside. Everything is elusive. There is nothing to take hold of, nothing solid to stand on."

Struggling for metaphors, Steed concluded that Austria was "like Hegelian philosophy," meaning, presumably, that it is full of trapdoors and hidden passages. One might add too, full of strange, terrifying, enchanting, and profoundly religious dreams.[42]

---

41. John W. Dixon, *Art and the Theological Imagination* (New York: Seabury, 1978), 1-2.
42. Henry Wickham Steed, "The Quintessence of Austria," *The Edinburgh Review* 454 (October 1915): 225-29.

Chapter 5

HIEROGLYPHS

Single words floated around me, they congealed into eyes which stared at me and into which I was forced to stare back — whirlpools which gave me vertigo and, reeling incessantly, led into the void.

Hugo von Hofmannsthal, *Ein Brief*[1]

Newspaperman Karl Kraus hated newspapers. Kraus devoted much of his own newspaper, *Die Fackel*, to attacks on other newspapers. Kraus was hard-pressed to find anything nice to say about Vienna's media. He hated their hucksterism and hypocrisy; he loathed the jargon and clichés of the daily papers; he was horrified by their grisly sensationalism. The problem with the media, Kraus thought, was itself part of a wider crisis, a crisis of language, a crisis in which a rupture has occurred between the realities around us and the symbols we have available to describe those realities. Reinhard Merkel writes of Kraus that he

> understood language, as did Wittgenstein, as a kind of symbolic substratum to our shared lives. Language provides the basis for spiritual coherence and on this basis alone permits the chaos of

1. Hofmannsthal, *Ein Brief*, in Otto Breicha and Gerhard Fritsch, eds., *Finale und Auftakt. Wien 1898-1914* (Salzburg: Otto Müller, 1964), 33-43.

space and time and motive to be structured and made into an endurable world.[2]

As Kraus scholar Frank Field notes, for Kraus, "a sensitivity to the mysteries of language was a necessary condition of religious awareness."[3] A crisis of language, then, is inevitably a crisis of faith.

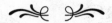

In turn-of-the-century Vienna, where everyone gossiped, everyone talked, and visiting was a highly cultivated art, words were life's very blood, especially among the avant-garde. This class had a voracious appetite for words. In 1890, for instance, when Vienna's population stood at around 1 million, the city had some 863 newspapers and magazines, 622 in German, the rest in a whole miscellany of languages. In 1914, when the city's population was closer to 2 million, there were some 1,500 publications, 1,475 in German, the rest in other languages. Education for the cultural elite was above all an education in languages. Vienna's better private schools demanded that students master German, of course, but also Latin and Greek and at least another modern language. Hugo von Hofmannsthal, for example, as a high school student, easily shifted from French to German to Latin to Greek. He was a genius, to be sure, but in living among several different word streams he was typical. Politics too centered on languages. Languages were electric symbols of tribal identity in the Austro-Hungarian ethnic hothouse. The language you spoke — and the language you didn't speak — defined who you were. The 1897 riots triggered by the Badeni language decrees — the decrees that demanded that German-speaking bureaucrats in Czech lands learn to speak Czech

2. Reinhard Merkel, "Die Welt im Wort erschaffen — Karl Kraus als Sprachdenker," in Peter Berner, Emil Brix, and Wolfgang Mantl, eds., *Wien um 1900. Aufbruch in die Moderne* (Vienna: Verlag für Geschichte und Politik, 1986), 132.

3. Frank Field, *The Last Days of Mankind: Karl Kraus and His Vienna* (New York: St. Martin's, 1967), 13.

— were riots over words. To move from language to language meant to move from identity to identity. For many Jewish Viennese, for instance, to abandon their grandparents' Yiddish and to adopt German meant to die as a member of a persecuted minority and to be reborn as a member of a cultivated and powerful majority.[4] Meanwhile, the avant-garde was hard at work inventing new languages in almost every imaginable field. According to Jean Maheu, "From 1880-1934, Vienna was a Babel where every possible language flourished: millenarianism and scientific positivism; symbolist poetry and grand novels; the rediscovery of minimalist form and giant works of grand synthesis."[5]

In this Babel, words suddenly tore off from things, signs from the things they signified; all the culture codes were scrambled, and this fed into the confusions about identity, both personal and collective. As Janik and Toulmin argue, "the problem of shattered identity and communication plagued Viennese society at all levels, the political and social, as well as the individual."[6] But isn't there some necessary link among thoughts and words and objects? In a pioneering three-volume work he called *Beiträge zu einer Kritik der Sprache* (*Contributions to a Critique of Language*),[7] Fritz Mauthner said no. We are afloat in a sea of words and signs and symbols, and how and when and if they form a coherent message is uncertain.

Vienna's trial of the century, at least as far as the avant-garde was concerned, began in a packed courtroom on February 22, 1901, and it was all

4. Statistics are from Mark E. Blum, *The Austro-Marxists, 1890-1918* (Louisville: The University Press of Kentucky, 1985), 8-9.

5. Jean Maheu, "Preface," in Jean Clair, ed., *Vienne 1880-1938. L'Apocalypse Joyeuse* (Paris: Editions du Centre Pompidou, 1986), 6.

6. Allan Janik and Stephen Toulmin, *Wittgensteins Wien*, trans. Reinhard Merkel (Munich: Carl Hanser, 1984), 80.

7. Fritz Mauthner, *Beiträge zu einer Kritik der Sprache* (Stuttgart: J. G. Cotta, 1901-1903). For more on Mauthner, see Johnston, *Austrian Mind*, 196-99.

about words. The plaintiff was Hermann Bahr. The defendant was Karl Kraus. Everyone knew there would be fireworks, and everyone enthusiastically looked forward to them.

Karl Kraus was haunted by the bizarre sensation that he lived in a maze, a funhouse, of multiple worlds, some of which were real and some of which were illusion. He wasn't alone, of course; everyone, it seems, had the same strange feeling. "Characteristic of the period," writes Petrus Tax,

> is . . . the awareness — pained, thrilled, problematicized or compulsive — that there is — or must be — or should be — this dualism, the dual presence of upper and underworld; the respectable, sober, rational, decorous, noble, possibly even sublime exterior or facade, and the vital, or demonically pathogenic, the bestial or ecstatically demonic other or nether sphere, and hence the need, temptation, or compulsion to play . . . with both . . . to hide and show.[8]

But maybe it's not simply that there are two worlds, upper and lower. Maybe they intersect, and if we fail to distinguish illusion from reality, we will plunge into disaster. But how can we tell the one from the other? By thinking carefully and critically, by deploying our thoughts into words, perhaps we can feel our way cautiously around reality and illusion. But what if the very words we use are themselves tainted by illusion? How can we think honestly if the very words in our heads are frauds? How can we ever speak and write clearly if the ocean of language around us, the ocean of language that feeds us, is polluted, not only by illusions, but by lies, deceptions, and fantasies? Words are the key. They are the nexus between thought and world. Kraus had, according to his biographer Harry Zohn, an "almost mystical fascination with words."[9]

Kraus began publishing his outrageous newspaper, *Die Fackel*, in order to purify thought by purifying language. As he wrote in his first editorial,

> This is our political program: we don't say: "here's what we're for," rather, we say: "here's what we're going to demolish." . . . What we

---

8. Petrus Tax, in Petrus Tax and Richard Lawson, eds., *Arthur Schnitzler and His Age* (Bonn: Bouvier, 1984), 3.

9. Harry Zohn, *Karl Kraus* (New York: Twayne, 1971), 60.

have in mind is nothing less than draining the vast swamp of jargon and rhetoric . . . maybe that way the *Fackel* can enlighten a land in which — unlike the Empire of Charles V — the sun never goes up.[10]

Kraus hated political rhetoric, bureaucratic double-speak, commercial hype, and ultra-precious avant-garde jargon. Vienna's media, he thought, was infected with all of it. And one Typhoid Mary of this plague was the avant-garde's guru, Hermann Bahr.

Hardly an issue of Kraus's *Die Fackel* went by without a shot at Hermann Bahr. To Kraus, Bahr was a charlatan, a poseur, and a tireless self-promoter. Bahr, and indeed much of cultural Vienna, did its best to ignore Kraus (Kraus called this being "silenced to death"). But in the summer of 1900, Bahr had had enough.

In an article called "Vom Wechselgastspiel" ("Guest performers"), Kraus wrote about an exchange arranged between Vienna's Volkstheater and Berlin's Deutsches Theater. In the course of the article, Kraus accused Bahr of outrageous self-promotion. Bahr, according to Kraus, attacked or defended theater directors simply on the basis of whether or not they staged his own plays. Even worse, Kraus alleged, Bahr had a cozy financial deal with the head of Vienna's Volkstheater; no wonder Bahr's theater reviews were so friendly!

For Kraus, this was an archetypical example of the corruption that was killing Vienna. In the arts, in politics, in business, merit and talent counted for nothing. What really mattered was influence, private deals, winks and nods, special privileges, and backroom payoffs (Kraus once joked that if there ever were a resurrection from the dead, he expected to see, when he popped out of his casket, a Viennese undertaker standing there looking for a tip). Cliques of patrons and clients, self-promoters and their sycophants, ran the city — the empire, for that matter — solely for their own enrichment, and the fact that the whole enterprise was about to crash and burn bothered them not in the least. It was all part of Vienna's cloying hypocrisy: on the surface, things looked normal enough, but behind the surface, all was corruption.

10. *Die Fackel*, April 1, 1899, 1.

For years, Kraus and *Die Fackel* needled Bahr, and finally, Bahr had had enough. He sued Kraus for libel.

In court, Bahr and Kraus were stars. Bahr was by now an imposing man. He had put on weight, and with his flowing beard and unruly mane of hair he really did look like some sort of prophet. He had spent much of his life around actors, and there was something grandly theatrical about him. Kraus, on the other hand, was thin and jittery, and with his twisted spine he looked fragile. He would become, in time, a famous public speaker — after 1910 or so, his public lectures would become major cultural events in Vienna — but in the courtroom in February 1901 he hardly seemed serious competition for Hermann Bahr.

Kraus, the defendant, piled a mountain of books and files on the table in front of him. In his statement, he said:

> My aim here is to attack the System of which Mr. Bahr is the most important representative. I fight this battle alone against an entire league. First they tried to "silence me to death," then they attacked me physically, yes, I have been attacked. . . . *Die Fackel* wages war against corruption, against the power of money and the power of the press, which are laying waste the country. . . . I have never written a word for my own personal benefit, and I am prepared to stand on my record. . . . My record will show that one profits much more from corruption than from fighting against corruption. . . . For the past ten years, without interruption, I have pursued Mr. Bahr.[11]

Bahr countered that he had always praised or blamed a dramatic work solely on its merits, never because of his personal friendships or financial interests. Arthur Schnitzler and other character witnesses testified on Bahr's behalf.

Bahr performed well in court; his testimony was repeatedly interrupted by laughter. For example:

> BAHR: I met Mr. Kraus some ten years ago. In those days, I used to frequent literary coffeehouses, a habit, thank God, I've since managed

11. The press was filled with accounts of the trial; see for example, "Ein Ehrenbeleidigunsprozess gegen *Die Fackel*," *Arbeiter Zeitung*, February 23, 1901, 5ff. See also accounts of the trial in Fischer, *Kraus*, 23ff.

to break! [Laughter] In those days, among assorted journalists and writers, sat a young man said to be a "great admirer" of my work. Then he suddenly disappeared. So one day I asked, "Where's little Kraus?" And someone said, "He's afraid you're going to punch him in the nose!" I then learned that somewhere he had published an article attacking me. I replied, "Don't worry, I have no intention of punching him in the nose!" Then I didn't see him for a long time, until I started editing *Die Zeit*. Then Mr. Kraus came to my office and asked to be hired. I liked his reviews, but my co-editors didn't like the idea. They were especially irritated when Mr. Kraus insisted that his name be printed in heavy type with each of his articles. I myself said to him one day, "Instead of making jokes about authors all the time, once in a while you ought to report what they actually write." Well, from that time on, his attacks on me became increasingly lively. He published a little brochure called *Die demolierte Literatur*, which included dozens of terrific jokes. I can say that because . . . they were all our jokes, mine and Schnitzler's and Beer-Hofmann's, so I'm allowed to praise them! [Laughter]

KRAUS [interrupting]: Remember, you're under oath![12]

Bahr insisted that the whole thing was a matter of envy. He and his coffeehouse friends had actually liked Kraus at first; they loved his jokes and imitations of actors. But Kraus, according to Bahr, was a frustrated man who only knew how to mock. And he had irrationally and unfairly picked Bahr as the target for a personal vendetta.

Kraus denied everything Bahr said. No, they hadn't met the way Bahr described. No, he had never gone to Bahr looking for a job; to the contrary, Bahr "in his cynical manner" had tried to buy Kraus off by giving him a job. But the jury agreed with Bahr. Kraus was convicted of libel and fined 1,800 crowns. While the court acknowledged that some of Kraus's accusations might have been made in good faith, his reporting was wrong.[13]

To be sure, most of Vienna's nearly two million inhabitants had more

---

12. "Ein Ehrenbeleidigunsprozess gegen *die Fackel*," *Arbeiter Zeitung*, February 24, 1901, 8ff.

13. "Ein Ehrenbeleidigunsprozess gegen *die Fackel*," 8ff.

important things to do that February than follow a catty libel trial between two writers. It was, after all, just a literary squabble, just a matter of words.

But to avant-garde Vienna, words mattered a very great deal.

Words had long been a problem in the sprawling, multiethnic Austro-Hungarian Empire. German-speakers, descended from Bavarians who had migrated eastward down the Danube in the Middle Ages, formed the linguistic core of the empire, and German was, more or less, the imperial lingua franca. But as the empire absorbed Czechs and Slovaks and Hungarians and Croats and Slovenes and Italians and Poles, more and more languages were added to German as official languages. Northern Germans, visiting Vienna, were surprised not only by Viennese German, which (to northern ears) was spoken in a singsong way and was peppered with Czech and Hungarian borrowings; they were amazed that all you had to do was turn a corner and you could hear Czech, Hungarian, Yiddish, Croatian, Italian, and, it seems, every imaginable language under the sun. Added to this, of course, were Greek and Latin, still the core languages in the better schools. Catholics worshiped in Latin; Jews, in Hebrew. Government decrees and army commands had to be issued in at least a dozen different versions. Czechs in Prague were enraged when imperial bureaucrats insisted on using German only; German-speaking bureaucrats were furious when the 1897 Badeni decrees forced them to learn Czech. German-speaking assimilated Jews were embarrassed by their Yiddish-speaking cousins. After 1867, when Hungary became an autonomous kingdom, linked to the empire only through loyalty to the House of Habsburg, the Hungarians quickly began to impose Hungarian throughout their kingdom, infuriating Slovak-speakers in the north.[14]

What mattered was not simply grammar, syntax, and vocabulary, but

14. See Emil Brix, "Der Gleichheitsgedanke in der Österreichischen Sprachpolitik um 1900," in Berner, *Wien*, 184-86.

tone as well, and here the demagogue Georg von Schönerer was something of an innovator. Schönerer had introduced a "new tone" in politics, a tone of ranting and shouting, which had nothing to do with reasoned persuasion and everything to do with violent assertion of one's own prejudices and obsessions. It was this new tone as much as objective political problems that had paralyzed the empire's fledgling democracy and pushed the empire back in an authoritarian direction. Words mattered.

But which words?

In 1897, Adolf Loos, aged twenty-seven, returned from his great adventure in America and began his lifelong mission of utterly, totally, and radically re-making Vienna's aesthetic vocabulary.

Adolf Loos, architect and culture critic, was in some ways utterly typical. Born in a small town (Brünn, now Brno), into an artisan, middle-class family (his father was a stonemason and builder), Loos was apprenticed as a mason before studying architecture in Dresden.

But, like so many of his generation, young Adolf Loos found his world stifling. As a young Central European, Loos not only had family and relatives, but generations of relatives and ancestors, ancestors often with grievances against someone else's ancestors. Loos's cities were already built with a dozen different architectural styles; literature, music, the visual arts — they were all already densely packed with the works of centuries. Though people lived cheek to cheek, class and tribe and faith made each alien to the other. Loos would later write, for instance, that to city people, the peasants out in the countryside were "more foreign to us than people who lived thousands of miles away"; Central European peasants, he wrote, were treated "like Negroes in America."[15]

Young Loos was suffocating. So, like so many other Central Europeans, Adolf Loos set out for America, the land of unlimited opportunity. At

15. Adolf Loos, *Trotzdem* (Innsbruck: Brenner Verlag, 1931), 9.

twenty-three, in 1893, Loos began a three-year stay there that would alter his life forever, and provide him with a stock of tall tales that he would tell for the rest of his life.

Loos's uncle was a clockmaker in Philadelphia, and young Adolf stayed with him for a time. Then he set off for parts unknown. Loos lived in New York City for a while, making a starvation living as a freelance music critic for one of New York's many German-language newspapers, the *New Yorker Bannerträger*. Before leaving Europe, a wise old man had advised him that whenever Americans asked whether he could do this or that, he should instantly reply, with a beaming smile, "Why yes, of course, that's my specialty!" Loos had asked for work from the *Bannerträger*, but it was only when the paper's regular music critic suddenly got a new job that the paper's desperate editor turned to young Loos. Did Loos know anything about the "Great Melba," the fabulously popular Australian soprano Nellie Melba? Or *Carmen*, the opera she was starring in? "Of course," Loos responded, "that's my specialty!" The skeptical editor had no choice; he handed Loos a standing-room-only ticket and sent him off to review Melba's performance.

Loos had never written a music review in his life. He frantically ran off to the public library and read every review he could get his hands on. He began to memorize what he assumed were the key terms: "counter-point"; "dynamic"; "crescendo"; "after three hours," he later wrote, "I knew enough."

Then he dashed off to the Metropolitan Opera, where he met a friend. The friend was actually a minor player in the opera, a soldier, but tonight the opera was short soldiers, did Loos know anything about soldiering? Marching around and so on? "Why yes," Loos replied, "that's my specialty!" So the opera hired him on the spot, dressed him up in a soldier suit, and marched him on stage. That, Loos joked, was the time he appeared on stage with the great Melba.

But he still had his review to write. He dashed home and packed it with all the disjointed jargon that he had memorized; the paper printed it as written. His roommate thought it was a spoof and laughed uproariously; Loos was terrified that someone would actually read it. The next morning (so Loos told the story), another German-language paper, the *New Yorker Staatszeitung*, reported that its rival, the *Bannerträger*, had published a hilarious satire of a music review. The *Bannerträger*'s regular reviewer was awful, the *Staatszeitung* wrote, but the new satirist was terrific! And later (Loos swore) the New York Music Critics Association made him an honorary member![16]

It was during his American stay that Loos experienced his epiphany. This is the way Robert Scheu reported it in Kraus's *Die Fackel* in 1909:

> Enlightenment came to him in America. He remembers how, his head still full of the notions of "ideal beauty" that he had learned in art school in Europe, he would wander through exhibitions in America of the latest technology... and he would think that "this is still a young land, this is a land where they use technology resolutely, this is a land where they chop down trees in ancient forests and run railroads over them. Here they build steel bridges over chasms and waterfalls, here they string telegraph wires across prairies. And it's beautiful. It's lightning-bolt beauty, a rushing together of high technology and the wild earth. . . ."
>
> In New York City, he spotted a suitcase. He was fascinated. A finely crafted leather suitcase with copper rivets. Suddenly he had it! That suitcase is modern! That's what "the modern" is all about! And at that moment, all those false and phony ideas he had about art and beauty, they tumbled away. Now he knew his way. "The Functional is the Beautiful!"[17]

Loos returned to Austria-Hungary via Britain in 1896; he had been called up for military service, and to dodge the draft would have meant loss of his citizenship. After his year's service, now 27, Loos began looking for work in Vienna, not only as an architect but as a journalist. For Loos, armed with his insight, had become a cultural prophet, burning with prophetic rage. Like Kraus in *Die Fackel*, like Freud in his *Psychopathology of Everyday Life*, Loos focused on the vocabulary of everyday life in his city, in his day, in his time.

He began writing about everything from fashion to interior design to plumbing to men's hats. No matter how diverse his subjects, though, his

16. "Mein Auftreten mit der Melba," in Adolf Loos, *Ins Leere Gesprochen* (Innsbruck: Brenner Verlag, 1932), 206-13.

17. Robert Scheu, "Adolf Loos," *Die Fackel*, June 26, 1909.

theme remained the same: "the modern." "What does it mean to be well dressed?" he asked in an article called "Die Herrenmode" ("Men's Fashion"). To be well dressed, he answered, means to dress modestly, practically, simply, and tastefully. "To wear a red jacket in a ball room is to immediately call attention to yourself, and therefore to be 'unmodern.'"[18]

Interior design ought above all to be honest — that's what "modern" style is all about, Loos argued in a piece called "Die Intereurs in der Rotunde" ("Interiors in the Rotunde"), a review of an interior design show. Furniture and objects in a person's space must be related to that person and his or her life. "Every piece of furniture, every thing, every object, tells a tale," and that tale must honestly reflect people who live among that furniture and those objects. Too often, people live in the midst of anonymous, mass-produced bric-a-brac that has nothing at all to do with them; to live like that is to be dishonest and unmodern.[19]

Furniture ought to be, first of all, practical:

By beautiful, what we mean is that something has achieved fullness, completion. But no useless, impractical object can really be described as "full" or "complete." . . . To be sure, practicality alone isn't enough. More is needed. A Renaissance art critic put it best: "when nothing can be added to or removed from an object, only then is that object 'beautiful.' Then we can say the object is fulfilled, complete, fully harmonious."[20]

What makes Greek vases so beautiful? Not their uselessness! Quite the contrary, their beauty resides precisely in their combination of simplicity and practicality. "Yes, Greek vases," Loos wrote, "are beautiful, like machines, like bicycles."[21]

"Modern" means truthful; it means that an object genuinely reflects the needs and aspirations of this day and this generation. To do this well, though, an object needs to be direct, simple, and clean; it needs to be free of useless clutter and decoration; it needs to be practical and well-made.

18. Adolf Loos, "Die Herrenmode," (May 22, 1898), in Loos, *Leere*, 11-15.
19. Loos, "Die Intereurs in der Rotunde," in Loos, *Leere*, 39.
20. Loos, "Das Sitzmöbel," in Loos, *Leere*, 48.
21. Loos, "Glas und Ton," in Loos, *Leere*, 56.

Take hats, for instance. You hear that fashions in men's hats come and go — that's the thing about modern times. But that's exactly wrong! Something really modern — that is, really relevant to our times and our needs — cannot be evanescent and episodic. The trivial is evanescent and episodic; the modern is solid. "You hear sometimes that a piece of clothing will be out of fashion next season, that it won't be 'modern' any more, but what that really means is that it wasn't really 'modern' to begin with."[22]

The first rule in design ought to be honesty, a radical honesty beginning with materials themselves. To disguise materials, to paint them over, to cover them with decorations, to make them look like what they are not, is fundamentally dishonest, and unmodern. But alas, everything around us is fake, false, untrue, disguised, and distorted. Where do you see this pervasive falsehood at its worst? asked Loos. In women's fashion.

In his day, he insisted, the only tool women had to better their lives was getting the attention of men. At that moment, for whatever reason, men seemed attracted to adolescent-looking, rather hermaphroditic persons, to young girls no longer children but not yet adults, feminine but also boyish. In such a situation, every woman wants to look like this regardless of the reality of her age and body. Women's clothing, consequently, is designed to disguise and deceive. Women's fashion is thoroughly ornamental. But ornamentation is a kind of atavistic survival from primitive times; "ornament is something that must be overcome." A bicycle is free of ornament; a steam engine is free of ornament; a genuinely progressive culture is a culture that repudiates ornament. Unfortunately for both men and women, women's only route to fulfillment at that time was to use some sort of sensual ornamentation, some sort of erotic disguise, to attract men. "But," Loos predicted, "we are headed for newer and better days. A woman will no longer have to attract a man but will win her independence through their own work, and that way she will be man's equal. The worth of a woman will no longer be tied to her sensuality. And then, silk and satin, flowers and ribbons, feathers and colors will all become irrelevant, they will all disappear."[23]

Loos published in Hermann Bahr's newspaper, *Die Zeit*, an important

22. Loos, "Die Herrenhüte," in Loos, *Leere*, 80.
23. Loos, "Damenmode," in Loos, *Leere*, 174.

review of a recent show sponsored by the Museum für Kunst und Industrie and its educational affiliate, the Kunstgewerbeschule, the school for applied arts. The review was not so much a review as a manifesto. He angrily criticized the Museum and the Kunstgewerbeschule precisely because he admired them so much. Their mission was what Loos insisted ought to be the mission of every contemporary artist: to express the contemporary, modern spirit of technology and industry, to unite the functional with the beautiful. But alas, Loos complained, more and more the Museum and the Kunstgewerbeschule were forgetting their mission and aping the Kunstakademie, the Academy of High Arts, with its pretentious and utterly outdated ornaments and fakeries.

Throughout 1898, and for that matter to the end of his long life, Loos published a host of reviews and commentaries, focused on the stuff of everyday life. He wrote about glassware and teapots and cooking utensils, about interior decoration and office design. He was fascinated by the textuality of everyday life; like Sherlock Holmes, he loved teasing out the clues lurking beneath the seemingly mute surface of things. Objects around us, Loos thought, are not mute at all but eloquent. They and the spaces that hold them ceaselessly whisper about the values we have, and profoundly shape the values we will develop.

In "Our Young Architects," Loos denounced the total commercialization of architectural work. Of course, architecture is of necessity the most commercial of arts; if architects want to do anything beyond sketches and blueprints, they need investors, and they need to bow to the investors' tastes. But architects need as well to insist on their own integrity, their own values as persons and artists. As a minimum, architects need to be creative, and courageous, and above all truthful. If architects want to be thought of as "artists," they have to be willing, Loos insisted, to draw the line somewhere, to refuse to bow to the taste of the highest bidder, and so suffer for their art, the way painters and sculptors and musicians do.[24]

In 1898, Loos designed the interior of the Café Museum, not far from the enormous museums of art and natural history. His interior was minimalist and stark, with no decorations allowed. He later recalled,

24. "Unseren Jungen Architekten," in Burkhardt Rukschcio and Roland Schachel, *Adolf Loos* (Vienna: Residenz Verlag, 1982), 47.

In 1898, every piece of wood was painted red, or green, or blue, or violet — architects made use of a whole palette. When I designed the Café Museum, and insisted on an interior done in undecorated mahogany, the Viennese suddenly learned that there are not only different colors in the world, but different materials too.[25]

Rivals called Loos's Café Museum "Café Nihilism."

In that same year, 1898, Loos published one of his most famous articles, "The Potemkin City," in the Secession's new journal, *Ver Sacrum*. In "The Potemkin City," Loos compared Vienna to the fake cities Russian Empress Catherine the Great's minister, Potemkin, presented to her. Vienna had undergone an immense urban renewal just the generation before; now the vast Ring and a dozen new buildings surrounded the old historic center, and the result, Loos thought, was a disaster. The grand buildings around the Ring — the Opera, the Parliament, the City Hall, and all the others — were fakes.

Loos's argument was both architectural and moral. An architect is a kind of artist, and what ought to matter most to an artist is truth. To be "truthful" as an artist meant, among other things, to be "true to" one's own age, to its particular needs and hopes and challenges. For ancient Greeks to build Greek buildings was fine; for twentieth-century Viennese to ape Greek or Gothic or Renaissance buildings, Loos thought, was deeply fraudulent. The Ring buildings might have said something modern and relevant; they might have spoken to their own generation's experience of industry and technology and rapid change. Instead, the Ring buildings did nothing more than imitate earlier styles in a hodgepodge way. The structures were hailed as great art, but they were fake art, they were frauds, façades, that only barely concealed both a complete lack of imagination and an inability — or unwillingness — to speak directly to the challenges and problems of the day. "Every city has the architects it deserves," he joked sarcastically. Maybe the fundamental fraudulence of the Ring's architecture arose from something fundamentally fraudulent deeply embedded in Viennese culture.[26]

At first it appeared that Loos and the Secessionists were soulmates.

25. Rukschcio and Schachel, *Loos*, 67.
26. "Die Potemkinische Stadt," in Rukschcio and Schachel, *Loos*, 46.

Both were unhappy with Viennese culture and society; both demanded radical cultural change; both thought of cultural change in moral terms. But it quickly became apparent that there were profound differences between the two. Loos had expected to be asked to help design the new Secession building, but he wasn't; the commission went to Josef Olbricht instead. Loos couldn't abide the Secession's other leading architect, Josef Hoffmann, and the two became bitter rivals. At one point, the writer Felix Salten tried to arrange a truce, and invited Loos and much of the rest of the avant-garde to a dinner at the Weisse Rössel restaurant. As the dinner discussion heated up, Loos jumped up, grabbed a chair, and waved it in the air. He pleaded with the others to respect the natural materials from which the chair was made. He insisted that to disguise the natural materials with glossy ornaments — precisely the kind of glossy ornament the Klimt-inspired artists had come to admire — was only another kind of lie. "Perhaps you'll recall," Loos later wrote Salten, "that the only thing I achieved was for the Secessionists, without exception, to brand me as a 'non-artist.'"[27]

Like the Secessionists, Loos insisted that the task of the artist is to see through, beyond, within, and below the here and now, the way things are, and the powers that be. Like the Secessionists, Loos insisted that surface reality is only one level of reality, that the artist must probe level on level, layer on layer, of reality. The Secessionists, inspired by Klimt, saw these other layers of reality in dazzling Byzantine light; they saw fantastic images and gaudy colors and vibrant forms. Loos did not. All this dazzling style, he increasingly worried, was nothing more than typical Viennese façade. The Secessionists, even as they claimed to be exploring the truth, were only perpetuating lies.

In 1908 Loos published his most radical work to date, a long essay called "Ornament und Verbrechen," "Ornament and Crime." Did Vienna's arts, its fine arts and architecture, help the Viennese to understand reality, to comprehend the specific reality, or realities, of their generation? Did Vienna's arts express the specific imperatives of the early twentieth century? Or did Vienna's arts delude and dazzle and divert people's attention from reality? There could be no doubt, Loos insisted, how one

27. Rukschcio and Schachel, *Loos,* 53.

had to answer. The older, Ring-style art, with all its fake buildings, was fraudulent, but so too were the newer arts, with their passion for gaudy decoration.

Loos demanded a radical demolition of Viennese culture. Decoration and ornament were like the tattoos of savages. Serious art, modern art, is above all an art that repudiates ornament. Ornament is not only frivolous; ornament is crime. Ornament obscures revelation, and revelation is the architect's imperative: revelation of the truth.

An artist — specifically, an architect — must above all be truthful, Loos insisted. To be truthful meant speaking the truth as it appears in one's own time. Though he did not coin the phrase, Loos was convinced that form should not conceal function, but should follow function. To be truthful, an architect should reveal, not conceal, a structure's materials; therefore finding the right materials is imperative. To be truthful meant to reveal, not hide, a work's inner form. To be truthful meant to shatter convention, to defy authority, and to express not simply psychological realities but external, metaphysical realities experienced by the artist. An artist who was content with imitation, convention, decoration, and ornament was a criminal.[28]

By the time of "Ornament und Verbrechen," 1908, Loos had angrily broken with the Secessionists. His great ally in Vienna's culture wars was critic Karl Kraus. Kraus, Loos, and the great eccentric writer Peter Altenberg became a kind of triumvirate, challenging the Klimt Secessionists. Eventually they would recruit young Oskar Kokoschka.

Loos was far more influential as a journalist than as a working architect; his commissions were only periodic, and usually small. He designed the Museum Café, and private homes and shops as well. They were all stark structures, constructed with fine materials, functional and geometrical. In his passion for simplicity, Loos increasingly thought not in terms of objects but in terms of space. As critic Françoise Very writes, Loos did not design attractive objects to fit in some empty space, but rather he designed space in which to work and live. Loos once remarked, "I don't project plans . . . I project space." He preferred to speak not of a "floor plan"

28. Loos, "Ornament und Verbrechen," in Adolf Loos, *Trotzdem* (Innsbruck: Brenner Verlag, 1931), 93-111.

but of a "space plan." In 1913 he remarked, "I try to teach students to think in three dimensions, in cubes."[29]

In 1910, Loos was working on what would be, up to that time, his most important commission. The Michaelerplatz is just inside what used to be the old city walls, nestled next to the massive Hofburg complex. The old city theater had been on the Michaelerplatz, and catty-corner from it was Young Vienna's favorite gathering place, the Griensteidl café, "Café Megalomania." Café Megalomania was demolished as part of a redesign of the Michaelerplatz, and in 1909, the firm of Goldman and Salatsch commissioned Loos to build them a commercial and residential building on Michaelerplatz, right across from the Hofburg.

Vienna was full of mixed-use commercial and residential buildings. In typical Viennese buildings, the ground floor was for shops, while the upper floors were for apartments. But nothing in Vienna looked like Loos's Michaelerplatz building. Every other mixed-use building was covered with decorations and ornaments, most often Greek-looking figures prancing about the façade, or pretending to hold up the upper floors. Conventional design clearly distinguished not only the commercial part of the building from the upper apartments, but the more exclusive apartments on the lower floors from cheaper apartments at the top of the building.

Loos did accept one convention: the commercial first floor was set off from the rest of the structure, though only by highly polished marble, not by decorative figures. But the upper floors were fiercely uniform, completely without decorations — no putti, no mythic figures, no flower boxes, nothing. The language was pure Loos: uncompromisingly stark.

The building's next door neighbor, the emperor, was not impressed. Loos's building, the emperor allegedly said, had "no eyebrows." Other critics were far more ferocious. The Loos building on Michaelerplatz was plain, ugly, emaciated, naked; some city council members denounced it as "monstrous." Loos's allies rallied to his defense. Richard Schaukal wrote that it took courage to construct a sober, unadorned, "naked" building. In its very simplicity and coldness, Schaukal argued, the building participated in the eternal beauty first expressed in ancient Greek architecture. Karl Kraus, always ready for battle, laughed that in the uproar about the

29. Clair, *Vienne*, 520-21.

building, "mediocrity rebels against functionality." A young architecture student, Paul Engelmann, even wrote a poem about the building:

> Let them scream and cry as they will,
> You remain standing proudly for me,
> The first sign of a new age[30]

No one was more impressed by signs and wonders than Sigmund Freud. Freud had experimented with drugs in treating his patients, but he had little faith in pharmaceutical cures. He had experimented as well with hypnosis, but was convinced that hypnosis might well distort rather than reveal. In the end, Freud hit upon words.

Freud carved out the basic elements of psychoanalysis (he first used that term in 1896) between 1900 and 1905. In 1900, in *The Interpretation of Dreams,* he had identified the anatomy of the unconscious and its modes of expression. In 1905, in *Three Essays on the Theory of Sexuality,* he described psychic physiology.

What is most striking about *Three Essays* is not so much Freud's stress on sexuality as his focus on history. Like most of his Darwinian contemporaries, Freud was sure that the organization of basic human instincts and appetites (broadly defined as "sexuality") is central to human personality. Infants are pure unorganized appetite; they are polymorphously perverse. Over time, unorganized appetite is channeled and structured in precise ways, and the result is a coherent human personality. Poorly structured personalities produce both dysfunction and psychic pain. "Neurotics" suffer from the past. Their pain is the result of unresolved conflicts, unmastered crises, from the past which persist into the present. To repair the past, the patient and the therapist must both become historians; they must plunge into the past in order to redeem the present and future.

30. Rukschcio and Schachel, *Loos,* 153-55.

But psychoanalysis was more than a theory. Freud insisted that it was a practice, a set of specific techniques and skills one could use to effect the redemption of a person's history.

Psychoanalysis was a "talking therapy." Reclining on the famous couch, Freud's patients spoke freely, unguardedly, prompted at most by an occasional suggestion from Freud. In their forests of words, Freud tried to track the spoors of their malady.

Josef Breuer had first experimented with the talking cure in 1881, when he treated Bertha Pappenheim, whom Freud would refer to as "Anna O." Anna O. suffered from a wide range of strange symptoms: a nervous cough, a loss of appetite, headaches, partial paralysis, disturbed vision. No treatment seemed to help until Breuer allowed her to talk freely about herself and her life. Strangely enough, this talking seemed to relieve, if not cure, her symptoms.

By 1892, Freud depended almost entirely on the therapeutic powers of words. The case of "Elizabeth von R." was the first full-length analysis of hysteria he had ever undertaken. Freud encouraged his patient to speak freely and randomly; it was precisely in this "free association" that Freud searched for clues. "The hysteric," he and Breuer wrote, "suffers mainly from reminiscences." Past events continue to press on the patient in the present; the doctor's task is to "excavate" remembered material, identify the troubling memory, vent its emotional charges, and bring it under rational control.[31]

Freud had long been amazed by the way in which words came unbidden, virtually on their own, when people relaxed their guard; he was fascinated by the way in which words concealed as much as they revealed, the way seemingly simple jokes or nervous laughs suggested things much more complex, lurking beneath the surface, as he explained in the *Psychopathology of Everyday Life*.

But more and more he was astonished by the way in which everything became a word, the way gestures, customs, facial expressions, dream-visions, all were, in a sense, "words," all charged with meaning, even more meaning than the mere spoken word.

This is why, for Freud, therapy was a matter of translation, not manip-

31. Peter Gay, *Freud: A Life for Our Time* (New York: Norton, 1988), 71.

ulation. The analyst's task, he had become convinced, was not to impose a cure, but rather to assist in the translation of languages speakers spoke but could not themselves understand. This was no easy task. As he helped patients excavate their buried cities of dreams, Freud began to discover the extraordinary tricks of the human mind. Patients "resisted" approaching the very things they needed to face. Often patients "transferred" to Freud the emotions they felt for others. Simply identifying the problem was never enough; the emotions attached to the problem had to be discharged, "worked through," and that took time. In the process, everything was disguised, distorted, and inverted. In the coming years, with the cases of "Little Hans," the "Rat Man," and the "Wolf Man," Freud would explore worlds as bizarre as those of Sherlock Holmes. In each case, the clues were in the words.

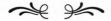

Karl Kraus heartily despised both Freud and psychoanalysis, but one thing Kraus shared with Freud was a fascination with words. Ideas move history, ideas are shaped by words, and Kraus, of course, was a writer, a person of words, and like all writers he was deeply impressed by the magical power of language. "Language is the mother of thought, not its handmaiden," he would write; "my mission is a profane one and my realm is entirely of this linguistic world."[32] Hermann Bahr, so different from Kraus, once wrote in words Kraus certainly would have approved of:

> Education, which focuses so much on reason, which so stresses merely the use and manipulation of words, has robbed us of a sense of the inner life of words, their prior life, one might say. For words first emerge in ancient times, directly from the mouths of our primitive ancestors, they emerge as pure sound, long before they

32. Zohn, *Kraus*, 61-62.

are coined into concepts. Every word is a tone-community of vowels and consonants; tones secretly attract one another, they secretly repel each other, and out of this loving attraction and repulsion emerges language, at first more gesture, more form than sense. . . . It is this primitive "ur-life" of language which repeats itself in poets; the poet hears in words their secret being.[33]

But with Kraus, there was even more. Words, Kraus thought, live quite independently from us; words lead lives of their own, we inherit them, and when we do they are already charged with layers of meanings which come from our ancestors and which we then transmit to our heirs. For Kraus, the proper use of words is a moral issue; their misuse is a hideous crime. In this regard, the press was the worst offender of all.[34]

Karl Kraus spent a lifetime at war with the media, and at the turn of the century, the media were the newspapers. The press, he would write, was "the goiter of the world."[35] The greatest goiter of them all was the *Neue Freie Presse*, of course, though in Vienna there were all those other newspapers as well. The coffeehouses offered their customers the latest papers from Vienna and abroad; newsboys prowled the Ring hawking the day's papers. Kraus read the papers angrily, snipping out articles for *Die Fackel*. A favorite technique was to print a paragraph or two from an article, then comment on it; or, on other occasions, to print two contradictory selections side by side without comment.

Some thought Kraus's vendetta against the press was personal, and there may well be truth in that. As a boy, his ambition had been to write for the *Neue Freie Presse;* when he wasn't hired, so the story goes, he determined to wage war against it. There were other motives as well: the *Presse*, edited by Moritz Szeps, expressed the views especially of those liberal and prosperous Jewish Viennese whom Kraus, Jewish himself, had come to detest.

But there was also substance in Kraus's one-man war on the media.

33. Hermann Bahr, *Selbstbildnis* (Berlin: Fischer, 1923), 228-29.
34. Reinhard Merkel, "Die Welt im Wort Erschaffen — Karl Kraus als Sprachdenker," in Berner, *Wien*, 132. See also Peter Kampits, "Sprachphilosophie und Literatur als Sprachkritik im Wien um 1900," also in Berner, *Wien*, 119-26.
35. Cited in Zohn, *Kraus*, 57.

Kraus's first accusation against the papers, and especially against the *Neue Freie Presse*, was rampant hypocrisy. The *Presse* was proud of its propriety; it was serious, humorless, and earnest. Reading its front pages, one might well assume that it was edited by English Puritans. But flip to its back pages, the advertisements and "personals," and you discover a bizarre world of only modestly disguised ads for prostitutes and abortionists, personal notices reflecting a world of adultery, despair, and suicide. Curious, Kraus noted, that the pompous *Presse* would carry ads offering the services of "Carola Prügler" (Carola the "whipper"), and "Wanda Schläger" (Wanda the "beater").[36] To be sure, Kraus mocked, "I have never denied the fact that contraceptive ads are the only decent, sensible, and tasteful contribution which the daily press makes year in and year out."[37]

But hypocrisy was the least of the media's sins. Far worse was the media's inevitable distortion of reality. In Kraus's view, the media did not merely respond passively to public tastes; the media actively shaped and molded public taste. The papers constantly exaggerated the trivial and trivialized the important. The result was a fascination with the bizarre and the grotesque.

Ah, but wasn't the media merely providing what its readers wanted? Kraus would not let the press off so easily. Yes, readers seemed to want the grotesque, but they did so in part because the media consciously appealed to and cultivated the voyeurism of its readers. The press appealed to the very worst in its readers, and given the enormous power of the media, it was little wonder that the worst thrived.

The exaggeration, deception, and distortion of the media were echoed in the new techniques of mass advertising — indeed, news reporting was increasingly a variant of advertising. The "jungles of commerce" spread everywhere. There was no escape — they colonized one's own consciousness. Try to close your eyes to escape the incessant huckstering, and what do you see and hear?

A shaggy head appears and moans: "I used to be bald!" And again: "On this side there are still pimples, on that side they have disap-

36. Cited in Zohn, *Kraus*, 44.
37. Karl Kraus, "Der Biberpilz" (1910), in Kraus, *In These Great Times*, ed. and trans. Harry Zohn (Manchester: Carcanet Press, 1976), 64.

peared after using. . . ." Now the maelstorm of slogans bursts forth unrestrained: "Be sure to ask for . . . !" "Once you try it you'll buy it!" . . . "For acid indigestion . . ." A gun dealer notices I no longer know what is going on and drowns out the din with his own slogan: "Be your own murderer!"[38]

Worse still, in its insatiable hunger to discover the grotesque and bizarre, the media was profoundly inhumane. Persons existed for the press merely as fodder for its never-ending freak show. A child dies, a mother is distraught, and hordes of reporters rush in, invading the mother's life, intent on capturing and exposing the mother's moment of grief. No one is safe, no story too vile, no subject too delicate for the hyenas of the press. The tortures the press could impose were far worse that those of the Middle Ages; the "Middle Ages only had thumb screws, not the media."[39] A child falls from a window and lies dying in a pool of blood. Somehow reporters make it to the scene before the boy is moved. They crowd around the dying child looking for a quote.

> He is already drowning, but he still had to answer the questions of the human sharks . . . the press struggles with death in order to beat it to the death-bed of a bleeding child for the sake of getting the news. Before this spectacle all hatred and contempt of the press falls silent. Nothing is left but sadness.[40]

Perversely enough, reporters were not really interested in the stories so much as they were interested in themselves. Inflated with their own sense of importance, reporters reported not the news but their feelings about the news, convinced that they alone possessed the sensitivity needed to comprehend events. In 1910, in an essay he called "Heine und die Folgen," ("Heine and the Consequences"), Kraus traced the presumptuousness and self-absorption of the press back to the great nineteenth-century writer Heinrich Heine. Heine made his living in part by writing for newspapers. That Heine was brilliant Kraus would not deny. The problem is

---

38. Karl Kraus, "Die Welt der Plakate" (1909), in Kraus, *Times*, 45.
39. Cited in Zohn, *Kraus*, 44.
40. Karl Kraus, "Interview mit einem sterbendes Kind" (1912), in Kraus, *Times*, 67.

that hordes of little Heines had come along, convinced that *their* impressions, *their* sentiments, *their* feelings were what news was all about.[41] Yet the clue to their dishonesty was their own language — jargon-filled, clichéd, obscure, sentimental, trite, self-absorbed, sensationalist, superficial, and utterly humorless — the language not of truth but of hypocrisy and deceit. "It is uplifting," Kraus remarked in one of his famous aphorisms, "to lose one's faith in a reality which looks the way it is described in a newspaper."[42]

But Karl Kraus was not one to despair. He was on a crusade. His aim was nothing less than the redemption of humanity by redeeming language, and reuniting language — beaten, bruised, and abused as it was — with the truth.

Arthur Schnitzler's characters are fragmented souls who typically never quite find a psychological center. They experience this fragmentation as psychic pain, but they are never quite sure either of the cause of or the therapy for this pain. Schnitzler once wrote:

> A lot of people seem to me to be put together from an odd assortment of floating parts, which never quite fit together, never quite group themselves around a coherent center. They have no center, no identity. These people have no identity and they experience that as a kind of terrible loneliness. Most people are like that. Sometimes, though, some really unusual individuals become acutely conscious of this.[43]

Schnitzler's fictional universe, Gerhart Baumann explains, is

41. Karl Kraus, "Heine und die Folgen," in Kraus, *Times*, 87.

42. Karl Kraus, "Lob der verkehrten Lebensweise" (1908), in Kraus, *Times*, 33.

43. Cited in Gerhart Baumann, *Arthur Schnitzler: Die Welt von Gestern eines Dichters von Morgen* (Frankfurt: Athenäum, 1965), 3.

a world of deception and self-deception in which characters have neither the certainty of a coherent "I" or of a coherent "you." And so characters tend to act not as individuals but rather as types, which flow all together, so that it takes work to distinguish them from each other. Characters tend to flow together, as do waking and dreaming, appearance and reality, wishes and facts, they all flow in and out of each other.[44]

No wonder that they have such a hard time saying who they are.

This is the world Hugo von Hofmannsthal explored, in 1902, in a peculiar little prose work he called "Ein Brief," better known as the "Chandos Letter." It purported to be a letter written in 1603, by Philip, Lord Chandos, to Francis Bacon. In it, Philip tries to explain why he has forsaken writing. Philip is only twenty-six. He has already become famous as a brilliant writer. Yet now, his earlier works seem utterly foreign to him, and he cannot imagine writing anymore. He had wanted to study ancient literature:

> I wanted to decipher the fables, the mythical tales bequeathed to us by the Ancients . . . decipher them as hieroglyphs of a secret, inexhaustible wisdom whose breath I sometimes seemed to feel as though from behind a veil.

There was a time when Philip, as an artist, could see the connections among all things, could see how words related to nature and nature to human beings. But something has happened to him, something dreadful. He writes: "My case, in short, is this: I have lost completely the ability to think or to speak of anything coherently."

It was a terrifying process. First, abstractions like "spirit" and "soul" suddenly became strange to him. He no longer quite knew what they meant; even talking about them became distasteful to him.

Worse followed. He began to pay close attention to what people really said, and what he discovered is that much of what they — we — say is trite, conventional, and false.

---

44. Baumann, *Schnitzler*, 18.

My mind compelled me to view all things occurring in such conversations from an uncanny closeness. As once, through a magnifying glass, I had seen a piece of skin on my little finger look like a field full of holes and furrows, so I now perceived human beings and their actions. I no longer succeeded in comprehending them with the simplifying eye of habit. For me everything disintegrated into parts, those parts again into parts; no longer would anything let itself be encompassed by one idea. Single words floated around me, they congealed into eyes which stared at me and into which I was forced to stare back — whirlpools which gave me vertigo and, reeling incessantly, led into the void.

At the very same time, this strange experience includes elements of extraordinary wonder. Suddenly everything around him seemed strange, new, amazing — a pitcher, a farmer's plow, a dog in the sun, a peasant's hut — all could become "vessels of revelation." At night, there are moments when

I feel as though I myself were about to ferment, to effervesce, to foam and to sparkle. And the whole thing is a kind of feverish thinking, but thinking in a medium more immediate, more liquid, more glowing than words. It, too, forms whirlpools, but of a sort that do not seem to lead, as the whirlpools of language, into the abyss, but into myself and into the deepest womb of peace.

But such moments are rare. Instead, he leads a life mixed of boredom and vacuity. He goes about the routines on his estate, scarcely able to think. He will never be able to write again. He will never be able to write because

the language in which I might be able not only to write but to think is neither Latin nor English, neither Italian nor Spanish, but a language none of whose words is known to me, a language in which inanimate things speak to me and wherein I may one day have to justify myself before an unknown judge.[45]

45. Hofmannsthal, *Ein Brief,* in Breicha, *Finale,* 33-43.

But there was life among the fractured shards of language, among the shattered narratives and broken words. Amid that rubble of words is where fin de siècle's archetypal bohemian, Peter Altenberg, lived.

Like everything else in Vienna, Peter Altenberg was a puzzle and a contradiction. To begin with, his name wasn't Peter Altenberg at all; it was Richard Engländer. At thirty-one in 1890, Engländer/Altenberg was older than most of the Young Vienna artists; he was also far more peculiar. By 1890 he had taken to wearing a broad brimmed hat and a sweeping cape and (even in the coldest winter) sandals. He awoke at noon, made it to the coffeehouses by early evening, and by midnight he was wandering the city, exploring the demi-monde, chatting with the prostitutes and petty thieves and shipwrecked people of the night. Sitting in a café (his favorite was the Central), he had taken to scribbling down his impressions on scraps of paper that he then shoved deep into his pockets. People noticed. Schnitzler, Kraus, and others read what Engländer/Altenberg wrote and they were deeply impressed. He wrote not novels, not short stories, not plays, not poetry, but episodes, fragments of life, momentary impressions. He wrote them with such freshness that the fractured moments seemed to come alive.

Kraus arranged to have some of the pieces published, but Engländer insisted on a pseudonym. He had one in mind. He explained that when he was a boy, he and his family vacationed in "Altenberg," and the word conjured up for him all sorts of childhood nostalgia. And while on vacation, he once met a young girl jokingly called "Peter" by her brothers. She was Engländer's first love. Even more, "Peter" became the very incarnation of childhood innocence and innocent love. Much like Lewis Carroll, Engländer was fascinated by adolescence, by that in-between moment in life that is no longer childhood but not yet adulthood. He was especially fascinated by adolescent girls — replicas, perhaps, of "Peter," alluring but not yet erotic, innocent but on the verge of awakening. Like Lewis Carroll, Engländer collected pictures of young girls and pasted them up in his room at the Hotel London. He had a pseudonym in mind; he would be "Peter Altenberg."[46] And he would be a prophet. He said of his work: "If

---

46. Peter Altenberg, *Reporter der Seele*, ed. Gunther Martin (Vienna: Stiasny-Verlag, 1960), 14ff.

you understand me, you will understand yourself! Look! I am your silent heart, now beating!"[47]

His sketches were moments snatched out of context; they were records of voices overheard. In "Vor dem Konkurse" ("On the Concourse") he writes about a family in a public garden, awaiting a concert. In "Im Volksgarten" ("In the Volksgarten") he recreates an image of a girl releasing balloons into the sky. Some sketches skirt the very edge of cliché but somehow never quite tumble over. For instance, in "Ein Schweres Herz" ("A Heavy Heart"), Altenberg recreates an encounter he witnessed between a young girl and her father. The young girl is in boarding school. Her father is visiting. He quizzes her about school, about history and arithmetic, and feigns interest. She rattles off the meaningless details of school, but then interrupts herself and says quietly, "Daddy, I want to go home, with you." But the father responds "No, you're a big girl now . . ." and then, at that precise moment, genuine communication is lost. Altenberg injects himself in a postlude: the father says it's time for the girl to go to ballet class. She doesn't want to go. Altenberg walks up to the father and pleads with him to relent, this once, and let the little girl skip her class. The father agrees, but still insists that education and such involve "principles" which simply have to be obeyed. "When it comes to matters of the soul," Altenberg responds, "the best principle is to be free of principles."[48]

Yet even in the very process of communicating, Altenberg was touched by just how difficult communication is, even communication between friends, even communication about the most trivial details. The problem is that one longs for intimate communication, but intimate conversation is very, very difficult.

In a comic sketch he called "Nacht Theater" ("Night Theater"), a wealthy woman bustles into the café where Altenberg is sitting and hastily asks him to watch her poodle for her while she goes to the theater. Off she goes. Altenberg looks at the poodle, and the poodle looks at Altenberg, each taken aback by their sudden relationship. The poodle whines and cries and Altenberg imagines it saying: "is she ever coming

47. Hans Bisanz, *Peter Altenberg: Mein Ausserstes Ideal* (Vienna: Verlag Christian Brandstätter, 1987), 17.

48. Altenberg, *Reporter*, 33-36.

back for me?" After several painful hours she does return, and without a word of thanks, she snatches up the dog and hurries away. But, Altenberg wrote,

> what struck me most was that intense feeling of longing, yearning, yearning that seems to stream out of the heart of people and animals too. Where does it all go, all this yearning? Does it all flow into space, the way water evaporates into the clouds? The way the air is filled with water, so the world is filled with longing.[49]

In "Der Nebenmensch" ("The Person by your Side") he reproduces a shard of conversation. Two girls chatting — about cheese. One likes Gorgonzola; the other can't understand how her friend could ever like Gorgonzola. "No one," Altenberg writes, "no one can ever understand another; in fact, the person right by your side is the person farthest away from you."[50] Novelist Robert Musil wrote in his vast novel, *Der Mann ohne Eigenschaften (The Man Without Qualities):*

> It wasn't simply a question of mistrust of your neighbor; it was also a matter of mistrusting yourself and your fate. People acted in this land quite differently from the way they thought, and thought quite differently from the way they acted. . . . Yes, of course, "Kakania" was a "land of genius"; that's probably why it collapsed.[51]

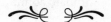

Vienna's waves of innovation in the visual arts paralleled, fueled, and reflected this crisis in language. Gustav Klimt and the Secession artists were convinced that the visual arts had reached a dead end in Vienna; they had become conventional, routine, clichéd, and false. The Secession artists ex-

49. Altenberg, *Reporter,* 58.

50. Cited in Harry Zohn, *Der farbenvolle Untergang* (Englewood Cliffs, N.J.: Prentice-Hall, 1971), 44-53.

51. Cited in Zohn, *Untergang,* 35.

propriated as much as they rejected, to be sure; they were as fascinated by Greek iconography, for example, as their predecessors and more conventional rivals. But what drove the Secession was a determination to reconnect art to life, to create a *Gesamtkunstwerk*, a "total work of art" — not, however, by imposing life on art (as "Naturalists" might argue), but by imposing art on life.

The Secession's *jugendstil* was an enthusiastic attempt to aestheticize and thus renew life. Its favorite images were images of youth, vitality, sensuality, and rejuvenation, its colors bold and brilliant. Viennese *jugendstil* was self-consciously artistic, and purposely "all surface"; Klimt, for example, loved the luminous glow of Byzantine mosaics and reproduced it endlessly in his work. As life became art, ordinary life was raised to the level of symbol, routine action to hieroglyph, and dream and mystery became as much a part of *jugendstil* as youth and vitality.

This effort to raise life to the level of art could be found everywhere in the early years of the Secession and its allies — in Otto Wagner's rose-covered apartments and in his gaudy tram-stops, and especially in his spectacular Church am Steinhof completed between 1905-07; in Josef Olbricht's Secession building itself; in the Secession's journal, *Ver Sacrum*; in the stunning posters announcing each new Secession show.

But its greatest triumph was in the creation of the Wiener Werkstätte, the Vienna Workshops, in 1903.

Vienna had two art schools — the Art Academy, which stressed painting and sculpture, and the Kunstgewerbeschule, the crafts school. In response to industrial mass production, artists and artisans throughout Europe had struggled to preserve handcrafts partly by defining them as "art," partly by arguing that traditional artisan skill ought to be applied to industrial objects; the way to humanize technology was to aestheticize it. The "arts and crafts movement" was especially strong in Britain, but it flourished in France and Germany as well. Vienna created a Museum of the Applied Arts (Museum für Kunst und Gewerbe) as part of the urban renewal associated with the construction of the Ring, and the Kunstgewerbeschule had been created in 1867 as the educational arm of the new museum.

The Art Academy was the prestigious art school in Vienna, but also the more conventional and academic. Though the Kunstgewerbeschule was less prestigious, it was also the more experimental and progressive; its instructors taught a wide range of skills beyond painting and sculpture, and they stressed integrating life and art.

Given the Secession artists' hopes of reconnecting art and life, it is no surprise that they flourished in the Kunstgewerbeschule. Josef Hoffmann and Kolo Moser were two Secessionists who taught at the Kunstgewerbe-schule, and it was they who hit on the plan to set up a business to market Secessionist art. Supported by industrialist and art-lover Fritz Waern-dorfer, they called the new business "the Wiener Werkstätte."[52]

The Wiener Werkstätte was born with a predictable burst of enthusi-asm on May 19, 1903. The Wiener Werkstätte commissioned scores of art-ists and artisans to design postcards, women's fashion, and household items; the products were sold at several shops around the city. Wiener Werkstätte women's fashion, for example, helped shift women's fashion from the Victorian matron look to much freer, much more flowing "garçon" look.[53]

The Wiener Werkstätte even set up its own cabaret, the "Fledermaus" (The "Bat"), on elegant Kärtnerstrasse. The Fledermaus was quite a place. Located in a basement, its interior was carefully designed by Wiener Werkstätte artists. The walls were covered with mosaics, the floors tiled in black and white squares, and there was, of course, a theater. Everyone, nat-urally, came to the Fledermaus sooner or later, and as proof of its popular-ity, Karl Kraus even joked about it in *Die Fackel*. All the artists, Kraus wrote, argued about the design of the lavatory:

> there has long been a debate about whether the [lavatory] is better served by the paper on which Zuckerkandl's art reviews are printed or by a costume for the lady lavatory attendant which Professor Hoffmann ought to design. In the end, however, it was agreed that

52. See Elisabeth Schmuttermeier, "Die Wiener Werkstätte," in Berner, *Wien,* 340-41; Angelo Völker, "Die Mode-Abteilung der Wiener Werkstätte," in Berner, *Wien,* 340-41; Peter Vergo, "La Wiener Werkstätte 1903-1913 — le paradis terrestre et le chemin de la ruine," in Clair, *Vienne,* 274-83.

53. Tegina Forstner, "Von der Tournüre zur 'Garçon' — Wiener Damenmode von 1870 bis 1930," in Robert Waissenberger, ed., *Wien 1870-1930. Traum und Wirklichkeit* (Vi-enna: Residenz Verlag, 1984), 209-14.

the cistern was to be painted white and a chequerboard pattern printed on it.[54]

Wiener Werkstätte design and fashion brought the world of art into the world of daily life, and everyday objects began to speak with a whole new vocabulary.

Precisely this crisis of language, and the fragmentation and disorientation it produced, was also the source of a stunning explosion of energy. Hermann Bahr recognized this in his 1904 collection of essays, *A Dialog on Tragedy*. In art, he wrote,

> All divisions are transcended. The physiological and psychological run together, events and experiences merge, the "I" dissolves and everything becomes a single flood, which here seems dammed, but there rushes freely, and everything becomes a vast movement of colors and tones and warmth, and feelings, of space and time, all of which we experience as intuition, feeling, and will.[55]

The crisis of language paralyzed Arthur Schnitzler's fictional musician, George von Wergenthin. In *Der Weg ins Freie (The Way to Freedom)* Wergenthin can never quite complete a musical composition. Partly, to be sure, this is because Wergenthin is lethargic and self-absorbed. But it is also because the musical language he had inherited no longer sufficed; neither the classicism of Brahms nor the turbulent innovations of Wagner provided the language Wergenthin needed to express what was in him.[56]

54. Cited in Frank Whitford, *Oskar Kokoschka* (New York: Atheneum, 1986), 25.
55. Hermann Bahr, *Tagebuch* (Berlin: Paul Cassirer, 1909), 17.
56. Marc A. Weiner explores this issue in his *Arthur Schnitzler and the Crisis of Musical Culture* (Heidelberg: Carl Winter, 1986); see William Johnston's comments in his introduction to Arthur Schnitzler, *The Road into the Open*, trans. Horace Samuel (Evanston: Northwestern University Press, 1991), xiv.

Yet it was precisely this crisis of language that impelled much of Gustav Mahler's vast work.

In the early years of the new century, Mahler was exhausting himself in Vienna. He directed the Hofoper; eventually he directed the Symphony as well. During the season he ran through a crushing round of rehearsals and performances; in the brief summers he composed frantically. He was the target of endless complaints and abuse, but he was also the subject of extraordinary fascination. Max Graf, for example, describes Mahler conducting:

> When the house drew dark, the small man with the sharply chiseled features, pale and ascetic looking, literally rushed to the conductor's desk. His conducting was striking enough in his first years of activity in Vienna. He would let his baton shoot forward suddenly, like the tongue of a poisonous serpent. With his right hand, he seemed to pull the music out of the orchestra. . . . He would let his stinging glance loose upon a musician who was seated far away from him, and the man would quail. Giving a cue, he would look in one direction; at the same time pointing the baton in another. . . . Mahler was always in full movement, like a blazing flame. Later he became calmer. Evidently he controlled himself, which only augmented his inner tension.[57]

Mahler was the last of the great romantic symphonists. His theatrical spirit was at home above all in the grand structures of the classical symphony. By 1906, Mahler had composed seven symphonies, the first four inspired by the *Wunderhorn* fairytales, the next three especially by the poetry of Friedrich Rückert. In these seven magnificent works, Mahler had pushed the symphony to frontiers never yet explored. He had altered the symphonic form (instead of the normal four movements, there are five in Symphony No. 2, and six in Symphony No. 3). He expanded the length of several of his symphonies; the Second runs some 85 minutes; the third, 100 minutes. He introduced folk melodies and a wide variety of other musical materials not commonly found in sym-

57. Max Graf, *Legend of a Musical City*, cited in Gartenberg, *Gustav Mahler: The Man and His Music* (New York: Schirmer Books, 1978), 136.

phonies (for example, the "Frère Jacques" theme in Symphony No. 1). He had added all sorts of new instruments, especially horns and bells, and in the Second Symphony he even had an off-stage ensemble play with the on-stage orchestra.

Above all, Mahler brought human words into the symphony. This was, of course, no innovation of his; Beethoven's Ninth Symphony concluded with a chorus, and that work immediately became a model of artistic perfection for generations of musicians. But few composers were so captivated by the human voice as Mahler. The Second Symphony is scored for soprano, contralto, and chorus; the Third includes both a male and female choir; the Fourth includes a solo soprano. If Kraus was a "word mystic," Mahler was a "tone mystic." His symphonic avalanche of tones pressed, somehow, insistently toward speech, as if the notes echoing in his imagination spoke in a wondrous language he could transcribe but not quite comprehend. But the speech in the symphonies is not mere words; it is words become music, and as music, transcendent and ethereal.

The first four symphonies, the so-called "Wunderhorn" symphonies, are filled with vibrant experiments. The next three, the "Rückert" symphonies are, by comparison, much more austere, more purely orchestral.

The Sixth is both powerful and disturbing.[58] Mahler composed it in 1903-04, and it is, in a sense, a simple work. It is by Mahler's standards not unusually long (eighty minutes); there are only a few extra instruments (his beloved horns). It is structured in the traditional four movements, and built around a single key, A-minor.

But in many ways it is one of the most moving works Mahler ever composed. It begins with a march, but the confident, triumphant rhythm is constantly undermined by dissonance, and a much more ominous, even grotesque mood develops. After a distant, quiet second movement, the third movement begins with a "horror" scherzo, a whirlwind of pounding, wild tones, interrupted only by a wistful childlike melody. The final movement brings back the march, but it is a grim, doomed march,

---

58. For a synopsis of the Sixth, see Deryck Cooke, *Gustav Mahler: An Introducton to His Music* (New York: Cambridge University Press, 1988), 83-87; Michael Kennedy, *Mahler* (New York: Oxford University Press, 2001), 139-44; Constantin Floros, *Mahler: The Symphonies* (New York: Amadeus Press, 2003), 161-86.

punctuated by three hammer blows (the percussionist actually uses a hammer); the symphony ends grimly with trombones and tympanis fading into silence.

Mahler's Sixth is perhaps his only truly "tragic" symphony. Symphonies normally end with at least a pleasing mood; Beethoven's titanic acoustic struggles concluded triumphantly. Brahms's Fourth Symphony has a grim conclusion, and Tchaikovsky's *Pathétique* is bleak enough. But Mahler's Sixth ends in catastrophe.

Mahler himself was deeply shaken by the Sixth. When he discussed it with his wife they both burst into tears; she later wrote: "Not one of his works came as directly from his inmost heart as this. We both wept that day. The music and what it foretold touched us so deeply."[59] Bruno Walter wrote of it:

> The Sixth is deeply pessimistic. . . . The mounting tension and climaxes of the last movement resemble, in their grim power, the mountainous waves of a sea that will overwhelm and destroy the ship; the work ends in hopelessness and the dark night of the soul. "Non placet" is his verdict on this world; the "other world" is not glimpsed for a moment.[60]

The Seventh, then, is a surprise. Composed in 1904-05, it is large (five movements, eighty minutes), progresses from minor to major, and is, compared to the turbulent Sixth, remarkably serene. It includes two "Night music" movements, separated by a strange scherzo. While a gentle work, the Seventh is in its own way very strange indeed. Critic Deryck Cooke writes of it:

> The prowling nocturnal patrol of the first Nachtmusik, amidst echoing horn-calls and the indeterminate noises of night; the Hoffmanesque spookiness of the scherzo, with its opposition between "things that go bump in the night" and puppet-like waltz music; the gurgling streams, the tinkling guitar and mandolin serenades of the second Nachtmusik — all these are haunting, uncanny

59. Cited in Cooke, *Mahler*, 84.
60. Cited in Cooke, *Mahler*, 85.

music, opening magical windows on imagined worlds behind the visible world.[61]

Theologians have long had deeply ambiguous understandings of the "word." On the one hand, theologians are struck by the utter inability of words to capture the sacred. John Dixon, for example, writes that theologians have, or ought to have, the same problem as the avant garde artists. Theology's task is, of course, to talk (*logein*) about God (*theos*), Dixon writes, but if, as at least the Jewish and Christian traditions maintain, God is ultimately beyond human comprehension, any theology must be limited and partial. Unlike science, which can produce ever more precise descriptions of phenomena, theology can at best circle and circle, now perhaps closer, now perhaps more distant, but never fully describing, let alone comprehending, its subject. Theologians, Dixon thinks, are prone to two fatal errors. The first he calls the "idolatry of words," that is, the conviction that words — rather than, say, images or tones — are the best tools for theological work. The second error is the conviction that theology must consist primarily of precise definitions and carefully scaffolded propositions:

> The claim to talk seriously and adequately about the omnipotent God is itself sufficiently startling, for to reduce God (or for that matter, anything) to the content of a proposition is to replace omnipotence with a new authority since the content of a proposition is subject to the authority that produced the proposition in the first place. A god described is a god subdued to the act of description.[62]

And yet, at the very same time, at least the major monotheisms are insistently religions of the Word. Judaism's God, after all, is the God whose Word called the cosmos into being, whose continuing Word reveals the Sacred to the Profane. Christianity experiences Jesus not only as the Christ but also as the Logos, the incarnate and revelatory Word. Islam, Judaism, and Christianity are not so much faiths of the book as faiths of the word. Language is utterly fallible; language is potentially revelatory; from

---

61. Cooke, *Mahler*, 89.
62. John Dixon, *Art and the Theological Imagination* (New York: Seabury, 1978), 2.

a religious perspective, both these insights of the Viennese avant-garde are true.

And both can be seen, for example, in Gustav Mahler's heroic struggles both to use to the absolute fullest the musical vocabulary he had inherited and to explode that vocabulary in the quest for revelation. By 1906, Gustav Mahler had all but exhausted the possibilities of the symphony, just as many of his contemporaries became convinced that they had exhausted the potentialities of their own artistic languages. Mahler was tired and depressed that summer of 1906, as he began his usual struggle to compose. The unending battle with musicians and critics was finally wearing him down. What else could he do? He had a rich mass of music, including seven remarkable symphonies; he had pushed the symphonic form as far as it could go. But then the extraordinary happened. It was almost, he liked to say later, as if he had become possessed. What he composed that summer would explode the language of music, and after that explosion would emerge in music something the likes of which hardly anyone had ever imagined.

What are artistic revolutions? Hermann Broch, writing about Hugo von Hofmannsthal, argues that such revolutions are about much more than styles:

> Artistic revolutions take place when preexisting conventions of symbolic language are thrown overboard, and art sets to work once more to search for primal symbols with which to build a new direct language aimed at attaining a higher artistic truthfulness; this alone is at stake in art.[63]

In fin de siècle Vienna, "primal symbols" were erupting from the souls of seemingly secular artists, primal symbols groping for a "higher truthfulness" in a way one might fairly describe as a search for the sacred.

---

63. Hermann Broch, *Hofmannsthal und seine Zeit* (Frankfurt: Suhrkamp, 1974), 41.

Chapter 6

THE FEMININE DIVINE

Das Ewig-Weibliche
Zieht uns hinan.

(The Eternal Feminine
Draws us on.)

From Goethe's *Faust*,
sung by the "Chorus Mysticus"
in Mahler's Eighth Symphony

It was February 1902, and the entire avant-garde was aquiver with antici-pation. Isadora Duncan, that shocking and wonderful experimental dancer, was coming to Vienna! Every man in Vienna's avant-garde — and the avant-garde was almost exclusively male — was in love with Isadora Duncan, and her performances were major occasions. In February 1902, for example, Hermann Bahr acted as her interpreter; his introduction of her included a discussion of ecstasy and its relationship to dance. Adolf Loos was there, and years later recalled:

> It was a remarkable collection of people who otherwise had noth-ing in common. When Isadora Duncan appeared, we all held our

breaths. Then, a sudden turn, her chiton flowed higher around her, and we all heard an older woman in the first row mumble "what a scandal!" Isadora stopped suddenly, stood still, and said: "I refuse to dance another step if this woman does not leave the theater!" The tension suddenly released itself in a burst of applause, the woman left, we were all relieved that we weren't the ones who had said it, the enthusiasm was intense and honest.[1]

Art critic Ludwig Hevesi, who was there too, wrote that Miss Duncan, in her diaphanous gown, "looked like an image from Secession art."[2]

Secession art was filled with Isadora Duncans because the bright young men in Vienna's avant-garde were obsessed with women. Young, beautiful women represented, for most of them, a whole host of concerns and themes and aspirations — first of all, not surprisingly, sex. But not just sex. For the Viennese avant-garde, women also represented the sacred.

Yes, Freud's Vienna was sex-drenched. In 1886, the year Freud began his medical practice, Viennese doctor Richard von Krafft-Ebing published his monumental *Psychopathia Sexualis*. Krafft-Ebing did not claim that every neurosis was sexual in origin, but he did insist that sexual neuroses were pervasive. By 1905, the indefatigable sex researcher Magnus Hirschfeld had compiled a 1,000-plus-page yearbook outlining current sex research.[3] Arthur Schnitzler's fiction is above all a fiction of intimacy, and sexuality. In 1906, Schnitzler sent Sigmund Freud a note congratulating him on his fiftieth birthday. Freud responded with a note of his own, thanking Schnitzler for the kind thoughts, and congratulating him in

1. Cited in Burkhardt Rukschcio and Roland Schachel, *Adolf Loos* (Vienna: Residenz Verlag, 1982), 77.

2. Ludwig Hevesi, *Acht Jahre Sezession* (Vienna: Carl Konegen, 1906), 368.

3. Edward Tannenbaum, *1900: The Generation before the War* (New York: Doubleday, 1976), 252.

turn for exploring that "secret knowledge" Freud too found so important. Freud continued: "I have been aware of the far-reaching agreement between your and my conceptions of quite a few psychological and erotic problems."[4] Historian Susanna Partsch describes Gustav Klimt as a "painter of women," and Klaus Albrecht Schröder insists that "eros and passion" powered Egon Schiele's work. Karl Kraus entitled his first important essay *Sittlichkeit und Kriminalität (Morality and Criminality)*; it was devoted especially to issues of sexuality and moral hypocrisy.[5]

Arthur Schnitzler's early plays had introduced the "sweet young girl" to the Viennese stage; living in the poor, working-class suburbs, Schnitzler's young women invariably became entangled in unhappy affairs with rich bourgeois men. Peter Altenberg's famous photo collection was filled with images of adolescent women.[6] Leopold von Adrian, one of the Young Vienna writers, stressed, in his *Garten der Erkentnis (The Garden of Knowledge)* the explicit connection of youth, love, and women.[7] Everyone seemed absorbed with the "woman question," from the avant-garde artists to the racist and anti-Semitic press.[8] The dramatic change in women's fashion brought the *jugendstil* woman — willowy, youthful, athletic — to the streets of the city.[9] Though the organized feminist movement was relatively small in Vienna compared to, say, London, it certainly was alive and well; many feminists found allies among the male avant-garde.[10] The

4. Peter Gay, "Sex and Longing in Old Vienna," *The New York Times Book Review*, July 11, 1999, 39.

5. Susanna Partsch, *Gustav Klimt: Painter of Women* (Munich: Prestel, 1994); Klaus Albrecht Schröder, *Egon Schiele: Eros and Passion* (Munich: Prestel, 1999); Karl Kraus, *Sittlichkeit und Kriminalität* (Vienna: Die Fackel, 1923).

6. Hans Brisanz, *Peter Altenberg: Mein Ausserstes Ideal. Altenbergs Photosammlung von geliebten Frauen, Freunde und Orten* (Vienna: Verlag Christian Brandstätter, 1987), 38-39.

7. For a thorough discussion of Andrian's work, see Carl Schorske, *Fin de Siècle Vienna: Politics and Culture* (New York: Vintage, 1980), 304ff.

8. For example, see Adolf Harpf, *Das Weibwesen* (Vienna: Ostra, 1906).

9. See Regina Forstner, "Von der Tournüre zur 'Garcon' — Wiener Damenmode von 1870 bis 1930," in Robert Waissenberger, ed., *Wien 1870-1930. Traum und Wirklichkeit* (Vienna: Residenz Verlag, 1984), 209-14.

10. For more on Vienna's turn-of-the-century feminists, see, for example, Erika Weinzierl, "Österreichische Frauenbewegungen um die Jahrhundertwende," in Peter Berner, Emil Brix, and Wolfgang Mantl, eds., *Wien um 1900. Aufbruch in die Moderne* (Vienna: Verlag für Geschichte und Politik, 1986), 226-31.

beautiful Empress Elizabeth owed part of her popularity to the fact that she seemed to embody the Viennese New Woman.[11] It would be difficult to find a Viennese avant-garde artist who was not fascinated by sexuality and all it involved — identity, relationships, courting, intimacy, desire, images of the human body, love.

Men, meanwhile, were undergoing, according to modern historians, a "crisis of the male ego." Turn-of-the-century men were suddenly unsure of their social roles. The New Woman challenged their power; the whole culture of patriarchal domination began to shiver. As common as the New Woman around the turn of the century was the uncertain, drifting, very nervous young man, such as Schnitzler's Anatol, or the terrified, naked, emaciated, young man staring out from Schiele's self-portraits. Friedrich Nietzsche rants against women; Edvard Munch sees women as vampires. When he was a teenager, Oskar Kokoschka wrote:

> there opened to me a rich, and dangerous depth, which I had to explore. Woman, in all her erotic proximity . . . threatened my hard-won equilibrium. It was odd — with men, I could see in their faces, even if those faces were a mask, character, experience, and sufferings. Men could never so terribly confuse me the way women could.[12]

Men still dominated cultural production, so that most cultural products were shaped by nervous men trying to comprehend New Women. All the female stereotypes and archetypes vigorously reappear: the Virgin returns especially as the art nouveau and *jugendstil* spirit of innocent springtime; Eve returns as that distinctively fin de siècle sinister figure, the "femme fatale" — Judith, Salome, exotic, sexually voracious, and castrating.

Vienna's obsession with sexuality, intimacy, gender roles, assertive New Women, and nervous young men is hardly unique. Nevertheless, it was intense. Nowhere were women so condemned as nearly demonic. And nowhere were women so sacralized, so identified with the divine.

11. See E. M. Cioran, "Sissi ou la Vulnerabilité," in Jean Clair, ed., *Vienne 1880-1938. L'Apocalypse Joyeuse* (Paris: Editions du Centre Pompidou, 1986), 14-19.

12. Oskar Kokoschka, *Mein Leben* (Munich: Bruckmann, 1969), 62.

Some of what the avant-garde had to say about all this was shocking. In 1905, for instance, Sigmund Freud published his daring *Three Essays in the Theory of Sexuality*. He had already, in *The Interpretation of Dreams* (1900), established, to his own satisfaction at least, the tremendous power of the unconscious, and in *The Psychopathology of Everyday Life* (1901) and in *Jokes and Their Relationship to the Unconscious* (1905) he had argued that the unconscious is everywhere, intrusive and eruptive. It is not our "I" that moves us; it is not reason and cold logic and what Freud would later call the cautious and calculating "reality principle" that motivates us. Most of our lives we are driven by the appetites, yearnings, and terrors of our unconscious. But what drives the unconscious?

In his *Three Essays*, Freud tried to explain: what drives the unconscious is sex. Freud used the term "sex" in a complicated way. On the one hand, by "sex" Freud meant an intense yearning for relationships, and intimacy, and shared lives, what he might better, perhaps, have called "love." But on the other hand, by "sex" Freud really did meant "sex" in its most graphic biological sense. Our unconscious craves physical pleasure — specifically, the physical pleasure that arises from bodily stimulation. This hunger for sexual arousal is intense, pervasive, and insistent. The clever unconscious disguises it in a thousand ways; sexual desire might take on a thousand forms; but beneath them all is a primal hunger for sexual gratification.

And when is this hunger born? At birth. Infants, Freud thought, find intense physical pleasure in the most basic physical actions: drinking at their mother's breast; cuddling; expelling waste. The location of these physical pleasures shifts over time. In the earliest years, oral pleasure shifts, as toddlers are toilet-trained, to anal fascination, and then eventually to genital fascination. There is, eventually, a period of "latency" in childhood, but in adolescence, these fundamental physical yearnings are all reborn.

Infants are bundles of raw appetites. Mothers satisfy these appetites and therefore are the cynosures of infants' cravings. But after several years, certainly by the age of three or four, children go through a shocking trauma. Fathers invade the mother-child world. Fathers' affection is "conditional," unlike mothers' unconditional affection. Fathers insist that children control and defer their ravenous appetites.

Children respond with homicidal rage. They become ravenous for their mother — and wish to annihilate their father. Is this ravenous hunger "sexual"? Of course it is, Freud argued. The hunger infants have has its origins in the most elementary and intense physical pleasures. Is this wish to annihilate the father really homicidal? Yes it is. The child really does wish the father to be destroyed. To be sure, children articulate none of this; these remain unconscious urges and furies, not conscious desires. They are expressed in odd symbols, strange dreams, and eruptive behavior. But, Freud graphically insisted, this experience is absolutely real. This is the famous "oedipal crisis," and how it is resolved fundamentally determines each child's fate. The child is the parent of the adult; the Oedipus crisis is the mother of all crises. All of us are scarred by it; most of us resolve it effectively, but some don't — and they, of course, were the people who came to see Freud.

Eventually, adults learn to satisfy their hunger for sexual pleasure in any number of ways, some "respectable," others less so. While many people satisfy their hungers, for instance, within the context of heterosexual marriage, that is not the only road to satisfaction. There is no single and simple way to allay ubiquitous and impertinent sexuality; each of us must forge a coherent sexual identity in the turmoil of experience.

To be sure, the Viennese weren't the only sex-crazed Europeans. It seems fair to say that no generation before 1900 talked quite as openly about sex, and probably no generation after 1900 was so surprised by sex. Partly this is yet another product of the modernization sweeping through Europe around the turn of the century. Young, urban Europeans had ideas very different from their parents and grandparents about sexual identity and sexual behavior. While historians have regularly found "sexual revolutions" cropping up here and there in the forests of European history, it does appear that some such thing really did occur around 1900. And it seems accurate to say that people invest an enormous amount of emotional energy in sexuality; for most people, the single most powerful moments in their lives are moments of desire, intimacy, and love. Because of this, the tremors of the turn-of-the-century sexual revolution shook the very foundations of European life.

All across Europe, artists, especially male artists, were fascinated by the New Woman. Young, urban, bright, ambitious, but also deeply frustrated with her inherited social role, eager for change, unhappy with Victorian asceticism, hungry for experience, the New Woman attracted writers as diverse as Henry James, Leo Tolstoy, Theodor Fontane, Gustave Flaubert, and Henrik Ibsen. Ibsen was especially crucial to the Viennese avant-garde; Bahr, Schnitzler, and all the others were fascinated by Ibsen's grim insights into love, marriage, and intimacy.[13]

The fin de siècle New Woman became an archetypal figure. According to historian Karl Beckson, writing about turn-of-the-century London:

> the New Woman insisted on alternatives to the traditional roles for women. Her smoking in public, riding bicycles without escorts, or wearing "rational dress" . . . was not the result of mere whim or self-indulgence but of principle, for she was determined to oppose restrictions and injustices in the political, educational, economic, and sexual realms in order to achieve equality with men.[14]

In Central Europe, there was a small but vigorous feminist movement, entirely aware that its demands for women's rights affected virtually every aspect of life. Natalie Milde, writing in 1902, noted that even the most mediocre men insist that their patriarchal authority is rooted in "nature." Nonsense, Milde replied; they were wrong. Patriarchy was cultural, not natural. Indeed, Milde continued, the categories "natural" and "cultural" badly needed careful rethinking.[15]

Nationalists in general, and racial nationalists in particular, took an intense interest in the "Woman Question." Adolf Harpf, a racial theorist, insisted that no one was more "feminist" than he and his fellow racists. Like everyone they wanted what was "best" for women. What was "best," though, Harpf insisted, was inherently a biological and racial question,

---

13. Ibsen's impact on Europe was truly amazing. For his English reception, see Karl Beckson, *London in the 1890s: A Cultural History* (New York: Norton, 1993), 138.

14. Beckson, *London*, 129-30.

15. Natalie Milde, *Gegenwart und Zukunft der Familie* (Weimar: Selbstverlag, 1902).

and in his view, what was "best" for women was for them to play their crucial role in reproducing and rearing the superior race, and in combating the terrible danger of racial pollution.[16]

Viennese Bertha von Suttner was a leader in the international peace movement and won the Nobel Prize in 1905.[17] Vienna's Marianne Hainisch was a leading European educational reformer. Adelheid Popp was a leader in Austria-Hungary's labor movement.[18] Austrian "New Women" really were everywhere, and they touched everything.

A whole literature grew up around the New Woman in fin de siècle Vienna. In the mid-1890s, *Wiener Mode,* the city's fashion magazine, published a guide to womanhood entitled *Die Frau "comme il faut,"* written by Natalie Bruck-Auffenberg.[19] "Modern times," Bruck-Auffenberg began,

> powerfully shape everything traditional. The familiar crashes to the ground, and women especially are now shaking the gates which for centuries have been both their protection and their prison. "The changing situation of women," and "modern relationships!" These are the mighty words that ring in our ears every day![20]

They call our century the "century of nerves,"[21] and with good reason, she continued. For nowadays it is not only the man who must daily go out into the dangerous world, but today even the "defenseless woman" has to venture out.[22] It is vital, therefore, she explained, for women to know how to conduct themselves.

Bruck-Auffenberg then proceeded to describe the ideal bourgeois woman. Of course, "the man must remain the center point of the household," she insisted.[23] A woman's primary task was to become a mother —

---

16. Harpf, *Das Weibwesen,* 32.

17. For an introduction to Suttner and the peace movement, see, for example: Brigitte Hamann, "Pazifismus in Wien um 1900," in Berner, *Wien,* 226-31.

18. Erika Weinzierl, "Osterreichische Frauenbewegungen um die Jahrhundertwende," in Berner, *Wien,* 221-25.

19. Natalie Bruck-Auffenberg, *Die Frau "comme il faut"* (Vienna: Verlag *Wiener Mode,* undated).

20. Bruck-Auffenberg, *Die Frau,* 1.

21. Bruck-Auffenberg, *Die Frau,* 122-23.

22. Bruck-Auffenberg, *Die Frau,* 2-3.

23. Bruck-Auffenberg, *Die Frau,* 117.

"a woman who has never been a mother has no idea what life is all about"[24] — and she extended her deepest sympathies to single women.

Women's work is inordinately complex, what with children to rear and a household to run. One must have a plan! One must systematically cultivate virtues like punctuality, orderliness, and frugality. The woman, much more than the man, must learn tact, must know how to generate a comforting and nurturing atmosphere in the home.

Above all, a woman must watch herself. She must observe herself daily to make sure that she not only performs her tasks properly but that every detail of her own person is in perfect order. The slightest flaw, the slightest misstep, will bring, at least ridicule, at worst, shameful scandal.

Watch your speech carefully, Bruck-Auffenberg advised: "it is astonishing just how much feminine charm rises or falls based on our speech." Women must avoid dialects and accents and of course every sort of vulgarity. "Every woman ought to cultivate a pleasant, feminine tone of voice and a gentle manner of speech . . . what comes from our voices must be first and last feminine."[25] Proper dress at all times was absolutely crucial. Too many married women, Bruck-Auffenberg scolded, let themselves go, but if they do, the respect of others and their own self-respect will be shattered. In marriage,

> the first danger is for a woman to neglect her appearance . . . clumsy, ill-kempt hair early in the morning, when a proper hairstyle is called for; or a comic, wrinkled, or extravagant negligée, or other pajamas which are not designed for the feminine form, all these things are far worse than the derangement that comes from real work, even if they don't seem as bad.[26]

Everyone is watching, so constant self-surveillance is essential. A woman needs to practice "the swift glance in the mirror to determine whether everything is in order; the constant checking of hair and dress repeatedly during the day."[27]

24. Bruck-Auffenberg, *Die Frau*, 44.
25. Bruck-Auffenberg, *Die Frau*, 474.
26. Bruck-Auffenberg, *Die Frau*, 113.
27. Bruck-Auffenberg, *Die Frau*, 113-14.

There were, in fact, hundreds if not thousands of rules a true woman had to follow: what to do during courtship; how to arrange a marriage; how to raise children; how to manage the household money; how to host a dinner; how to cope with illness; how to deal with servants; how to choose jewelry, fashion, hats, and cosmetics; Bruck-Auffenberg had advice on all this and more.

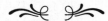

Bruck-Auffenberg's elaborate manual rested on the assumption that there is a fixed "feminine" nature. "There is in the nature of woman," she wrote,

> a certain something that even the most profound change cannot alter, something eternal and unchanging: namely true womanhood. . . . Woe to her who herself destroys that nimbus of gentleness, calm, propriety, and softness . . . how easily are borders crossed! A single wrong word, the wrong scent, and the magic will disappear as in a fairytale![28]

By the 1890s, biologists insisted that masculinity and femininity were hard-wired into human beings. For example, Professor Paul Mantegazza's *Die Physiologie der Liebe* explained that the "drive to reproduce" is a fundamental and inescapable human drive. "The urge to reproduce," Mantegazza wrote, "is overwhelming and irresistible."[29] Professor Mantegazza was an Italian who taught in Florence; translated into German, his text was popular in Vienna by the 1890s.[30]

Humans call this instinctual drive to reproduce "love," and like every other instinctual drive, erotic impulses must be controlled by reason. Indeed, the failure to harness eros to reason produces madness. The "gigantic power of love," he argued,

28. Bruck-Auffenberg, *Die Frau*, 2.
29. Paul Mantegazza, *Die Physiologie der Liebe*, trans. Eduard Engel (Jena: Costenoble, 1885), 4.
30. Mantegazza, *Liebe*, 3.

is, of all human passions, the least well controlled. We humans seem too weak, too small, to control it. And, just like savages drop to their knees or flee in terror at the sound of thunder, so we modern, civilized people cower at the storms of love which seem to prove our impotence and ignorance . . . a thick fog surrounds the temple of love, which we always seem to enter as thieves, and almost always leave as slaves. Modern love is a mix of one part hypocrisy and one part lust.[31]

Women, Mantegazza wrote, were the "high priestesses" of love. Far more sexual than men, far more concerned with emotions and relationships, driven far more than men by the urge to reproduce, it was women, ultimately, who controlled love relationships. On the one hand, instinctual sexuality had to be controlled by masculine reason if it were not to lead to madness; on the other hand, masculine reason was all but powerless when faced with feminine eros. Thus, while men had to be extraordinarily careful about love (lest they lose their reason), women had to rigidly control their own erotic natures (as Bruck-Auffenberg warned, the slightest slipup could be fatal). "A man in love is more beast than angel," according to Mantegazza; "a woman, more angel than human."[32]

Everyone seemed to want to talk about women. In 1898 Adolf Loos published an article on women's fashion. Like Freud, Loos was curious about the textures of everyday life. Why is it, he asked, that men and women have such different costume? Loos argued that difference in costume was rooted in the fundamental and undeniable differences between men and women. Women, he thought, are essentially "sensual"; men are essential "rational." Thus women's dress is ornamental, luxurious, and impractical, and men's dress is sober, ascetic, and practical. "But," Loos continued, "we are moving to a greater, newer time." Women will achieve equality with men not by relying on feminine sensuality but by economic independence, by becoming more like men. And as they do so they will be able to abandon "silks and satins, flowers and ribbons, feathers and colors."[33] They will abandon ornament and adopt the spare, ascetic style

31. Mantegazza, *Liebe*, 2-3.
32. Mantegazza, *Liebe*, 222.
33. Adolf Loos, "Damenmode" (1898), in Rukschcio, *Loos*, 78-79.

Loos identified with the masculine and the modern. Loos thought of himself as a friend to women; he looked forward to the day when women could finally repudiate the "feminine" and replicate the "masculine."

Karl Kraus wrote frequently about women. For Kraus, sexuality and gender roles were foundational issues in any culture. All the stifling limits on women, Kraus thought, were expressions of old Vienna's brutal effort to destroy anything new and alive. Kraus attacked all the old inhibitions regarding sexuality; he denounced the government's snooping intrusions into private life. Kraus rejected Vienna's criminalization of homosexuality, and for a time, he engaged in a running battle with Berlin's Maximilian Harden over Harden's none-too-veiled accusations that homosexuals dominated Emperor Wilhelm II's court. Though Kraus admired Harden in many ways (Kraus's *Die Fackel* was modeled after Harden's own crusading journalism), Kraus insisted that whether or not someone was homosexual or heterosexual was none of the media's business. When actress Annie Kalmar died young in 1901, Vienna's scandal press published long speculations on her intimate life; Kraus, who deeply loved Kalmar, was appalled.[34]

Kraus was especially contemptuous of Vienna's laws regulating prostitution. Vienna, like every other big city, had had prostitutes for centuries. Most were poor working-class girls desperate to make a living. In Kraus's opinion, prostitution was a victimless crime, and sexual relations among consenting adults nobody's business, and the government's clumsy attempt to regulate them only another sign of Viennese hypocrisy.

In 1909 Kraus published a hilarious story, called "The Good Conduct Medal," which mocked both Vienna's prostitution laws and its hypocritical obsession with respectability. In Vienna, the story explained, the police regulate prostitution. Any woman practicing prostitution is supposed to report to the vice squad and obtain a license. Licensed prostitution is legal; unlicensed prostitution is a crime.

Now, Kraus continues, he had heard about a young girl who joked to a man that she was a licensed prostitute. Unhappily, the man was a detective who immediately investigated; he discovered that she had, in fact, no license, and was, for that matter, not really a prostitute. Still, the public

---

34. Many of Kraus's pieces on these and related issues were published in his essay collection entitled *Sittlichkeit und Kriminalität* (Frankfurt: Fischer, 1966).

prosecutor brought charges against her for "making false statements." Had she been a licensed prostitute she wouldn't have been in trouble, since she would simply have been telling the truth, but since she didn't have a prostitution license, because she wasn't a prostitute, well, she was in trouble. At the hearing, when the judge asked her what she was thinking of when she made her false claim, she replied, "nothing." The judge let her go. Kraus added:

> Now, to recapitulate: the girl had claimed that she was under the supervision of the vice squad. Because that turned out to be a lie, an investigation was launched on suspicion of immoral conduct. She was able to prove that she was not immoral enough to engage in immoral conduct, but not that she was moral enough to be registered with the vice squad. So that's why she was charged with "making false statements," which in Austria, after all, is the basis for charging even murderers if it cannot be proven that they have committed a murder.

Let's go a step further, Kraus wrote:

> Let's say that a woman is, in fact, a licensed prostitute. But suppose that she, for some reason, doesn't admit that she is so licensed. In that case she would be engaging in immoral conduct (lying) for which she had no authorization, when, in fact, she is authorized to engage only in the immoral conduct (prostitution) for which she has a license.

Now, let's consider a fascinating case from Wiener Neustadt. Quoting and parodying news reports, Kraus wrote:

> In a local brothel worked a young woman who was a licensed prostitute. She had never been in trouble, never engaged in any immoral conduct for which she was unlicensed, never made false statements about the immoral conduct for which she was licensed. One fine evening, she appeared in the brothel's parlor with a "Good Conduct Medal" pinned to her blouse.
> "By doing so she aroused in her customers" — and so on. Well,

what do you suppose she aroused in her customers? No, not what you think, but the very opposite — annoyance. One of the customers immediately complained to the police. "She was charged with an arousal for which she was not licensed."

The public prosecutor charged the girl with unlawful wearing of an official medal. The lower court judge ruled her innocent, however, explaining that a Good Conduct Medal was not a military decoration, since it was awarded to civilian civil servants, and therefore the young woman hadn't violated any laws, which, it seemed, dealt only with the unauthorized wearing of military medals. But the prosecution appealed the case to the superior court, insisting that the Good Conduct Medal was the equivalent of a military medal. The superior court agreed and fined the woman twenty crowns, which was, ironically, precisely the fee she normally charged for her services. When asked what she was thinking of, the woman answered "nothing," but unlike the earlier case, this "nothing" did not impress the judge. It would appear, Kraus concluded, that "it is better that a respectable girl presume to be a prostitute than that a prostitute presume to wear a Good Conduct Medal."

But how did she get the Good Conduct Medal in the first place? It seems that a customer was a little short of cash, and so gave her the medal in payment, part of what the newspapers called her "wages of shame." She should have stuck it in her stocking, Kraus said, since according to the court "only the customers in a bawdyhouse are entitled to wear a Good Conduct Medal," not the prostitutes. Should a prostitute pin on the medal, the court decided, she would have to pay the state a fee of twenty crowns. Kraus concluded: "For 'justice' is a whore that won't be stiffed, and will demand the 'wages of shame' even from the poor."[35]

35. Karl Kraus, "Das Ehrenkreuz" (1909), in Kraus, *In These Great Times*, ed. and trans. Harry Zohn (Manchester: Carcanet Press, 1976), 38-42.

No one who saw Otto Weininger clutching his books, scuttling across the Ring on his way to the university, would have guessed that this slight young man had discovered the key to the universe. In 1900 Weininger was a student, struggling to complete his dissertation. He was small and thin; in photographs he looks like a handsome teenage boy, his lip marked by his wisp of a mustache more ambition than hair.

In 1903, Weininger had finished his dissertation, a massive, 600-plus-page work, 20 dense chapters long, heavily laden with vast stocks of footnotes. The dissertation plunged doctoral candidate Weininger's academic advisors into crisis. They were deeply divided. No one denied Weininger's industry or seriousness. Everyone agreed that the dissertation was, one might say, eccentric, but some thought it brilliant too, while others thought it the most extravagant, pompous hodgepodge of crackpot ideas they had ever read. There was a tremendous fight, but finally, perhaps to be rid of Weininger entirely, the faculty committee accepted the dissertation, and Weininger officially became Dr. Weininger. As was the custom throughout Central Europe, freshly minted Dr. Weininger hurried to a printer and had the dissertation run off as a book.

And then a miracle happened. No one, other than scholars, ever bought dissertations, but Weininger's instantly became a bestseller. The publisher hurried to bring out edition after edition — by 1914, the dense work would be up to its fourteenth run — and overnight, intense young Otto Weininger had become the talk of Vienna.

The work was called *Geschlecht und Charakter (Sexuality and Character)*.[36] Its core argument was that sexuality determined character, and character, in turn, shaped society and culture. At the root of everything, in other words, was sex.

The book was written in the turgid style so beloved of German academics; it drew on an immense store of biology, sociology, and philosophy to make its case. No one could deny Weininger's enormous, if eccentric, erudition.

His discussion was complicated. Human embryos, Weininger began, are plasma, neither male nor female. But very quickly, human fetuses take

---

36. Otto Weininger, *Geschlecht und Charakter* (Vienna: Wilhelm Braumüller, 1918); this was the seventeenth edition of the work.

on distinctive male or female qualities; indeed, every *cell* of the human body is either "male" or "female," he claimed.[37] Thus, in the abstract, "maleness" and "femaleness" are biological givens.

Then Weininger made a surprising move. When considered concretely, in the real lives of real people, "maleness" and "femaleness" are not simply opposites, and points on either end of a long continuum. In specific cases, human beings include both "maleness" and "femaleness" in varying portions within themselves: "every person swings, or one might say, oscillates, between the 'male' and the 'female.'"[38] Every human being, then, is actually "bisexual." Homosexuality, thus, is not a "perversion" but rather a common variation of normal sexuality.

This claim, incidentally, would cause no end of trouble. When Sigmund Freud's one-time associate and former friend, Wilhelm Breuer, read Weininger's text, he was furious. The notion that all persons are biologically bisexual was, he exploded, *his* idea! Yet Weininger didn't even mention Breuer in the text! The only person Breuer had shared the idea with was Freud — so, Breuer thought, Freud must have told Weininger Breuer's idea! Breuer wrote an angry letter to Freud, blaming him for giving the idea to Weininger; Freud wrote back that he had indeed spoken with Weininger, but that Freud was not responsible for Weininger's use of the notion. Breuer was not appeased, and his already sour relationship with Freud soured even more.[39]

But now Weininger made another turn. If, admittedly, in actual life, bi- or even multi-sexuality occurs, what must interest the scientist are the ideal types of sexuality, that is, "masculinity" and "femininity." There is an infinite variety of frogs in the woods, but the biologist is not interested in all the individual frogs but in the abstract "frogness" that they all share. So too the sexologist needs to focus not on all the varieties of sexual behavior and identity, but on the foundations of sexual behavior and identity, "maleness" and "femaleness." These, Weininger insists, are the poles between which all humans move. Put differently, just as we must have some notion of health in the abstract before we can discuss deviations from

37. Weininger, *Geschlecht*, 19.
38. Weininger, *Geschlecht*, 64.
39. See Peter Gay's discussion of this affair in Peter Gay, *Freud: A Life for Our Time* (New York: Norton, 1988), 154-56.

health, so too we must have some idea of "masculinity" and "femininity" before we can understand all the variations of each.

For Weininger, biology was destiny. To understand "masculinity" and "femininity," one needs to begin with biology, with the structure and function of the human body. And here, the distinctions between male and female were clear. Women's bodies were designed exclusively for child-bearing and child-nurturing. Both anatomically and physiologically, women were creatures designed by nature for reproduction. Sexual reproduction is the entire meaning of a woman's body. That is not true of men. Neither anatomically nor physiologically is the male body so centered on reproduction. "The woman," Weininger wrote, "is *only* sexual . . . the man is *also* sexual."[40]

Women are *only* sexual. From that, for Weininger, followed a host of conclusions. Women are more intensely driven by sexuality than are men. Driven by their sexual hungers, women are much more attuned to their bodies than men are, much more aware of their biological states, their emotions, their appetites.

Women are *only* sexual. Men are *also* sexual. And this makes all the difference! Of course men have sexual appetites. But men's bodies are nowhere near as sexual as women's bodies. And this is why men are capable of transcending their bodies, of moving beyond the physical and emotional to the rational, while women cannot. This explains, Weininger continued, why men dominate the arts and sciences, why men control business and politics, why men debate philosophy and morals. Men are capable of all this because their biology permits them to transcend their bodies; women are incapable of any of this because they *are* their bodies. Women are incapable of logic; they can never achieve any sort of abstract thought; artistic creativity is beyond them.

"Man is form," Weininger insisted, "woman is matter."[41] The "absolute woman has no 'I,'"[42] no personality as such, because woman is fundamentally incapable of thought or self-awareness. Woman, as matter and appetite, is the very negation of thought, awareness, creativity, logic, and art.

40. Weininger, *Geschlecht*, 114.
41. Weininger, *Geschlecht*, 399.
42. Weininger, *Geschlecht*, 240.

"The pure man is the image of God, the absolute 'something'; the woman . . . is the symbol of 'nothing.'"[43]

Women are the negation of everything cultural and creative; they are, in this sense, "pure negation," "nothing," and "nothingness and nihilism are of course related. Thus we see the deep connection between the 'criminal' and the 'female.'"[44] Women, for their own good, and for men's good too, need to be under masculine authority. Men need little education, since they instinctively engage the wider world; women, however, desperately need education, that is, training in controlling their sexuality.[45] Thus Weininger emerges as an advocate for women's education.

But, on the other hand, there is nothing more preposterous, nothing more destructive, than for women to want to have what men have, to want to be like men. Just look, Weininger writes, at so-called "feminists." Women who claim to be "feminists," Weininger argues, are perverse; though women, they are all distinctly "manish"; their dress, their habits, even their physical appearance is masculine. True, it is understandable that women would want to be like men, since men are "all" and women "nothing." But any woman who tries to deny her biological fate is doomed to frustration and failure. Real "emancipation" for women, Weininger continued, will thus occur only when women realize that they have only two possible destinies: either to be a mother, or to be a whore.

Now let us consider whores. Actually, a whore is "pure woman." A whore is pure sexuality (which is what woman *are* by nature). A whore is "criminal," not because she is sexual — as a woman, poor thing, she can't control that — but because she is independent of, outside of, male control. Only when a woman's inexorable sexuality is subjected to male control, only when a woman becomes the mother of the man's children, can a woman truly achieve happiness. As mother, a woman achieves identity and meaning (through adopting the man's identity), security and purpose (by supporting the man's profession).

As for men, their primary task in life is to mold the "matter" of woman into the "form" of man. This transformation of women by men is

43. Weininger, *Geschlecht,* 403.
44. Weininger, *Geschlecht,* 405.
45. Weininger, *Geschlecht,* 399.

what is known as "love," and indeed love is at the heart of every great male creative act.

> Every man driven by Eros is a genius, and all genius is fundamentally erotic, even when his love finds expression in eternity, in the cosmos, instead of in a woman's body. The relationship of "I" to the world, of subject to object, is basically a repetition of the male-female relationship, raised to a higher and grander sphere.[46]

What in heaven's name is one to make of all this? Weininger's work is so riddled with contradictions that almost anyone can find anything in it. Some feminists actually applauded his focus on gender; anti-feminists endorsed his defense of patriarchy. Weininger supported education for women (a rather radical idea then), but called for an education designed to bring women under masculine control. His argument that bisexuality and homosexuality are normal variations of human sexuality certainly seemed daring; but his fierce advocacy of "true manhood" encouraged the most desperate homophobe. He thought prostitutes were only doing what was natural — reformers like Karl Kraus quoted Weininger in their campaign for the decriminalization of prostitution — and yet his insistence that all women were either mothers or whores outraged almost everyone.

"Woman," Weininger thought, is the very key to the cosmos. Understand her, and you can comprehend reality. "Woman," thus, is more than a biological or sociological term; "woman" is a metaphysical term. When men encounter women, they encounter being-as-such, primal reality, and primal reality is very, very dangerous. No wonder that, confronted by the Primal Feminine, strong men shiver.

Weininger, as eccentric as he seems, was also representative of his age, gender, and class. "Woman," for fin de siècle male intellectuals, was a simultaneously attractive and frightening term. Fascinated by "woman," shaken men also fled woman, hurling epithets behind them. Max Nordau, writing about "degeneration," identified degeneration and all that came with it — disease, crime, syphilis, adultery, and social disorder — with sexual anarchy, and with the "feminization" of men and the "masculiniza-

---

46. Weininger, *Geschlecht*, 337.

tion" of women.[47] Haunting the whole discussion was the "femme fatale," the man-eater, the castrator, "Judith" and "Salome," shockingly erotic figures that were both alluring and terrifying.

The turn-of-the-century "woman" was a bewilderingly multivalent symbol. In the male imagination of the time, there were indeed those awful Judiths and Salomes, but there were also Arthur Schnitzler's "sweet girls," the poor girls of the working-class suburbs seduced and discarded by effete bourgeois young men, like Schnitzler. The women who march through Karl Kraus's social criticism are emblems of injustice and hypocrisy. The Viennese artist, though, who was most fascinated by "woman" was Klimt. In Klimt's work, women emerge as dangerous, to be sure, but also redeeming. For Klimt, "woman" is not only both Eve and Mary; if there is a Messiah, for Klimt, she is a woman.

In 1899, two years after the birth of the Secession, Gustav Klimt completed his aforementioned "Nuda Veritas." Standing, facing the viewer, is a nude young woman, her long auburn hair falling turbulently over her shoulders, flowers scattered in her hair. Her eyes stare out from the painting. In her right hand, she holds a mirror toward the viewer. A snake encircles her feet.

The image, though not pornographic, is clearly erotic — like all Klimt's women, this young woman is beautiful in a vibrantly sensual way; she is no cold Greek statue, no abstract woman, but a living, human person. The title, "Nuda Veritas," links "truth" not only with "woman" in general but particularly with this erotic image of a young woman. The mirror she holds is odd; perhaps in approaching her, do we, as viewers, somehow approach

47. See Shearer West's discussion of this in Shearer West, *Fin de Siècle: Art and Society in an Age of Uncertainty* (Woodstock, N.Y.: Overlook Press, 1994), especially 23ff. For more on gender during the fin de siècle, see for example: Bram Dijkstra, *Idols of Perversity: Fantasies of Feminine Evil in Fin-de-Siècle Culture* (New York: Oxford University Press, 1986), and Elaine Showalter, *Sexual Anarchy: Gender and Culture at the Fin de Siècle* (New York: Viking, 1990).

ourselves? Do men, in particular, learn with her the truth? Whatever the answer, the serpent winding around the woman's feet in the image suggests something dangerous to be sure, but also something chthonic.

Klimt is rightly thought of as "a painter of women." Women fill his imagination. Whatever truth we hope to find, Klimt seems to argue, that truth will be found in and through women.

There are plenty of terrifying women in Klimt's work: nightmarish harpies, multiple Judiths. *Judith I* (1901), for instance, is a burst of golden light. Under the heading "Judith und Holofernes," a beautiful woman stares out at the viewer. Her eyes are partially closed, her lips parted, her jewel-encrusted choker glows, her gown is opened. She holds, at her waist, to the viewer's right, the severed head of Holofernes. Somehow, in the work, luxurious eroticism is linked, at least for Holofernes, with violent death and implied emasculation. Judith's claw-like fingers in *Judith II* (1909) make scary Judith even scarier.

Among the most terrifying of his female images are those in *Justice* (1907), the third of his university pictures. One might argue that the concept of the picture is to show law dawning on a world of violence and revenge. Women personify law; there they are, far off in the upper right-hand corner of the work, in a small blaze of color and light. But what dominates the work is the dark mass that includes the broken old man in the center of the image, ensnared by a bizarre octopus-like creature; observing the scene are three harpies, two of them dreamy and detached, the central one seemingly viscous and cruel.

Sometimes too, Klimt, like Weininger, associated women not so much with danger and violence as with raw sensuality, and he did hundreds of skillful and quite pornographic sketches.

Yet, if Klimt's male ego was in crisis, he seemed to survive that crisis well. However frightened he may have been of women, he seems to have been fundamentally fascinated by them. If Arthur Schnitzler is the artist of the crisis of intimacy, Gustav Klimt is the artist of intimacy restored.

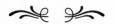

Perhaps Klimt could imagine intimacy restored because, by the turn of the century, he had fallen in love.

People whispered that Klimt, like many male artists who employed nude female models, was licentious. He had had a variety of intimate relationships as a young man (at the time of his death, some fourteen paternity suits were filed against Klimt's estate, and four were affirmed by the courts). But Klimt was in many ways a very shy man. He lived most of his life with his mother and sisters, and one sister wrote of him,

> He was not a person for company, more of a loner, and as his sisters our concern was to relieve him of the burdens of everyday life. He came home to us every evening, ate his meal with very few words, and went to bed early.[48]

Klimt's brother, Ernst, had married Helene Flöge. The Flöges were a respectable, middle-class clan; Helene's father manufactured meerschaum pipes, and the family owned both a city home and a country house. In 1892, Ernst died suddenly; he had had an unusually bad cold, and then contracted the pericarditis which killed him. Gustav, by that time close to the Flöge family, did what he could for Helene. And in the process, he became very close to Helene's younger sister, Emilie.

At first they were simply brother-in-law and sister-in-law; then close friends; then soulmates. By 1900 they were inseparable. As good Bohemians, they never married; they kept their individual homes, and yet they remained for the rest of their life together as comfortable with each other, as affectionate, and as committed as any conventional married couple. They were deeply in love.[49]

Flöge was interested in clothing design and set up, with her sisters, a fashion shop in Vienna. Klimt and others worked with her on the design both of the shop and of the clothing. Flöge's designs were a radical departure from the heavy, voluminous, Victorian style so typical of Franz-Josef's Vienna. Flöge's costumes were simple and fluid and finely hand-crafted, displaying bold colors and striking patterns. The Flöge sisters'

---

48. Cited in Partsch, *Klimt,* 17.
49. See Partsch's comments in her *Klimt,* 11-17.

fashions, in fact, became one of the crucial links between the experiments of the avant-garde and the aesthetic renewal of popular culture.

A photograph shows Klimt and Flöge dressed in flowing painters' smocks, his a single color, hers gaudily striped and checked. She smiles at the photographer; Klimt smiles at her. They appear to be dancing.[50]

Klimt made his living partly as a portrait painter, and his subjects were typically wealthy women. He painted scores of portraits over the years, and of course to get paid for his work he would have to produce something pleasing to his customers. But Klimt's portraits of women reflect much more than just commercial concerns. The women in his paintings are not all beautiful in any conventional sense, but they are dignified and treated with respect by the painter. Klimt thought of this work as much more than mere hackwork. In all of his portraits he experimented with form and color. The portrait of *Sonja Knips* (1898) reveals a handsome young woman in a flowing gown, but strikingly placed off center in the work. Later portraits, such as *Fritza Riedler* (1906) and especially *Adele Bloch-Bauer II* (1912) are occasions for compositional experiments in which Klimt presents the portrait in an increasingly abstract style. Perhaps his most striking portrait is of his beloved Emilie. *Emilie Flöge* (1902) is an elongated, full-length portrait. The figure stands with one hand at her side, the other on her hip. She looks rather seriously out at the viewer. She is gowned in a spectacular mosaic-like dress of blue and yellow in riotous design, making her look not only like a strikingly handsome person, but almost like a being from another dimension.

Undoubtedly Klimt's most famous painting — one reproduced endlessly it seems — is *The Kiss*. In 1904, architect Josef Hoffmann won a spectacular commission. Adolphe Stoclet, the young son of a Belgian industrialist, had just inherited a fortune. Stoclet wanted a house designed and built for him on Avenue de Tervueren in Brussels. Stoclet was fascinated by the work of Vienna's avant-garde and hired Hoffmann to do the work.

The Palais Stoclet was an artist's dream. Money was never a problem, Stoclet rarely interfered in the work, and Hoffmann quickly recruited vir-

---

50. The photograph is widely reproduced; see, for instance, Gottfried Friedl, *Klimt*, trans. Hugh Beyer (Cologne: Benedikt Taschen, 1991), 170.

tually all of the Secession's artists to help him with the project. The result was extraordinary. The Palais Stoclet was yet another "total work of art," a symphony in which each detail related to the whole, a brilliant memorial to art nouveau and *jugendstil;* everything in the vast, three-story, forty-room house, from door knobs to china to cutlery, was designed by an artist. Not everyone, to be sure, admired it. Adolf Loos was disgusted by the building's lavish and ostentatious ornament that represented everything he found repugnant about the Secession. Others complained that the Palais was utterly impersonal, so "perfect" that it was almost inhumane.[51]

Hoffmann asked Klimt to design a mosaic for the dining room. From 1905-1907 Klimt worked on it off and on. He could use any material he wanted, and he wanted a lot: gold, metal, glass, pearls, and semiprecious stones. The result was probably the most impressive decorative work Klimt ever did. Its most famous part was *The Kiss.*

For Klimt, as for many artists, a kiss between two persons is the classic physical expression of human intimacy. In an earlier work, for instance, *Love* (1895), he had presented a rather clichéd embrace and kiss. The Stoclet Palais *Kiss* (1905-09) is a kiss of another kind. It is a riot of abstract color, the embracing figures themselves barely emerging from the background design. Both the man and woman are dressed in gowns not unlike those designed by Emilie Flöge. The male figure, to be sure, seems to absorb the female figure, yet only the female figure is given a face, and the work's tone is one of gentle intimacy, the brilliant and glowing colors creating a mood of joy and exhilaration. Klimt did a second *Kiss* in 1907-08, the figures now side-by-side, surrounded by the same pandemonium of gaudy color.

Athena, the goddess of wisdom, is one of Klimt's recurring images; she appears, for example, on the poster he designed for Secession I, the first Secession-sponsored art show. To be sure, he used the figure as part of the struggle to snatch the rich symbols of classicism from conventional artists, but he used it as well because Athena, the young goddess of wisdom as well as military guile, fascinated him. He would do Athenas repeatedly. His other mythic women, such as the priestess figure "Hygeia" in

51. See Frank Whitford, *Klimt* (London: Thames and Hudson, 1990), 100-108.

his *Medicine*, are typically young, vital, and arresting, all of them looking not like textbook reproductions of mythical images, but instead like very attractive, and very contemporary-looking, flesh-and-blood women.

In 1902, the Secession artists organized their most spectacular show to date. Secession XIV was to be a *Gesamtkunstwerk*, a total work of art. The entire show, to be exhibited in the Secession's own new building, was centered around the monumental, polychrome statue of Beethoven sculpted by Max Klinger. A German, not a Viennese, Klinger was well known in Vienna. He shared with the Viennese artists the conviction that Beethoven was the ultimate artist, the hero-artist, virtually a demi-god.

Klinger's statue was the centerpiece. It was, to say the least, an odd piece. Klinger's Beethoven was seated, and semi-nude, draped only from the waist down. He sat on an oversized throne, perched on a stone precipice, an eagle at his feet, a cross between Wotan and Zeus. Some viewers couldn't decide whether the sculpture was comic or vulgar. But the secessionists loved it. The entire Secession worked enthusiastically on the show. Josef Hoffmann designed much of the interior, creating a temple-like design to parallel the building's temple-like exterior; Gustav Mahler arranged and conducted selections from Beethoven's music. Some 58,000 people visited the show.

Gustav Klimt designed a frieze for one of the side "chapels." He designed the frieze musically; form and color begin quietly, and then become much more turbulent, but conclude in harmony. He thought of the frieze narratively as well; as the viewer moved along it, a story unfolded. The panels portray human beings, nude and defenseless, who are confronted by "hostile powers," represented as harpies and an immense, gorilla-like monster. But a hero saves them, a knight quite literally in shining armor. In the last panel, the knight embraces a woman, while a female chorus appears to sing in the background.

The "Beethoven Frieze" is not Klimt's greatest work. Technically well crafted and visually powerful, the work is not particularly successful. The gorilla in the "hostile powers" resembles more Hollywood's King Kong than anything really evil. The muscular knight is a rather too clichéd image of the warrior-male who wins the swooning girl. By one reading, the frieze crudely implies that female submission to male dominance is the key to cosmic harmony.

Such a reading is certainly justified, but it is also incomplete. For all its clichéd and even comic bathos, the frieze does conclude with harmony and not simply male domination; the embracing couple are themselves embraced by a chorus of women. Moreover, seen in light of Klimt's entire artistic and personal life, the work seems, however clumsy, to be a movement beyond *jugendstil* innocence and idols of perversity toward harmony and intimacy, even love.

The most touching of Klimt's woman images are the series he simply entitled "Hope" and "The Virgin." His *Hope I* (1903) is a nude and vastly pregnant young woman. Above her are death's heads that add a chill to the image, but she seems unaware, or unafraid of them, as she looks out at the viewer. In *Hope II* (1907-1908) a pregnant woman, draped in a brilliant, abstractly designed gown, stands against a golden, star-like background. The stars and the dazzling color suggest that this figure is more than a pregnant woman, but has achieved some sort of transcendent quality. *The Virgin* (1913) shows a young woman, her dress a blaze of spectacular color, sleeping, it seems, her head on her shoulder, her eyes closed. Around and behind her are five other young women, the entire ensemble of figures arranged in an approximate circle, brilliant with color, a Jungian mandala of youth and grace and life, a visual summary of Klimt's experience of the feminine reality of the sacred.

In 1906, Gustav Mahler began work on what would prove to be perhaps the single most extraordinary symphony he ever composed. It would be his eighth. Scored in E-flat, it was written for, in addition to a normal symphony orchestra, a tenor, a baritone, a bass, two contraltos, three sopranos, a boys' choir, a double-sized adult choir, and an organ. No wonder that it quickly earned the nickname "Symphony of a Thousand." It was first performed under Mahler's direction in Munich in 1910, at a time when he knew himself to be dying. The premiere was a triumph.

The Eighth is a choral symphony; indeed, it might be thought of as *the* choral symphony of the twentieth century, as Beethoven's Ninth was the choral symphony of the nineteenth century.[52]

Mahler's Eighth consists of two seemingly different parts. Part I is based on the ancient Christian hymn *Veni Creator Spiritus* (*Come, Holy Spirit*). The hymn is a passionate invocation of the Holy Spirit — "Come, Creator Spirit! Dwell in our minds! Fill with divine grace the hearts of your servants!"

Part I "bursts out with a mighty choral invocation," writes Deryck Cooke, and the fundamental tone of Part I, with variations of course, is both expectant and jubilant. The grimness of the Sixth Symphony and the nocturnal moods of the Seventh are overwhelmed by this passionate invocation of the Divine: "Accende lumen sensibus/Infunde amorem cordibus/Veni Creator Spiritus!" ("Illuminate our senses/Pour love into our hearts!/Come, Creator Spirit!")

Part II, at first sight, seems oddly juxtaposed to Part I. While Part I is an ancient hymn, the text in Part II Mahler takes from the conclusion of Goethe's *Faust*. Part I is liturgical and medieval; Part II is secular and modern. Yet the two texts — carefully woven together musically — are complementary. Part I calls for the descent of the Divine to the human; Part II recounts the ascent of the human to the Divine.

Goethe's Faust, like Christopher Marlowe's Faust, is that folkloric figure who, in exchange for worldly knowledge and power, sold his soul to the devil. He ought, like Don Juan, to be condemned. But in the conclusion of his massive poem, Goethe saves him. It is this text of salvation that Mahler's choruses sing in Part II.

The music in Part II is stranger and more rhapsodic than the music in Part I. Mahler's notes describe several different voice roles: there is a "Chorus of Anchorites"; then "Pater Ecstaticus" ("Ecstatic Father"), and "Pater Profundus" ("Profound Father") and "Doctor Marianus"; there are "Angels," "Blessed Boys," "Younger Angels," and "More Perfect Angels."

---

52. Deryck Cooke, *Mahler: An Introduction to His Music* (New York: Cambridge University Press, 1988), 91. For more on Mahler's Eighth, see Michael Kennedy, *Mahler* (New York: Schirmer Books, 1990), 149-54; Henry-Louis de La Grange, *Gustav Mahler. Vienna: Triumph and Disillusion* (New York: Oxford, 1999), 911-25; Egon Gartenberg, *Gustav Mahler* (New York: Schirmer Books, 1978), 319-32; Constantin Floros, *Gustav Mahler: The Symphonies* (Portland, Ore.: Amadeus Press, 1985), 213-37; Karl-Josef Müller, *Mahler: Leben-Werke-Dokumente* (Munich: Piper, 1989), 328-30, 409-16; also Cooke, *Mahler*, 91-102.

Women play a central role in the drama narrated in Part II. Gretchen, the young girl wronged by Faust in Goethe's text, in the Eighth is referred to as "A Penitent (once named Gretchen)" who pleads for Faust's salvation. Three other women appear, not like Klimt's awful furies in *Justice*, but transformed by Mahler into saved, and saving, figures.

First appears the "Magna Peccatrix" ("A Great Sinner"). She is the unnamed woman who appears in the New Testament (Luke 7:36-44), where she is described as having "sinned much." This unnamed woman from Luke is sometimes mistakenly identified with Mary Magdalene, the demon-possessed woman (Mark 16:9; Luke 8:2), who ministered to Jesus (Luke 8:2), was a witness to the crucifixion (Matt. 27:56), and was among the first to see the risen Christ (Matt. 28:9).

The "Mulier Samaritana," the "Samaritan Woman," appears in John 4:2-26. She too is a "sinful woman." Jesus asks to see her husband; she replies that she has no husband; Jesus replies that she's quite right, the man she lives with is not really her husband because she has actually had five different husbands. Yet, oddly enough, it is to this triply estranged person — a woman (Jewish men would rarely speak to strange women in public), a Samaritan (ancient Jews considered Samaritans to be traitors), and an adulteress (adultery under the ancient law was a capital offense) — that Jesus reveals himself. (The woman says: "I know the Messiah . . . is coming" and Jesus says to her: "I who speak to you am he.")

"Maria Aegyptiaca," "Mary of Egypt," is a legendary fifth-century Christian saint. Historical data about her is fragmentary. She was, it appears, a courtesan and prostitute, perhaps from the Egyptian city of Alexandria. She traveled to Jerusalem with pilgrims — not, though, as a pilgrim herself, but as a prostitute intent on expanding her market. While in Jerusalem she experienced, according to legend, a radical conversion inspired by an icon of the Blessed Virgin. Devoted now to the Virgin, Mary repudiated her former life and rushed off to the Jordanian desert to lead a life of prayer. A monk named Zosimus discovered her and learned her story; he buried her when she died. Zosimus spread her story and over the centuries an immense body of legendary and iconographic material grew around these historical shards.

In popular imagination, all three, combined with Mary Magdalene, became variations on a single theme. All were ancient femmes fatales; all were sexual sinners; all were, moreover, sexual sinners who corrupted both themselves and the men around them; all are, in a sense, Weininger's women, erotic, predatory, even demonic.

Yet all are saved. Their passionate eroticism is not destroyed but transformed; Jesus says of the unnamed "sinful woman," "I tell you, her many sins have been forgiven — for she loved much. But someone who has been forgiven little loves little" (Luke 7:47). Though the Jesus of the Gospels very rarely reveals his identity as Messiah, he does share this "Messianic secret" with, of all people, the Samaritan adulteress. And Mary of Egypt becomes the iconic image of "the prostitute redeemed."

All three plead the case of "A Penitent (once named Gretchen)." In Goethe's *Faust, Part I*, Gretchen, an innocent, is seduced and transformed into a criminal. When Faust first meets Gretchen, lust overwhelms him and he not only seduces her but also even convinces her to give her mother a sleeping potion that proves fatal. Faust engages in a brawl with Gretchen's brother and kills him. Having all but destroyed Gretchen, Faust flees and is led by Mephisto to a witches' sabbath, a *Walpurgisnacht*, where he can satisfy his lusts as he wishes. But he cannot shake Gretchen's image, and returning to her, he finds her in prison — for infanticide. Faust tries to free her, but cannot. Even as Mephisto drags Faust away, though, a voice from heaven says that Gretchen "ist gerettet," is saved.

Mahler's three women plead again for Gretchen. An awesomely terrifying sinner, complicit in the deaths of her mother, brother, and child, Gretchen remains nevertheless an innocent and penitent. Forgiven, Gretchen, shockingly enough, then appeals for Faust's forgiveness.

All four women now appeal to the figure central in all their lives, the "Mater Gloriosa," the "Glorious Mother."

Mahler is, of course, revisiting the archetypes of whore and mother, Eve and Virgin, but he has both moved these archetypes into the celestial plane and transformed whore and Eve into mother and Virgin, and reprising Goethe, he makes Faust's salvation directly contingent on their saving action. The cliché of the wicked man saved by the good woman has become, for Mahler, a spiritual truth. If wicked men, and women, are to be saved, they will be saved by saving women. In the Eighth Symphony, the economy of salvation really is driven by feminine action.

Angels, blessed boys, the four converted women, the Anchorites, all join in a chorus of praise for the "Mater Gloriosa." She responds:

Komm! Hebe dich zu höhern Sphären!
Wenn er dich ahnet, folgt er nach.

[Come! Into higher spheres outreach him!
He must sense you to find the way].[53]

To be sure, some Christians might well cringe at Goethe's and Mahler's conclusion. The centrality they accord the Virgin is not, to be sure, unprecedented, even in Christian history. The Virgin is a central figure in both Orthodox and Roman Catholic spiritual imaginations; Beatrice and the Virgin are the key figures in Dante's *Divine Comedy;* Gothic architects dedicated their work to "Notre Dame," "Our Lady"; and Renaissance artists saw in both Madonna and Pietà images extraordinarily powerful portals to the Divine.

It is, though, in the context of fin de siècle Vienna that this transformation is especially striking. Mahler's culture was confused by and terrified of women. Freud thought that Mahler's marital problems might be rooted in Mahler's troubled relationship with his mother. Nevertheless, like Klimt, Mahler not only affirms women as creative spirits but, in his Eighth, he has come to think of the Divine as feminine.

The penultimate lines sung at the conclusion of the Eighth Symphony belong to Dr. Marianus, who "bows in adoration":

Blicket auf zum Retterblick,
Alle reuig Zarten,
Euch zu sel'gem Glück,
Dankend umzuarten!
Werde jeder bess're Sinn
Dir zum Dienst erbötig;
Jungfrau, Mutter, Königin,
Göttin, bleibe gnädig!

---

53. This and the following English translations are by David Luke; see de La Grange, *Gustav Mahler. Vienna: Triumph and Disillusion,* 903-4.

(Gaze aloft — the saving eyes
See you all, such tender
Penitents; look up and render
Thanks, to blest renewal rise!
May each noble spirit never
Fail to serve thee; Virgin, Mother,
Queen, oh keep us in thy favour,
Goddess, kind for ever!)

And finally, the "Chorus Mysticus" concludes this vast work with Goethe's, and now Mahler's, final image of salvation and the Divine:

Alles Vergängliche
Ist nur ein Gleichnis;
Das Unzulängliche,
Hier wird's Ereignis;
Das Unbeschreibliche,
Hier ist's getan;
Das Ewig-Weibliche
Zieht uns hinan.

(All that must disappear
Is but a parable;
What lay beyond us, here
All is made visible;
Here deeds have understood
Words they were darkened by;
Eternal Womanhood
Draws us on high.)

Chapter 7

THE UNCANNY

"Religious dread" (or "awe") . . . first begins to stir in the feeling of "something uncanny," "eerie," or "weird." It is this feeling which . . . forms the starting-point for the entire religious development in history. "Daemons" and "gods" alike spring from this root.

Rudolf Otto, *The Idea of the Holy*[1]

Writing after the end of the Great War, the German philosopher Rudolf Otto attempted to describe the Holy. Virtually every human culture, Otto argued, expresses some sense of what it calls the "Holy." The Holy is not simply an idea. It is, above all, an experience. People don't think the Holy; they experience the Holy. When humans experience the Holy, Otto thought, they attempt to recount this experience. They generate scriptures, doctrines, and liturgies. But fundamental to all this is the primal experience of the Holy. And though it is a very intimate, personal, and interior event, this experience is also both social and historical — that is, others share it and it occurs in time.

Humans experience the Holy in a multitude of ways; now the experi-

---

1. Rudolf Otto, *The Idea of the Holy,* trans. John Harvey (New York: Oxford University Press, 1969), 14-15.

ence is a whisper, now it is a shout; to some it is overwhelming, to others it is diaphanous and elusive; for some it is a recurring thing, for others, it occurs only once. However humans experience the Holy, the recurring theme in their descriptions, Otto thought, is that the Holy is experienced as the "Other." To experience the Holy is to experience something, or someone, that is radically different, that transcends the normal, the daily, and the routine. Otto, of course, here echoes earlier writers, such as Emile Durkheim. To Durkheim and his school, human beings exist in more or less homogeneous groupings; it is precisely this homogeneity that provides identity and orientation. The heterogeneous is threatening and dangerous, but also tempting and intriguing. The "radically heterogeneous," the "radically other," is charged with dangerous but enticing electricity; to Durkheim, the "radically other," the "sacred," is "sheer heterogeneity."[2] To experience the Holy, Otto writes, is to encounter the wholly other, the *mysterium tremendum fascinans* (the terrible and fascinating mystery), the uncanny.[3]

The uncanny ran loose in fin de siècle Vienna from the moment when Crown Prince Rudolf shot himself to the eruption of the Great War. Arthur Schnitzler, for example, is more than just a dramatist of the beautiful and decadent aesthetes. Schnitzler the realist is, as Michael Imboden argues, also a surrealist. His fictions are pervaded by a kind of "magical realism," in which the oddest things happen in the midst of mundane life. What characterizes Schnitzler's imagination, Imboden writes, is the "disappearance of the border between the 'real' and the 'unreal'; the play of magical powers; and the intrusion of the daemonic into everyday life."[4] His characters are swept along by what one, in *Die Traumnovelle (Dream Novel)*, calls the "incomprehensible winds of fate."[5] Schnitzler discovered "the ordinary in the

2. On all this, see Alexander Irwin's important study of Georges Bataille and Simone Weil, *Saints of the Impossible* (Minneapolis: University of Minnesota Press, 2002), especially xxiiff.

3. Otto, *Holy*, 14 See also: Gerardus van der Leeuw, *Religion in Essence and Manifestation*, trans. J. E. Turner (New York: Harper and Row, 1963); Louis Dupré, *The Other Dimension* (New York: Doubleday, 1972); Mircea Eliade, *Patterns in Comparative Religion* (New York: Meridian, 1958); Paul Ricoeur, *Figuring the Sacred* (Minneapolis: Fortress Press, 1995).

4. Michael Imboden, *Die surreale Komponente im erzählenden Werk Arthur Schnitzlers* (Frankfurt: Lang and Cie, 1971), 23.

5. Imboden, *Die surreale Komponente*, 48.

bizarre and the bizarre in the typical";[6] his constant themes were the "secrets of everyday life," the "workings of unknown powers."[7]

Hugo von Hofmannsthal, especially in his early works, is, if anything, even more a magical realist than Schnitzler. He recalled that as a little boy he was deeply religious and deeply superstitious. Remembering his childhood, he wrote:

> Those were the days when the eyes of the Madonna sometimes threatened and sometimes smiled. Those were the days in which what happened seemed somehow connected to other, unrelated, things; somehow it mattered whether the fourth house on the street were three stories high, whether a raindrop fell right in the center of a flagstone . . . then too there was a recurring dread of death.[8]

His early poems and sketches are not only sensually precious, filled with strange glows and odd scents; they also have, as in *Gerechtigkeit (Righteousness)* (1893), the occasional angel.

Critic Lorna Martens notes how Freud, Schnitzler, Musil, and Kafka seemed obsessed with spatial metaphors when they talked about "reality." All four, Martens writes, thought in terms of a Here and an Out There. Here is normal and safe; Out There is dark and dangerous. "Typically, the dark area appears not as a delicate thing, a fragile unity susceptible to disintegration, but as something powerful and rather frightening."[9] The dark is not nothing, the dark is something, palpable and dense. The dark Out There constantly threatens to invade and extinguish the little light that illuminates the familiar Here. In the work of all four writers, Martens thinks, "the dark area is seen to be primary . . . it is accorded the status of a spatial 'ground' or temporal 'origin' or both."[10] In Schnitzler's work, for instance,

---

6. Gerhart Baumann, *Arthur Schnitzler. Die Welt von Gestern eines Dichters von Morgen* (Frankfurt: Athenäum, 1965), 3.

7. Imboden, *Die surreale Komponente*, 9.

8. Hugo von Hofmannsthal, *Loris. Die Prosa des jungen Hugo von Hofmannsthal* (Berlin: Fischer, 1930), 9.

9. Lorna Martens, "Irreversible Processes, Proliferating Middles, and Invisible Barriers: Spatial Metaphors in Freud, Schnitzler, Musil, and Kafka," in Erika Nielsen, ed., *Focus on Vienna 1900* (Munich: Wilhelm Fink, 1982), 46.

10. Martens, in Nielsen, *Focus*, 47.

typically, the afflicted character seeks unsuccessfully to come to terms with a traumatic experience, that is, to establish rational control over the irrational. In several early stories, the power and wholly alien otherness of the irrational is dramatized by the introduction of a third thing, which might be described as an obsessional image. The image presents itself to the subject with the force of a message from the other world.

This "third thing" — a strange object, a mysterious person, a recurring dream — comes to play a key role in the typical Schnitzler story. On the one hand, it serves as a bridge between the rational and irrational, but at the same time, it becomes an obstruction, a malevolent growth, that makes it impossible for the Schnitzler character to heal and regain stability. The "third thing's" effect, Martens writes, "is to transform the original traumatic event into a mysterious source, into a kind of abyss which casts forth questions to which there are no answers."[11] As Young Vienna's Richard Beer-Hofmann wrote, "Things don't simply have form and color. Behind everything is a kind of secret sense, which shines through and illuminates everything."[12]

Perhaps the uncanny's greatest moments were two great art shows, *Kunstschau 1908* and *Kunstschau 1909*. Nowhere was the uncanny so powerful as in the work of the artists who emerged in those years, Oskar Kokoschka, Adolf Loos, Egon Schiele, Arnold Schoenberg, and Georg Trakl. True, not every encounter with the uncanny is necessarily an encounter with the Holy. But the uncanny pervaded the work of these Viennese artists, and to them at least this uncanny was unmistakably Holy.

Oskar Kokoschka exploded onto the Viennese art scene the very same year as Egon Schiele. Historian Carl Schorske writes that Kokoschka's ar-

11. Martens, in Nielsen, *Focus,* 47.
12. Esther Elstun, *Richard Beer-Hofmann* (University Park: Pennsylvania State University Press, 1983), 36.

rival was a kind of "explosion in the garden." Schorske recounts a telling incident from Kokoschka's childhood: Oskar Kokoschka was a poor boy from a rough Vienna neighborhood. He played in what once had been the luxury garden of an aristocratic estate. It was in the park that he first experienced a crush on a girl. She would swing on a swing strung from a tree. Young Kokoschka fell head over heels in love:

> One day, equipping himself with homemade gunpowder, Oskar went to the palace garden where his friends were at play. Beneath the tree where the swing was hung was a huge ant colony. Under it Oskar placed his explosive charge. When all was prepared . . . Oskar "cast the torch into the world." The explosion was immense . . . the burning city of ants flew into the air with a clap of thunder. "How hideously beautiful!" Singed bodies and severed limbs of ants fell writhing over the well-kept lawn. And the innocent temptress was found unconscious beneath her swing.
>
> The forces of civilization rallied. The mother summoned the guard of the park. Oskar was "banished from the Garden of Eden."
>
> But young Oskar was not defeated.
>
> Behind the garden lay a city dump, with a bluff that Oskar might scale to enter the garden from the rear. He climbed the bluff; but disaster awaited him. He lost his footing.
>
> Only the expressionist fantasy could have contrived what followed. Plunging back into the dump, Oskar landed upon the bloated carcass of a rotting pig. A swarm of vicious flies rose from its body, stinging the hapless boy. Oskar went home to bed with a serious infection.
>
> Lying in bed, the fevered second Adam had psychological experiences that have the tortured glow of the Expressionist's painterly vision: At the root of his tongue sat a fly that incessantly turned round itself, leaving its grubs as it went. The wallpaper burned with revolving suns of green and red. The victim felt his brain dissolve into a vile gray fluid.[13]

13. Carl Schorske, *Fin de Siècle Vienna: Politics and Culture* (New York: Vintage, 1980), 323-24.

Schorske is of course right: Oskar Kokoschka was a phenomenon, even wilder than Egon Schiele. Born in 1886, Kokoschka's childhood memories were filled with grotesqueries, though whether these were real events, or hallucinations, is difficult to say. He would say that his mother told him about a mysterious fire which erupted not long after his delivery, a fire from which he and his mother and his older brother just barely escaped (most likely, writes Kokoschka's biographer, Frank Whitford, "the fire never happened"[14]). An older brother died in infancy. Kokoschka insisted that he had been a terrified witness to the birth of a younger brother; through "a dreadful accident," he wrote in 1908, his mother had "given birth beside me . . . the blood made me faint. Ever since then I have been unable to get along properly with people."[15] He told people about his possessive mother and bitter father, about bleak Christmases, grinding debts, and constant moving from one dingy Viennese apartment to another. How much is true, how much is invented, how much is self-dramatization, how much is self-pity, how much is hoax, how much is trauma, is almost impossible to sort out. What is clear is that all this was part of what Kokoschka saw as a "pattern of strange, inexplicable events which punctuated and seemed to give significance to his entire life."[16]

He was a talented boy with a knack for drawing, and he was accepted into the arts and crafts academy, the Kunstgewerbeschule, in 1904.

Kokoschka vividly remembered one drawing lesson in human anatomy — the lesson's model was a human cadaver. Kokoschka remembered "being sick when the professor demonstrated on a corpse; the air had entered the knee-joint with a hissing sound, and I had caught sight of the severed head, lying open-eyed in a pail under the marble slab."[17]

Kokoschka was an enthusiastic member of the Wiener Werkstätte, and performed in the Fledermaus cabaret. Shortly after the café's opening night, Kokoschka performed a fairytale play in the Fledermaus, which he called *The Speckled Egg*. The show was a Balinese-style puppet show. It was a disaster — the puppets didn't work, and the audience laughed Kokoschka off the stage.

14. Frank Whitford, *Oskar Kokoschka* (New York: Atheneum, 1986), 2.
15. Whitford, *Kokoschka*, 4.
16. Whitford, *Kokoschka*, 2.
17. Whitford, *Kokoschka*, 16.

In those days, Kokoschka, like Mahler, was fascinated by fairytales. In the late fall of 1907, he had been commissioned by the Wiener Werkstätte to produce a fairytale book. He was to be both author and illustrator. He finished it the following spring.

He called his little fairytale *Die Träumenden Knaben, The Dreaming Youths*. It was without a doubt the world's most bizarre fairytale. The lithograph illustrations are straight Secession — bright, stylized, vibrant with the Secession's distinctive curving lines and Klimt-like geometric designs. The text is utterly hallucinatory. Incantational, dense and obscure, filled with idiosyncratic and shocking symbols, the text has far more to do with, as Carl Schorske writes, adolescent nightmares than childhood dreams.[18]

In the text, the poet dreams. He dreams a series of dreams filled with violence, blood, and sexual arousal. He dreams he has become a monster, a werewolf, who invades a garden:

When the evening bell dies away
I steal into your garden
Into your pastures
I break into your peaceful corral
My unbridled body
My body exalted with pigment and blood
Crawls into your arbors
Swarms through your hamlets
Crawls into your souls
Festers in your bodies
Out of the loneliest stillness
Before you awaken my howling shrills forth
I devour you.[19]

Not surprisingly, Kokoschka's employers at the Wiener Werkstätte were taken aback. But the illustrations were so arresting, and the text so shockingly powerful (if utterly obscure), that they decided to produce it. It was sold at the summer 1908 *Kunstschau*, the art show which would be one of the most dramatic moments in Oskar Kokoschka's tumultuous life.

18. Schorske, *Vienna*, 330-32.
19. This is Carl Schorske's translation; see Schorske, *Vienna*, 332-33.

In 1905, Gustav Klimt and his closest friends had seceded from the Secession. Klimt had become convinced that the secession group he had founded in 1897 had itself become too rigid and conventional; what had begun as a demand for freedom had become obsessed with its own sort of orthodoxy. When they seceded from the secession, Klimt and his friends again found themselves without an exhibition space. After a two-year hunt, Klimt and allies found a free plot of land on the Schubertring, near the Schwarzenbergplatz. Josef Hoffmann quickly designed some temporary buildings, and in the summer of 1908, the Klimt group, together with the faculty and students from the Wiener Werkstätte and the Kunstgewerbeschule, hosted an exhibition entitled simply *Kunstschau/Wien*.

It was a very big show: 179 artists participated; their work filled 54 separate rooms; there were paintings, graphics, posters, religious art; there was even a garden and a theater. Kolo Moser designed the central space, which displayed Klimt's work.[20] Kokoschka's *Die Träumenden Knaben* was on sale. And he, like many other Kunstgewerbeschule students, also had work on display.

Kokoschka's debut was a success, but it was a scandalous success. Klimt had had nice things to say about his work, and the critics commented on Kokoschka's obvious talent. But what Kokoschka remembered was all the abuse showered on him. People called him an outlaw, a cannibal, an *Oberwildling* (savage), and though he later wrote that he was wounded by all this, he quickly embraced his outlaw, bad-boy image.[21]

For the 1909 *Kunstschau*, Kokoschka decided to live up to his "savage" image. The *Kunstschau* site had a stage, and Kokoschka prepared two plays. They were perhaps the most bizarre plays, if indeed plays they were, ever staged in Vienna.

The first and better-known play he called *Mörder, Hoffnung der Frauen* (*Murderer, the Hope of Women*). What made it famous was Kokoschka's poster for the play. It is, in Frank Whitford's phrase, a kind of "pagan pietà," in which a ghastly looking woman holds a blood-red, flayed-looking, male corpse. Whitford explains:

20. Whitford, *Kokoschka*, 27.
21. Whitford, *Kokoschka*, 28-29.

The man is a bloody red, that is the life-color; but he's lying dead in the lap of the woman, she's white, the color of death. If the slogan "expressionism" really means anything, this is the earliest example of it. The poster . . . threw the Viennese into a rage.[22]

Later generations would describe the play as a "happening," or "improvisation." Kokoschka provided his intense student actors with the basic idea: a woman lusts after a man; the male chorus brands the woman on the breast; the woman stabs the man; but the man survives; the woman is killed, and the man then slaughters the chorus. Everything was grotesquely stylized and exaggerated, from the torn costumes to the scary makeup — the actors' bodies were painted to highlight nerves and veins. Kokoschka designed the stark scenery. Later, Kokoschka would remember the play's performance as utterly chaotic, the audience booing, the actors shrieking, everything in turmoil, though contemporary reports don't quite confirm Kokoschka's enflamed memory. He and his troop staged another event, this one called *Sphinx und Strohmann* (*Sphinx and Strawman*) in which, among other things, a man dies after being betrayed by his wife.[23]

Kokoschka also had a number of works on display. Although several looked Secessionist, two works, a painted clay portrait bust, and an oil portrait, called *The Trance Player*, marked a revolution in Kokoschka's style. Though recognizable images of their subjects — the clay bust was supposed to be a self-portrait, and the oil painting was of Kokoschka's friend, Ernst Reinhold — the two works were profoundly different from anything seen before in Vienna. They were purposely grim, even ghastly; they had a distinctly "unnerving" effect. One reviewer described them as "disgusting plague sores" and "puddles full of foul stench."[24]

Kokoschka would remember the 1909 exhibition as a chaotic epiphany. Before 1909, Kokoschka was unknown; after 1909, Kokoschka was notorious.

Kokoschka's work represented both an endorsement of, and a violent

22. Oskar Kokoschka, *Mein Leben* (Munich: Bruckmann, 1969), 64.

23. Whitford, *Kokoschka*, 36.

24. Whitford, *Kokoschka*, 35; Tobias Natter, ed., *Oskar Kokoschka: Early Portraits from Vienna and Berlin, 1909-1914* (New Haven: Yale University Press, 2002), 17.

turn away from, Klimt and the Secession. Like Klimt and the secession-ists, Kokoschka was convinced that when he looked at reality he saw layer upon layer of images. Behind each plane of vision was another plane, and another plane, and each carried its own distinct emotional charge. But, where Klimt saw colors with a Byzantine glow and fantasy figures swirling, Kokoschka saw, or rather felt, power and energy, raw, dangerous, and fierce.

Like all the other artists, including Gustav Klimt, Kokoschka had to make a living, and making a living typically meant doing portraits of Vi-enna's well-off. So Kokoschka did portraits. But they were very unusual portraits.

His *Father Hirsch* (1907), for example, is an image of an old man. The background is dark, the surface texture is thick, and the lines are jagged. The subject's eyes are oversized and staring; the teeth protrude beneath the mustache; the left hand is held in an unnatural position. The *Portrait of Professor Forel* (1909) is similar — dark colors, thick and rough textures, the same jagged line, the same stylized hand gesture, though the subject's face seems weathered and wearied rather than frightening. The *Portrait of Adolf Loos* (1909) has much the same tone as *Professor Forel*; the *Loos* portrait is rough, jagged, dark, and stylized too, but as with *Professor Forel* the emo-tional tone, at least in the subject's face, is calm.

What was Kokoschka trying to do in these remarkable works? Ac-cording to critic Thomas Trummer,

> Kokoschka interpreted his models as individuals, but even more im-portantly as phenomena of a deep, invisible dimension that he hoped to reveal in an attitude of self-forgetting. And in so doing, he effected a paradigmatic shift of large scope. Instead of the iconic real-ity of the image, which attempts a comparison with and likeness of reality (finally culminating in the photographic image) Kokoschka practiced an apparent indexical reality,

that is, Kokoschka was trying to create an image which corresponded to the invisible reality surrounding and penetrating the subject.

> The image appears to be a vibrating field of something behind or beneath it. It seems as if it is a direct medium upon which some-

thing in movement, perhaps something disturbing, inscribes itself
. . . the image is no longer understood as a likeness but as an imprint
and track.[25]

Consider, for example, *Still Life* (1909). The title *Still Life* suggests a routine work, the sort of thing artists have cranked out by the millions, a picture of vegetables or dead rabbits or flowers or some such things. The central image in this *Still Life* is one of "a dead and partially flayed sheep, a
tortoise, a brown jug, a white mouse, a tomato, a white axolotl in a small
glass tank, and a white hyacinth in a pot, arranged on a table that is vaguely
suggested . . . the colors, especially the dominant whites, reds, blues, and
greens contribute to a shimmering, opalescent effect."[26] Kokoschka had
been at a friend's home, Oskar Reichel, when the image came to him.
Reichel was getting ready for the Passover feast, and there was a dead lamb
in his kitchen. Kokoschka was both fascinated and horrified:

> I was left alone in the kitchen for a while. The corpse lay on the ta-
> ble. It was Good Friday, and my mind turned to the Son of Man
> whose fate was not very different. Every Sunday in the Holy Mass
> the faithful eat his body and God be thanked that Christ can no lon-
> ger feel it, even in sympathy. The lamb's eyes seemed to cloud over
> and become lifeless as I watched. But the thought that this dead
> thing was now to be roasted and consumed! When the master of
> the house lifted it by its stiff legs to give me a better view of it, blood
> dripped out of its mouth. I had had enough.[27]

A traditional still life included a variety of objects: sometimes dead
animals as in traditional kitchen scenes, but always everything neatly and
tidily arranged. In this still life, the animals have nothing to do with each
other; they are juxtaposed in a visually disturbing way, as if the visual
planes in which they exist are not parallel but colliding. The sight is un-
pleasant and upsetting. The figures are, to be sure, well rendered, and in
isolation some might even be attractive (it is a rather nice little mouse, for

25. Thomas Trummer, "A Sea Ringed about with Visions," in Natter, *Kokoschka*, 38.
26. Whitford, *Kokoschka*, 48.
27. Whitford, *Kokoschka*, 48.

instance). Together, they're odd and scary. They look poisonous; the overwhelming theme of the work seems to be that of death and decay. According to critic Werner Hofmann:

> The colours look as though poisonous essences had been added to them which eat into the canvas. The animals appear to glow from within. . . . All this morbid charm gives the picture its threatening beauty. It is that residue of animality which Hofmannsthal had discovered as early as 1902 in his *Letter from Lord Chandos:* "In these moments a worthless creature, a dog, a rat, a beetle, a stunted apple tree, a stone overgrown with moss mean more to me than the most beautiful, submissive mistress in the most happy night ever did."[28]

Kokoschka is depicting death, that death which obsessed the fin de siècle avant-garde; he not only depicts it, though, but also evokes it emotionally. Viewing *Still Life,* we not only think about death, but we can see, and feel, and smell it in all its corrupt presence.

In 1912, in a rambling talk he called "Vom Bewusstsein der Gesichte" ("On the Nature of Visions"), Kokoschka tried to explain what he was trying to do in his work. Human beings have, Kokoschka argued, a kind of "awareness of vision." This visionary quality is a kind of mental ability, every bit as powerful and important as more familiar cognitive abilities. This visionary ability, Kokoschka insisted, is not a kind of systematic, detached thought, not a kind of distanced analysis, not a kind of calculus. No, it is more a kind of immediate awareness, a kind of sensual and emotional experience aroused by vision. Nor is this visionary ability a kind of remembering; it's not that we recall something by seeing again. In fact, this visionary ability is not exactly a kind of seeing; Kokoschka isn't talking about simply recounting in a painting what we happen to see around us. What Kokoschka had in mind were visions; we all have the ability to receive visions; these visions come to us somehow from deep inside us or from some world beyond us. The experience of vision "cannot be fixed; for the vision is moving . . . it can be evoked but never defined," he writes.

At one level, this visionary capacity which we all have is actually a

28. In Whitford, *Kokoschka,* 49.

kind of waiting, a sort of heightened, sensitive receptivity. Receptive to what? To everything, to the boundless.

Visions live independently of us. They come to us of their own accord, and then they vanish, but not into nothingness; instead "they continue as though with a power of their own, awaiting the focus of another consciousness. There is no more room for death; for though the vision disintegrates and scatters, it does so only to reform in another mode." Therefore, Kokoschka warned,

> We must harken closely to our inner voice. We must strive through the penumbra of words to the core within. "The Word became flesh and dwelt among us." And then the inner core breaks free — now feebly and now violently — from the words within which it dwells like a charm. "It happened to me according to the Word."[29]

It was in 1909, in that extraordinary second *Kunstschau,* the show that highlighted Kokoschka's *Mörder, Hoffnung der Frauen,* the show in which Kokoschka and Adolf Loos became friends (Loos would introduce the uncanny Kokoschka to Kraus and Altenberg, and by 1914, with their help, Kokoschka would become one of Vienna's most talked about young artists), that Egon Schiele exploded on Vienna's art scene.

A photograph of young Egon Schiele in the art academy depicts a thin, fragile, sensitive, handsome young man, a shock of jet-black hair, loose shirt and tie, a Viennese Rimbaud. When his stunning work first appeared in 1909, Schiele was nineteen.

He had been born in Tulln, a little town west of Vienna, in 1890. His father was a railroad official, and Egon was born on the second floor of Tulln's railroad station. Outwardly the Schiele household seemed normal enough. But in fact, this normal civil servant household was haunted.

The marriage between Schiele's parents, to begin with, was unhappy. Schiele's mother, Marie Soukup, had, it seems, little love for her husband. She had only been seventeen when she married Adolf Schiele, and her family had disapproved; they were not rich but they were modestly well off, and they were convinced that Marie was marrying beneath her. Though

29. In Markus Neuwirth, "Oskar Kokoschka: From Jugendstil, 'Style of Youth,' to Unmediated Expression," in Natter, ed., *Kokoschka,* 234-36.

she married Adolf, whatever affection she had for him disintegrated over the years. The marriage was punctuated with grief; three children died very young. Four others survived: Elvira, Melanie, Gertrude, and Egon.

Far worse was Adolf's illness. He retired from the railroad at fifty-two with some unknown malady. Whatever it was, he began to act strangely and frighteningly. There were bursts of rage; once, he snatched up all the family's papers and money and important documents and hurled them into the fire. He gibbered to himself, and not only to himself but to imaginary houseguests, and he furiously insisted that the children talk to these specters as well. He was slowly going insane. There were rumors of syphilis. He died in 1905, when Egon was fifteen.

Schiele's relationship with both parents was turbulent. On the one hand, he developed an intense hatred of precisely the kind of person his father was, a minor official in a small town. Schiele remarked to his friend and agent, Arthur Roessler,

> I don't know of anything more disgusting, more galling to life, nothing more destructive, no greater impediment to human progress, than arrogant, sadistic, little petty bourgeois bureaucrats! . . . [A]s soon as you turn into a bureaucrat, you abandon all human qualities, you become a brainless and heartless automaton, in your veins flows not human blood but ink, you become a bureaucrat, uncritically, mechanically obedient to whatever the rules say . . . just go to a post office . . . there you can see wonders of sadism! Every one of them, sitting behind the windows, every one is convinced that he is a superior sort of person, infinitely superior to the mere citizen . . . it's even worse with the bureaucrat behind a desk. It's like he's sitting on a throne. Like he's a king, granting favors to whoever is groveling before him. I know, I've experienced it hundreds of times. I've learned all their tricks, I've learned to despise them, hate them. They're all perverse, all sadists, all they want to do is to "get someone," to hurt you, to humiliate you. You can imagine how hard it is for me to admit this, since my own father was a bureaucrat just like this.[30]

The perfect description of a computer which run [in] the 21st century rules all over lives!

30. Arthur Roessler, *Erinnerungen an Egon Schiele* (Vienna: Wiener Volksbuchverlag, 1948), 70-71.

There was little love between son and mother. Young Egon went off to study art in Vienna when he was sixteen. He was under the vague supervision of his eccentric uncle, Leopold Czihaczek. Uncle Leopold was wealthy and famous for his two African hounds, which he walked every day around the Ring. Uncle and nephew didn't get along, and Egon quickly was on his own. He was penniless.

"I'll tell you the truth," he remarked to Roessler,

> my mother is, well, remarkable. She has lots of peculiarities. For me she hasn't the least understanding. And not much love . . . since I've been on my own, I've haven't gotten a penny from her, not a piece of bread, absolutely nothing.[31]

Those teenage years in Vienna were hard. "When, against the wishes of my mother and my guardian, I went on my own," Schiele told Roessler,

> when I decided to live as an independent artist, I was as poor as a dog. My uncle gave me some old second hand clothes, and shoes, and a hat, all of which were way too big for me. My clothes just hung around my skinny arms and legs. My shoes were worn out, the tops had rips, the soles had holes in them, so I had to sort of slide along in them. I had to stuff newspapers in the beat-up old hat I had, so it wouldn't slide down over my eyes. I had a particularly delicate problem with my underwear. I don't even know whether you could call those old torn shreds clothing. My inheritance from my father was a used collar, way too big for my skinny neck. So, on Sundays and "special occasions," I wore homemade collars I made out of paper, they were actually nice looking and at least they were clean, but they didn't last long. And on top of all this, my hair was long, I didn't shave, I certainly didn't look like "a nice young man from a nice civil service family," which I suppose I really was. And then there was my room. It was a tiny single room, and the sunlight could hardly get in through the filthy windows. Torn wallpaper hung from the walls. Little by little I tore the wallpaper off and painted the walls white. Whenever I saw my mother,

31. Roessler, *Erinnerungen*, 21-22.

all she had for me were complaints and rebukes. From my uncle, I got five Crowns each week. I bought cigarettes with that, I couldn't go a week without them. At the end of the week, if I were without cigarettes, I'd fish some butts out of the garbage and smoke them.[32]

He lived a bohemian life, purposely designed, it seemed, to outrage the sensibilities of his mother and her respectable friends. He was close to an odd young man named Erwin Osen, a sometime artist fascinated by insanity, a homosexual and drug-user; Osen, his dancer friend called "Moa," and Schiele were frequent companions. Schiele fell in love with one of his models, a poor young girl named Wally Neuzil. They moved in together, shocking their families.

Schiele had an extraordinary gift. He experienced the world not through words or ideas but through visions, through colors and shapes and lines, and he had the remarkable ability to translate onto paper what his inner eye saw. Even as a little boy, he delighted in sketching the trains he saw coming and going from his father's station; his father, in his terrifying bursts of madness, often snatched the sketches up and destroyed them.

As an adolescent, Schiele did not simply sketch what was around him, but rather what was inside him. And what was inside him was often terrifying.

He was obsessed by love, or rather the absence of love; by relationships of love, between men and women, not just in the abstract, but in their most physical and sexual manifestations; by madness and its sudden explosions into ordinary life; and above all, by himself, by his moods and impulses and terrors. And all of these things Schiele experienced and expressed not in words but in color, form, and line.

His style was unique and instantly recognizable. His colors were juxtaposed, vibrant blocks. His lines were electric, jagged, and jittery; they conveyed to the viewer a visual energy found in few other works, and a nervousness that seemed ready at any moment to explode off the canvas.

32. Roessler, *Erinnerungen*, 64.

He began studying art in Vienna in 1906, and his early work clearly reflects Klimt's influence. But rapidly young Schiele found his own mode of nervous expression, and in 1909, he was discovered by the critic and dealer Arthur Roessler.

In some ways, Schiele's work was horrifying. O yes, critics remarked, he was a talented draftsman. But his images! His themes! His obsessions!

He was obsessed with not just love in the tidy abstract, but with physical and sexual love. Like all artists, he painted female nudes, but his nudes were most often not only erotic but sometimes blatantly and explicitly pornographic. (There were rumors, which were true, that as an adolescent, when he couldn't afford models, his sisters posed nude for him. Though there was no evidence of any sexual perversion, it certainly seemed to the neighbors, well, odd.)

And when not absorbed by sexuality, he seemed absorbed by himself. Again and again he returned to self-portraits, often nude self-portraits, as if the greatest mystery in the world was his own existence, and more specifically, his own body.

Worst of all, some critics thought, was the tone of the works. All his works, especially his self-portraits, seemed grotesque, horrifying. He saw his own body as emaciated, all parchment skin and jutting bone. He saw his face leering and grinning monstrously. Everything in his work seemed twisted and contorted; his famous nervous line made his works look like hallucinatory, nightmare visions of some madman. There was something ghastly about them.

But this, Roessler insisted, was precisely the point. Wasn't it appropriate for an artist to take fear, grief, and unhappiness as his themes? Couldn't an artist attempt to deal with sexuality and passion? Must art deal only with nice, pleasant, harmless topics? Schiele, Roessler argued vehemently, was "a seer . . . who carries dreams inside himself . . . a wanderer with great staring eyes in the secret realm of shadows."[33]

Sensitive viewers, Roessler insisted,

will perceive Schiele to be a messenger from an unknown land, they will recognize him as someone resurrected from the dead,

33. Roessler, *Erinnerungen*, 5.

who now, filled with chaotic pain, brings a mysterious revelation to humanity, but who has not had the proper opportunity to express his message.[34]

Schiele's topics, he added, may be shocking, but they are not perverse. His visual explorations of love and sexuality and identity were done with not only remarkable technical skill and striking imagination but with an intensely serious purpose; Schiele in fact is, Roessler argued, "a moralist."[35]

> It would be false and utterly misleading to judge him only by a few works from a single moment in his development as person and artist. In Schiele's total work, delicate and chaste compositions and striking landscapes far outweigh those images that reflect unrepressed sexuality or the terrors of a suffering soul.[36]

True enough, but it was horror and eroticism that became associated with Schiele, especially after the terrible scandal that swept over him in 1912.

That year, Schiele, then 22, was living with Wally Neuzil in the little village of Neulengbach, outside Vienna. He and Wally had moved there to avoid the noise and confusion of Vienna. Their neighbors took an instant dislike to them. Egon and Wally were bohemians from the big city; they were living together in sin; worst of all, Egon, like most artists, employed nude models, and stories of wild orgies and worse quickly swept through the village.

Partly it was Schiele's own fault. He enjoyed being outrageous. His models were young women, sometimes teenagers, sometimes even preadolescents. Friends warned him that he had to be more careful using such young girls, that he had to make sure that they were of legal age, but Schiele blithely ignored their warnings.

In April 1912, police raided his studio. They confiscated scores of sketches, nudes mostly, some explicitly sexual. He was charged with sexual abuse of minors, and locked in jail.

The charge itself was terrible; even worse was the fact that if con-

34. Roessler, *Erinnerungen*, 5.
35. Roessler, *Erinnerungen*, 8.
36. Roessler, *Erinnerungen*, 8-9.

victed, Schiele could spend most of the rest of his life in prison. A trial was held within a few weeks, and most of the charges against him were dropped. There was no evidence of sexual abuse; for all his fascination with sexuality, Schiele's habits were conventionally heterosexual and monogamous. He was convicted of displaying erotic pictures in places where children could see them, and for that he was sentenced to time served plus four days; he spent, all totaled, about three weeks in jail.

In retrospect, his suffering was trivial. But for those few weeks, charged with a disgusting crime and threatened with imprisonment for decades, Schiele was terrified. He captured something of that terror in some thirteen watercolor self-portraits. They are remarkable and frightening works. The image in the portraits has cropped hair, sunken cheeks, and eyes simultaneously vacant and terrified. For all the world they look like photographs of concentration camp inmates; it is almost as if, mysteriously, for a moment, Schiele was able to see through his own fear into something much more terrible coming in the future.

And yet, as Roessler insisted, there was much more to Schiele's work. His personal life slowly became more regular, and, he seemed to shake some of his demons. In 1915, he met Edith Harms. Edith was a bright young woman from a respectable family. Egon and Wally broke up; Egon and Edith were married. It was by all accounts a happy marriage, and Schiele's work increasingly took on a tone of, if not joy, then at least hope. To be sure, he was still capable of self-pitying introspection (expressed, for example, in his famous portrait of himself as St. Sebastian), but his portraits of Edith, his landscapes, his experiments with photography all show much more confidence than terror, much more love than fear. Perhaps his single most poignant work is a painting of himself and Edith, done near the end of both their lives. They sit together, nude, facing the viewer, looking sober and concerned. Before them is a child. It is a family portrait of a family that would never be. It was done when Edith was pregnant, and in that sense it is a portrait of the future, of hope. That hope was destined to be dashed. In 1918, both Edith and Egon were struck down by the influenza epidemic that ravaged Vienna; Edith died on 28 October, and the child she was carrying died with her. Egon died, age twenty-eight, three days later. Wally Neuzil, his first love, had died a year earlier. When the Great War began, Wally had become a Red Cross nurse. In December 1917, in a hospital in Split, in the Balkans, she contracted scarlet fever, and died at the age of twenty-three.

Egon Schiele was above all an artist of nerves. In 1911, Roessler had written: "The entire nervousness of a rapid and yet sure and confident hand lives and vibrates in Schiele's lines."[37] Schiele, Roessler continued,

> is different. His paintings are the visual manifestations of a nervous sensibility, they are sensitive impressions. They arise from instincts and drives, without pose, without bitterness, utterly hopeless. They appeal to those who consider it important that invisible and often-times hidden moments of life achieve visual manifestation. . . . His is an art of monologue, an art driven by his own demons. His art brings to visual clarity what occurs in the darkest levels of consciousness. He senses the power of fate looming above daily life, and gives this sensation a sensuous expression of almost pious simplicity.[38]

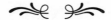

Oskar Kokoschka's biographer, Frank Whitford, notes that 1908-09 marked a fundamental turning point in Vienna's culture. Those years were the years of the two great *Kunstschauen*, the years when Kokoschka and Schiele erupted on the art scene, the years when Adolf Loos, in "Ornament und Verbrechen," called for a rebellion against the secessionist rebels. They were also the years in which Arnold Schoenberg introduced Vienna to radically new tones.

Arnold Schoenberg, a dozen years older than Kokoschka, was closer to the first generation of the avant-garde, to Klimt, Schnitzler, and Hofmannsthal. Like them, he experienced that odd dizziness that opened the fin de siècle. As Carl Schorske points out, Schoenberg shared with this first generation "a diffuse sense that all is flux, that the boundary between

37. Arthur Roessler, "Egon Schiele" (1911), in Christian Nebehay, ed., *Egon Schiele. Leben, Briefe, Gedichte* (Vienna: Residenz Verlag, 1979), 169-70.

38. Roessler, "Egon Schiele," 169-70.

ego and world is permeable. For him as for them, the firm traditional co-
ordinates of ordered time and space were losing their reliability, perhaps
even their truth."[39] Yet Schoenberg's response to all this is much more
reminiscent of Kokoschka and Schiele than Klimt.

The son of a shoe manufacturer, Schoenberg as a musician was largely
self-taught. His parents were practical people and had little hope that he
would have a career in the arts. At sixteen, they put him in a bank as an ap-
prentice.

But Schoenberg worked hard not at banking but composing; his first
surviving work was written when he was seventeen, in 1893. It is a work
for voice and piano that sets to music a text by Alfred Gold. The piece is
called "In hellen Träumen hab ich dich oft geschaut" ("In clear dreams I've
often seen you").

The next year, in 1894, Schoenberg met his artistic mentor, Alexander
von Zemlinsky. Zemlinsky would encourage young Schoenberg to quit
banking and commit himself to art; Schoenberg and Zemlinsky would
eventually become brothers-in-law when Schoenberg married Zemlinsky's sister, Mathilde.

In 1895, at nineteen, Schoenberg finally abandoned banking and followed Zemlinsky's advice, turning to music.

Schoenberg, in these early years, set a variety of texts to music in a series of songs and symphonic poems. Already his early works, such as
Verklärte Nacht (1899), *Gurrelieder* (1901), and *Pelléas und Mélisande* (1903),
sparked controversy both because of their content (praise of uncon-
strained love, for example) and their style. Even in these early works,
Schoenberg had begun experimenting with odd tones and unusual musical structures. In those years, Schoenberg became a key member of the
avant-garde. He taught, for example, at the Schwarzwald School, where
Oskar Kokoschka and Adolf Loos occasionally lectured. He became close
to Gustav Mahler. Schoenberg and his students, especially Alban Berg and
Anton Webern, joined the circle around Kraus, Loos, and Altenberg.[40]

In 1909, Schoenberg completed a song cycle called *The Book of the*

39. Schorske, *Vienna*, 345.
40. Jane Kallir, "La Vienne d'Arnold Schoenberg," in Jean Clair, ed., *Vienne 1880-1938.*
L'Apocalypse Joyeuse (Paris: Editions du Centre Pompidou, 1986), 445.

Hanging Gardens, which Carl Schorske compares to Kokoschka's *Träumenden Knaben.* The frightening images in Kokoschka's text are echoed by the increasingly frightening tones emerging in Schoenberg's music. Schoenberg's song cycle marked, according to Schorske, "the erosion of the old order in music, the diatonic harmonic system. Schoenberg's most revolutionary act, accomplished in *The Hanging Gardens,* was a rejection of tonality, an act which he himself called, significantly, 'the emancipation of dissonance.'"[41]

Schoenberg was also a visual artist, and the very same dissonance loose in Schoenberg's music invaded his painting. In the first years of the new century, Schoenberg did a series of self-portraits. They are typically entitled "Stare" or "Vision." In *Red Stare* (1910), for instance, a skull-like, triangular form, with blazing red eyes, stares out at the viewer; the staring head is detached from its body and floats against a roughly stroked opaque background.

These strange images and musical pieces emerged from Schoenberg's increasingly strange life. His marriage was in ruins. He discovered that his wife, Mathilde von Zemlinsky, was having an affair with the artist Richard Gerstl. Gerstl was a deeply troubled young man, whose tortured self-portraits are reminiscent of those by Egon Schiele. Schoenberg plunged to the brink of suicide; somehow, his student, Anton Webern, was able to reunite Arnold and Mathilde, but then Gerstl collapsed, and in November 1908 he committed suicide.[42] Meanwhile, Schoenberg was plagued by money problems, and his artistic work was driving him into ever more unexplored and frightening terrain. Critics and audiences were increasingly hostile.

On January 14, 1910, Arnold Schoenberg's Second String Quartet premiered in Vienna. The audience was stunned; the soprano completed the performance in tears; Wassily Kandinsky was so excited by it that he immediately became a Schoenberg enthusiast (and helped Schoenberg exhibit his paintings). The Second String Quartet, influenced by Mahler's use of disembodied solo voices, set to music texts by poet Stefan George. According to Allen Shawn, "The last movement's text, George's

41. Schorske, *Vienna,* 345.

42. Jane Kallir, "Arnold Schoenberg et Richard Gerstl," in Clair, ed., *Vienne 1880-1938,* 454-70.

Entrückung, with its unforgettable line "ich fühle Luft von anderem Planeten" ("I feel the air from other planets") was set to some of the eeriest music yet composed by anyone."[43] Schoenberg, writing in the midst of his personal crises, later explained that his composition was inspired by a kind of mysterious "inner compulsion" inspired by an "ideal" which had "hovered before" him for several years. Whatever it was that inspired him, then, was deeply interior and simultaneously exterior, part of him yet somehow independent of him. It was not simply his soul that Schoenberg wanted to express; it was "air from other planets."[44]

For the next several years, as Schoenberg's music became even more odd, his performances became ever more dangerous. In 1912, for example, he completed another song cycle, *Pierrot lunaire*. Like so much avant-garde work, *Pierrot lunaire* is self-consciously childlike. The text tells the story of the clown Pierrot, famous in European folklore. And like so much avant-garde work, the text focuses on a strange, visionary moment in Pierrot's life; the moon makes him drunk; moondrunk, he dreams strange dreams. Schoenberg wanted a stunningly different sort of voice for *Pierrot lunaire*. He wanted a voice that was midway between speaking and singing, but he wanted the voice to strike tones rarely if ever heard in either speaking or singing. He called this new declamation *Sprechstimme*, and to an audience, *Sprechstimme*, eerie and otherworldly, sounds just like a voice that might very well come from *Red Stare*.

Meanwhile, Richard Beer-Hofmann, one of the Young Vienna writers circle, had just completed a long poem called *Jaakobs Traum (Jacob's Dream)* (1909). In the poem, Jacob, in his famous dream, struggles with God. Jacob's problem is not any lack of faith in God; that, in fact, would be no problem at all. If only God were some minor puzzle, whose existence, like that of the Loch Ness Monster, one could wonder about at odd free moments! Alas, for Jacob, God is no minor puzzle, no Loch Ness Monster; God is a terrifying and inescapable force. But a force for creation or annihilation? God is fate; God is chance; God is the sum of those transcendent planes of reality that extend infinitely beyond, and beneath, surface real-

43. Allen Shawn, *Arnold Schoenberg's Journey* (New York: Farrar, Straus, and Giroux, 2002), 48-49.

44. Shawn, *Schoenberg's Journey*, 54.

ity. But is this God good? Jacob wants to flee but exclaims, "I cannot escape Him!" Jacob is "chosen," but is horrified at being chosen: "Chosen — what does that mean? Never to know dreamless sleep; visions in the night, voices around me in the day.... Chosen for what? ... For suffering?" In the end, Jacob, despite everything, responds with love, not only love of self and neighbor, but love of this massive, impenetrable, inexorable God. Jacob concludes: "I love Him, as he is. Terrifying and gracious, pure light and deepest abyss."[45]

Pierrot lunaire reflects strikingly similar concerns. With *Pierrot lunaire*, Carl Schorske writes, Schoenberg "established the identification of the artist and Christ by a related religious symbolism: that of the Mass." The work is organized more or less like a Catholic Mass, and "the second part, equivalent to the consecration, is replete with hallucinatory killings. At the very center of this section, and thus of the whole cycle, is a song (no. 11) entitled 'Red Mass.' In it, Pierrot climbs upon the altar, 'rends the priestly raiment,' then 'shows to the frightened souls the dripping red host: his own heart in bloody fingers, for (their) gruesome communion.'"[46]

For the next two years, from 1912 to 1914, Schoenberg worked on what he hoped would be a symphony that would celebrate the death of the Bourgeois God. The dead Bourgeois God is the God Nietzsche described as dead, the idolatrous, respectable, middle-class, human-imagined God. But, is this God really God, or is this God really an idol? Does the death of this so-called God actually then make possible the revelation of the true God? It is this that Schoenberg seemed to have in mind, at least according to Schorske's reading of the symphony. Schoenberg wanted to show that the whole machinery of human thought, all the values and categories and prejudices, all the "isms" we humans impose on the world, are all falsehoods and idols. "By virtue of the collapse of these categories, Schoenberg's modern man seeks God again: but his own, metaphysical God, who stands for the mysterious, unitary plenitude of reality, which no principle can comprehend."[47]

45. Elstun, *Beer-Hofmann*, 130-36.
46. Schorske, *Vienna*, 356-57.
47. Schorske, *Vienna*, 359.

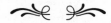

In 1908, the year of the first *Kunstschau*, a young man, twenty-one years old, named Georg Trakl moved to Vienna, and joined the ranks of the avant-garde. Among that collection of the odd and eccentric, Trakl stood out as singularly bizarre. He heard voices; he talked to himself; he paid prostitutes to listen to him talk to himself.

He had been born in Salzburg. His father, Tobias, was a shopkeeper, a Protestant. After his first wife died, Tobias became involved with a young Catholic woman named Maria. Maria was married at the time. When she discovered that she was pregnant with Georg, she got a divorce, abandoned Catholicism, converted to Protestantism, and married Tobias. Maria and Tobias would share six children and a deeply unhappy marriage. Tobias's sole interest was his store. Maria, haunted by her past and profoundly depressed, experimented, rumor had it, with opium. The children, neglected by their parents, grew up wild.

People said that Georg was strange from the beginning. Once, as a little boy in a trance, he wandered into a pond and almost drowned. He jumped in front of horses; once he jumped in front of a train. People said that he probably took some of his mother's opium.

Trakl's brain seemed shattered into fragments and shards. According to one biographer, Frank Graziano, Trakl "reported to friends that he never saw people's faces and had no notion of their physiognomy, and that until the age of twenty he saw nothing in his environment except water."[48] Once, "standing before a mounted calf's head at a peasants' festival celebrating the construction of a church . . . Trakl, shivering and apparently dumbstruck, uttered 'that is our Lord Christ!'"[49]

He heard voices and bells. He insisted that his parents were not his real parents, that his real father was a Catholic cardinal. He had a terrible time in school, his grades were awful, his friends were few. He often talked about suicide.

48. Frank Graziano, ed., *Georg Trakl* (Durango, Colo.: Logbridge-Rhodes, 1983), 9.
49. Graziano, ed., *Trakl*, 19.

Visions would tear into his mind, and perhaps the one thing that kept Trakl functioning was his ability to scribble them down in shocking and riveting language. What he wrote were not stories, and not exactly poems, either, but hallucinations and nightmares. They were idiosyncratic, the cries of a troubled soul. But as Trakl himself discovered as he read Baudelaire and Verlaine, his nightmares were not his alone.

His parents apprenticed him to a pharmacist in Salzburg. In 1909, he moved to Vienna, hoping to attend pharmacy school. His sister Grete, perhaps the only person who could actually communicate with him, moved to Vienna to study piano. Briefly in the army, Trakl later drifted about Vienna, penniless, unemployed, chattering to himself, scribbling down his visions.

The avant-garde was fascinated by him. Like tribal people gathered around a madman, the avant-garde was convinced that Trakl was not simply insane but that he had a strange sort of second sight, that he could see more deeply into reality than so-called "normal" people. Archenemies Hermann Bahr and Karl Kraus both helped get Trakl's poems published. Oskar Kokoschka became Trakl's friend. Young Ludwig Wittgenstein, heir to a vast family fortune, gave him money. Commenting about Trakl's poems, Wittgenstein remarked: "I do not understand them . . . but their tone delights me. It is the tone of a man of real genius."[50]

Trakl's poems are incandescently visual; they recreate Schiele's awful nudes and Kokoschka's frightening *Still Life*. For example, Trakl writes in "De Profundis":

There is a stubble field on which a black rain falls.
There is a tree which, brown, stands lonely there.
There is a hissing wind which haunts deserted huts —
How sad this evening.
Past the village pond
The gentle orphan still gathers scanty ears of corn.
Golden and round her eyes are gazing in the dusk
And her lap awaits the heavenly bridegroom.
Returning home
Shepherds found the sweet body

50. Graziano, ed., *Trakl*, 10.

Decayed in the bramble bush.
A shade I am remote from somber hamlets
The silence of God
I drank from the woodland well.
On my forehead cold metal forms.
Spiders look for my heart.
There is a light that fails in my mouth.
At night, I found myself upon a heath,
Thick with garbage and the dust of stars.
In the hazel copse
Crystal angels have sounded once more.[51]

Nasty things crawl through Trakl's poetry, in the moonlight, on dark, icy nights. His poems typically take on a religious tone, and for all their grotesquerie, they sometimes include a quiet note of hope. The uncanny in Trakl, like the uncanny throughout the work of the avant-garde, is much like Rudolf Otto's uncanny — mysterious, dangerous, and totally other, yet fascinating. If Otto is correct that the encounter with the uncanny is the very womb in which religion is conceived, then Trakl's work, and the work of the whole avant-garde, is indisputably religious work, though one has to admit that it is religious work filled with visions unlike any others. Listen to Trakl's "Amen":

Corruption gliding through the crumpled room;
Shadows on yellow hangings; in dark mirrors
The ivory sorrow of our hands is arched.
Brown beads trickle through fingers that have died.
In the stillness
An angel's blue opium eyes unclose.[52]

---

51. Translation by Michael Hamburger, in Graziano, ed., *Trakl*, 24.
52. Translation by David Luke, in Graziano, ed., *Trakl*, 27.

Chapter 8

THE ARTISTS' HOUR

The artists ruled the day. They wanted to make life itself a work of art!

Peter Altenberg[1]

S omehow, in fin de siècle Vienna, languorous decline energized a whole generation of artists. Historian Edward Crankshaw explains it this way:

> "Decadence" may be defined in many ways, but this is its most striking and revealing feature — the metamorphosis of the artist from entertainer to prophet. The artist is always, in whatever phase of society, a creature of vitality. He is alive and growing. But in a healthy society, others who are not artists are also alive, they grow with the artist, a little behind him, but understanding him; where he goes they are going. Then, later, when decline sets in, the artist still climbs, but the people have ceased to climb. His is no longer the voice of the people, but that of a prophet crying alone.[2]

1. Peter Altenberg, *Reporter der Seele*, ed. Gunther Martin (Vienna: Stiasny-Verlag, 1960), 9.
2. Edward Crankshaw, *The Fall of the House of Habsburg* (London: Longmans, 1963), 189.

Around 1900, Vienna's avant-garde passionately embraced this lonely role. In Vienna, artists would be more than artists or intellectuals; artists would be shamans, prophets, and priests, who would lead the way to the divine.

Bertha Zuckerkandl made it a point to know everyone who was anyone in turn-of-the-century Vienna. Her father was Moritz Szeps, the editor of the *Neue Freie Presse,* Vienna's equivalent of the *London Times.* Her husband, Emil Zuckerkandl, was an eminent scientist, and through him she met Vienna's leading academics. Her sister, Sophie, married Paul Clemenceau, brother of Georges Clemenceau, who would be France's Prime Minister during the Great War. Sigmund Freud was an acquaintance. Bertha herself was a talented journalist and translator. Her home became one of Vienna's leading salons, where everyone sooner or later met everyone else.

It was no surprise, then, that when young Hermann Bahr, in the early 1890s, returned to Vienna after several years of travel, one of the first people he contacted was Bertha Zuckerkandl.

She remembered his call quite well. She would later write of Bahr:

> He seemed to emit spiritual energy and at the same time he seemed to absorb everything. . . . Bahr's experience, his thoughts and feelings were in constant flux. People accused him of constantly changing, like a weather-vane, they said he was always full of contradictions and paradoxes. Once, when he was asked to sign someone's guest book, he wrote beneath the good wishes expressed . . . "always the same, never the same."[3]

The call came one morning late in 1891, or perhaps early in 1892. Bahr breathlessly introduced himself.

3. Bertha Zuckerkandl, *Österreich Intim. Erinnerungen, 1892-1942* (Frankfurt: Propyläen, 1970), 5.

She had asked him what he thought of Vienna after being away so long.

"That's why I'm calling you so early!" Bahr enthusiastically replied. "Vienna's a cemetery! No, a cemetery has something solemn about it; at least a cemetery is a reminder of something that was alive once. But in Vienna you don't even get that impression!"

"Vienna's like Sleeping Beauty, you mean?" Zuckerkandl asked jokingly.

"Sleeping?" Bahr retorted. "Sleeping! Why Vienna's snoring!"

"Well, you're back now. I suppose you'll wake everyone up?"

"I'll wake them up, I swear to God. Not that God would pay any attention to me, God's snoring too!"

"Ah, more atheist jokes," Zuckerkandl laughed, "I'll bet anything you'll end up a saint yet."[4] (Zuckerkandl was more prescient than perhaps even she knew. Bahr's youthful atheism faded into an increasing concern with myth and symbol, which in turn changed into explicit religious faith. But all that would take some time.)

There are some people who influence other people because they seem to express in their lives things other people want to express, need to express, but for some reason can't quite express. Some people have influence because their lives in microcosm reflect, incarnate, what hundreds or thousands of other people feel and think and hope for. Such was the case of Hermann Bahr. He seemed to be a mirror, a sounding board, a weathervane, and in the early 1890s, more and more people looked to him to see which way the winds of the world were blowing. He was the "man from tomorrow," who somehow had the knack of translating tomorrow into today.

Like just about everyone else in the Vienna of his day, Hermann Bahr was a small-town boy who moved to the big city. "You'll never understand the whole tone of the period from, say, 1880-1890," Bahr wrote,

> if you don't recall that we all came from small towns, that we were all raised in tidy little rooms filled with carefully arranged white gardenias, that we all grew up in tidy little artificial worlds which thought of themselves as realms of "honesty" and "loyalty." But

4. Zuckerkandl, *Österreich*, 11.

then, suddenly, were torn from this Biedermeier little world and hurled into life. And we screamed.[5]

Hermann would be a difficult adolescent, and his father, Dr. Alois Bahr, was consistently shocked. Bahr senior was in many ways the archetypical Austrian middle-class civil servant. Of humble background, he had worked his way up, first up the academic ladder, then up the bureaucratic ladder. Educated as a lawyer and accountant, he had served in the Austrian civil service, and then gone into private practice. He considered himself a "liberal" in the Austrian sense of the term, that is, a man who was rational and self-controlled, who believed both in order and hierarchy, but also in progress and science. Loyal to the empire and His Imperial Majesty Franz Josef, contented with the way things were, a firm believer in propriety and respectability, Dr. Alois Bahr had firmly hoped that his son, Hermann, would replicate all these values.

Hermann didn't.

Born in Linz, in northern Austria, on July 19, 1863, Hermann was a bright little boy and did well at the Benedictine Gymnasium in Salzburg (where the family moved), earned his Abitur "with distinction," and was even his graduating class's valedictorian. He recalled years later, though, that even as a little boy in Linz he felt odd and out of place. He was barely five years old, in 1868, when Linz's great son, the writer Adelbert Stifter, committed suicide. Writing of himself in the third person, Bahr said:

> One dark winter's night, Stifter cut his throat with a razor blade. And so, nearby, the child had his first encounter with the demonic. It would become the great theme of his life — to move through that shallow optimism of his epoch, so that he could learn to experience the demonic powers with his own body. . . .
>
> I felt everything around me to be somehow strange. It was all very nice, but I didn't fit in. I was always very nice, but in my heart I was always far away. I still have that same odd sensation today. Sometimes I think that I wasn't born where I was but was brought there by gypsies. Gypsies from Mars. . . .

5. Hermann Bahr, in Eduard Castle, *Die Neue Generation um Hermann Bahr* (Vienna: Carl Fromme, undated), 165.

What separated me from the other boys in Linz, I suppose, was this metaphysical intuition, this sense that the world around us all was somehow not really real, that it was a kind of play, a game, without any meaning to it at all, but that maybe our job would be to bring meaning to it.[6]

In October 1881, aged eighteen, Bahr enrolled at Vienna University. Two years later he was expelled. It was a tremendous humiliation for Dr. Bahr. He was a good and patient man, and did his best to understand his tempestuous son. For years, he would continue to support his son financially. But more than once, he must have asked himself what had happened to young Hermann.

What had happened to young Hermann was Vienna. When he enrolled in the University of Vienna in 1881, he entered more than the classroom. Among many other things, he entered a full-throated, hormone-charged, generational rebellion.

The generational rebellion going full steam in the 1880s was a predictable if nevertheless frightening phenomenon. Times were changing; the worlds parents grew up in seemed increasingly remote from the worlds their own children grew up in. Europe was changing, the Austro-Hungarian Empire was changing, Vienna was changing. Change itself was changing: it was accelerating, reaching into more and more lives, and transforming everything. The most obvious and immediately apparent product of all this change was an enormous gap between parents and their children. The rural Austria Dr. Bahr had been born into was rapidly becoming, at least in parts, an industrialized, market-driven, technological society. The tidy little Vienna Dr. Bahr had known was, by his son's day, a throbbing metropolis. Foreigners and strangers were rare in Dr. Bahr's world; the world of his son was filled with the foreign, the strange, and the new. The values Dr. Bahr valued — order, respectability, hierarchy — were not quite as obviously valuable to Hermann.

"Young," by the late nineteenth century, certainly in Vienna, was no mere adjective. It had become an accolade, a compliment, an aspiration. "Young" was infinitely different from "old." Eduard Michael Kafka, who

6. Hermann Bahr, *Selbstbildnis* (Berlin: S. Fischer, 1923), 43-44.

edited the literary magazine everyone in the avant-garde read and wrote for, *Moderne Dictung (Modern Poetry)*, wrote in 1890 that the key to the new literature was precisely this yawning generation gap. "From day to day, it gets wider and wider, the gulf between young and old. It's not just a question of artistic tastes. What divides young and old are entirely different world views, radically different understandings of truth and morality."[7]

"Young" carried with it a host of connotations. It meant "spring," while "old" meant winter. It meant that the concerns of adolescence, concerns about identity and sexuality in particular, took precedence over the concerns of age. Frank Wedekind's 1891 play, *Frühlings Erwachen (Spring Awakens)*, for instance, with its (for those days) explicit references to sexuality, shocked the "old" and fascinated the "young." In Central Europe in particular (though not only there), an entire generation was emerging, acutely conscious of its difference from its parents, noisily convinced of its own righteousness and innocence, a generation idealizing its own youth, contemptuous of age, and fascinated by "change," "revolution," and "tomorrow."[8]

In Central Europe's patriarchal societies, "young and old" translated especially into "son and father," and no polarity so fascinated turn-of-the-century Viennese as the tensions between sons and fathers. Everyone, of course, whispered about the tensions between Crown Prince Rudolf and his father, the emperor, and every family, it seemed, somehow replicated those very tensions. "Expressionist" and "Futurist" literature would be filled with themes of youthful rebellion and parental revenge; the Great War brutally exacerbated generational tensions; postwar extremist movements would play on violent parent/children tensions. Little wonder that Sigmund Freud would see the conflict between parents and children, and especially between fathers and sons, as one of the keys to understanding human psychological development.

When he was a young man, for example, Arthur Schnitzler was determined to be a writer. His head was filled with made-up stories which he obsessively scribbled down. But Schnitzler's father, Dr. Schnitzler, was de-

7. E. M. Kafka, in Robert Waissenberger, ed., *Wien 1870-1930. Traum und Wirklichkeit* (Vienna: Residenz Verlag, 1984), 45.

8. For an introduction to the rich literature that describes this turn-of-the-century youth rebellion, see especially Robert Wohl, *The Generation of 1914* (Cambridge: Harvard University Press, 1979).

termined that his son would be a doctor. The elder won; the younger grudgingly submitted and attended medical school, and only abandoned medicine for literature when his father died. In January 1890, the young Schnitzler wrote in his diary:

> Friday afternoon, January 17, 1890.
>
> My father has recovered from a severe lung infection. But he's still in poor condition. Our conflicts are ever more burning . . . my disgust with . . . doctors and medicine is worse and worse, I shudder when I think of the future. My literary ambitions are unwelcome at home, our relations are terrible. And I still have no success to show. . . . Still, I know what I have to do. Inside, I'm finished with medicine.[9]

Home from college, Hermann Bahr got into a ferocious argument with his father. Bahr later recalled what was to generations of European young men an archetypical scene, a scene reported in a thousand memoirs, a scene straight out of Turgenev's *Fathers and Sons*. Bahr recalled himself shouting:

> "Liberalism is finished! A new age is coming. We want room for us!" And I can still see the utterly confused look of my old father, and I can still hear his voice ask: "What in the world have they done to you in Vienna?" And then he stood up, walked back and forth in our little garden at home, and kept saying again and again: "What's happened to you in Vienna?" I walked behind him, full of enthusiasm, my hat bobbing back and forth, I shouted again and again, "Yes! We're here now! And now everything's got to change!" His friends began to show up, old Liberals like he was, fathers of sons, and all these sons had brought back home with them ideas like mine, all of them said that liberalism was dead. And all the old fathers sat together and couldn't understand what had happened to their sons, they couldn't understand the world anymore.[10]

9. Cited in Bernard Denscher, "Literatur um Jung Wien," in Waissenberger, *Wien*, 54.
10. Hermann Bahr, cited in Castle, *Die neue Generation*, 165.

Anyone visiting the University of Vienna in the early 1880s, when Hermann Bahr was a student, would instantly see all the signs of generational rebellion underway: passionate student rallies, angry student marches, clashes with the city police, confrontations with university administrators, heated arguments with teachers. But generational rebellion is energy, not direction. What direction did young Hermann Bahr expect this energy to take?

One current of youthful rebellion swept to the political left, in the direction of liberty, equality, fraternity, and democracy. Since bourgeois, capitalist liberalism was so weakened after the economic crisis of 1873, these democratic energies found their home in Austria's labor-oriented, social-reformist Social-Democratic movement.

The case of Bahr's contemporary, Victor Adler, is representative. Adler was a medical student. After medical school, he began investigating issues of public health and was shocked by what he discovered. Especially in big cities like Vienna, slums had suddenly grown up around the new factories, filled with exhausted and impoverished factory workers, with crime, alcoholism, and every imaginable disease. Victor Adler quickly became a reformer. Deeply concerned with issues of poverty and wealth and social class, he turned to Marx for inspiration. In 1889, Adler and his friends organized Austria's first socialist party, and for the rest of his long life, Victor Adler struggled to turn the socialist party into a genuine tribune for the poor and the workers.

But other, much grimmer energies flowed to the political right. The most vehement institutions on German university campuses were the fraternities. There had been student cooperatives in German universities since the Middle Ages. But in the early 1800s, in the midst of the Napoleonic Wars, entirely new student groupings began to appear, and they were peculiar things indeed.

When Napoleon and his Grande Armée invaded Germany, they triggered a vehement xenophobic response (the same thing would happen in Spain and Russia as well). Germans perceived the French troops not as bearers of the revolutionary ideals of liberty, equality, fraternity, but as foreign invaders bent on imposing an alien tyranny on the German people. Young men, filled with nationalist ardor, rushed to the standards to expel the foreign French. And when the students among them returned to their studies, they organized themselves into groups that were as much young veterans' associations as student groups. They wanted to preserve the heroic memories of the war against the hated French; they wanted to inculcate younger students with their own militant patriotism.

These young veterans forged the new fraternities. They were part student association, part veterans' group, and part secret society. They were highly exclusive groups, intensely aware of their exclusivity. Who could join? There were great debates about that in the early days. Obviously only students could join — male students, that is, since there were no women students. Only "patriotic" male students could join, champions of the German people. But who were the "German people"? The young fraternity veterans insistently defined "German" in cultural terms — language, folk customs, and place of birth determined one's "Germanness." Non-Germans, obviously then, could not be fraternity brothers.

Was religion a marker of "Germanness"? For many young veterans, though not all, it was indeed. "Real Germans" were Protestants. Catholics were unwelcome, though grudgingly some fraternities eventually accepted Catholics. What about Jewish Germans? Virtually without exception, the fraternities excluded Jews. No matter how German they were, and even if they were entirely German, they simply weren't "fully" German, since they were not Protestant Christians.

From the beginning, then, the fraternities were hothouses of a kind of paramilitary, xenophobic chauvinism. They taught their members powerful lessons in exclusiveness and social hierarchy. Potential new members underwent a grueling initiation process, designed to shatter their sense of individuality and replace it with an intense identification with and submission to the larger group. Fraternity brothers were expected to be unhesitatingly loyal to the fraternity and its officers, come what may. Whatever aggression or frustration members might feel was directed outward, toward that world of "outsiders" and "non-brothers."

It was warm inside those brotherhoods. Fueled by intense male bonding, the fraternities typically exhibited an adolescent puritanism and moral self-righteousness as well. Fraternity members were to be "morally upstanding": they were to be serious and live cleanly, they were not to associate with "low class" people, they were to give up carousing and smoking and loose women. In Jena, in March 1819, for example, members organized protests in front of the city's bordellos and demanded that they be closed down.[11] At the same time, within the fraternity, a kind of orgiastic release was periodically permitted, especially through the fraternities' beer evenings, marked by drunken male camaraderie.

The fraternities preserved their quasi-military qualities even after the founders' generation had long since departed. Most fraternities were organized into strict hierarchies, and fraternity officers expected instant obedience from new members. New members were subjected to brutal hazing. All fraternities encouraged ritual duals. To have a dueling scar on one's face was the tribal mark, the tattoo, that symbolized both personal bravery and membership in an elite and exclusive male organization.

For adolescent males, being accepted by a fraternity was akin to a religious conversion. Fraternities were secretive groups, and getting into one of them, passing through their terrifying initiation rituals, being accepted as a "brother," meant a great deal to young men. Fraternity brothers stuck together; brothers, years later, looked after each other; fraternities fed into those old-boy networks that were of immense help years later.

These fraternities first began to appear in Vienna around 1859, when a handful of young ethnic Germans from the far eastern stretches of the empire learned to their horror that the boundaries of their home town were to be redrawn to make room for ethnic Poles. Furious and shocked, these young men determined to organize a "German" student group to advance "German" awareness and culture. They modeled their organization after the fraternities in Germany.[12]

By the time Hermann Bahr came to the University of Vienna, the fraternities had become vehement champions of German ethnic consciousness. Habsburg authorities viewed them as subversive and periodically restricted them or banned them outright — making them, of course, all the more attractive to young men like Hermann Bahr.

When Hermann Bahr went off to university in 1881, the University of Vienna was in the midst of an enormous expansion. Its roots went back to 1365, and for centuries it had been a very small institution, hidden away in

11. Hermann Haupt, ed., *Quellen und Darstellungen zur Geschichte der Burschenschaft und der deutschen Einheitsbewegung*, Volume 1 (Heidelberg: Carl Winter, 1910), 78-79.

12. On Vienna's fraternities, see Haupt, *Quellen*; see also Franz Gall, *Alma Mater Rudolphina, 1365-1965. Die Wiener Universität und Ihre Studenten* (Vienna: Austria Press, 1965).

the old Inner City near the Dominican Church. But with the transformation of the city in the 1860s, the University of Vienna was transformed as well. The university was moved from the Inner City to the newly constructed Ring, from its ramshackle old buildings in the Inner City to the grand pseudo-Renaissance buildings near the grand pseudo-Gothic City Hall. Entirely new departments were created, enormous numbers of new faculty were hired, and by the turn of the century, the student body had expanded from a few hundred students to nearly 10,000.[13]

As the university grew, more and more layers of bureaucracy separated administrators and faculty from students. As Franz Gall, the university's historian, wrote about this gulf between administration and students, "the height of this development can be seen in the fact that, when the University celebrated its 500th birthday in August 1865, the festivities were held 'excluding students.'"[14]

Strutting about campus dressed in their military-looking costumes, armed with their swords, the fraternity brothers were a force to be reckoned with. The fraternities were student advocacy groups; they provided their members with a sense of community and identity; they helped with practical issues like housing and jobs. Above all, though, they channeled adolescent rebellion in the sinister direction of ethnic narcissism, authoritarianism, and militarism. Little wonder that one of the fraternities' favorites was the demagogue and anti-Semite Georg von Schönerer.

Fraternity members thought Schönerer's scurrilous anti-Semitism "patriotic"; they considered his bombast "heroic"; they thought his aggression and rhetorical violence "manly." The fraternities fully endorsed Schönerer's rejection of the Habsburg's multiethnic empire and his adulation of the newly created, almost ethnically pure, German Empire.

In October 1881, Hermann Bahr was accepted into the "Alba" fraternity. By the next year he had become a Schönerer enthusiast.

But it would be a mistake to see too much logic to young Bahr's radicalism. For all his nationalist militancy, he was also strongly attracted to socialist reforms; for all his enthusiasm for some sort of "socialism," he remained what he thought of as a "German patriot."

13. Gall, *Alma Mater Rudolphina*, 25ff.
14. Gall, *Alma Mater Rudolphina*, 5.

In fact, Bahr became increasingly bored with political questions. In 1888, he wrote to his long-suffering father:

> I've gone from one political party to the other, because I always try to look at things, as it were, from the perspective of eternity, and all I've ever found is daily routine. It's no different with the socialists. O yes, outwardly, they're for Freedom, Equality, and Fraternity, but inwardly, what they're really interested in are bakers' working hours, or the pay-rates for smiths. They're not interested in the real revolution in the human spirit that Ibsen talks about, they're only interested at most in the things of the body.[15]

Part of young Bahr's frustration with politics grew out of the extraordinary discovery he made at the university, a discovery that grew into a passion, a passion that he shared with his entire generation. Bahr discovered Richard Wagner.

It is hard, now, to understand the fin de siècle Wagner mania. Our more informed, if not necessarily wiser, age recognizes Wagner as a great artist to be sure, but also a narcissist, a poseur, a racist, an anti-Semite. It is hard to understand the extraordinary spell Wagner cast over an entire generation.

But cast a spell he did. The French avant-garde was enraptured with him. Charles Baudelaire, that progenitor of bohemian Paris, wrote an effusive pamphlet in 1861, called "Tannhäuser à Paris," which praised Wagner's operas.

> Languishings and delights, blended with fevers shot through with anguish, incessant returnings to voluptuousness, almost promising to quench one's thirst for it, but never doing so, raging palpitations of the heart and sense, imperious commands of the flesh — the entire dictionary of onomatopoeias identified with love is heard here. Finally, the religious theme slowly regains its empire, gradually absorbing the other in a peaceful and glorious victory, as an irresistible being does over a sickly, disordered one.[16]

---

15. Hermann Bahr, *Prophet der Moderne — Tagebücher 1888-1904*, ed. Reinhard Farkas (Vienna: Böhlau, 1987), 8.

16. Cited in Karl Beckson, *London in the 1890s* (New York: Norton, 1993), 275-76.

Symbolist poet and novelist Edouard Dujardin edited Paris's *Revue wagnérienne;* most of Paris's poets and artists not only read it and contributed to it, but also undertook the pilgrimage to Bayreuth to honor the Master.

The British were equally swept away. Algernon Swinburne, James MacNeil Whistler, Aubrey Beardsley, Oscar Wilde, W. B. Yeats — indeed virtually all of London's dandies, aesthetes, and decadents were fascinated by Wagner. George Moore, for example, wrote,

> The fanfare of the Rhine told me something undreamed of had come into my life, and I listened as a child listens, understanding nothing, for my poor ears could not follow the intricate weaving and interweaving; my reason tottered like one in a virgin forest, for there seemed to be no path to even a partial understanding of the fulgurate orchestra, predicting at every moment wars and rumors of wars, giants against gods.[17]

For many young people in German-speaking Europe in the 1880s, Wagner was a star, an idol, even a god. Friedrich Nietzsche's fascination with Wagner, for example, is well known. In October 1868, Nietzsche, then twenty-three, heard a performance of the overture to Wagner's *Die Meistersinger.* He was swept away. "I cannot bring myself to take a critically cool view of this music," he wrote. "It sends a thrill through every fiber, every nerve, and for a long time I have not had such a sustained feeling of being carried away as the Overture gave me."[18] Swept away, Nietzsche became obsessed with Wagner, an obsession that would profoundly shape his life and thought. And in this, as in so much else, Nietzsche's experience became paradigmatic for the next generation.

No one, it seemed, had ever made music the way Wagner made music. Admirers called Wagner's work the "Music of the Future." His vast musical fantasies offered a heroic and mythic alternative to the staid and proper

---

17. Cited in Beckson, *London,* 284-85; Beckson provides a fine discussion of the London Wagnerians in ch. 12, "Imperfect and Perfect Wagnerians," in *London,* 272-91.

18. Nietzsche made the comment in a letter to Erwin Rohde, written on October 27, 1868; see Ronald Hayman's account in his *Nietzsche: A Critical Life* (New York: Penguin, 1980), 97.

world of late Victorian Europe. The operas' explicitly liturgical and ritual qualities provided a surrogate religion to people intensely religious but alienated from conventional piety. Wagnerian operas, structured around surging emotions rather than rational argument, propelled not by linear narrative but by recurring musical "leitmotifs," appealing to the unconscious, relying on myth and symbol instead of abstract concepts, reflected the pervasive yearning for a mode of discourse and experience richer and deeper than that of one-dimensional, routine, conventional life. The redemptive eroticism of the operas, their explosions of passionate love that saved not only souls but also entire universes, was infinitely more compelling than political dogma or conventional churchly pieties. Wagner's struggle to create a "total work of art," a *Gesamtkunstwerk*, was far more than an artistic enterprise; what Wagner had in mind was the aestheticization of the cosmos, the salvation of the universe by means of art.

For the young and artistically inclined at the end of the nineteenth century, trapped in a stifling Victorianism, Richard Wagner was a prophet, an idol, and a messiah. For them, entering a Wagnerian opera was to enter a magical universe of compelling sounds and sights, of intoxicating rhythms and haunting melodies.

Anton Bruckner, for example, was an odd country boy who came to Vienna with a passion for organ music. Bruckner was an eccentric to say the least, whose close-cropped hair, too short trousers and absent-minded manners quickly became the butt of children's taunts. When he was nervous, which was often, he felt compelled to sort things and count things, and he would fire off telegrams to friends pleading with them to count the numbers of windows in certain buildings and report back to him so he could ease his mind. He was an old bachelor, looked after by an irritable housekeeper, but he had a magnificent musical imagination. And he was passionate about Richard Wagner. In his own music he tried to replicate the cosmic power of the Master. Bruckner, critic Oskar Lang wrote, saw music as a "revelation of that divine creativity which governs the world,"[19] and Bruckner conveyed this sacred passion to his students, especially to Gustav Mahler.

Young Mahler was an ardent Wagnerian, despite the fact that Mahler

19. Oskar Lang, *Anton Bruckner* (Munich: Beck, 1943), 41.

was Jewish and Wagner an anti-Semite. Mahler not only echoed Wagner's music in his own creations, he mimicked Wagner's manners and habits. Wagner, for instance, was a vegetarian (and hypochondriac), so Mahler was a vegetarian. (And so would be another young resident of Vienna and Wagner enthusiast, Adolf Hitler.)

Hugo Wolf, at one time Mahler's roommate, was a passionate Wagnerian. Wolf had a gift for song; his *lieder* are some of the most haunting songs of the era. According to one story, Wolf, when he heard that Wagner would be staying at Vienna's Imperial Hotel, hung around the hotel's entrance to see his idol, then ran along the Ring to the Opera ahead of Wagner's coach so he could catch another glimpse of the Great Man. Adolf Loos too was a Wagner enthusiast. He claimed that he had seen Wagner's *Tristan* dozens of times.

Wagner was, to be sure, a sign of contradiction. If his thousands of youthful admirers adored him, many people also despised him. In Britain, Queen Victoria rather liked the music of Felix Mendelssohn, and was not pleased when Wagner, in an anti-Semitic tirade, denounced Mendelssohn in an 1850 pamphlet entitled *Judaism in Music*.[20] Karl Marx, working away in the British Museum, thought Wagner a charlatan and a fraud.[21] Friedrich Nietzsche, shaking off his obsession with Wagner, would come to think of Wagner not only as fraudulent, but as sinister, as a kind of "disease."[22] In Vienna, most of the music establishment, led by the titanic Johannes Brahms and music critic Eduard Hanslick, thoroughly despised Wagner and all his works. The rivalry between Brahms and his many allies on the one side and Vienna's Wagnerians, led by Bruckner and his friends, on the other rocked Vienna's musical world in Bahr's student days.

But for Hermann Bahr and many others, Wagner was the single most important influence in their lives. He seemed to them a genuine radical, an ardent patriot, and above all, a master who introduced them into the realm of the spirit.

20. Beckson, *London*, 275.

21. Beckson, *London*, 273.

22. Nietzsche's obsession with Wagner never really ended; even when denouncing Wagner, Nietzsche was still fascinated by him. *Der Fall Wagner (The Case of Wagner)* is Nietzsche's most sustained attack on Wagner, but the attack occurs in most of Nietzsche's later works. See also Hayman, *Nietzsche*, 206; 316-37.

For Wagner was indeed a great and powerful artist, and he insisted again and again, in essays such as *Die Kunst und die Revolution (Art and Revolution)* and *Das Kunstwerk der Zukunft (The Art of the Future)*, that if there is to be human salvation it is to be found through the spirit, expressed above all through the imagination. Politics, economics, social structures, philosophies are all secondary to art; real revolutions are revolutions of spirit; genuine transformations are spiritual transformations; it is in imagination and art that ultimate values are to be found, to be created, to be expressed. "Here," Bahr would later write, "here flowed the springs of life."[23]

Bound up with Wagner, for Bahr's generation, were Nietzsche and Arthur Schopenhauer. Like hammer blows, these three names struck the imaginations of Bahr's cohorts. Schopenhauer, years before, had demonstrated in his massive *Die Welt als Wille und Vorstellung (The World as Will and Representation)* that external reality is ultimately a product of human consciousness and imagination; Nietzsche called for an entirely new generation of "singular persons" who could "break with the herd" and who, through creative action, would recreate the world; Wagner demonstrated the extraordinary emotional and spiritual power that great art could have. For Hermann Bahr this was the real stuff of revolution.[24] Through Wagner, Bahr was converted from politics to art.

To be a college student in the early 1880s in Vienna, to live in that turbulent city suspended between "no longer" and "not yet"; to live in a spiritual world shaped by Schopenhauer, Nietzsche, and Wagner, was a passionate, emotional, tremendous thing. Bahr would write about himself and his generation:

> With God, we were quickly finished. "Science," we were sure, had proven that the concept of God was outdated, "modern science" had no room for him. . . . We were sure that it was up to us to unmask all myths. . . . It wasn't worth the trouble to be "anti-clerical," we laughed when the Liberals expressed their fears about "the

23. Cited in Donald G. Daviau, *Der Mann von Übermorgen*, trans. Helga Zoglmann (Vienna: Österreichischer Bundesverlag, 1984), 54.

24. For a more detailed discussion of the impact of Schopenhauer, Nietzsche, and Wagner and Bahr, see Daviau, *Der Mann von Übermorgen*, 46-69; and Farkas, *Bahr*, 55ff.

priests" ... all we wanted to do was serve Art ... the only things we had were Ibsen and Wagner.[25]

In the early 1880s, all this was still jumbled up in Bahr's young mind. And the jumble would get him into trouble.

In March 1883, Richard Wagner died. The German fraternities in Vienna jointly sponsored an emotional memorial service that quickly turned into a German nationalist rally. Georg von Schönerer was an honored guest. Vienna's police turned out in force.

Hermann Bahr was the last speaker. After tearfully praising the dead Master, Bahr launched into a passionate plea (laced with Wagnerian metaphors) for Bismarck and his New Germany to come south and rescue their German cousins trapped in the rickety, multiethnic Habsburg Empire. Wagner, Bahr insisted, had advocated a nation for all Germans, a greater Germany, and he urged his listeners never to rest until they had fulfilled Wagner's dream.

That was enough for the police. This sort of talk was treason against the House of Habsburg. The police waded into the crowd and announced that the memorial was over; students leapt to their feet and began singing "Die Wacht am Rhein"; police swung nightsticks, students swung chairs, and the memorial turned into a riot. Suddenly someone grabbed Bahr and pulled him away from the fighting. It was Schönerer himself, savagely swinging a club at the police, "enraged," Bahr would later remember, "somehow elemental in his wildness, the image of his unchained rage stays with me even today."[26]

Bahr was expelled from the university. His father was horrified. Look, his father wrote him some years later, "I am middle-class, maybe I am a little bit of a philistine, but what I keep in mind is that one needs to earn his daily bread; I would have loved to see you become a professor."[27]

His father tried unsuccessfully to get him into the University of Graz; he briefly attended the University of Czernowitz, but was invited to leave given his anti-Habsburg attitudes.

Finally, in May 1884, Bahr went off for the Friedrich-Wilhelm Univer-

25. Bahr, *Selbstbildnis*, 25.
26. Daviau, *Der Mann von Übermorgen*, 54.
27. Cited in Bahr, *Prophet der Moderne*, 93.

sity in Berlin to study government and economics. He would stay in Berlin for some four years, leaving in 1887 without completing his doctorate. He fulfilled his one-year obligatory military service, and then, in November 1888, still supported by his father, he moved to Paris. He would spend two critical years in Paris, and then, by way of Spain and Russia, he would finally return to Vienna in the fall of 1891.

In these seemingly unfocused years, Bahr made a crucial career choice, and even more important, a critical spiritual discovery. The career choice he made was for literature. In Berlin, for example, he found the coffeehouse debates of writers already being called "modernists" much more interesting than lectures on political economy. And in vibrant Paris, already in the midst of a tremendous cultural revolution, he dedicated his life to art.

To earn his daily bread (as his father would put it), Bahr turned to journalism. While still in Berlin, the twenty-three-year-old Bahr began writing for socialist Victor Adler's new newspaper, *Die Gleichheit*. He discovered that he had the journalist's talent of writing reams of prose every day, and from then on Bahr would be an inexhaustible writer; he would produce, over the years, an avalanche of book reviews, theater and art reviews, travelogues, and cultural criticism. But his real love was imaginative literature. He began writing plays and poetry; he drafted a novel.

It was in Paris that Bahr discovered the simple truth that would transform his life: things aren't really what they seem.

Hermann Bahr was hardly the first person to be surprised by the distinction between "seeming" and "being." The distinction is so obvious that most people take it for granted and then ignore it. Yet the rapid and accelerating changes underway throughout Europe suddenly made this distinction inescapable. Rural life was dying, hounded to its death by urban industrial life; railroads swept masses of people across the continent, and steamships carried them across oceans; electricity turned night into day. Nothing solid, it seemed, remained; "all that is solid melts into air."[28] What seemed fixed proved to be fluid; what seemed clear became obscure; what had been taboo became permitted; what seemed unchangeable disappeared into smoke.

28. Marshal Berman, *All That Is Solid Melts Into Air: The Experience of Modernity* (New York: Penguin, 1988).

Things are not what they seem to be. Taken seriously, brooded about and puzzled over, the distinction between "seeming" and "being" is dynamite.

It meant to Hermann Bahr that all the "certainties" he had been taught by his parents and teachers — the virtues of thrift and hard work; the importance of sexual self-discipline; the eternal truths of Christianity; the rightness of monarchy, hierarchy and authority; the inevitability of progress — all these things were no certainties at all but human creations, illusions, chains of illusion.

The worst error one could make, he became convinced, was to take such human constructs as eternal verities. To assume that "normal" life was "real" was ignorance, hypocrisy, or ultimately madness. To confuse "seeming" and "being" would produce precisely the kind of narrow, closed, one-dimensional society that late Habsburg Austria had become.

Later, he would write that even as a boy he sensed that what he was being taught as true was only a charade.

> It was clear to me that everything that they told us children was nonsense. . . . Our lessons were designed to divert our attention; it was a kind of game to disguise the seriousness of truth. It always struck me how different adults' faces were when they thought we weren't looking: sad and terribly tired. But, with us children watching, they would immediately pretend to be happy.[29]

But this respectable world, which parents and teachers taught was the only possible world, was not the real world at all. Reality extended far beyond middle-class respectability; it included much more than pursuing a good career in the imperial bureaucracy, making a proper marriage, and owning a smart apartment in the Schwarzenburg Platz in Vienna. This "proper" world, in fact, was a fraud, a cage, and a trap.

Schopenhauer had taught Bahr, of course, that external realities are really products of human creation, and he knew enough about Marx to understand that "reality" is simply a disguise for the interests of the ruling classes. All this was why the respectable world had to be challenged, why

29. Cited in Bahr, *Prophet der Moderne*, 96; the comments are from Bahr's 1890 essay, *Die gute Schule*.

it had to be destroyed, why its obvious faults and failures were occasions for celebration.

In Paris, Bahr became a "decadent." Decadents were those who celebrated the decay of social norms, who applauded the violations of social taboos, who scoffed at proprieties and conventions. The "decadent" was daring and outrageous, a precursor for a new reality.

In an 1889 play called *Die grosse Sünde (Great Sins)*, Bahr's protagonist shouts, "I will be an honest man!" That became Bahr's motto. To be honest meant above all to be open to experience — all experience, no matter how strange — to hunger for experience, to think of oneself as a receptor for the multiplicity of reality.

Bahr not only was a decadent; he also became a "dandy." Decadents tended to be dandies. The fin de siècle dandy was a distinctive social type. The dandy was a young male, literate, sophisticated, resolutely uncommitted to anything or anyone, but eager to taste experience. The dandy was a hedonist, but not a glutton. The dandy was a connoisseur, whose life consisted of satisfying ever more precious appetites, appetites of all sorts — intellectual, artistic, culinary, or sexual. Exquisitely groomed and cologned and manicured, witty and charming and ultimately cynical, dandies were thick on the ground in Paris in Bahr's day, and he would soon find plenty of dandies back in Vienna. Oscar Wilde was the archetypal dandy; Hermann Bahr became a Viennese Oscar Wilde.

But Bahr was far too serious to assume that dandyism was anything more than yet another pose. For if indeed reality were fluid, multifarious, and elusive, then no single lifestyle, no single set of mores, no given artistic approach could capture it. But could reality at least be pointed to, hinted at?

The 1880s were the great years of artistic "Naturalism." Naturalists like Zola and Ibsen struggled to replicate in their art the precise and dispassionate descriptions of the natural scientists that seemed to that generation to have finally comprehended truth. Bahr was impressed with Naturalism, and would remain an admirer of Ibsen and Zola, but by his last days in Paris he became convinced that Naturalism itself would have to be transcended. Something new had to be created, a style, a manner sensitive and open, attuned not only to reason but to passion — an artistic style that accepted that "reality" was elusive but that nevertheless used metaphor and symbol (and not mere description) to point to it.

Young Bahr was fascinated by the "-isms" flowing through Paris: Impressionism, Naturalism, and Symbolism. He was, he wrote to his father in 1888, "a man, rushing wildly, torn and tortured by a thousand crisscrossing ideas."[30] But by January 1889 there was one thing he was sure of. He wrote in his diary:

> I am modern. And that means that I am utterly different from what has come before. . . . "Modern" — that means that I abandon everything that has been, every model, every thought, and obey only one law in art, the law of my own sensations, my own impressions. These I follow without question. If we can change our fashions every few years, we certainly can change our art every century, and if we eat, live, speak, sing, and love differently from our ancient ancestors, why in the world should we still compose like they did?[31]

"Modern" in fact became Bahr's talisman. The sudden and stunning realization that the world was radically different from the way it had been in his father's day, that every day the world was different from what it had been the day before — that realization transformed Hermann Bahr.

In March 1889, he wrote to himself: "The *Modern* is what exists since the collapse of individualism. Everything that is not yet, but will be. A nameless wish, a struggle for a new world view, and a new art."[32] In the dizzying whirl of the Modern, Bahr noted, "we all want a synthesis, a synthesis of the outer and the inner, of world and self, of the wildest power (brutal and unbroken) and the tenderest sensitivity."[33]

This was Hermann Bahr's great discovery: this grand synthesis would not be found in politics or economics or science; no, this synthesis, if ever it could be found, would be found in art. And the discoverer of this cosmic synthesis would be the artist.

In January 1889, Bahr had been reading Emile Zola, the great French "realist" novelist. A phrase suddenly leapt out, which Bahr hurriedly scribbled in his diary: "Une phrase bien faite est une bonne action," "a well-

30. Bahr, *Prophet der Moderne*, 28.
31. Bahr, *Prophet der Moderne*, 43.
32. Bahr, *Prophet der Moderne*, 48.
33. Bahr, *Prophet der Moderne*, 48.

made phrase is a good action."[34] What struck him was the insight that artistic beauty, "une phrase bien faite," is a moral act, a "bonne action." "This," he wrote, "was my Paris experience, decisive for my entire future — I discovered the Secret of Form."[35] He continued,

> And on that day a new life began for me. This phrase had suddenly awakened me. It reminded me of "good" and "bad." Even before we had heard of the formula from Nietzsche, we young people had lived "beyond good and evil." That was why we had no use for a materialistic point of view. But when we tried to live "beyond good and evil" we forgot the distinction between the beautiful and the ugly. "Fair is foul and foul is fair"; we could never get beyond this formula of Macbeth's. But Zola's phrase suggested that even "modern" artists could, indeed, should, distinguish between the beautiful and the ugly.[36]

This "discovery of form" was decisive not only for Bahr but for the whole avant-garde. What is art? Art is stuff, stories, objects, tones. But what makes art art is the way this stuff is organized. Random tones are noise; formed tones are music. The making of stuff into art is an aesthetic act, but also a morally good act. To make art is to redeem the world.

Philosopher Richard Viladesau insists that an awareness of artistic form is a kind of religious awareness. The experience of art, Viladesau writes, is about being moved by "beauty." The beauty in question may be terrible or gentle or something else entirely, but what provokes our fascination is not content alone, but form as well. "The experience of beauty," Viladesau continues, "is a kind of delight: a joy in the experience of 'form.'" Beauty, in fact, arises not from the stuff of the art, but from the form that stuff has taken on. The experience of beauty is precisely an experience of form.

Form is invisible, but it is nevertheless real. Form, in fact, is "what corresponds to the mind's quest for intelligibility." We literally cannot com-

---

34. Bahr, *Prophet der Moderne*, 40.
35. Bahr, *Selbstbildnis*, 221.
36. Bahr, *Selbstbildnis*, 226-27.

prehend the formless. Following Plato, Viladesau argues that a delight in beautiful things leads to a delight in abstract form, which leads to a delight in beauty as such, which is above all intelligible form. This real but not physical form, which provokes such wonder and joy in us, is simultaneously "in" us as human beings, but also "out there" in the trans-human universe. The act of reflecting on this form is an act of transcendence — we "ascend" (to be Platonic about it) from the formless chaos of the quotidian to the timeless delight of pure form.[37] Many eventful years later, well into middle age, after his long bout of atheism and religious experimentation, Bahr would find a religious home in Catholicism. Some of his artist friends were shocked, but one remarked that he had always known that Bahr was a good Catholic, that it was only a matter of time until Bahr himself finally found that out.

Writing about this secret of form, Bahr himself would wax Platonic, almost Heideggerian:

> My conscience awoke, at least artistically. I suddenly had a passion for quality, for quality based not on my own taste or whims, but for quality in and of itself. . . . For the first time in my life, I felt a kind of power over me, I felt that one ought to serve this power. . . . Being appeared to me, I could almost grasp it with my hands; Being, before which time stood still; Being itself, which, appearing in the middle of all the illusions of life, gave me at least a brief taste of eternity. Now my life had purpose, a mission was emerging for me.[38]

Bahr's mission was to spread the good news of Form. Art would both reveal and transform reality. Later, writing about tragedy, Bahr would say about the new art in general:

> All divisions are here transcended. The physiological and psychological flow together, stuff and sensation become one, the "I" dissolves and everything is eternal flow, that which is here seems to slow, and then suddenly rushes, everything becomes a movement

---

37. Richard Viladesau, *Theology and the Arts* (New York: Paulist Press, 2000), 42.
38. Bahr, *Selbstbildnis*, 226-27.

of color, tone, warmth, feeling, space and time, all of which appear to us as impressions, feelings, and will.[39]

Art would reveal Reality — "Being," in Bahr's language — and thus transform the mundane. Art's priest and prophet was the artist.

Bahr did not return to Austria and Vienna immediately. From Paris he traveled to Spain, and from Spain to Russia. His conviction that he had hit on something profound increased on his travels. He wrote compulsively: he wrote in his diaries; he wrote essays and book reviews; he sketched novels and plays. As his ideas began to take on more solid form, he became calmer and more confident. The religious tone increased. While on his way to St. Petersburg, like St. Paul on the way to Damascus, it appears, Bahr was finally converted and decided to return to Vienna to preach the word of art. In May 1891, he wrote to his long-suffering father: "The time of searching and experimenting is over. Now begins a calm, still, productive time. Petersburg is my Damascus."[40]

He had remained in touch with friends in Vienna, friends from his turbulent college days, young men and women now in their later twenties: aspiring actors, hopeful novelists, ambitious poets, Wagnerians, and aesthetes. While on his travels, Bahr had learned that two young poets, Eduard Michael Kafka and Julius Kulka, wanted to start a little magazine they enthusiastically hoped would revolutionize Vienna. They intended to call it *Moderne Dichtung (Modern Poetry)*. Bahr contacted Kafka and Kulka. They invited him to send something. He sent a great deal.

Bahr's essays on "modernism," printed in *Moderne Dictung* in the early 1890s, revealed modernism to young Viennese artists who had experienced its power but hadn't quite yet learned its name. Bahr was certainly not the only prophet of modernism. In 1886, for example, Eugen Wolff had published an essay called "Die Moderne. Zur Revolution und Reformation der Literatur" ("Modernism: On Revolution and Reformation in Literature"), and two years later he published a book called *Die jüngste deutsche Literaturströmung und das Prinzip der Moderne (Recent Currents in German Literature and the Principle of the Modern)*. Wolff insisted in both that dramati-

39. Bahr, *Prophet der Moderne*, 15.
40. Bahr, *Prophet der Moderne*, 35.

cally new times needed dramatically new forms of expression.[41] *Moderne Dichtung* would quickly be filled with titles like "Toward a Criticism of the Modern," "Modern Types," and "Modern Individualism."[42] But still, it was Bahr's articles in particular that fueled the passionate discovery of the wonders of modern art.

In January 1890, *Moderne Dichtung* published Bahr's groundbreaking article called simply "Die Moderne." It was written in an at times breathless Nietzschean style, aphoristic and apocalyptic. "It may be," Bahr began,

> that we are at an end, that we are at the end of an exhausted humanity, and that what we witness around us are merely death rattles. But it might be that we are at the beginning, that we are witnessing the birth of a new humanity, and that the snows are melting, that we are witnessing the avalanches of spring. Perhaps we will ascend into the divine; perhaps we will fall into night and annihilation. But we will not remain unchanged. That somehow salvation will come from suffering, that grace will come from doubt, that day will come again after this terrible darkness, that art will be reborn — belief in this glorious and holy rebirth, that is the faith of the Modern.[43]

Modern art meant "life":

> life has changed profoundly, and changes all around us constantly, restlessly, hungrily. But the human spirit is old and inflexible and refuses to move, refuses to change, and so the spirit suffers helplessly, because it is alone and separated from life itself. . . . We want to throw the windows wide open. . . . We want to open wide all our senses, all our nerves.[44]

---

41. For a thorough collection of materials related to Young Vienna and the discussion of "modernism," see Gotthart Wunberg, ed., *Das junge Wien*, Volume 1 (Tübingen: Max Niemeyer, 1976). Wolff is discussed in the introduction, liii-liv.

42. E. M. Kafka, "Zur Kritik der Moderne," February 1890, in Wunberg, *Junge Wien*, 42-46; Robert Fischer, "Moderne Typen," June 1890, in Wunberg, *Junge Wien*, 81-84; E. M. Kafka, "Von Modernen Individualism," July 1890, in Wunberg, *Junge Wien*, 85-87.

43. Hermann Bahr, "Die Moderne," in Wunberg, *Junge Wien*, 30.

44. Hermann Bahr, "Die Moderne," 33.

Modern art, Bahr explained in other articles, meant "youth.[45] Modern art overcame the dichotomy between "inner world" and the "outer world." Modern art transcended the narrow materialism of "naturalism": "the power of naturalism is over," Bahr wrote in "Die Krisis des Naturalismus" ("The Crisis of Naturalism") in 1891; "its role is over, its magic is broken."[46] Modern art meant nervousness and mysticism. "I believe," he wrote, "that naturalism will be transcended by a nervous romanticism, or rather, through a mysticism of nerves."[47]

Modern art meant a bold rupture of routine and convention and relentless experiment. Human imagination, Bahr insisted, was paralyzed by the contradiction between romanticism and naturalism. The modern task was to transcend this contradiction because both parts of it were inadequate alone. A new experiment had to be tried, an experiment which would reunite romanticism and naturalism.

> This experiment can only be made at that point where people and the world confront each other, at that point between persons and the world . . . there where something occurs which is neither personal alone nor worldly alone but both. One calls the sparks which occur at that point between person and world, sparks which are neither one nor the other but both, one calls these sparks "impressions" or "sensations." In German, we have no single word for them. This is the zone of experiment . . . and experiments here characterize the new life of the spirit. The new life of the spirit abandons simple objective "being" so beloved of materialism and naturalism, but it doesn't simply flee inward to the "I"; the spirit has no intention of simply repeating the old romanticism. No, what the new spirit wants to do is approach the "I" through the process of becoming, in the process of thinking; where the spirit wants to act is in that place that is neither "outer" alone nor "inner" alone but both.[48]

45. Hermann Bahr, "Die Alten und die Junge," May 1890, in Wunberg, *Junge Wien*, 53-58.

46. Hermann Bahr, "Die Krisis des Naturalismus," 1891, in Wunberg, *Junge Wien*, 155.

47. Bahr, "Die Überwindung des Naturalismus," in Wunberg, *Junge Wien*, 157.

48. Hermann Bahr, "Kritik," 1894, in Wunberg, *Junge Wien*, 420-21.

E. M. Kafka summarized Bahr's book, *Die Überwindung des Naturalismus (Overcoming Naturalism)*, in 1891, this way:

> In this book, there is much talk about nerves. For the modern person is according to Hermann Bahr, a "nervenmensch," a person who is nothing but nerves. The classical person may have been a person of reason, and the romantic a person of emotion, but the modern person is above all a person of nerves. The modern person reacts according to nerves, experiences through nerves, acts only through nerves. The sensations of the nerves, the instantaneous impressions of the ganglia, the swift shifts of moods, the chaotic onslaught of associations that shape thoughts and emotions, these are the stuff that must be grasped and shaped and conveyed to others.[49]

Bahr's sense of religious mission became, if anything, more intense as Vienna's modernists gathered around him. They thought of him as the "Man from Tomorrow"[50] who had invaded the present to lead his converts off into the future. And Bahr couldn't help himself; he really did see himself as a prophet. In February 28, 1894, for instance, Bahr noted in his diary:

> The streets are all closed for the funeral of [Mayor Johann] Prix. The first warm sun shines with the vehemence of an adolescent spring on the yellow houses . . . the ordinary mass of people are there to awaken the person of genius. . . . It's foolish, I think, to think of God as somehow finished, unmovable, fixed. No, God is in constant motion. God is constantly re-creating Creation, and the tools for this constant re-creation are artists.

On May 15, 1894, he wrote, "Each of us is a kind of gesture of God. And so, each of us has the duty to express as clearly as we can this divine action."[51]

---

49. E. M. Kafka, "Der Neueste Bahr," 1891, in Wunberg, *Junge Wien*, 242.
50. It appears that Maximilian Hardenberg coined the nickname.
51. Hermann Bahr, *Tagebücher* (Berlin: Paul Cassirer, 1909), 67-69.

No life is just like every other life, but Hermann Bahr's life was very much like the lives of the other members of the *Wiener Moderne*. Small town beginnings; tension with fathers; thrilling moves to the big city; the terrifying but delicious sense that one's life is radically different from one's parents' lives — indeed, radically different from all lives that have gone before; above all, the passionate, intense sense that the odd gift for story or verse or drawing or song that one possesses can be the source not only of revolution, but even more important, revelation. As historian Hans Brisanz writes,

> This "genius-cult" of Schopenhauer and Nietzsche found widespread enthusiasm around 1900 in Vienna, especially among the artists of the Secession, who considered themselves a "'knowing minority of elect, who considered it a sacred duty to teach the unknowing majority through their actions.'"[52]

Everything about the Viennese avant-garde exuded this priestly and prophetic self-image, from the night-long debates at "Café Megalomania," where artistic questions assumed the intensity of theological definition, to Mahler's vast musical liturgies, to the exhibitions at Olbricht's temple-like Secession building, designed as a place where you could purge yourself of daily concerns and focus your mind, by means of the magic of art, on the divine.[53]

The Viennese artists enthusiastically embraced the Nietzschean ideal of artist as *übermensch*, as an inspired figure outside and above normal humanity. Hermann Bahr quite early began to play the role of sage, turning in his dandy bowler and Oscar Wilde suits for a long white beard and a flowing gown. This is how Hermann Bahr, for example, writing of himself in the third person, explained his mission in 1893: "The moral renewal of

---

52. Hans Brisanz, *Peter Altenberg: Mein Ausserstes Ideal. Altenbergs Photosammlung von geliebten Frauen, Freunde, und Orten* (Vienna: Christian Brandstätter, 1987), 13. Brisanz is citing an observation by Marian Brisanz-Prakken.

53. Gottfried Friedl, *Klimt*, trans. Hugh Beyer (Cologne: Benedikt Taschen, 1991), 102.

humanity can only occur when people are led by an aesthetic elite. His mission would be the formation of that elite."[54] Gustav Klimt too liked to work in a long flowing gown. No doubt to a painter the gown had utilitarian value, but its vestment-like quality contributed to Klimt's semipriestly status. In 1898, Adolf Loos, thinking along these same lines, called on "our young architects" to be something much more transcendent than people with a career. Of course, young architects need to make a living. But, to the ideal architect,

> whether or not his employer endorses his artistic ideals is irrelevant. Most young architects don't have an employer anyway! . . . But if our young architect has the moral courage to pursue his artistic calling, cost what it may, then real blessings would shower on our profession. Young architects — look to young painters and sculptors and musicians. If they have to, they'll starve, they'll sacrifice their lives, for their art! And that's precisely what you will have to be willing to do, if you want to earn the most beautiful title anyone can win: "Artist."[55]

Vienna's artists defined their roles in priestly and prophetic ways. As they did so, they began to realize not only that prophets are rejected in their own countries, but also that priests themselves are sacrificial victims. Violence and suffering were intimately bound up with the artists' prophetic and priestly mission.

Consider, for example, the work of artist Richard Gerstl. Gerstl was a talented if deeply troubled young painter. He became involved in a painful relationship with Mathilde Schoenberg (Arnold Schoenberg's wife); when it became apparent that the relationship was doomed, Gerstl committed

54. Bahr, *Tagebücher,* 63.
55. Adolf Loos, "Unseren Jungen Architekten," in Burkhardt Rukschcio and Roland Schachel, *Adolf Loos* (Vienna: Residenz Verlag, 1982), 47.

suicide, leaving behind a series of troubling pictures. The self-portraits are especially powerful, such as *Self-Portrait, Semi-nude against a Blue Background* (1901) and *Self-Portrait, Naked* (1908), the first completely male nude ever painted in Austria before 1910. In the first self-portrait, Gerstl stands at relaxed attention in the center of the image, nude from the waist up, covered with a white shroud from the waist down. He stares without expression at the viewer. The background is dark blue, preventing the viewer from locating the image in any particular time and place. There is an odd, halo-like lighter blue around the image's head. The halo is even more striking in the second self-portrait, *Self-Portrait, Naked*. The shroud around the figure's waist is gone, the genitalia are exposed, but there is nothing indecent about the image; to the contrary, the stark whiteness of the body and even more the blue and white background make the image fairly glow. As critic Klaus Albrecht Schröder suggests, there is an important iconography at work here. Clearly the visual reference in these images is hagiographical. Only saints, persons infused with the divine spirit, glow like the Gerstl images. Only saints — and Christ — glow.[56]

The artist as Christ is even more explicit in Kolo Moser's *Self-Portrait* (1916). The image is similar to Gerstl's *Self-Portrait, Semi-nude*, except that it is much closer to the viewer. The image stares impassively at the viewer, the white shirt is open, baring the chest. Striking again, though, is the glow behind the figure.

Egon Schiele's terrifying self-portraits — he did scores of them — seem at first sight to be radically different. Whether clothed or nude, his images are twisted and distorted. The head and hands contort at impossible angles; often the body is not simply nude but naked; the genitalia obscenely highlighted; often the colors are jarring.

Yet this too, as Schröder writes, is intensely "christic." It is a kind of "hagiography of the 'accursed artist,'" an "iconography of mangled flesh."[57] Schiele intensely felt outcast and rejected, yet he found in this very rejection his redemption. In his ghastly self-portraits, Shiele becomes the "man of sorrows"; he becomes Christ. Schröder explains:

56. Klaus Albrecht Schröder, *Egon Schiele: Eros and Passion*, trans. David Britt (Munich: Prestel Verlag, 1999), 54.

57. Schröder, *Schiele*, 58, 74.

The mutual incomprehension of artist and public was the catalyst behind the whole iconography of the artist as outcast. The child, the obsessive, the savage, proclaimed the artistic virtues of the future: naivety, spontaneity, and freedom. . . . The literary prototypes of these masks of the artiste maudit were Baudelaire and Arthur Rimbaud: the latter was much prized by Schiele, whose own far from extensive library included a copy of a German translation of Rimbaud's poems. . . . The Christian imagery of artistic self-interpretation ranges from the artist as Demiurge to the artiste maudit, plagued by existentialist doubts. In the Classical Modernism of Western Europe, the use of such identification figures as the Monk, the Hermit, the Prophet, the Seer, the Preacher, the Voice Crying in the Wilderness or the Martyr was abandoned as "literary"; but in Vienna, Expressionists such as Schiele and Kokoschka kept Symbolism alive.[58]

Certainly the most famous artist-as-"man-of-sorrows" is Oskar Kokoschka's grotesque self-portrait in the poster he did for the magazine *Der Sturm* (1910). Denounced as a "criminal" by critics, young Kokoschka embraced the criminal image, and presented himself in the poster with his head shaven and his body scarred. In Christ's archetypal gesture, the image points with its left hand to a wound in his chest. The gesture is typically found in images of the risen Christ; in the *Sturm* poster, Kokoschka is both the "man of sorrows" and the "risen One." He is, then, doubly Christ.

Peter Altenberg was, no doubt, the most eccentric member of Young Vienna. He was an archetypical café bohemian. He slept until noon, only got himself going by late afternoon, and spent the evenings in a café or bar, arguing and writing. Indifferent to money and to appearance, Altenberg wore sandals and capes year-round regardless of the weather. As he got

58. Schröder, *Schiele*, 77.

older, his friends, including Karl Kraus, Adolf Loos, and Arthur Schnitzler, were forced to look after him.

Yet for all his oddity, Peter Altenberg was exactly like all the rest of them in his conviction that art was a sacred calling and that artists were modern saints. Their mission was to transform daily life in light of artistic revelation: "Art is art and life is life, but to lead life artistically, that is the art of life! We want the artistic, the exceptional, to pervade the everyday!"[59] Indeed, it is Peter Altenberg who offers one of the best summaries of the artist-saint-priest-prophet-shaman's mission in fin de siècle Vienna:

> Most people reach the summit of their life's energy, the limit of their emotional ability, only in rare and fleeting moments of their lives. It might be as they dress for their first ball, or the first time they touch the hand of their beloved. It might be while they travel to the theater or a morning trip . . . when they suddenly receive unexpected riches or when a loved one dies. In those moments, for just a moment, they inwardly become artists, they are torn, they experience a rush of joy or pain, they are shattered, they grow and develop. But artists are always at this kind of summit; everything can be such a moment for them. The fate of the world echoes in them, every suicide who plunges into the Danube is their murdered child. Maybe fifty times, an ordinary person becomes for a moment an artist. But for the artist, this is eternal, until the artist's day of death, this passion and intensity, this being torn apart and rising again![60]

59. Brisanz, *Altenberg*, 46.
60. Altenberg, *Reporter*, 65.

Chapter 9

SONG OF THE EARTH

Die liebe Erde allüberall
Blüht auf im Lenz und grünt aufs neu!
Allüberall und ewig blauen licht die Fernen!
Ewig . . . ewig . . .

(The dear earth everywhere
Blossoms in spring and grows green again!
Everywhere and forever the distance shines bright and blue!
Forever . . . forever . . .)

Gustav Mahler, *Das Lied von der Erde*

"Cosmic optimism," writes philosopher John Hick, is the mark of the world's great religious traditions. "Each tradition," Hick explains,

draws a radical distinction between the state from which we desire to be saved or released, or out of which we need to awaken, and the limitlessly better state to which it shows a way. There is a deeply pessimistic view of our present predicament, combined with a highly optimistic view of what is ultimately open to us. The pessimism understands ordinary human life to be fallen into sin and

277

guilt, or lived in disobedience and alienation from God, or caught
in the unreality of spiritual blindness . . . and the consequent round
of anxious suffering existence. . . . But there is also affirmation of a
limitlessly better possibility available to us because the Ultimate is,
from our human point of view, benign. By divine grace or divine
mercy, or by a gradual transcending of the ego point of view and a
realization of our own deepest nature, we can attain or receive our
highest good. And in so far as this limitlessly better state is said to
be available to everyone, the message of each of the great religions
constitutes good news for humankind.

I mean by cosmic optimism . . . then, that in each case, if their
conception of the nature of the universe is basically correct, we can
be glad to be part of it and can rejoice in and be thankful for our
present human existence. For the meaning of life is such that we
can have an ultimate trust and confidence, even — at least in principle — in life's darkest moments of suffering and sorrow.[1]

Hick refers here not to cosmic naiveté but to cosmic optimism, to a kind
of stance toward "the real" that fully accounts for pain and suffering and
death but which insists that "the real" can, despite everything, be trusted,
even loved.

Transfiguration is integral to this cosmic optimism. The believer not
only is optimistic about reality; the believer is profoundly converted,
transfigured, and transformed by the real. For Christians, of course, the
central metaphor for this transformative process rooted in cosmic optimism is resurrection. We will indeed die as Jesus died; we will not just
seem to die, or partly die, or pretend to die, but we will indeed be annihilated. And yet even in the process of annihilation we will somehow be re-
created. We will not only be resuscitated but resurrected; we will not only
be immortal but be utterly transformed.

It would be impossible to speak of a cultural movement's religious dimension in the absence of a process of conversion and cosmic optimism.
Can we speak of conversion and cosmic optimism in fin de siècle Vienna?

---

1. John Hick, *The Fifth Dimension* (Boston: Oneworld Publications, 1999), 51-52.

In 1862, Rudolf von Eitelberger, Vienna's first professor of art history, returned home from a visit to London, aquiver with energy and ideas. The 1860s witnessed the brief flowering of middle-class Viennese liberal optimism. Newly wealthy from Austria-Hungary's jump into capitalism, bubbling with confidence in human reason and ingenuity, fascinated by science and technology, secular, progressive, and cautiously democratic, Vienna's liberals were determined to transform stodgy old Vienna into a modern city. They turned Vienna inside out, ripped down the moldering old city wall and replaced it with the splendid Ring, and for a brief moment seemed to have Austria-Hungary's fate well in hand.

Rudolf von Eitelberger was one of these energetic liberals. In London Eitelberger had attended the *Exposition* of 1862, and had been deeply impressed by the South Kensington (now Victoria and Albert) Museum. The museum was designed both to showcase and to advocate the latest developments in science, technology, and industry. Just the sort of thing, Eitelberger was convinced, that Vienna needed. In 1863, prodded by Eitelberger's vigorous lobbying, the government agreed to create a *Museum für Kunst und Industrie,* a Museum for Art and Industry. In 1868, the museum generated its own craft school, the Kunstgewerbeschule, the School of Applied Arts.

From the beginning, the Kunstgewerbeschule was the rival of the older and far more prestigious Akademie der bildenden Künste, the Academy of Fine Arts. Fine arts students had infinitely more social prestige than mere craft students. Yet by the end of the century, the Kunstgewerbeschule had become a hothouse of artistic experimentation. Oskar Kokoschka was educated at the Kunstgewerbeschule, and so was another of the key artists of the fin de siècle, Koloman Moser.

Moser, born in 1868, was one of those rare creatures, a native Viennese. His father was an official at the Nobelgymnasium Theresianum auf der Wieden, the famous Theresianum gymnasium, in the Wieden section of the city, attended by Vienna's aristocratic elite. A born artist, young Moser enrolled in the Fine Arts Academy, but when his father unexpectedly died, Moser realized that he had a better chance at making a living were he educated in craft and design. When he was twenty-four, in 1892, Moser transferred to the Kunstgewerbeschule.

Moser studied with Franz Matsch, who, together with Ernst and Gustav Klimt, had founded the *Künstlercompagnie,* the "Artists' Company." Very quickly the same spirits that inspired Gustav Klimt whispered to Koloman Moser. Klimt and Moser, for example, both were commissioned to produce illustrations for *Gerlach's Allegorien.* Moser was fascinated by Klimt's imagination, and the two artists quickly became close friends. In 1897 Moser, with Klimt, was one of the enthusiastic leaders of the Vienna Secession, and many of the secession exhibition posters and *Ver Sacrum* covers were designed by Moser. The fluid line, the lithe female figures, the glowing colors, the springtime motifs, the floral arabesques, which have become iconic for the early secession, were in large part the creation of Kolo Moser. Josef Olbricht designed the Secession building, but it was Moser who enlivened its severe geometry with a frieze (now destroyed) of garlanded maidens and stylized owls. Moser was a participant in and organizer of all the major secession shows. But perhaps Moser's most important role was as organizer of the Wiener Werkstätte, the Vienna Workshops.

Moser, by the turn of the century, had become a professor at his alma mater, the Kunstgewerbeschule, and he and his colleagues and students were eager to play a more powerful role in the work of the avant-garde. They were designers and artisans, and in particular they wanted to expand the role of the crafts in the secession. The omnipresent Hermann Bahr fully endorsed their hopes. Bahr saw the crafts as the ideal bridge between the avant-garde arts and the textures of daily life. If art were to transform life in Vienna, the crafts would play the decisive transforming role. With all his typical energy, Bahr argued that

> What we need is the broad organization of an association between art and handicraft. . . . Give us a bridge! The two must finally come together. A gigantic studio, a colony of workshops, where artists work with craftsmen, teaching them and learning from them, craft growing out of art, art growing out of craft . . . so it is a matter of finding three or four artists, firstly free from historical constraints,

secondly, very lively modern people, and thirdly completely Austrian, and then giving these artists some trained craftsmen, and then arranging the influence of the one upon the other and creating a link between the arts and the crafts.[2]

The very modern Austrian artist, free from historical constraints, that Bahr had especially in mind to lead the project was Koloman Moser. The idea wasn't new; in fact, crafts such as Bahr had in mind already existed in Britain, and Moser, Klimt, and many others were thinking along the same lines as Bahr.

According to legend, the Wiener Werkstätte was born, appropriately enough, in a café, the Café Heinrichshof opposite the Opera on the Ring, when in 1902 Kolo Moser met with textile tycoon Fritz Waerndorfer. Wealthy and energetic, and an art patron, Waerndorfer had long supported the secession. At that meeting in the Heinrichshof, he agreed to bankroll Moser's experiment.

On May 19, 1903, the Wiener Werkstätte was born. The Wiener Werkstätte was registered with the city as a private, for profit company; its directors were Josef Hoffmann, Fritz Waerndorfer, and Koloman Moser. After a brief stay in temporary quarters on Heumühlgasse in Wieden, the Werkstätte moved to its permanent home on Neustiftgasse.

The first years were a time of boundless energy and exciting experiment. The Werkstätte was to translate art into daily life and daily life into art. Moser and Hoffmann, who actually ran the Werkstätte, insisted that everything, from office design to the showrooms to the workshops themselves, reflect the Werkstätte's artistic ambitions. There was to be no gap between the merely functional and the artistic, the mundane and the unique, the mechanical and the beautiful. If art were to transform life, that transformation, Moser and Hoffmann insisted, would begin with the Wiener Werkstätte.

The Werkstätte produced its own products for sale, and accepted special commissions. Its artisans made everything from candlestick holders to lamps to furniture to vases to jewelry boxes to mustard pots. Each item was to be, first of all, an item of daily life, something functional and useful.

2. Maria Rennhofer, *Koloman Moser*, trans. David Wilson (London: Thames and Hudson, 2002), 69.

Each item, though, was to be made of the finest materials available, and hand-crafted. Above all, each object was to be transformed, brought to life, energized, by a distinctive Wiener Werkstätte design, a design that was clean and crisp and geometrical, but a design that also made colors glow and lines shimmer.

Two years after its founding, the Wiener Werkstätte began a joint venture with the Flöge sisters, Helene, Pauline, and Emilie. The sisters had started a fashion shop at the Café Casa Piccola, on Mariahilfer Strasse. Helene was Ernst Klimt's widow, and Emilie was Gustav Klimt's beloved. The Flöge Salon's design philosophy was almost identical to that of the Wiener Werkstätte; the showroom itself was thought of as a work of art, the clothing was made of fine material, hand-crafted, and brought to life by the vibrant geometry characteristic of the secession. Moser worked with the sisters in designing the salon, its furniture, and the textiles for the clothing. Moser also became an active fashion photographer, and did a series of photos of Emilie Flöge modeling the salon's fashions.

In 1907, Moser left the Werkstätte to teach full-time at the Kunstgewerbeschule. He brought to his teaching an extraordinary ability to work in virtually any medium, which is why Hermann Bahr nicknamed Moser the "thousand-artist." Moser and his students designed advertising posters, handicrafts, furniture, and books. Moser designed postage stamps, banknotes, and playing cards. Eventually he would collaborate too with Vienna's elder statesman of architecture, Otto Wagner.

Otto Wagner was Vienna's master builder. Born in 1841, Wagner was twenty-seven years older than Kolo Moser. In fact, Wagner belonged to the generation before Moser and Klimt and the rest of the avant-garde.

Wagner began his career as simply another workaday Viennese architect. By the time he was a young man, Vienna was booming, people were flooding into the city from all over central Europe, the demand for housing was insatiable, and real estate speculators, contractors, builders, and architects made fortunes.

Wagner designed the hurriedly constructed apartment buildings typical of the time. Vienna's central historic district and the elegant Ring were home to the rich; workers and poor immigrants lived in the sprawling suburbs which grew up along the main roads which led, like spokes from a wheel, from the city center. The apartment buildings grew up along those spokes. Several stories high, they were built according to a standard formula: cheap materials were used; there was a strict and obvious division between the more expensive apartments on the second floor and the cheaper apartments at the top; there were usually two staircases, one for the expensive apartments, one for the cheaper ones; once up, the building was decorated with vaguely Greek-looking figures. Wagner proved to be a very effective builder; his projects came in on time, within budget, and he prospered. By the time he was fifty, he had become a prosperous and highly respected architect. He seemed hardly the man to spark a revolution.

Vienna's burst of expansion in 1890, though, inspired the radical angel in Wagner. The city had annexed the immense working class suburbs that were growing so uncontrollably. Now part of the city, these suburbs would need streets, sewers, and trams, and the city council wanted not a hodgepodge of projects but a single, coherent urban development plan. Otto Wagner and his colleagues won the competition and Wagner became, for a moment, Vienna's urban-planning tsar. Alas, as in so much of Viennese history, not much came of the huge project. Wagner's comprehensive urban plan, though, marked a fundamental break in the city's design and a profound shift in his architectural work.

Wagner's plan ruptured the whole mental world of the Ring. The Ring's designers had purposely erected monumental buildings in a variety of historical designs — Greek, Gothic, and Renaissance — everything, it seemed, but "modern." Yet it was precisely "modern" architecture that Wagner championed. In 1895, he published the book that would make him famous, *Die moderne Architektur* (*Modern Architecture*). In it, he argued that contemporary artistic creation must be rooted in contemporary life. It is the artist's task, and the architect's task, to help their contemporaries comprehend their world. Therefore, architecture must reflect not some other epoch; it must reflect its own time. "The task of art," Wagner wrote, "and therefore modern art too, remains always the same. Modern art must represent to us Moderns our abilities, our actions, forms that we ourselves have created."[3]

Architects, in fact, had no choice. Whether they willed it or not, times were changing. As Wagner wrote in a re-issue of *Modern Architecture* in

3. Otto Wagner, *Moderne Architektur* (Vienna: Anton Schroll, 1896).

1898: "Only three years have gone by, and everywhere the Modern has emerged victorious!"[4]

Modern life, Wagner argued, is dominated by science and technology, by speed and efficiency. Therefore, buildings, tram stations, and apartment buildings must, if they are to honestly speak to their own times, reflect these distinctly "modern" qualities. Here, of course, Wagner anticipated Adolf Loos's attack on the whole Ringstrasse historicist aesthetic.

Yet, at the very same time, Wagner insisted that the technological and functional had to be transformed from dead things into living forms. What he had in mind, of course, was what had already been nicknamed art nouveau, or *jugendstil*, the style that would become identified with Gustav Klimt and the secession. Wagner's architecture of the mid-1890s was a kind of three-dimensional echo of Klimt's paintings. Wagner's famous *jugendstil* tram station at the Karlskirche, for example, is both a functional object and yet, because of its vibrant line, somehow alive, energetic, playful, and humming.

In 1898, Wagner began building an apartment house on the Linke Wienzeile. Nicknamed the Majolika House, the building was supposed to be a normal Vienna apartment building, with shops below and apartments above. But Wagner, with the help of Kolo Moser, converted the Majolica House into something unique.

For this project, Wagner rejected most of the apartment building design conventions. In a striking nod to democracy, he insisted that all the apartment windows, whether looking out from the lower (and more expensive) or upper (and cheaper) apartments, be the same; there would be only one staircase, not one for the wealthy and one for the poor. But Wagner's most striking innovation was in collaboration with Moser. The front of the house was decorated, not with the fake Greek-looking statues, but with secessionist patterns: large medallions with stylized female heads and geometric floral patterns, all in bright gold.

In 1904, Wagner began work on a huge and seemingly endless project, the construction of Vienna's Postal Savings Bank. He worked on the project from 1904 to 1906 and then again from 1910 to 1912. The Postal Savings

4. Wagner, "Modern Architektur," in Otto Breicha and Gerhard Fritsch, *Finale und Auftakt: Wien 1898-1914* (Salzburg: Otto Müller, 1964), 190.

284

Bank was simply a utilitarian building, but Wagner transformed it into a monument of modern architecture. Like Loos, Wagner championed a clean, simple structure, and, as Carl Schorske writes, the Postal Savings Bank reflected its bureaucratic function:

> The imposing uniformity of bureaucratic rationalism was reflected in the very surface of the building, with its equalized, unobtrusive casements, its unadorned walls of marble slabs anchored by rich but simple aluminum bolts, its entrance efficiently capacious, yet unostentatious by comparison with the monumental portals favored in the Ringstrasse's earlier public buildings.[5]

Yet this was simultaneously an art nouveau building. The prominent bolts on the façade, which presumably held the building together, were, of course, purely decorative. The interior space, with its great vaulted ceiling, curved lines, and marble surfaces, is an enlivened and not simply structured space. The functional items in the interior, heaters and lights, for example, all call attention to themselves in a decorative, even playful way. This is indeed primarily a bureaucratic structure, but Wagner transformed deadened bureaucracy into something alive and joyful.

Even while he was working on the Postal Savings Bank, Otto Wagner simultaneously created one of his most remarkable structures, the St. Leopold Kirche am Steinhof. Steinhof was a psychiatric hospital in one of Vienna's outer districts. A church, dedicated to St. Leopold, was to be built on the hospital's grounds. Wagner won the contract.

Wagner's Kirche am Steinhof is clearly related to Josef Olbricht's Secession building; indeed, the church is a dazzling example of the seces-

---

5. Carl Schorske, *Fin de Siècle Vienna: Politics and Culture* (New York: Vintage, 1980), 91. Schorske notes that the building was encased in a dense political agenda. Its purpose was to provide state-supported inexpensive banking services, which would free the Viennese from the power of the big, commercial banks. This would seem to be a "populist" and anti-capitalist measure. At the same time, though, many of the big banks were associated with prominent Viennese Jewish families, and the postal-savings bank movement was entangled in populist anti-Semitism. Georg Coch, the government official who sponsored the postal-savings bank project, was, as Schorske says, a "martyr-hero" of the Christian anti-Semitic movement; a bust honoring him was placed in a small square across from Wagner's bank.

sion's "decorative functional style."[6] The church is basically a rigidly geometrical cross, formed by two intersecting rectangles. Atop the building is a large, gold dome. Though the church was built of brick, the brick is covered by glistening white marble, so that the entire building gleams in the sun. Two Assyrian-looking towers mark the entrance. The windows, based on designs by Kolo Moser, and the angels, by Othmar Schimkowitz, are all done in Viennese Secession style. The interior is breathtaking. Everything is white and gold. A gold baldachino covers the main altar; behind the altar is an immense Byzantine and very Klimt-like mosaic, again predominantly white and gold.

The construction of the church was plagued with controversy. Church officials especially complained about Kolo Moser's designs for the stained glass windows, partly no doubt because Moser had converted from Catholicism to Protestantism, making him a bit suspect to Catholic purists, and partly because, according to one church official, Moser's angels "are not angels but ladies blowing kisses!"[7] Critics mocked the church as a "memorial for an Indian maharajah," and ridiculed its style as "assyrian-babylonian-insane." Despite all the controversy, though, Wagner's art nouveau church was a remarkable achievement. It and the Postal Savings Bank are, in Carl Schorske's opinion, "perhaps the most radically modern monumental buildings built by a European state since the erection of the Eiffel Tower in 1889."[8] But, especially given its location in the midst of psychic pain, the Kirche am Steinhof is, more than anything else, a monument to the possibility of healing, conversion, and resurrection. Just as Wagner and his collaborators could transform mere stone and glass into a breathtakingly beautiful structure, so perhaps could the suffering patients in the state mental hospital at Steinhof be cured, and not only medically cured but psychically, and spiritually, saved.

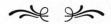

6. For a brief description and images of the church, see http://www.jugendstiltheater .co.at/kirche.htm.

7. Rennhofer, *Moser*, 159.

8. Schorske, *Vienna*, 239.

A sense that conversion and redemption through love were possible can be found too, even in the work of those most ferocious fin de siècle artists, Oskar Kokoschka and Egon Schiele.

In 1912, Oskar Kokoschka fell head over heels in love with Alma Mahler, the widow of Gustav Mahler.

Alma Mahler had been born Alma Schindler. Her father, Emil Schindler, was a respected artist. When he died, Alma's mother married one of Emil Schindler's pupils, Carl Moll.

As a young girl, Alma Schindler lived in the heart of Vienna's artistic world. She grew up to be a shockingly beautiful, talented, and ambitious woman; it seemed that every man in Vienna fell in love with her, and it appeared that she rather encouraged those many falls. She would later claim that Gustav Klimt had pursued her — her father, Emil Schindler, and her stepfather, Carl Moll, were artists and friends with Klimt. She studied music with Alexander von Zemlinsky — Arnold Schoenberg's teacher too — and Zemlinsky fell in love with her and even proposed marriage. But just before Christmas in 1901, Alma Schindler became engaged to Gustav Mahler. They were married in March 1902.

Gustav was forty-one; Alma was twenty-two. Obsessed with his own music, he explained to her (according to Alma) that he simply could never marry another musician, and that the only way they could marry would be if she abandoned her music. She agreed. Gustav and Alma had two little girls. Gustav and Alma no doubt loved each other; there is also no doubt that their marriage was stormy. Gustav Mahler was no easy person to live with, and neither was the beautiful, charming, and ambitious Alma Mahler. In 1910, deeply frustrated with her marriage, Alma went off for a cure at a resort in Toblach. As therapy for her depression, her physician prescribed dancing, of all things. Dancing, she met a young architect four years her junior named Walter Gropius. Gropius would of course be famous one day as one of the founders of the Bauhaus school of modern architecture; in 1910 he was a lovesick young man with a frantic crush on Alma Mahler.

Their relationship proceeded along lines Arthur Schnitzler could have invented. They met secretly and exchanged passionate letters. At one point, Gropius wrote her a heartbroken emotional letter, pleading with her to leave Mahler and run off with him. The letter he addressed, alas, for some odd Freudian reason, to "Herr Gustav Mahler." Gustav read the letter. Gustav insisted that he, Alma, and Walter meet; Alma agreed. Gustav insisted that Alma decide between him and Walter. Alma abandoned Gropius.

Gustav was exhausted both physically and mentally; his physician recommended a consultation with Sigmund Freud. Freud and Gustav Mahler met briefly in August 1910. Mahler explained that his life, and his marriage, were about to collapse. Freud encouraged Mahler to talk about his intimate life and his childhood, and suggested that maybe Mahler's trouble with Alma was partly a reflection of Mahler's trouble with his own mother. Their meeting was very brief, and Mahler later remarked that he was entirely unimpressed by psychoanalysis.

Gustav became a far more attentive husband. He began to encourage Alma's music, and helped her get some songs published. He left love notes on her pillow when he left in the mornings. But their marriage was doomed. Mahler was dying. On May 18, 1911, Mahler, aged fifty, died in Vienna.[9]

Walter Gropius immediately returned, and though they resumed their intense relationship, Alma Mahler insisted on remaining the respectable widow and heir to Gustav Mahler, at least for a time.

In 1912, Alma Mahler met Oskar Kokoschka.

Alma's stepfather, Carl Moll, was still an active artist. He had been impressed by Kokoschka's work, and invited him to do a portrait of Alma. They met in Moll's home in the lovely neighborhood of Hohe Warte. Kokoschka got his materials ready; Mahler sat for him. Here, according to her, is what happened next:

> He had brought some rough paper with him and wanted to draw. After a short time I told him that I couldn't be stared at like that and asked if I might play the piano while he worked. He began to draw, coughing all the time, and whenever he hid his handkerchief there were spots of blood on it. His shoes were torn, his suit was ripped.

9. The story of Gustav and Alma's troubled marriage is basic to every biography of either Gustav or Alma. See, for example, Michael Kennedy, *Mahler* (New York: Schirmer Books, 1990), 97-99; Henry de La Grange, *Gustav Mahler. Vienna: Triumph and Disillusion, 1904-1907* (New York: Oxford University Press, 1999), 86-91; 234-36; Norman Lebrecht, ed., *Mahler Remembered* (London: Faber and Faber, 1987), 280-84.

We scarcely spoke and he was nevertheless unable to draw. He stood up — and he embraced me suddenly and violently. I found this kind of embrace strange. . . . I returned it in no way, and precisely that appears to have affected him. He rushed out and in an hour I had the most beautiful letter of love and supplication in my hands.[10]

For Kokoschka, the next years were years of emotional torture. He was obsessed with Mahler. She was attracted to him, but she had, in part, defined herself as the keeper of Gustav Mahler's memory, and Kokoschka felt haunted by the dead composer. Anyway, Alma was still involved with Walter Gropius; there were rumors that she was somehow involved with composer Franz Schreker too; she did volunteer work with biologist Rudolf Kammerer, and Kammerer's wife insisted that Mahler and Kammerer were intimately involved.

And so, awkward, unsure, lovesick, and fabulously talented, Oskar Kokoschka very nearly went crazy. The affair was the talk of the avant-garde. Adolf Loos warned him to stay away from Alma Mahler. Kokoschka's mother urged her son to break with her. But Kokoschka dreamed that one day Alma would reject all the others and marry him, that they would have a home together, and children.

His dreams would be blasted. With regard to the home together: Alma Mahler was indeed building a villa in Vienna's Semmering district. Somehow Kokoschka got it into his head that the Semmering villa would be their home. But Alma was already sharing at least part of the villa with biologist Kammerer, who was studying toad reproduction. According to Kokoschka's biographer, Frank Whitford:

One day [Kokoschka] arrived at the house alone to find the living-room full of glass tanks with toads in them. Many of the toads had escaped and were mating. Obscenely coupled, they hopped and slithered across the floor and over the furniture. Kammerer, as Kokoschka well knew . . . must recently have been at the house conducting his experiments. In a rage, Kokoschka chased the creatures into the garden and smashed all the tanks.[11]

10. Frank Whitford, *Oskar Kokoschka* (New York: Atheneum, 1986), 89.
11. Whitford, *Kokoschka*, 94.

He would never share the villa with Alma. He was ecstatic when Alma told him she was pregnant with, according to her, his child. He was desperate to have the baby. Alma had an abortion.

Alma appears constantly throughout Kokoschka's art in those years. Their relationship is the subject of the most powerful painting of his early career, *Die Windsbraut (The Bride of the Wind)* (1914). In the image, a couple embrace. They seem to be floating in air (or is it water?), the air or water behind them turbulent and swirling. In the background, there are suggestions of other objects, mountains perhaps, lightning, and the moon, but they are obscured by the general chaos. The rough brushstrokes contribute to this tumultuous feel. The couple in the center is nude but partly draped. They seem oblivious to the turmoil through which they are floating. The woman's eyes are closed; she seems in deep repose. The man's eyes are open and his face seems fixed but expressionless. Is he sad? Resigned? At peace? Kokoschka's extraordinary friend, the poet Georg Trakl, stared at the image and suggested its title, *Die Windsbraut*.

The pairing of turmoil and love is entirely appropriate to Kokoschka's terrible experience. In the painting, the turmoil is externalized and becomes part of nature; love has become calm and peaceful. Perhaps, as Frank Whitford suggests, Kokoschka was thinking along Wagnerian *Liebestod* lines. *Liebestod* — literally "love-death" — is, of course, an archetypal Wagnerian theme. True love is spiritual love; the chaos of daily life constantly interferes with spiritual love; spiritual love, then, can only be fulfilled when the lovers are free of life's chaos around them; but one can only be freed from the pains of life by death; therefore, spiritual love can only find fulfillment in death. Perhaps these floating lovers, floating in but free of the riotous air around them, are spirits, joined at last in spiritual unity.

Multiple readings of the work are of course possible. The male figure's expression is especially difficult to read. One might argue that, while the woman sleeps, he cannot, and that his inability to sleep is a sign not of happiness but of a troubled spirit. But Kokoschka himself thought of the work in much more positive terms. He thought of it as a testimony to love and peace, to the love and peace he never could find with Alma, but which he longed for desperately. To Kokoschka, his painting is a painting of transformation and reconciliation through love. This is what Kokoschka wrote to Alma:

> The picture is slowly being finished . . . we two with a very strong, peaceful expression, our hands entwined, on the edge, in a semi-circle, a sea illuminated as though by Bengal fire, a water-tower, mountains, lightning, and the moon . . . in the midst of the confusion of nature, to trust one person eternally and through faith to make oneself and the other secure.[12]

Schiele was, to be sure, the painter of pornographic images and obscene, nude, self-portraits. Yet there was much more to Schiele's work than that. Like Klimt and Kokoschka, Schiele supported himself partly by painting portraits, and his portrait work, such as the picture of his father-in-law, *Johann Harms* (1916), or *Marga Boerner* (1917), suggest a certain calm, even repose. Schiele did a variety of landscapes, and though done with his signature jagged line and blocky colors, the landscapes express peace and even serenity. But perhaps Schiele's most striking expression of hope and redemption was one of his very last works, *The Family* (1918).

Some of *The Family*'s power is simply biographical. For all his obsession with identity and intimacy, for all his raw sexual fantasies, Schiele's personal life was remarkably stable. For years, his great love was Wally Neuzil. Though they never married, Wally was his model, his companion, his fellow bohemian. But as Schiele entered his mid-twenties, he changed.

A less generous interpretation is that Schiele was becoming respectable. His work was selling, some of his reviews were glowing, and his reputation was slowly shifting from *enfant terrible* to serious artist. He had tired of the bohemian life; he wanted stability and respect; Wally, poor girl and artist's model, simply didn't fit in any longer. A more generous interpretation is that Schiele, by his mid-twenties, was finally growing out of adolescence, but unfortunately, his and Wally's relationship, for whatever reason, just did not grow as well.

Schiele fell in love with another, Edith Harms, the daughter of a respectable middle-class family. Edith loved Egon, she admired his work, she

12. Whitford, *Kokoschka*, 95-96.

was even quite willing to pose for him as Wally had, but Edith had no interest in living a bohemian life, and certainly had no intention of entering some bizarre ménage à trois with Wally. Egon would have to decide. He did. Egon and Wally broke up; Egon and Edith were married in 1916.

Their marriage was a happy one. They looked forward to having a baby; astonishing as it might seem, Schiele, the perennial troubled adolescent, looked forward to being a dad. The 1918 portrait *The Family* is an expression of this marital love, and this hope for children.

The Family is a multiple-nude portrait. Schiele sits in the background, his right arm raised and his right hand shaped in that rigid gesture typical of his portraits. He looks directly at the viewer. But this nude self-portrait has none of the horror of his earlier self-portraits. His genitals are modestly hidden by Edith, sitting in front of him, and his body is almost in a relaxed pose. His facial expression too is calm, perhaps even slightly inquisitive. Before him, nude as well, sits Edith. She looks away from the viewer with a tired air. What is astonishing, though, is what is at Edith's feet — a baby, with a remarkably sweet face. Edith and Egon had no children when Egon did the portrait. The child in the picture, then — indeed, the picture itself — is an image not of the present reality but of the future hope.

The Family is an amazingly poignant image. It is poignant because of its contrast to Schiele's earlier tortured and tormented work. It suggests that Schiele was emotionally capable now of something well beyond screams. The picture is poignant too because of its hope, expressed by the child. The viewer knows, as Egon and Edith did not, that their hope would not be fulfilled, and that makes the picture all the more touching. There is no exuberance in *The Family*; Edith's expression is weary, Egon's is wondering; the colors are muted; the emotional tone is tranquil but perhaps a little sad as well. And yet, for all that, the most powerful message in *The Family* is the message that change is possible, that love is possible, that a future founded on love, however unlikely, can at least be imagined, that one's imagination can, in fact, be charged not only by what is, but by what may come to be.

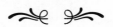

The single most compelling statement of conversion, love, and transcendence, however, was composed by Gustav Mahler in 1907, during the single most horrible year in his often deeply painful life.

The year 1907 was a dreadful year for Gustav Mahler. To begin with, his ten-year run as Vienna's greatest conductor ground to an unhappy end. Conducting in Vienna had been Mahler's life's dream. He had arrived in Vienna in 1897, at the young age of thirty-seven, first as the opera's conductor, then as the philharmonic's conductor too. The next years had been intense beyond belief. Driven, a perfectionist, Mahler had made some of the greatest music in the world, and many bitter enemies too. Small things angered some people, like his refusing to let latecomers bumble into the concert hall. Larger things, like breaking up the claques which performers often hired to applaud them, seemed to rupture long-held traditions. He could be brutally demanding of his performers. Working furiously all season long, and then frantically writing his own music all summer, Mahler had exhausted himself. In 1907, Mahler resigned his positions in Vienna and announced that he would be leaving for America, to conduct in New York City.

In July 1907, his little daughter Maria, whom Mahler called "Putzi," came down with scarlet fever and diphtheria. The family was on summer holiday. Mahler and "Putzi" were especially close. Every morning she would march into her father's study and the two would have long talks. She suffered for two weeks, and died on July 5. She was only four and a half years old. Both Gustav and Alma were very nearly destroyed by her death.

Meanwhile, that same year, something ominous seemed to be happening to Mahler's health. In January he had gone to the doctor — he had chronic throat infections, some of them very severe — and the doctor had detected some sort of heart irregularity. Gustav assured Alma that it was nothing, though in March both Bruno Walter and Alfred Roller saw him, according to biographer Michael Kennedy, "suddenly stand still while he was on stage directing the chorus in a rehearsal of *Lohengrin* . . . turn white as a sheet and clutch his heart."[13]

Then, that summer, the summer that little "Putzi" died, Mahler again

13. Kennedy, *Mahler*, 80.

went to a doctor, who sent him to a heart specialist. What happened be-tween them no one knows, though it is almost certain that Mahler learned that he had an irreparable heart defect that would kill him very soon.

Gustav Mahler left Vienna in December of that ghastly year. A whole host of admirers, virtually all of the fin de siècle avant-garde, turned out to wave goodbye — Arnold Schoenberg, Bruno Walter, Alfred Roller, Alex-ander von Zemlinsky, Gustav Klimt, and several scores of others. As the train pulled away, someone heard Klimt mutter "Vorbei," "it's all over."[14]

Over the next two years, Mahler would complete two remarkable symphonies, *Das Lied von der Erde* and his Ninth Symphony; he would, as well, leave notes behind for a tenth symphony. Of all these, *Das Lied von der Erde* (The Song of the Earth) especially serves as Mahler's final word about his life, his death, and his hope.

In 1906, Mahler had completed his enormous Eighth Symphony, the "Symphony of a Thousand," with his passionate call for divine inspiration, "Veni, creator spiritus," and its triumphant assertion that all of us, even great sinners like Faust, can be saved, saved especially by the divine ex-pressed through the "eternal feminine." By the end of the very next year, 1907, Mahler knew he was dying.

Death was hardly a new topic for Mahler, but now he had to face the experience of his own imminent death. The first thing that he felt was a deep disturbance in his soul, as calm and peace fled and left only agitation and apprehension behind. Mingled with this agitation and apprehension were a host of other, uncontrollable feelings: loneliness, terror, anger, a heart-broken nostalgia for joys long past, grief for his little life which had flown by so quickly, resignation, a determination to face what he had to face with dignity, a persistent hope that this death would not mean annihi-lation, and, strangely enough, an intense love: love for his life, for his loved ones, for nature and the human comedy within it. As he wrote to his friend Bruno Walter:

> If I am to find my way back to myself, I have got to accept the hor-rors of loneliness. I speak in riddles, since you do not know what

14. Kennedy, *Mahler*, 82. Also La Grange, *Gustav Mahler*, 792.

has gone on and is going on within me. It is, assuredly, no hypochondriac fear of death, as you suppose. I have long known that I
have got to die. . . . Without trying to explain or describe something
for which there probably are no words, I simply say that at a single
fell stroke, I have lost any calm and peace of mind I ever achieved. I
stand vis-à-vis de rien and now, at the end of my life, I have to begin
to learn to walk and stand.[15]

It was in that terrible year, 1907, that Mahler's friend, Theobald Pollak,
gave him a copy of Hans Bethge's *The Chinese Flute*. Things Chinese were all
the rage in Europe around the turn of the century. The book was a collection of eighty-three Chinese poems that Bethge had accumulated from
French, German, and English translations. Chinese experts have since
pointed out that the translations vary in quality and the attributions aren't
always accurate, but nevertheless, Mahler found the poetry enchanting. It
was precisely the kind of poetry he had always loved, fairytale like, seemingly naïve and childlike, and yet, in its ability to articulate moments of
human feeling, very touching. He selected six of them, and, as he had always done, he began reworking them, rearranging these lines, deleting
those, adding some of his own. He began setting them to music.

As the music developed, it was clear that Mahler was working on a
ninth symphony. Always superstitious, Mahler was frightened by the
phrase "ninth symphony"; his great hero, Beethoven, had completed only
nine symphonies before his death; Mahler's friend and teacher, Anton
Bruckner, had completed nine symphonies and then he died. To call this
new work his "ninth" symphony seemed to Mahler to be nothing less than
courting death. Besides, though constructed like a symphony, the work
was really a kind of song cycle, and so Mahler began to refer to the work as
Das Lied von der Erde (The Song of the Earth).

The musical material in *Das Lied von der Erde* is strikingly new — indeed, critics would later argue that much of the music really belonged to
the "new music" just then emerging especially in the work of Schoenberg
and his pupils Alban Berg and Anton Webern. It is gentle and often heartbreaking music:

15. Deryck Cooke, *Gustav Mahler: An Introduction to His Music* (New York: Cambridge
University Press, 1988), 106; the letter was written in 1909.

The clarity of the instrumentation (for normal orchestra with extra wind) is as masterly as ever, but the hardness has practically vanished; in the main, the lines are sharper and thinner, or fainter and more disembodied. The material, evoking a quasi-Chinese atmosphere with the pentatonic scale, and often advancing further the tonal disruption of the Sixth and Seventh Symphonies, is full of deep heartache; this is Mahler's most purely personal style. The use of tonality is largely psychological, yet a "progression" can be discerned — inevitably a falling one: the tonal sequence of the first five movements (A minor, D minor, B flat, G, A) implies a finale in D (minor) but in fact it is a tone lower, in C minor.[16]

Das Lied von der Erde begins with the text "The Drinking Song of Earth's Sorrow," based on a poem by Li Tai-Po. The singer calls on the listeners to drink up! — but — first "sing ich euch ein Lied!" ("I'll sing you a song").

It is an unhappy song, a "Lied vom Kummer" (a song of sorrow), in the vein of "eat, drink, and be merry — for tomorrow we die." Sadness approaches; joy and song will die; the refrain reminds the listener that "Dunkel is das Leben, ist der Tod" ("Dark is life, is death"). The song contrasts the "eternally blue sky" with the shortness of an individual's life. Near the end, there is a moment of grotesque horror:

Seht dort hinab! Im Mondschein auf den Gräbern
Hockt eine wild-gespenstische Gestalt.
Ein Aff' ist's. Hört ihr, wie sein Heulen
Hinaufgellt in den süssen Duft des Lebens!

(Look down there! In the moonlight, on the graves
Squats a wild spectral figure.
It is an ape! Listen how his howling
Screams its way through the sweet fragrance of life!)[17]

---

16. Cooke, *Mahler,* 104.

17. Cooke, *Mahler,* 109. This and other translations of the texts are by Cooke. For other commentary on *Das Lied von der Erde,* see, for example, Egon Gartenberg, *Mahler: The Man and His Music* (New York: Schirmer Books, 1978), 336-46; Kennedy, *Mahler,* 155-65; Constantin Floros, *Gustav Mahler: The Symphonies* (New York: Amadeus Press, 2003), 243-70.

The music is built around a quiet and sad A minor; the text itself is bleak indeed; and yet there is, in Cooke's words, "an exquisite central section for orchestra, a shimmering vision of earth's beauty."[18] Michael Kennedy writes that *Das Lied von der Erde* "has everything: it is filled with indefinable sadness and longing yet ultimately it is not depressing; it is simple in design; it is fantastically beautifully scored; and it provides the soloists with wonderful opportunities."[19] Mahler had always spent the summers up in the mountains, in the midst of earth's beauty, composing. The summers were times of escape from the exhausting opera and philharmonic seasons, and the mountains calmed Mahler, and triggered in him a powerful sense of transcendence. Romantic that he was, Mahler always felt free in the mountains, and not only free but transformed. The superhuman size of the mountains, the limitless vistas, and nature's eternal cycle helped him feel the breath of the divine. And so this first song captures several of the many layers of emotions surging in Mahler: grief, and horror, yes, but also at least the possibility of peace provoked by recollection of his beloved mountains.

The second movement, the slow movement, is built around the song "The Lonely One in Autumn," attributed to Tschang Tsi. The text evokes the death of the year: mist covers the lake, frost covers the grass; the summer flowers are all dead; a cold wind blows. The mood, musically and poetically, is weary and resigned. "Mein Herz is müde," the singer sings, "My heart is tired." And yet, even here, at the onset of winter's death, the singer feels not simply resignation but yearning for another spring.

> Ich weine viel in meinen Einsamkeiten.
> Der Herbst in meinem Herzen währt zu lange.
> Sonne der Liebe, willst du nie mehr scheinen,
> Um meine bittern Tränen mild aufzutrocknen?
>
> (I weep much in my loneliness
> The autumn in my heart persists too long
> Sun of love, will you never shine again
> And dry up, tenderly, my bitter tears?)[20]

18. Cooke, *Mahler*, 107.
19. Kennedy, *Mahler*, 156.
20. Cooke, *Mahler*, 110.

The texts in the third, fourth, and fifth movements recall youth, beauty, and springtime; all are based on texts by Li Tai-Po. Musically they are scherzos in, respectively, B flat, G, and A. They recall, among many other things, Mahler's childlike love of forests and flowers and birdcalls. The fifth text, "Drunkard in Springtime," includes a remembered moment of innocent delight:

> Was hör' ich beim Erwachen? Horch!
> Ein Vogel singt im Baum.
> Ich frag' ihn ob Frühling sei,
> Mir is als wie im Traum.
>
> Der Vogel zwitschert: Ja!
> Der Lenz ist da, sei kommen über Nacht!
> Aus tiefstem Schauen lauscht' ich auf,
> Der Vogel singt und lacht!
>
> (What do I hear when I awake? Listen!
> A bird sings in the tree.
> I ask him if the spring is here;
> I feel as if I were dreaming.
>
> The bird twitters, "Yes!
> Spring is here — came overnight!"
> In deepest wonder I listen,
> The bird sings and laughs!)[21]

But death abruptly intervenes. The finale, the work's longest single part, is an adagio, sad and painful. The instrumentation, the melodies, the strained tonality, everything contributes to an overpowering sadness. This work is not about some titan defying fate. This is, instead, about a fragile and vulnerable human being, who loves life, and is heartbroken that his life is over.

The text is called "The Farewell"; it is attributed to Wang Wei. It tells of a speaker awaiting a friend; the friend is coming to say goodbye. It is night in the poem, the moon is up, and nature is fast asleep. The friend arrives.

21. Cooke, *Mahler*, 112.

The heartbroken speaker asks why the friend must depart. The friend, saying goodbye, explains:

> Du, mein Freund,
> Mir war auf dieser Welt das Glück nicht hold!
> Wohin ich geh'? Ich geh,' ich wand're in die Berge.
> Ich such Ruhe für mein einsam Herz!
> Ich wandle nach der Heimat, meiner Stätte!
> Ich werde niemals in die Ferne schweifen.
> Still is mein Herz und harret seiner Stunde!

> (Ah! My friend —
> Fortune was not kind to me in this world!
> Where am I going? I am going to wander in the mountains,
> I seek rest for my lonely heart!
> I journey to the homeland, to my resting place;
> I shall never again go seeking the far distance.
> My heart is still and awaits its hour!)

Then the text takes a surprising turn. The narrator, presumably the "I" who has said goodbye to his departing friend, returns to the image that has wafted throughout the entire work, the image of nature, dying surely, but just as surely blossoming again every spring, mixing with the certainty of death and decay the equally powerful certainty of new life. The text ends gently, hushed:

> Die liebe Erde allüberall
> Blüht auf im Lenz und grünt aufs neu!
> Allüberall und ewig blauen licht die Fernen!
> Ewig . . . ewig . . .

> (The dear earth everywhere
> Blossoms in spring and grows green again!
> Everywhere and forever the distance shines bright and blue!
> Forever . . . forever . . .)[22]

22. Cooke, *Mahler*, 113.

Das Lied von der Erde is the most intimate, most personal, and perhaps most poignant work Mahler ever created. His Ninth Symphony instrumentally expresses many of the same emotions. Mahler was as nervous about the magic term "ninth symphony" as ever, and he only half jokingly referred to this as, well, actually his "tenth," that is, if you counted *Das Lied von der Erde* as his ninth, which it wasn't exactly. This final work was unquestionably a symphony, and Mahler couldn't escape calling it his "ninth."

Technically, the Ninth continues to demonstrate Mahler's increasingly experimental approach not only to the symphonic form but also to the very stuff of western art music, tonality and harmony. Psychologically, the Ninth starkly reworks the materials from *Das Lied von der Erde*. Death, doom, and annihilation dominate the first movement. According to Alban Berg, "The whole [first] movement is permeated by the premonition of death. Again and again it makes itself felt."[23]

The two middle movements recall the grotesque ape shrieking over the graves in the first song in *Das Lied von der Erde*. Both are dances, but the dances are awkward and frightening. Though they include lovely moments, both are dominated by a shrill dissonance.

Mahler was working on a tenth symphony when he died in 1911. It is impossible to know how Mahler would have completed it, yet his notes are full enough to provide a strong sense of his ideas. His Tenth was to have five movements; it returned to the concerns and motifs of the Ninth; technically, it too included some of the "new music" dissonance and atonality. Part I would have an adagio followed by the first scherzo; Part II would begin with an allegretto moderato (Mahler scribbled "Purgatorio") at its head, followed by a second scherzo, and then the finale.[24]

The fourth movement ends with a single drum stroke. As Kennedy recounts, that simple note was charged with meaning. Gustav and Alma had been staying at the Hotel Majestic in New York. A funeral procession went by. A brave firefighter, Deputy Chief Charles Kruger, had died of in-

23. Cooke, *Mahler*, 114.
24. For more on the unfinished Tenth, see Kennedy, *Mahler*, 174-79; Gartenberg, *Mahler*, 357-66; Cooke, *Mahler*, 118-21; Floros, *Mahler*, 297-17.

juries while fighting a fire. The procession halted briefly by the Mahlers' hotel. A drummer tapped a single stroke on his muffled drum. Gustav Mahler burst into tears. Chief Kruger's drum stroke reappears in the Tenth Symphony.[25]

The finale, according to Cooke, "transmutes horror and bitterness into courageous acceptance and unquenched belief in life, musically as well as emotionally." The finale seems to be a conflict between a "lyrical melody of strange, unearthly beauty," and somber, shrill, sometimes frightening death music. That death music is powerful and intrusive, and yet, at the finale's conclusion, it is the "soaring lyrical melody" which returns, and which ends the symphony "with a sigh of great tenderness." As it concludes, it "fades into the distance, full of a profound peace."[26] According to Cooke, "this is not the music of death but — as is confirmed by Mahler's avowal of devotion to his wife written over the last bars — of love."[27]

Das Lied von der Erde, the Ninth Symphony, and the unfinished Tenth Symphony, all written in an astonishing burst of creativity as Mahler was dying, form a distinct trilogy. Cooke thinks that in the trilogy, certainly in *Das Lied von der Erde,* Mahler's "hard-won religious faith had deserted him."[28] In the trilogy, neither "God" nor any explicitly religious imagery appears. Certainly the trilogy is not about doctrine, or churches, or Scripture; the comforts a dying man might find in traditional religion are not found in the trilogy.

Still, all three works are about transfiguration, and specifically about the transfiguration of death and all its awful spawn — fear, pain, regret, despair — into life, and hope, and especially into love. Perhaps the most powerful expression of this occurs in the finale of the Ninth in which the death music is transfigured into a hymn to life.

Human life alone? Clearly not. Mahler obviously is not simply praising routine human existence, but whatever that force, that power is, that gives and sustains life. To speak ontologically, he is not simply praising "being," but whatever it is that makes "being" actually "be." Is it, then, na-

25. Kennedy, *Mahler,* 177.
26. Cooke, *Mahler,* 118.
27. Cooke, *Mahler,* 121.
28. Cooke, *Mahler,* 106.

ture that Mahler praises? Is he in some sense a pantheist? Mahler does indeed passionately love nature — he prefers to speak not of "resurrection" exactly but of "spring" — and no doubt there is more than a little pantheism in Mahler's religious imagination.

Yet it is not really nature either that Mahler praises, that comforts and sustains him. When the friend in the final poem in *Das Lied von der Erde* speaks of "returning home," he is referring of course to his grave, and thereby a return to the recurring cycles of nature. But "nature" is not the last word in *Das Lied von der Erde;* the last word is "ewig . . . ewig," which can be translated as "forever" or "eternal"; "Ewigkeit" is "eternity." The hushed conclusion of the Ninth, in which the music fades away into the distance, again evokes a sense of "eternity."

But what is this "ewig . . . ewig," this "forever" (as in "forever and ever, amen") and "eternity"? Is it nature? Or does it rather somehow include but also transcend nature?

Mahler's final trilogy, with its recurring evocation of nature, parallels classic landscape painting, particularly Dutch sixteenth- and seventeenth-century landscapes. The landscapes, like Mahler's trilogy, evoke nature. The landscapes, like Mahler's trilogy, are devoid of explicit "religious" content (the Dutch artists were sufficiently influenced by Calvinism to regard explicitly "religious" art as dangerously idolatrous). And yet, in the landscapes, as in Mahler's trilogy, the very absence of explicit god-references only heightens the presence of the divine. As Gene Veith explains, the Dutch landscape painters did not want to mimic Michelangelo and reproduce God as an old, if powerful male; such an image seemed not only idolatrous to the Dutch but also fundamentally inadequate. "God," they were sure, was transcendent, overwhelming, and eternal. How could one visually evoke an experience of the transcendent, the overwhelming, and the eternal? By removing from the image any reductionist god-image and replacing it with vistas of sky, plain, and ocean. In early modern Dutch landscape painting, vistas are not merely vistas; they are evocations of the eternal.[29]

To be sure, the analogy wobbles. But what is important to note is that

---

29. For a detailed discussion of this "art of transcendence," see Gene Edward Veith, *Painters of Faith* (Washington, D.C.: Regnery, 2001), especially chapter 2, "Images Not Graven," 19-34.

Mahler's turn to nature in his final trilogy does not simply mean that he had become either a materialist or a pantheist. Mahler indeed loved nature, but he also loved that to which nature pointed. As he prepared for the grave, what Mahler saw in and through his beloved nature was the "eternal," associated in his mind, as the conclusion of the unfinished Tenth suggests, above all with tenderness and love.

FINALE

Religion . . . is ultimate concern . . . religion is the substance, the ground, and the depth of man's spiritual life.

Paul Tillich[1]

Bertha Szeps-Zuckerkandl liked to tell this story:
In 1902, France's great sculptor Auguste Rodin visited Vienna. All the avant-garde turned out to greet him. They took him to the Secession building to see the Beethoven exhibition. They took him out to the Prater. They dined outdoors, in one of the Prater's gardens; Rodin flirted with the pretty girls; Gustav Klimt, acting as host, asked a friend to play some Schubert on the piano.

> Rodin leaned over to Klimt and said: "I've never felt what I feel here with you. Your *Beethoven-fresco,* so tragic and yet so holy. Your ex-hibit in that temple of art, and now this garden, these women, this music! Around you all, in you, this childlike joy. What is all this?"
>
> I translated Rodin's words for Klimt. Klimt nodded and said a single word: "Österreich" (Austria).[2]

1. Paul Tillich, *Theology of Culture* (New York: Oxford University Press, 1978), 5.
2. Bertha Szeps-Zuckerkandl, in Harry Zohn, *Der farbenvolle Untergang* (Englewood Cliffs, N.J.: Prentice-Hall, 1971), 135.

Klimt's Österreich did not survive the Great War.

On that chilly and sad December night in 1907, when Gustav Mahler and his family took the train from Vienna, when Gustav Klimt murmured "vorbei," "it's over," Klimt wasn't exactly right. The extraordinary cultural blossoming known as "fin de siècle Vienna" had some seven more years to live.

Chronology is always a tricky business, and not everyone would agree that the Viennese fin de siècle was finished by 1918. A case can be made that something of the fin de siècle mood survived until the Nazis took over Austria in 1938. After all, Freud stayed on in Vienna after World War I, and so did Karl Kraus and Arthur Schnitzler. Hermann Bahr and Hugo von Hofmannsthal remained in Austria too. Adolf Loos stayed in Vienna and became one of the great advocates of "modern" architecture. The whole experience of the dying Habsburg world continued to fire artists' imaginations; many of Josef Roth's novels, and Robert Musil's enormous work, *Der Mann ohne Eigenschaften (The Man Without Qualities)*, were written after World War I but evoked the old, still compelling, Habsburg ghosts. At the end of World War II, the great Austrian novelist, Hermann Broch, was asked to write an introduction to a collection of Hofmannsthal's poetry; the introduction turned into a two-hundred-page study of that long dead but somehow still living fin de siècle world.

Josef Roth once wrote that the Great War was called a "world" war "not because the entire world conducted it, but because, owing to it, we all lost a world, our world."[3] Actually, several worlds were destroyed by World War I, among them the world of fin de siècle Vienna.

Gustav Mahler, of course, died in 1911.

Poor Georg Trakl, schizophrenic and paranoid, was drafted into the army when the war began. Since he had been to pharmacy school, the army made him a medical corpsman. The sights he saw in the frontline hospitals to which he was assigned were more gruesome than anything even he had ever dreamed. In terror and panic he tried to flee, and when he couldn't flee, he tried to commit suicide. He succeeded late in 1914 with an overdose of cocaine. His beloved sister Grete committed suicide three years later.

3. Paul Hofmann, *The Viennese* (New York: Doubleday, 1988), 162.

In 1918, the Austro-Hungarian Empire not only lost the Great War, but was itself destroyed. Left behind was a preposterous creature, little Austria with the huge, former imperial capital, Vienna, as its head.

Otto Wagner died in 1918. In 1918, Kolo Moser was diagnosed with cancer and he was dead before the year was out. Klimt and both Egon and Edith Schiele died in 1918.

True, not everyone died. But the war and the destruction of the empire profoundly scarred everyone.

Consider, for example, Oskar Kokoschka's fate. Kokoschka, like so many other young people, saw the war at first as a glorious explosion. He joined the cavalry and sold *Die Windsbraut* to raise money for a uniform. Just before he left Vienna, he completed a strange painting he called *The Knight Errant* (1914). In it, Kokoschka, in armor, is sprawled out from left to right through the center of the painting, as if wounded. He appears to be on some sort of promontory; behind him is a roiling ocean. The sky above is dark and threatening. To the viewer's right, in the ocean, a strange female creature, half-human, but also half-beast — Alma Mahler? — seems to be retreating from the wounded knight. In the grim and scary air, an angel of death. The letters "E S" float in the sky — a reference, in Kokoschka's personal code, to the dying Christ's last words, "Eli, Eli, lama sabachthani" ("My God, my God, why have you forsaken me?").

If indeed the painting was done early in the war — and there is some dispute about the painting's actual date — it is, as Frank Whitford writes, "evidence for [Kokoschka's] visionary powers."[4] The vision was ominous, and the next years would be terrible for him.

He remained obsessed with Alma Mahler, but she had long since lost interest in him. In 1915, she married Walter Gropius, moved with him to Berlin, and the following year gave birth to a daughter.

In 1915 too, only eleven days after Alma had married Gropius, Kokoschka was in battle against Cossacks on the eastern front. His horse was shot out from under him. He was shot in the head. Many years later, he described what happened next:

---

4. Some critics argue that the painting was done later in the war; Kokoschka biographer Frank Whitford tentatively dates it early in the war. See Frank Whitford, *Oskar Kokoschka* (New York: Atheneum, 1986), 100.

I lay for some days on the ground until Russian Cossacks began to kill the badly wounded with their long bayonets. . . . I opened my eyes and saw an enemy soldier dispatching several of my comrades, who were screaming loudly, into the other world. Now I knew it was my turn. In my hand, the one that was not paralyzed, I felt my revolver which was pointing directly at the man's chest. He could not see the danger because I was in his shadow. He bent over me. I cocked the revolver, my finger squeezed the trigger. The bullet was in the chamber. Then his bayonet entered my jacket and I thought I could not bear the pain but knew that it was only the jacket. There was still time for me to save myself. But I could not shoot the enemy soldier because my mind was not so confused as to permit me to murder the Russian who was only carrying out an order. Now I felt the weapon very slowly penetrating the skin, the fat on my ribs and then going into the ribs. The pain was terrible . . . then [it] ceased as the weapon entered my lung . . . my head felt light. I was happy as I was never happy again. I floated on air. Blood flowed from my nose, ears and mouth and blinded my eyes. Dying was so simple and easy that I suddenly had to laugh in the soldier's face.[5]

Kokoschka obviously survived, though he suffered severe pain and constant hallucinations. Because of his head wound, he would suffer bouts of dizziness for the rest of his life. After he recovered, the army put him back on active duty, and he was nearly killed a second time. When the war finally ended, and Kokoschka got out of the army, he would leave Vienna forever. For a time, he dragged along with him an inflatable female doll that he painted and re-painted many times. He would prop it up next to him when he went drinking.

As for Alma Mahler, now Alma Gropius, her marriage lasted a matter of months. She discovered that she didn't love Walter Gropius after all; she thoroughly disliked his family, and she was unhappy in Berlin. By 1916, though still married to Gropius, she had become involved with writer Franz Werfel.

So, it is quite true that some survived the devastation of the Great

5. Whitford, *Kokoschka*, 105.

War: Freud, Schnitzler, Hofmannsthal, Bahr, Kokoschka, Alma Werfel, and others. Yet it seems hard to deny that by 1918, the drama had ended.

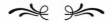

That the *Wiener Moderne* was an extraordinary moment would be impossible to deny. "Modernism" had many creators, but the role of the Viennese avant-garde in the creation of "modernism" was enormous. But was Viennese modernism in any sense "religious"? Can Viennese modernism be a text for theology?

Richard Viladesau notes that, at least until the mid-nineteenth century, art in Europe was typically an art *of* theology, that is, an art which explicitly dealt with religious themes. But in the eighteenth century, and certainly by the nineteenth century, saints and demons and madonnas began disappearing from the visual arts; composers less and less frequently composed hymns and masses; writers rarely wrote about God, or heaven, or spirits. Art largely ceased to be a text *of* theology.

But, Viladesau asks, can art still be a text *for* theology? That is, can theology still share common ground with arts that seem, at least on the surface, to be resolutely secular? Viladesau argues that the "modern" arts, despite their apparently secular nature, remain a rich text *for* theology for at least three reasons.

First, art and theology both share a deep concern with beauty, as well as with truth and goodness. Though some modern artists might only grudgingly agree that beauty, truth, and goodness have anything to do with art, and though some theologians might forget that beauty, as well as truth and goodness, is one of the traditional attributes ascribed to the divine, beauty, truth, and goodness remain central concerns for both artists and theologians.

Second, both theologians and artists share what Paul Tillich has called a "method of correlation." Theology, Tillich argues, attempts to comprehend those issues central to human life at any given moment and address those issues from the perspective of faith. Art attempts to do something similar. Artists do indeed express themselves subjectively in their work, but behind every work, as Viladesau says, is always a "world," that is, a set of assumptions and concerns, prejudices and hopes, that express questions and answers about the human situation. Both art and theology, then, share a common attempt to address the deepest human concerns.

Finally, both art and theology have as their central concern the transcendent. By the very act of creating something new, artists transcend the here and now, the way things are, and the powers that be. Artists, in the very act of creation, attempt to "incarnate" the immaterial but very real visions they experience. Theologians too are concerned with the transcendent, with expressing the transcendent's nature and actions, with articulating the human encounter with the transcendent. Therefore, Viladesau insists, yes, art, even apparently secular art, can indeed be fruitful text *for* theology.[6]

In fact, the whole "modernization as secularization" thesis may well be quite wrong. No doubt, all the great changes that swept Europe in the eighteenth and especially nineteenth centuries — the immense prestige of science and technology; industrialization; urbanization, and so on — fundamentally changed religious structures and values. Yet the assumptions that God had died, that the spiritual had become irrelevant, that religious phenomena had ceased, and that therefore theological language had lost any explanatory power, may themselves be dead. Not God but secularism has been the great myth of the modern age.[7]

But if religious phenomena remain potent in modern times, what about this one particular modern time, fin de siècle Vienna? Is it true to say that fin de siècle Viennese modernism was profoundly religious? As surprising as it may seem at first blush, one must conclude that fin de siècle Viennese modernism was an intensely religious phenomenon.

6. Richard Viladesau, *Theology and the Arts* (New York: Paulist Press, 2000), especially chapter 3, "Art as a Theological Text."

7. For an introduction to some of the literature on the debate about the "secularization hypothesis," see, for example, Peter Berger, ed., *The Desecularization of the World* (Grand Rapids: Eerdmans, 1999); Linda Woodhead and Paul Heelas, eds., *Religion in Modern Times* (Malden, Mass.: Blackwell, 2000); Philippa Berry and Andrew Wernick, eds., *Shadow of Spirit: Postmodernism and Religion* (New York: Routledge, 1992); Douglas McGaughey, "Through Myth to Imagination," *Journal of the American Academy of Religion* 56, no. 1 (2001); Edith Wyschogrod and John Caputo, "*Postmodernism* and the Desire for God: An E-Mail Exchange," *Cross Currents* 48, no. 3 (Fall 1998).

What Richard Viladesau has argued about art in general clearly applies to the work done by the Viennese avant-garde. The avant-garde were not simply entertainers, and for all their commitment to subjectivity, they were doing much more than merely "expressing themselves." They were intensely committed to beauty, truth, and goodness. Klimt, Mahler, Loos, and all the rest saw their work simultaneously in aesthetic, ontological, and ethical terms. They were determined to create new artistic modes of expression because those modes were beautiful, because they were true to reality, and because they were morally good.

The Viennese avant-garde, like theologians, used a kind of "method of correlation." They desperately wanted to speak to, and for, their age. With their distinctive obsessions and fears, especially those about death and rebirth, change, sexuality, identity, and intimacy, the avant-garde were mirrors of their generation.

But they also wanted to be physicians to their generation. Their repeated refrain was: "this is false, but this is true"; "this is fake, but this is genuine." Unlike some "postmodernists" who deny that we can distinguish between the "fake" and the "genuine," the Viennese modernists insisted that such distinctions, though difficult indeed, not only could be made but also had to be made.

The Viennese modernists wanted, like theologians and religious sages, to talk about, and to, the "real." They not only wanted to speak to and for the human condition; they wanted to speak to, and for, "reality." Not only reality as defined by the quotidian, but reality as defined as foundational — not the "seemingly real," but the "really real."

One of the most striking things they learned about the real is that it is alive. The real is intrusive and revelatory; its sudden and surprising appearances are "weird." The "real," "being itself," is hardly limited to humanity or human consciousness. The "real," "being," utterly transcends the human. Therefore, "being" is inherently mysterious and "weird." Transcendent and superhuman, the "real" is also everywhere, acting, moving, and changing things, intruding unexpectedly.

The weird both annihilates and engenders; it is both terrifying and fascinating. To nervous male minds it appears as feminine; to adolescent minds it appears erotic. The weird kills, but the weird impregnates too.

And in the end, despite all the terrors of invasion and annihilation, the

Viennese avant-garde experienced the intrusion of the "real" as love, and because they experienced reality as love they could endure reality with hope.

The Viennese avant-garde were doing ontology by metaphor. Ontology was born when a handful of ancient Greeks began to have the odd, frightening, yet simultaneously fascinating sensation that just possibly the world they were living in was somehow not the real world, that the lives they were living were somehow fake lives. But what then would be a "real" life? How can we distinguish between "illusion" and "reality," between "seeming" and "being"? From Plato's cave to late twentieth-century films like "The Matrix," humans have engaged in ontology, in the struggle to distinguish between "seeming" and "being," not simply out of some leisurely curiosity, but out of the urgent need to know how they should live, and how they should die, and whether any of it matters anyway.

"God," Paul Tillich famously argued, is not simply another being that, like unicorns, may or may not exist, no one knows for sure, opinions differ, who's to say, and so on. "A God about whose existence or nonexistence you can argue," Tillich writes," is a thing beside others within the universe of existing things."[8] But when we speak about "God" we speak about "reality," about "being," about that which makes the "real" real, that which makes "being" be. "God," to use Tillich's phrase, is the Unconditioned, that is, reality as it really is. Our awareness of the Unconditioned is a matter of "ultimate concern" because meaning, purpose, and trajectory to our lives can be found only in "being," not in "seeming," only in the Unconditioned, not in the conditional. A life lived according to "seeming" is not only fake but disastrous.

Therefore, to continue with Tillich, we are, or should be, "ultimately concerned" about the Unconditioned. Such "ultimate concern" about the Unconditioned is called faith. According to Tillich, "religion . . . is ultimate concern . . . religion is the substance, the ground, and the depth of man's spiritual life."[9]

All of us, sooner or later, confront the Unconditioned, either because we seek it, or much more likely, because it seeks us. The Unconditioned is

8. Tillich, *Theology of Culture*, 5.
9. Tillich, *Theology of Culture*, 7-8.

reality; if telling the truth means speaking in accord with reality, then the Unconditioned is the foundation of truth. Thus, it is not simply a logical parlor trick to note, as Augustine did, that whenever we say that "it's true that God doesn't exist," we are actually trying to be true, to be truthful; we are asserting that there is indeed truth (though we may be mistaken about it, to be sure); thus an atheism which appeals to some standard of truth is, in the end, an affirmation of God.[10]

No doubt, much that we claim to be true is false; much that we think real is an illusion; much that we say about God is really a human projection and distortion. God, the Unconditioned, transcends human institutions and categories, and therefore maybe we ought to retire the word "God," as Tillich suggested, and clean it as well as we can of human accretions. Maybe we ought even to think about "God beyond God" — that is, the Unconditioned that lurks behind our human ideas of God. Judaism, Christianity, and Islam all began as a kind of atheism: angry rejections of idolatry.

Every time we attempt to transcend the way things are, every time we become aware of the way the transcendent intrudes into the way things are, we experience the Unconditioned. There is nothing occult in this; it does not necessarily imply visions, speaking in tongues, or handling snakes (though it doesn't exclude those, either). An experiential awareness of the Unconditioned is not, and cannot be, humanly provoked (which would imply that we humans control the Unconditioned, that we can conjure it up at will — which is, in fact, magic). Though an awareness of the Unconditioned involves knowledge, it is more than a kind of cognition, because it includes ultimate concern. Being able to recite the capitals of the world's major countries is a (primitive) form of cognition, but such an activity has very little to do with me, with my life, with what or who I should love; such cognition does not engage my ultimate concern. An encounter with the Unconditioned, however, engages my ultimate concern, and thus engages me intellectually, emotionally, and spiritually.

Tillich argues that much modern thought, from Kierkegaard and Nietzsche to Heidegger, is an effort to understand the meaning of the Unconditioned. An encounter with the Unconditioned occurs, for instance,

---

10. Tillich, *Theology of Culture*, 12.

in an *Augenblick,* in that blink of an eye when time seems to pause, or rupture entirely, when things become terribly important. It occurs in that moment of *kairos,* the moment of "fulfilled time" when joy or sorrow or hope or despair seems especially intense. An awareness of the Unconditioned occurs in those odd times of *Gleichzeitigkeit,* or "simultaneity," when, through memory, time cracks and the past flows into the present; or when, through hope, the future rushes into the present and we are touched by the future and care deeply about that touching.[11]

Can we articulate this awareness? Such articulation is fraught with hazard, Tillich thinks. The danger involved "is the danger of every embodiment of the Unconditional . . . that it elevates something conditioned, a symbol, an institution, a movement as such to ultimacy."[12] The danger, in other words, is idolatry, confusing symbols with what they symbolize, thinking mistakenly that we should look at the finger instead of that to which the finger points.

We humans do not and cannot conjure up the Unconditioned. We can be, at times, grasped by the Unconditioned. "Faith," Tillich writes, "is the state of being grasped by an ultimate concern, and God is the name for the content of that concern."[13] To have no ultimate concern is to be in despair. To be ultimately concerned about that which is not ultimate is to be idolatrous. To be grasped by ultimate concern for that which is ultimate is to have faith.

We can articulate the experience of faith best through symbols. Symbolic expression is not simply an option we have; symbolic expression is really the only way we can express that which transcends expression. Symbols are more than mere signs, of course. Signs point to some specific and finite object. Symbols point to the Unconditioned, to the inexpressible, to the Holy. Symbols are intensely "subjective" and personal; they "work" only when they touch some cord in me for whatever biographical or psychological reason. Symbols that "work" for some do not work for all. Yet symbols are "objective" too in that they point not simply to me or to themselves but beyond me and them to the Unconditioned. Symbols

11. Tillich, *Theology of Culture,* 99-100.
12. Tillich, *Theology of Culture,* 29.
13. Tillich, *Theology of Culture,* 40.

are "realistic" in that they use forms of expression rooted in the familiar world around me, the world I know. But symbols are simultaneously "idealistic" — that is, they point to reality beyond the conventions of the here and now.[14]

Symbolic language, then, is precisely the language needed if we are to describe, or re-create, moments of awareness of the Unconditioned. Great art does ontology, then, by metaphor. And this is what occurred in the turbulent world of the avant-garde in fin de siècle Vienna.

In 1996, the Museum of Contemporary Art in Chicago hosted an exhibition entitled "Negotiating Rapture." The show focused on the work of a variety of late twentieth-century artists such as Francis Bacon, Joseph Beuys, Agnes Martin, Barnett Newman, and others. The premise of the show was that art can express and evoke extraordinary moments of understanding and enlightenment that in more traditional religious language might be described as moments of "rapture" — moments when we encounter the Unconditioned. The show suggested that what artists do is "negotiate rapture"; that is, they attempt to translate immediate, intensely personal experience into languages, images, colors, and tones others can understand. It is a very difficult type of mediation among, for instance, that which is experienced, the artist, the medium the artist uses, the wider culture, and the audience. Often it fails; sometimes it succeeds.

But isn't this what religion does? Indeed. But art does it as well, and there may be times when art does it even more powerfully that the institutions of religion. It is a commonplace to point out that "art became religion" during the Viennese fin de siècle, but it is a profound commonplace. Art did indeed become religion, and thereby assumed the grave dangers, and transcendent purposes, of religion.

Joseph Shapiro was the founding president of the Chicago Museum of Contemporary Art. His comments preface the catalog to the "Negotiating Rapture" show. They serve as a fitting conclusion as well to this long reflection on the *Wiener Moderne*:

> Art, "the mirror held up to nature," provides a reflection of the interior self. For of all man's endeavors, art, with its plenitude and reso-

---

14. Tillich, *Theology of Culture*, 71.

nance, has the capacity to articulate those primordial and eternal mysteries that inhabit the psyche — the soul, the secret realities — and make them perceptible through image, symbol, and metaphor. . . . We need art's organizing power to impose order on nature, both physical and human; to defend against the chaos of fragmentation and dissolution; and to clarify our perceptions and conceptions about existence, life, and death. . . .

Art in modern times bears a resemblance to religious ritual and the sense of deeply felt shared experience. As a surrogate for religion, art combats the emptiness and malaise that permeates these anxious, dehumanized times. In short, it creates a world of imagination that can transfigure the human spirit.[15]

---

15. Richard Francis, ed., *Negotiating Rapture: The Power of Art to Transform Lives* (Chicago: Museum of Contemporary Art, 1996), x.

BIBLIOGRAPHY

I. Primary Sources

A. Periodicals

Das Andere
Arbeiter Zeitung
Die Fackel
Die Neue Freie Presse
Neues Wiener Tagblatt
Reichspost
Ver Sacrum

B. Published Primary Sources

Der Adel und der Conservatismus in Osterreich. Vienna, Lechner, 1878.

Altenberg, Peter. *Reporter der Seele.* Edited by Gunther Martin. Vienna: Stiansny-Verlag, 1960.

Bahr, Hermann. *Gegen Klimt.* Vienna: Eisenstein, 1903.

———. *Tagebücher.* Berlin: Paul Cassirer, 1909.

———. *Selbstbildnis.* Berlin: S. Fischer, 1923.

———. *Prophet der Moderne — Tagebücher 1888-1904.* Edited by Reinhard Farkas. Vienna: Böhlau Verlag, 1987.

Beth, Karl. *Urmensch.* Berlin: Runge, 1909.

Bibliography

Braasch, August Heinrich. *Die religiösen Strömungen der Gegenwart.* Leipzig: B. G. Teubner, 1909.

Bresler, Johann. *Die Niederösterreichischen Landes- Heil- und Pflege-Anstalten für Geistes-und Nervenkranke "am Steinhof" in Wien.* Vienna: Psychiatrisch-Neurologische Wochenschrift, 1908.

Bruck-Auffenberg, Natalie. *Die Frau 'comme il faut.'* Vienna: Verlag Wiener Mode, undated.

Brüsselbach, J. *Religion und Wissenschaft.* Leipzig: Rust, 1893.

Capesius, Victor. *Die Zustände in der evangelische Gemeinde A.C. in Wien.* Wien: Selbstverlag, 1895.

Ehrhard, Albert. *Der Katholizismus und das zwanzigste Jahrhundert.* Vienna: Roth'sche Verlag, 1902.

"An English Officer." *Society Recollections in Paris and Vienna, 1879-1904.* London: John Long, 1907.

Fechner, Gustav. *Das Buchlein vom Leben nach dem Tode.* Hamburg: Voss, 1896.

Felden, Emil. *Protestantische Kirchen in Deutschland.* Frankfurt: Neuer Frankfurter Verlag, 1902.

Göhre, Paul. *Die neuste Kirchenaustrittsbewegung aus den Landeskirchen in Deutschland.* Jena: Diederich, 1909.

Harnack, Adolf. *Die Dienstentlassung des Pfarrers Lic. G. Traub.* Leipzig: Hinrich, 1912.

Harpf, Adolf. *Das Weibwesen.* Vienna: Ostara, 1906.

Haupt, Hermann, ed. *Quellen und Darstellungen zur Geschichte der Burschenschaft und der deutschen Einheitsbewegung,* Volume 1. Heidelberg: Carl Winter, 1910.

Hellmer, Erwin. *Die öffentliche Armenpflege in Osterreich im allgemeinen und die Armenpflege der Stadt Wien insbesondere.* Vienna: Zentralverband der Wiener Waisenräte, 1907.

Hellwig, Albert. *Verbrechen und Aberglaube.* Leipzig: Teubner, 1908.

Henning, Max. *Römische Afterreligion oder "Frankfurter Lümmeleien"?* Frankfurt: Neuer Frankfurter Verlag, 1909.

Herbatschek, Heinrich. *Ein Indizienprozess. Der Fall Sautner.* Vienna: Im Selbstverlag, 1913.

Hevesi, Ludwig. *Acht Jahre Sezession.* Vienna: Carl Konegen, 1906.

Hoensbroech, Paul Graf. *Des Jesuiten von Nostitz-Reineck Schrift: Graf Hoensbroechs Flucht aus Kirche und Orden.* Leipzig: Breitkopf und Härtel, 1913.

von Hofmannsthal, Hugo. *Loris. Die Prosa des jungen Hugo von Hofmannsthal.* Berlin: Fischer, 1930.

———. *Hugo von Hofmannsthal: Poems and Verse Plays.* Edited and translated by Michael Hamburger. New York: Bollingen, 1961.

———. *Gesammelte Werke.* Frankfurt: Fischer, 1979.

Bibliography

Hold, Karl. *Austria Sancta. Die Heiligen und Seligen Niederösterreichs*. Vienna: Mayer and Company, 1913.

Horneffer, Ernst. *Die künftige Religion*. Leipzig: Klinkhardt, 1909.

Jacobi, W. "Die Ekstase der Alt-Testamentlichen Propheten," *Grenzfragen des Nerven und Seelenlebens*, Vol. 108. Munich: Bergmann, 1920.

Kalweit, Paul. *Die Stellung der Religion im Geistesleben*. Leipzig: Teubner, 1908.

Kaminka, Rabbi Armand. *Wird das Gute Belohnt?* Vienna: Moriz Waizner, 1902.

Kappstein, Theodor. *Psychologie der Frömmigkeit*. Leipzig: M. Heinsius, 1908.

Kläger, Emil. *Durch die Wiener Quartiere des Elends und Verbrechens*. Vienna: Karl Mitschke, 1908.

Kokoschka, Oskar. *Mein Leben*. Munich: Bruckmann, 1969.

Kralik, Richard. *Heiliges Osterreich*. Vienna: Vogelsang, 1922.

Kraus, Karl. *Sittlichkeit und Kriminalität*. Frankfurt: Fischer, 1966.

———. *Die Demolierte Literatur*. Steinbach: Anabas Verlag, 1972.

———. *In These Great Times*. Edited and translated by Harry Zohn. Manchester: Carcanet Press, 1976.

Landsdale, Maria Horner. *Vienna and the Viennese*. Philadelphia: Henry T. Coates, 1902.

von Laveseye, Emil. *Protestantismus und Katholizismus in ihren Beziehungen zur Freiheit und Wohlfahrt der Völker*. Nördlingen: Beck, 1875.

Lebrecht, Norman, ed. *Mahler Remembered*. London: Faber and Faber, 1987.

Leitich, Ann Tizia. *Verklungenes Wien*. Vienna: Wilhelm Andermann, 1942.

Levetus, A. S. *Imperial Vienna*. London: John Lane, 1905.

Lipiner, Siegfried. *Buch der Freude*. Leipzig: Breitkopf and Härtel, 1880.

Loos, Adolf. *Trotzdem*. Innsbruck: Brenner Verlag, 1931.

———. *Ins Leere Gesprochen, 1897-1900*. Innsbruck: Brenner Verlag, 1932.

Mach, Franz. *Die Krisis im Christentum und die Religion der Zukunft*. Dresden: E. Pierson, 1908.

Mantegazza, Paul. *Die Physiologie der Liebe*. Trans. Eduard Engel. Jena: Costenoble, 1885.

Merschmann, Friedrich. *Die Idee der Unsterblichkeit*. Berlin: Heinersdorff, 1870.

Meyer, Jürgen Bona. *Der Mainzer Katholikentag, der Fall Harnack, und die Gottlosigkeit unserer Universitäten*. Hamburg: Richter, 1893.

Milde, Natalie. *Gegenwart und Zukunft der Familie*. Weimar: Selbstverlag, 1902.

Minichthaler, Josef. *Heilige in Osterreich*. Vienna: Tyrolina Verlag, 1935.

Moerchen, F. *Die Psychologie der Heiligkeit*. Halle: Carl Marhold, 1908.

Naumann, Viktor. *Die zweite Wahrmundbroschüre*. Vienna: Styria, 1908.

Pfleiderer, Otto. *Theorie des Aberglauben*. Berlin: Carl Habel, 1872.

———. *Die Religion, ihr Wesen und ihr Geschichte*. Two volumes. Leipzig: Fues' Verlag, 1878.

Pfungst, Arthur. *Ein Deutscher Buddhist. Oberpräsident Theodor Schultz.* Stuttgart: Frommann, 1901.

Popp, Adelheid. *Jugendgeschichte einer Arbeiterin.* Munich: Ernst Reinhardt, 1909.

Redlich, Hans. *Gustav Mahler.* Nürnberg: Hans Carl, 1919.

Roessler, Arthur. *Erinnerungen an Egon Schiele.* Vienna: Wiener Volksbuchverlag, 1948.

Salten, Felix. *Das Österreichische Antlitz.* Berlin: Fischer, 1909.

———. *Wurstelprater.* Vienna: Rosenbaum, 1911.

———. *Gestalten und Erscheinungen.* Berlin: Fischer, 1913.

Schlögl, Friedrich. *Aus Alt- und Neu-Wien.* Vienna: Carl Teufen, 1882.

Schmidt, Heinrich. *Der Kampf um die "Welträtsel."* Bonn: Emil Strauss, 1900.

Schneider, Georg. *Zweck und Ziel des Deutschkatholicismus.* Wiesbaden: Limbarth, 1884.

———. *Lehrbuch für den religiös-sittlichen Unterricht in freireligiösen Gemeinden.* Frankfurt: Neuer Frankfurter Verlag, 1904.

Seuse Denifle, Heinrich. *Das geistliche Leben.* Graz: Moser, 1879.

Seydel, Rudolf. *Religion und Wissenschaft.* Breslau: Schottlaender, 1887.

Sichler, Albert. "Die Theosophie (Anthroposophie) in psychologischer Beurteilung." *Grenzfragen des Nerven- und Seelenlebens* 112 (1921): 1-43.

Steed, Henry Wickham. "The Quintessence of Austria." *The Edinburgh Review* 454 (October 1915): 225-30.

Strunz, Franz. *Über antiken Dämonenglauben.* Prague: Deutscher Verein zur Verbreitung gemeinnütziger Kenntnisse, 1905.

Troels-Lund, Professor. *Himmelsbild und Weltanschauung im Wandel der Zeiten.* Translated by Leo Bloch. Leipzig: Teubner, 1899.

Wagner, Otto. *Moderne Architektur.* Vienna: Anton Schroll, 1986.

Wahrmund, Ludwig. *Religion und Klerikalismus.* Innsbruck: A. Edlinger, undated.

———. *Das deutsche Reich und die kommenden Papstwahlen.* Frankfurt: Neuer Frankfurter Verlag, 1903.

Weininger, Otto. *Geschlecht und Charakter.* Vienna: Wilhelm Braumüller, 1918.

Die Wiener Landes- Heil- und Pflegeanstalten für Geistes- und Nervenkranken "am Steinhof." Vienna, 1934.

Wiener Magistrat, ed. *Kurzgefasster Führer durch die Wiener öffentliche Armenpflege.* Vienna: Gerlach and Wiedling, 1909.

Wiesinger, Albert. *Das Anti-Christentum.* Vienna: Doll, 1895.

Windelbrand, W., ed. *Die Philosophie im Beginn des zwanzigsten Jahrhunderts.* Heidelberg: Carl Winter, 1907.

Zuckerkandl, Bertha. *Zeitkunst Wien, 1901-1907.* Vienna: Hugo Heller, 1908.

———. *Österreich Intim. Erinnerungen, 1892-1942.* Frankfurt: Propyläen, 1970.

"Zum 25. Jährigen Bestande der Wiener Landes- Heil- und Pflegeanstalt "am Steinhof." Vienna: Psychiatrisch-Neurologische Wochenschrift, 1932.

II. Secondary Sources

Anderson, Mark, ed. *Reading Kafka*. New York: Schocken, 1989.

Andics, Helmut. *Luegerzeit. Das schwarze Wien bis 1918*. Vienna: Jugend und Volk, 1984.

Bauer, Wilhelm. *Georg Ritter von Schönerer*. Klagenfurt: Das deutsche Volksbildungswerk, 1941.

Baumann, Gerhart. *Arthur Schnitzler: Die Welt von Gestern eines Dichters von Morgen*. Frankfurt: Athenäum, 1965.

Beckson, Karl. *London in the 1890s: A Cultural History*. New York: Norton, 1993.

Berger, Peter, ed. *The Desecularization of the World*. Grand Rapids: Eerdmans, 1999.

Berkley, George E. *Vienna and Its Jews*. Cambridge: Abt Books, 1988.

Berman, Marshal. *All That Is Solid Melts Into Air: The Experience of Modernity*. New York: Penguin, 1988.

Berner, Peter, Emil Brix, Wolfgang Mantl, eds., *Wien um 1900. Aufbruch in die Moderne*. Vienna: Verlag für Geschichte und Politik, 1986.

Berry, Philippa, and Andrew Wernick, eds. *Shadow of Spirit: Postmodernism and Religion*. New York: Routledge, 1992.

Bettelheim, Bruno. *Freud's Vienna and Other Essays*. New York: Knopf, 1990.

Blum, Mark E. *The Austro-Marxists, 1890-1918: A Psychobiographical Study*. Louisville: The University Press of Kentucky, 1985.

Boyer, John W. *Political Radicalism in Late Imperial Vienna*. Chicago: University of Chicago, 1981.

Breicha, Otto, and Gerhard Fritsch, eds. *Finale und Auftakt. Wien 1898-1914*. Salzburg: Otto Müller, 1964.

Brisanz, Hans. *Peter Altenberg: Mein Ausserstes Ideal. Altenbergs Photosammlung von geliebten Frauen, Freunde und Orten*. Vienna: Verlag Christian Brandstätter, 1987.

Brisanz-Prakken, Marian. *Gustav Klimt. Der Beethovenfries*. Vienna: Residenz Verlag, 1977.

Broch, Hermann. *Hofmannsthal und seine Zeit*. Frankfurt: Suhrkamp, 1974.

Bundespolizeidirektion Wien, ed. *80 Jahre Wiener Sicherheitswache*. Vienna: Jugend und Volk, 1949.

Castle, Eduard. *Die Neue Generation um Hermann Bahr*. Vienna, Carl Fromme, undated.

Clair, Jean, ed. *Vienne 1880-1938. L'Apocalypse Joyeuse*. Paris: Editions du Centre Pompidou, 1986.

Bibliography

Comini, Alessandra. *The Fantastic Art of Vienna*. New York: Knopf, 1978.

Cooke, Deryck. *Gustav Mahler: An Introduction to His Music*. New York: Cambridge University Press, 1988.

Copland, Aaron. *Music and Imagination*. Cambridge: Harvard, 1952.

Crankshaw, Edward. *The Fall of the House of Hapsburg*. London: Longmans, 1963.

———. *Vienna: The Image of a Culture in Decline*. London: Macmillan, 1976.

Daviau, Donald. *Der Mann von Ubermorgen. Hermann Bahr, 1863-1934*. Vienna: Residenz Verlag, 1984.

Dijkstra, Bram. *Idols of Perversity: Fantasies of Feminine Evil in Fin-de-Siècle Culture*. New York: Oxford University Press, 1986.

Dixon, John. *Art and the Theological Imagination*. New York: Seabury, 1978.

Dupré, Louis. *The Other Dimension*. New York: Doubleday, 1972.

Eckstein, Modris. *Rites of Spring: The Great War and the Birth of the Modern Age*. New York: Houghton Mifflin, 1989.

Edwards, Tudor. *The Blue Danube: The Vienna of Franz Josef and Its Aftermath*. London: Robert Hale, 1973.

Eliade, Mircea. *Patterns in Comparative Religion*. New York: Meridian, 1958.

Elstun, Esther N. *Richard Beer-Hofmann*. University Park: Pennsylvania State University Press, 1983.

Engel, Gabriel. *Gustav Mahler*. New York: The Bruckner Society of America, 1932.

Fenz, Werner. *Koloman Moser*. Vienna: Residenz Verlag, 1976.

Field, Frank. *The Last Days of Mankind: Karl Kraus and His Vienna*. New York: St. Martin's, 1967.

Fischer, Jens Malte. *Karl Kraus*. Stuttgart: Metzler, 1974.

Fischer, Wolfgang Georg. *Gustav Klimt und Emilie Flöge*. Vienna: Christian Brandstätter, 1987.

Floros, Constantin. *Mahler: The Symphonies*. Portland, Ore.: Amadeus Press, 2003.

Francis, Richard, ed. *Negotiating Rapture: The Power of Art to Transform Lives*. Chicago: Museum of Contemporary Art, 1996.

Friedl, Gottfried. *Gustav Klimt*. Translated by Hugh Beyer. Cologne: Benedikt Taschen, 1991.

Friedländer, Otto. *Letzter Glanz der Märchenstadt. Das war Wien um 1900*. Vienna: Molden-Taschenbuch-Verlag, 1969.

Fuchs, Albert. *Geistige Strömungen in Österreich, 1867-1918*. Vienna: Globus, 1949.

Gall, Franz. *Alma Mater Rudolphina, 1365-1965. Die Wiener Universität und Ihre Studenten*. Vienna: Austria Press, 1965.

Gartenberg, Egon. *Johann Strauss: The End of an Era*. New York: Da Capo, 1974.

———. *Gustav Mahler: The Man and His Music*. New York: Schirmer Books, 1978.

Gay, Peter. *Freud: A Life for Our Time*. New York: Norton, 1988.

———. *Schnitzler's Century*. New York: Norton, 2002.

Geretsegger, Heinz, and Max Peintner. *Otto Wagner*. Vienna: Residenz Verlag, 1983.

Graziano, Frank, ed. *Georg Trakl*. Durango, Colo.: Logbridge-Rhodes, 1983.

Grunfeld, Frederic V. *Prophets without Honor: A Background to Freud, Kafka, Einstein and Their World*. New York: McGraw-Hill, 1980.

Hayman, Ronald. *Nietzsche: A Critical Life*. New York: Penguin, 1980.

Hick, John. *The Fifth Dimension*. Boston: Oneworld Publications, 1999.

Hofmann, Paul. *The Viennese*. New York: Doubleday, 1988.

Hofmann, Werner, ed. *Experiment Weltuntergang. Wien um 1900*. Munich: Prestel Verlag, 1981.

Imboden, Michael. *Die surreale Komponente im erzählenden Werk Arthur Schnitzlers*. Frankfurt: Lang and Cie, 1971.

Irwin, Alexander. *Saints of the Impossible*. Minneapolis: University of Minnesota Press, 2002.

Janik, Allan, and Stephen Toulmin, *Wittgensteins Wien*. Translated by Reinhard Merkel. Munich: Carl Hanser, 1984.

Jenks, William A. *Vienna and the Young Hitler*. New York: Columbia, 1960.

Johnston, William M. *Vienna, Vienna: The Golden Age, 1815-1914*. New York: Crown, 1980.

Kann, Robert. *A History of the Habsburg Empire, 1526-1918*. Berkeley: University of California Press, 1974.

Kennedy, Michael. *Mahler*. New York: Schirmer Books, 1990.

Kern, Stephen. *The Culture of Space and Time*. Cambridge: Harvard University Press, 1983.

Kindermann, Heinz. *Hermann Bahr*. Graz: Böhlaus, 1954.

Kovach, Thomas A. *Hofmannsthal and Symbolism*. New York: Peter Lang, 1985.

La Grange, Henry-Louis de. *Gustav Mahler. Vienna: The Years of Challenge, 1897-1904*. New York: Oxford University Press, 1995.

————. *Gustav Mahler. Vienna: Triumph and Disillusion, 1904-1907*. New York: Oxford University Press, 1999.

Lang, Oskar. *Anton Bruckner*. Munich: Beck, 1943.

Lehne, Inge, and Lonnie Johnson. *Vienna: The Past in the Present*. Vienna: Bundesverlag, 1985.

Luft, David S. *Robert Musil and the Crisis of European Culture*. Berkeley: University of California Press, 1980.

Malinowski, Bronislaw. *Magic, Science, and Religion*. New York: Doubleday, 1954.

May, Arthur. *Vienna in the Age of Franz Josef*. Norman, Okla.: University of Oklahoma Press, 1966.

McGrath, William J. *Dionysian Art and Populist Politics in Austria*. New Haven: Yale University Press, 1974.

Bibliography

Mitchell, Donald. *Gustav Mahler: Songs and Symphonies of Life and Death.* New York: Boydell Press, 2005.

Morton, Frederic. *A Nervous Splendor: Vienna 1888-1889.* New York: Penguin, 1979.

Müller, Karl-Josef. *Mahler: Leben, Werke, Dokumente.* Munich: Piper, 1980.

Natter, Tobias, ed. *Oskar Kokoschka: Early Portraits from Vienna and Berlin, 1909-1914.* New Haven: Yale University Press, 2002.

Nebehay, Christian M. *Egon Schiele. Leben, Briefe, Gedichte.* Vienna: Residenz Verlag, 1979.

Nielsen, Erika, ed. *Focus on Vienna 1900.* Munich: Wilhelm Fink, 1982.

Otto, Rudolf. *The Idea of the Holy.* Translated by John Harvey. New York: Oxford University Press, 1969.

Rennhofer, Maria. *Koloman Moser.* Translated by David Wilson. London: Thames and Hudson, 2002.

Ricoeur, Paul. *Figuring the Sacred.* Minneapolis: Fortress Press, 1995.

Romein, Jan. *The Watershed of Two Eras: Europe in 1900.* Translated by Arnold Pomerans. Middletown, Conn.: Wesleyan University Press, 1978.

Roretz, Karl. *Das religiöse Erlebnis.* Vienna: Österrichische Wochenzeitung, 1966.

Roth, Michael S. "Performing History: Modernist Contextualism in Carl Schorske's *Fin de Siècle Vienna.*" *American Historical Review* 99, no. 3 (June 1994): 729-45.

Rozenblit, Marsha L. *The Jews of Vienna, 1867-1914.* Albany: State University of New York Press, 1983.

Rukschcio, Burkhardt, and Roland Schachel. *Adolf Loos.* Vienna: Residenz Verlag, 1982.

Schick, Paul. *Karl Kraus.* Hamburg: Rowohlt, 1965.

Schorske, Carl. *Fin de Siècle Vienna: Politics and Culture.* New York: Vintage, 1980.

Sekler, Eduard F. *Josef Hoffmann.* Vienna: Residenz Verlag, 1982.

Seliger, Maren, and Karl Ucakar. *Wien. Politische Geschichte, 1750-1934.* Two volumes. Vienna: Jugend und Volk, 1985.

Shedel, James. *Art and Society: The New Art Movement in Vienna, 1897-1914.* Palo Alto: SPOSS, 1981.

Showalter, Elaine. *Sexual Anarchy: Gender and Culture at the Fin de Siècle.* New York: Viking, 1990.

Simpson, Josephine M. N. "Peter Altenberg: A Neglected Writer of the Viennese Jahrhundertwende." Ph.D. dissertation, Edinburgh University, 1987.

Spiel, Hilde. *Vienna's Golden Autumn.* New York: Weidenfeld and Nicolson, 1987.

Swales, Martin. *Arthur Schnitzler: A Critical Study.* Oxford: Clarendon, 1971.

Tannenbaum, Edward R. *1900: The Generation before the Great War.* New York: Doubleday, 1976.

Bibliography

Tax, Petrus, and Richard Lawson, eds. *Arthur Schnitzler and His Age*. Bonn: Bouvier, 1984.

Timms, Edward. *Karl Kraus: Apocalyptic Satirist*. New Haven: Yale University Press, 1986.

Van der Leeuw, Gerardus. *Religion in Essence and Manifestation*. Translated by J. E. Turner. New York: Harper and Row, 1963.

Veith, Gene Edward. *Painters of Faith*. Washington, D.C.: Regnery, 2001.

Viladesau, Richard. *Theology and the Arts*. New York: Paulist Press, 2000.

Wagner, Nike. *Geist und Geschlecht. Karl Kraus und der Erotik der Wiener Moderne*. Frankfurt: Suhrkamp, 1982.

Wagner, Renate. *Frauen um Arthur Schnitzler*. Munich: Jugend und Volk, 1980.

Waissenberger, Robert, ed. *Vienna 1890-1920*. New York: Tabard, 1984.

———, ed. *Wien 1870-1930. Traum und Wirklichkeit*. Vienna: Residenz Verlag, 1984.

Werkner, Patrick. *Austrian Expressionism: The Formative Years*. Translated by Nicholas T. Parsons. Palo Alto: SPOSS, 1986.

West, Shearer. *Fin de Siècle: Art and Society in an Age of Uncertainty*. Woodstock, N.Y.: Overlook Press, 1994.

Whiteside, Andrew G. *The Socialism of Fools: Georg Ritter von Schönerer and Austrian Pan-Germanism*. Berkeley: University of California Press, 1975.

Whitford, Frank. *Oskar Kokoschka*. New York: Atheneum, 1986.

———. *Gustav Klimt*. London: Thames and Hudson, 1990.

Wien um 1900. Klimt, Schiele, und ihre Zeit. Katalog, Sezon (Japan) Museum of Art. 7 October–5 December 1989. Tokyo: Sezon Museum of Art, 1989.

Wohl, Robert. *The Generation of 1914*. Cambridge: Harvard University Press, 1979.

Woodhead, Linda, and Paul Heelas, eds. *Religion in Modern Times*. Malden, Mass.: Blackwell, 2000.

Wunberg, Gotthart, ed. *Das junge Wien*. Two volumes. Tübingen: Max Niemeyer, 1976.

von Wysocki, Gisela. *Peter Altenberg*. Vienna: Hanser, 1979.

Yates, W. E. *Schnitzler, Hofmannsthal, and the Austrian Theater*. New Haven, Conn.: Yale University Press, 1992.

Zohn, Harry. *Karl Kraus*. New York: Twayne, 1971.

———. *Der farbenvolle Untergang*. Englewood Cliffs, N.J.: Prentice-Hall, 1971.

INDEX

Abraham, Chaim, 128

Der Adel und der Conservatismus in Österreich (The Nobility and Conservatism in Austria), 71

Adler, Victor, 252, 262

Adrian, Leopold von, *Garten der Erkentnis (The Garden of Knowledge)*, 189

Akademie der bildenden Künste (Academy of Fine Arts), 75, 179-80, 279

Akademische Gymnasium, 101-2

Alps, 46, 61

Altenberg, Peter, 176-78, 189, 230, 245, 275-76; fascination with adolescence, 176-77; and Kraus, 88, 165, 176, 239, 276; and Loos, 165, 239, 276; pseudonym, 176-77

Altenberg, Peter, works: "Ein Schweres Herz" ("A Heavy Heart"), 177; "Im Volksgarten" ("In the Volksgarten"), 177; "Nacht Theater" ("Night Theater"), 177-78; "Der Nebenmensch" ("The Person by your Side"), 178; "Vor dem Konkurse" ("On the Concourse"), 177

Améry, Jean, 3

"Anna O.," 168

Anthropology, Victorian, 10-12, 13

Anti-Semitism: and anti-immigrant politics, 67, 253, 255; and the avant-garde, 10; and Depression of 1873, 67; and Lueger's populism, 68; and student fraternities, 253, 255; and Wagner's Postal Savings Bank, 285n.5

Art Academy (*Akademie der bildenden Künste*), 75, 179-80, 279

Artists' self-images in fin de siècle Vienna, 245-76; and Bahr, 247-73; dandyism, 264; decadence, 103-4, 105-6, 246, 265; and modernism, 265-71; priestly/prophetic images and roles, 272-75; suffering self-portraits, 273-75; and Wagner cult, 256-61; and youthful rebellion, 249-56. *See also* "Young Vienna"

"Art nouveau" (*Jugendstil*), 114-15, 179, 284, 285, 286

"Arts and crafts movement," 179

Athena, 95, 210

"Augenblick," 313

Augustine, 312

Augustiner Church, 28

Austro-Hungarian Empire, 306; and aristocratic elite, 71; and death of liberalism, 71-73; decline of, 31, 68-73,

88, 178; languages and people, 34; threats to, 69-70. *See also* Habsburgs

Avant-garde, Viennese, 8-10, 308. *See also* Modernism, Viennese; "Young Vienna"

Bacon, Francis, 314

Badeni decrees (1897), 150, 156

Bahr, Alois, 248-49, 251, 261

Bahr, Hermann, 187, 246-73, 305; and "Alba" fraternity, 255; and artistic Naturalism, 264-65, 270; in Berlin, 261-62; as "dandy," 264; on death of liberalism, 251; and the decadents, 103-4, 264; dedication to literature and art, 262; on dream of "Austria," 145-46; early life and background, 247-51; on his generation, 251, 260-61; as Klimt's defender, 141-43; and Kraus, 86, 88, 151-56; and "Loris," 100-101; and modernism, 99, 265-71; on Moser, 282; in Paris, 262-66; personality and influence, 246-47; politics of, 255-56; priestly self-image, 272-73; and religion, 267, 271; on the Secession, 115; seeming/being distinction, 262-64, 265; and Trakl, 243; at University of Vienna, 249, 252, 254-56, 261; and Wagner, 256, 259-61; and the *Wiener Werkstätte*, 280-81; on words/language, 169-70; and Young Vienna, 40, 86-87, 98, 100, 107, 111, 154-55

Bahr, Hermann, works: *A Dialog on Tragedy*, 181; *Die Grosse Sünde (Great Sins)*, 264; "Die Krisis des Naturalismus" ("The Crisis of Naturalism"), 270; "Die Moderne," 269; *Die Überwindung des Naturalismus (Overcoming Naturalism)*, 86, 271

Balkans, 69-70

Ball season, 39-40

Baroque imagination, 61-62

Barrès, Maurice, 105

Barth, Karl, 13

Baudelaire, Charles, 256

Bauhaus school, 288

Baumann, Gerhart, 173-74

Beardsley, Aubrey, 257

Beauty: and artistic form, 266-67; Loos's epiphany about function and, 159; and religiosity in modern art, 266-67, 308, 310

Bechstein, Ludwig, 91

Beckson, Karl, 193

Beer-Hoffmann, Richard: and signs/visions, 137-38, 221; and Young Vienna, 100, 107; *Jaakobs Traum (Jacob's Dream)*, 241; *Der Tod Georgs (George's Death)*, 137-38

Beethoven, Ludwig van, 183, 211-12, 295

Beiträge zu einer Kritik der Sprache (Contributions to a Critique of Language, 1901-1902), 151

Belvedere Palace, 37, 101, 128, 130, 132

Bellevue Hotel, 134

Berg, Alban, 239, 296, 300

Berger, Peter, 5n.15

Berner, Peter, 2

Berry, Philippa, 1

Bethge, Hans, 295

Bettelheim, Bruno, 55

Beuys, Joseph, 314

Bisexuality, 202, 205

Bismarck, Otto von, 31, 66

Boltzmann, Ludwig, 60

Bonhoeffer, Dietrich, 13

Boyer, John, 68-69

Braasch, August Heinrich, 7-8; *Die religiösen Strömungen der Gegenwart*, 7-8

Brahms, Johannes, 77, 184, 259

Breicha, Otto, 2

Brentano, Franz, 9

Breuer, Josef, 168

Breuer, Wilhelm, 202

Brisanz, Hans, 272

Broch, Hermann, 15, 73, 135, 186, 305; *Der Schlafwandler*, 15

Bruck-Auffenberg, Natalie, 194-96, 197; *Die Frau "comme il faut,"* 194-96

Bruckner, Anton, 258, 259, 295
Bucharest National Theater, 76
Burckhardt, Max, 94, 114

Café Casa Piccola, 282
Café Central, 30
Café Dobner, 40
Café Gabesam, 40
Café Griensteidl: demolishment of, 87, 166; and Young Vienna, 40, 86-87, 98, 100, 105, 107, 166
Café Heinrichshof, 281
"Café Megalomania." *See* Café Griensteidl
Café Museum, Loos's interior design of, 162-63, 165
Café Stadtpark, 40
Campbell, Joseph, 18-19
Carlota, daughter of King of the Belgians, 64-65
Carroll, Lewis, 176
Catholic Reformation, 62
Cavour, Camillo, 31, 66
The Chinese Flute (Bethge), 295
Chotek, Countess Sophie, 52, 130-32
Christian Social Party, 67-68
Clemenceau, Georges, 246
Clemenceau, Paul, 246
Clemenceau, Sophie, 246
Coch, Georg, 285n.5
Conversion and cosmic optimism in fin de siècle Vienna, 277-304; and Alma Mahler, 287-91; cosmic optimism in world's religions, 277-78; Mahler's final trilogy, 293-303; Moser and the *Wiener Werkstätte*, 280-82; Schiele's *The Family*, 291-93; Wagner's architectural philosophy, 282-87
Cooke, Deryck, 139, 184, 213, 297, 301
Correlation, method of, 308-9, 310-11
Cosmic optimism, 277-78
Crankshaw, Edward, 245
Cubists, 127
Czechs: and the Austro-Hungarian Empire, 46, 66-67, 68; Czech-language speakers, 34, 35, 150-51, 156; Prague Riots (1897), 68
Czihaczek, Leopold, 232

Dandyism, 86, 264
D'Annunzio, Gabriele, 105
Dante's *Divine Comedy*, 216
Danube River, 45-46
Death aesthetic in fin de siècle Vienna, 58-93; and Baroque imagination, 61-62; fin de siècle and death, 55-56, 63; Habsburgs and curse of death/disaster, 63-71; and Klimt, 79-82; and Kraus's social criticism, 85-88; and Mahler, 89-93, 294-95; and Schiele, 82-83; and Schnitzler, 83-85; suicides, 60-61; Vienna and the macabre/melancholy, 55-57, 59-73; weather and morbidity, 61
De Bleeckere, Sylvain, 7
Decadence, 103-4, 105-6, 245, 264
Depression of 1873, 67, 71, 101
Deutsches Theater (Berlin), 153
Dixon, John, 148, 185
Dreams, 132-40; and Beer-Hofmann, 137-38; Freud's interpretation of, 132-35; and Hofmannsthal, 136-37; and Mahler's Third Symphony, 138-40; in Viennese culture, 132-33
DuBois, W. E. B., 89
Dujardin, Edouard, 257
Duncan, Isadora, 187-88
Dupré, Louis, 12, 147
Durkheim, Emile, 10, 11, 219
Dutch landscapes, 302-3

Eckhart, Meister, 18
Education: and the cultural elite, 150; women's, 204
Edward VII, King, 25
Edwards, Tudor, 36
Ehrhard, Albert, 5-6
Eitelberger, Rudolf von, 279
Eliade, Mircea, 12

Elizabeth, Empress, 25, 52, 55, 65, 129, 190

"Elizabeth von R.," 168

Engelmann, Paul, 167

Engländer, Richard, 176. *See also* Altenberg, Peter

Exposition of 1862 (South Kensington Museum, London), 279

Expressionist literature, 250

Die Fackel (newspaper), 87-88, 159, 180, 198; attacks on Bahr, 153-54; attacks on other papers/media, 126, 149, 153, 170-73; and Hummel execution, 126; and Kraus-Bahr libel trial, 151-56; and purification of language, 152-53

Fairy tales: and Hofmannsthal, 109; and Kokoschka, 224-25, 239; and Mahler, 91; and Schnitzler, 84

Fashion, 197-98; Flöge Salon, 208-9, 283; Loos on, 160, 161, 197-98; and *Wiener Werkstätte*, 180, 282

Faust (Goethe), 187, 213, 215

Fechner, Gustav, *Das Buchlein vom Leben nach dem Tode (The Little Book of Life after Death)*, 135

Feld, Frank, 150

Feminine divine in fin de siècle Vienna, 187-217; female stereotypes and archetypes, 190, 193, 205, 215; and Freud, 191-92; images of young women/the *jugendstil* woman, 189; Klimt's images of women, 189, 206-12; Kraus's social criticism, 198-200, 206; Mahler's Eighth Symphony, 187, 212-17; the nature of women/the essential feminine, 196-98; nervous men and crisis of male ego, 190; the New Woman, 189-90, 193-96; obsession with women and sexuality, 188-206; sexual revolution, 192-93; and Weininger's dissertation, 201-5; the "woman question," 189-90, 193-94; women's advice manuals, 194-96

Feminist movement, 189-90, 193, 204, 205

Fenstergucker (coffeehouse), 40

Ferdinand I, Emperor, 64

Feuerbach, Ludwig, 122n.33

Field, Frank, 150

Fischer, Wolfgang, 3

Flaubert, Gustave, 193

Fledermaus, 180-81, 224

Flöge, Emilie, 208-9, 210, 282

Flöge, Helene, 78, 208, 282

Flöge, Pauline, 282

Flöge Salon, 208-9, 282

Fohleutner, Anna Maria Josefa, 101

"Föhn," 46, 61

Fontane, Theodor, 193

Fransiskaner Church, 28

Franz Ferdinand, Crown Prince, 52, 128, 129-32

Franz Josef, Kaiser: attachment to old ways and routines, 52; and Crown Prince Rudolf, 23-24, 52; and Franz Ferdinand, 52, 130, 131-32; long reign, 31-33, 63-68, 70-71, 129-30; and Loos building on Michaelerplatz, 166; marriage to Elizabeth, 52; and Nüll's suicide, 45, 60

Franz-Josef Gymnasium, 86

Fraternities, student, 252-56

Frazier, James, 10-11

"Free church principle," 135

Freud, Sigmund, 44, 220-21, 246, 305; and Breuer/Weininger's views of bisexuality, 202; on children and psychological development, 191-92, 250; and dream interpretation, 132-35; home on the Berggasse, 133-34; on the "I"/ego, 73; and Mahler, 216, 288; and "oedipal crisis," 192; and psychoanalysis/talking cure, 167-69, 288; on religion, 122n.33; and Schnitzler, 188-89; on the unconscious, 134, 191-92

Freud, Sigmund, works: *The Interpretation of Dreams*, 133, 167, 191; *Jokes and Their Relationship to the Unconscious,*

191; *The Psychopathology of Everyday Life*, 159, 168, 191; *Three Essays in the Theory of Sexuality*, 167, 191
Friedell, Egon, 53
Friedländer, Otto, 32-33, 35, 45-47, 53, 70-71
Friedrich-Wilhelm University (Berlin), 261-62
Fritsch, Gerhard, 2
Futurist literature, 250

Gall, Franz, 255
Garibaldi, Giuseppe, 66
Gay, Peter, 5n.15, 17
George, Stefan, 15, 240
Gerlach's Allegorien, 280
German Empire, 26, 69, 256
German-speakers, 34, 35, 150-51, 156
Gerstl, Richard, 273-74; affair with Schoenberg's wife, 239; self-portraits, 239, 274; suicide, 60; *Self-Portrait, Naked*, 274; *Self-Portrait, Semi-nude against a Blue Background*, 274
Gesamtkunstwerk, 108, 179, 211, 258
Die Gleichheit, 262
Goethe's *Faust*, 187, 213, 215
Göhre, Paul, 6
Gold, Alfred, 238
Goldmark, Karl, 77
Graben, 28, 34, 42, 97
Graf, Max, 182
Graziano, Frank, 242-43
Great War, 237, 250, 305-8
Grillparzer, Franz, 56; *Traum ein Leben (Life Is a Dream)*, 133
Gropius, Walter, 290, 291, 306, 307

Habermas, Jürgen, 16, 18
Habsburgs: cruelty to each other, 52; and curse of death/disaster, 63-71; and dying Empire, 68-73, 88; family marriages, 52; Franz Joseph's reign, 31-33, 63-68, 70-71, 129-30; and omens/signs, 129-32; and Spanish Baroque, 62. *See also* Austro-Hungar-

ian Empire; Franz Ferdinand, Crown Prince; Franz Josef, Kaiser; Rudolf, Crown Prince
Hainisch, Marianne, 194
Hanák, Peter, 59, 132-33
Hanslick, Eduard, 259
Harden, Maximilian, 198
Hardy, Thomas, 4
Harms Schiele, Edith, 236-37, 292, 306
Harnack, Adolf von, 5
Harpf, Adolf, 193-94
Heine, Heinrich, 172-73
Hellwig, Albert, 132
Henderson, Archibald, 144
Hermann, Marie, 89
Herrengasse, 98
Herzl, Theodor, 43-44, 56, 59-60; "Trudy's Tears," 59-60
Heschel, Abraham Joshua, 12
Hevesi, Ludwig, 79, 113, 141, 188
Hick, John, 277-78
Hirschfeld, Magnus, 188
Hitler, Adolf, 259
Hoensbroech, Paul, 5
Hofburg Palace, 22, 28, 32, 37, 39, 42, 70, 77, 98, 130, 166
Hoffmann, Josef: and Kunstschau/Wien exhibition, 225; and Loos, 164; and the Palais Stoclet, 209-10; Secession XIV exhibition interior, 211; and the *Wiener Werkstätte*, 180, 281-82
Hofmann, Isaak Löw, 101
Hofmann, Paul, 48
Hofmann, Werner, 80, 229
Hofmannsthal, Augustin Emil, 101
Hofmannsthal, Hugo August Peter von, 101
Hofmannsthal, Hugo von, 150, 186, 305; and crisis in language, 174-76; death/life themes, 107-9; and the decadents, 103-4, 105-6; early life and youth, 101-4; early writing, 104, 106-9; and fairy tales, 109; family of, 101; and fascination with dreams/visions, 136-37; as "Loris," 100-101, 104, 105;

and modernism/modernist aesthetic,
110-11; and notion of "Zusammenschauen," 108, 109; and the uncanny/
magical realism, 220; and Young
Vienna, 99-111

Hofmannsthal, Hugo von, works:
Alkestis, 109; "Ein Brief" ("Chandos
Letter"), 149, 174-76, 229; *Gerechtigkeit
(Righteousness)*, 220; *Gestern (Yesterday)*,
106, 107-8; "Leben" ("Life"), 106; *Der
Tod des Tizian (Titian's Death)*, 106,
108; *Der Tor und der Tod (Death and the
Fool)*, 106-7, 108-9

Hofoper Opera, 45, 60

Hohermarkt, 38-39

Holy, the, 12, 218-19, 222, 244-45

Homosexuality, 198, 202, 205

House of Hohenzollern, 66

House of Savoy, 66

Hummel, Anna, 124-25

Hummel, Juliane, 124-27

Hungarian-speakers, 156-57

Hygeia, 80, 210

Ibsen, Henrik, 193, 264

Idolatry, 185, 312, 313

Imboden, Michael, 219

Impressionism, 72, 100n.9, 265

Jackson, Andrew, 32

James, Henry, 193

Janik, Allan, 3, 29, 151

"Jesus Seminar," 7

Jewishness, 35, 36; and Depression of
1873, 67; Kraus, 85-86; and language,
151, 156, 185; Mahler, 89-90; and
members of avant-garde, 10;
Schnitzler, 84. *See also* Anti-Semitism

Johnston, William, 29, 72

Josefstadt, 78

Joseph II, Emperor, 98

Jugendstil, 114-15, 179, 284, 285, 286

Kafka, Eduard Michael, 40, 99, 104,
249-50, 268, 271

Kafka, Franz, 220-21

"Kairos," 4, 12, 313

Kalmar, Annie, 198

Kaminka, Rabbi Armand, 136

Kammerer, Rudolf, 289

Kandinsky, Wassily, 15, 240

Karl I, Emperor, 9

Kärtnerstrasse, 34, 42, 97

Kazin, Alfred, 5n.15

Kennedy, Michael, 92-93, 116, 294, 297,
301

Kern, Stephen, 2

Kirche am Steinhof, 286-87

Kläger, Emil, 36

Klimt, Ernst, 75-76, 78, 94, 208, 280,
282

Klimt, Gustav, 294, 304; Bahr's defense
of, 141-43; death of, 83; death theme,
79-82; early illustrations and paintings, 75-77, 94-95; early life and family background, 74, 78; and Emilie
Flöge, 75, 78, 208-9; erotic and intimate images, 77, 206-8, 209-10; images of mythic women, 80-81, 95,
210-11; and *jugendstil*, 284; and
Kokoschka, 225-26, 227; and the
Kunstgewerbeschule, 75; and the
Künstlercompagnie, 75-77, 78, 94-95,
280; and the *Künstlerhaus*, 112; and
Kunstschau/Wien exhibition (1908),
225-26; landscapes, 143-44; and
Moser, 112, 281; notes on self-portrai-
ture, 74; obsession with sex and
love, 75; and Old Burgtheater, 77;
personality/character and work habits, 75, 82; portraits of women, 127,
143, 209; and priestly self-image, 273;
and Schiele, 82-83; and Schnitzler,
83-84; and Secession, 112-15, 178-79,
225, 280; terrifying images, 80-81,
207; "University paintings," 73-74, 77-
82, 140-43; visions, 140-44; and
women, 189, 206-12

Klimt, Gustav, works: *Adele Bloch-Bauer
I*, 127; *Adele Bloch-Bauer II*, 209; "Bee-

thoven Frieze," 211-12; *Death and Life*, 81-82; *Emilie Flöge*, 209; *Fishblood*, 143; *Flowing Water*, 143; *Fritza Riedler*, 209; *Goldfish*, 142; *Hope I*, 81, 212; *Hope II*, 81, 212; *Judith I*, 80-81, 207; *Judith II*, 81, 207; *Justice*, 80, 81, 207; *The Kiss* (1907-08), 210; *The Kiss* (Stocket Palais), 209-10; *Law*, 142; *Love*, 210; *Marie Henneberg*, 127; *Medicine*, 80, 142, 210; *Mermaids (Whitefish)*, 143; "Nuda Veritas," 115, 206-7; "Organist," 95; "Pallas Athene," 95; *Philosophy*, 78-80, 140-42; "Sculpture" (1889), 95; "Sculpture" (1896), 95; Secession I exhibition poster, 114, 210; *Serena Lederer*, 127; *Sonja Knips*, 127, 209; "University paintings," 73-74, 77-82, 140-43; *The Virgin*, 212; "Youth," 95

Klinger, Max, 211

Des Knaben Wunderhorn (The Boy's Magic Horn), 91, 119

Kohlmarkt, 28, 42, 98

Kokoschka, Oskar: and Alma Mahler, 287, 288-91, 306; childhood of, 222-24; debut on Viennese art scene, 222, 225-26; and encounter with the uncanny, 222-30; and the Great War, 306-7; and Klimt, 225-26, 227; and Kraus, 88, 230; and the Kunstgewerbeschule, 224, 279; and Kunstschau 1909, 226-27; and Loos, 165, 230, 289; portraits, 226-28; and Schoenberg, 239; and summer 1908 Kunstschau, 225-26; and Trakl, 243; visionary perspective/ability, 227-30; and the *Wiener Werkstätte*, 224-25; on women, 190

Kokoschka, Oskar, works: *Father Hirsch*, 227; *The Knight Errant*, 306; *Mörder, Hoffnung der Frauen (Murderer, the Hope of Women)*, 225-26, 230; *The Portrait of Adolf Loos*, 227; *The Portrait of Professor Forel*, 227; self-portrait, 275; *The Speckled Egg*, 224; *Sphinx und*

Strohmann (Sphinx and Strawman), 226; *Still Life*, 228-29; *The Trance Player*, 227; *Die Traümenden Knaben (The Dreaming Youths)*, 224-25, 239; "Vom Bewusstsein der Gesichte" ("On the Nature of Visions"), 229-30; *Die Windsbraut (The Bride of the Wind)*, 290-91, 306

Krafft-Ebing, Richard von, 188

Kraus, Karl, 279, 305; and Altenberg, 88, 165, 176, 239, 276; attacks on newspapers/media, 126, 149, 153, 170-73; and Bahr, 86, 88, 151-56; and the coffeehouse intellectuals, 86-87; on the dying Empire, 70, 88; early life, 85-86; on the Fledermaus, 180-81; Jewishness, 85-86; and Klimt's university paintings, 142; and Kokoschka, 88, 230; libel trial, 151-56; and Loos, 88, 165, 166-67, 239; on prostitution laws, 198-200, 205; satirical talents, 86, 87-88; and the "Sirk," 97; social criticism on sexuality and moral hypocrisy, 189, 198-200, 206; and Trakl, 243; and words/language, 149-50, 151-56, 169-73. See also *Die Fackel* (newspaper)

Kraus, Karl, works: "Die Demolierte Literatur" ("Demolished Literature"), 87, 155; "The Good Conduct Medal," 198-200; "Heine und die Folgen" ("Heine and the Consequences"), 173; *Die Letzten Tagen der Menschheit (Humanity's Last Days)*, 97; "Overcoming Hermann Bahr," 86; *Sittlichkeit und Kriminalität (Morality and Criminality)*, 189; "Vom Wechselgastspiel" ("Guest performers"), 153

Die Kreuzeitung (newspaper), 22

Kruger, Charles, 301

Kulka, Julius, 268

Kunstakademie (Academy of High Arts), 162

Kunstgewerbeschule (School of Ap-

plied Arts), 162, 179-80, 224, 279-80,
282
Kunsthistorisches Museum, 76
Künstlercompagnie (the "Artist Com-
pany"), 75-77, 78, 94-95, 280
Künstlerhaus, 111-12
Kunstschau/Wien (1908), 225-26

Landsdale, Maria, guide to Vienna, 21,
34, 38-39, 41-42, 54-55, 62-63, 96-97
Lang, Oskar, 258-59
Language, crisis in, 149-86; and
Altenberg, 176-78; Freud and psy-
choanalysis, 167-69; and
Hofmannsthal, 174-76; Kraus and the
press/media, 149-50, 153, 170-73;
Kraus-Bahr libel trial, 151-56; lan-
guage and tone in politics, 157; lan-
guages spoken, 34, 35, 150-51, 156-57;
Loos, 157-67; Mahler, 182-86;
Schnitzler, 173-74, 181; and the Seces-
sion, 178-81; theological understand-
ings of the "word," 185-86; words
and meaning (reality/illusion), 151,
152
Laurence, Richard, 72
Lax, Petrus, 152
Levetus, A. S., 38; *Imperial Vienna*, 65
Liberalism: the liberal "I," 72, 73; modernism and death of, 17-18, 71-72, 251
Liebestod, 290
Lipiner, Siegfried, *Buch der Freude* (*Book
of Joy*), 135
Li Tai-Po, 296, 298
Loos, Adolf, 157-67, 239, 305; and
Altenberg, 165, 239, 276; in America,
157-59; architectural designs of, 162-
63, 165-67; early life, 157-58; epiphany
about function and beauty, 159; on
fashion, 160, 161, 197-98; and
Hoffmann, 164; and interior design,
160; and Isadora Duncan, 187-88;
and Kokoschka, 165, 230, 289; and
Kraus, 88, 165, 166-67, 239; the "modern" and design in everyday life, 159-

65; music reviews, 158-59; and the
Palais Stoclet, 209-10; and priestly
self-image, 273; reviews and com-
mentaries, 159-65; and Ringstrasse
aesthetic, 163, 284; and Secession
Building, 164; and Secessionists, 163-
65; and Wagner, 259
Loos, Adolf, articles: "Die
Herrenmode" ("Men's Fashion"), 160;
"Die Intereurs in der Rotunde" ("In-
teriors in the Rotunde"), 160; "Orna-
ment und Verbrechen," 164-65, 238;
"Our Young Architects," 162; "The
Potemkin City," 163
"Loris," 100-101, 104, 105
Ludwig, Archduke Charles, 65
Lueger, Karl, 67-69
Luft, David, 17
Luxury shopping, 42

Mach, Ernst, 72
Mach, Franz, 135
Maheu, Jean, 151
Mahler, Alma, 287-91, 301, 306; family
and youth, 287; and Gropius, 288,
289, 306, 307; and Gustav, 89, 90,
287-88, 294; and Klimt, 75; and
Kokoschka, 287, 288-91, 306; on
Third Symphony, 138-39; and *Die
Windsbraut*, 290-91
Mahler, Bernard, 89
Mahler, Ernst, 90-91
Mahler, Gustav, 116-23, 293-303, 305;
and Alma, 89, 90, 287-88, 294;
boundary-expanding symphonies,
182-83, 186; as conductor, 116, 182,
293; and crisis of language, 182-86;
daughter's death, 91, 293; death
themes, 89-93, 294-95; early life, 89-
91; and fairytales, 91; family, 89-91;
and Freud, 216, 288; health, 91, 293-
95; leaving Vienna, 293, 294; and nature, 138, 302-3; and omens/signs,
138-40; personality and character,
90, 91; resurrection/rebirth themes,

117-23; and Schoenberg, 140, 239, 294; and Secession XIV exhibition, 211; and Wagner, 258-59; works of religious transfiguration, 301-3

Mahler, Gustav, works: "Des Antonius von Padua Fischpredigt" ("St. Anthony Preaches to the Fishes"), 118; *Das klagende Lied (A Sorrowful Song)*, 91-92, 116; *Lieder eines fahrenden Gesellen* (Gesellen songs), 92-93, 116; *Das Lied von der Erde*, 277, 294, 295-300, 301-2; First Symphony, 91, 116-17, 183; Second Symphony, 117-23, 182, 183; Third Symphony, 124, 138-40, 182; Fourth Symphony, 183; Sixth Symphony, 183-84; Seventh Symphony, 184-85; Eighth Symphony, 187, 212-17, 294; Ninth Symphony, 294, 295-96, 300, 301-2; Tenth Symphony, 294, 300-301, 303

Mahler, Maria, 91, 293

Mahler, Otto, 60, 91

Majolica House, 284-85

Makart, Hans, 76, 111

Malinowski, Bronislaw, 1, 4, 58, 59

Mantegazza, Paul, *Die Physiologie der Liebe*, 196-97

Marcus Aurelius, 31

Martens, Lorna, 220-21

Martin, Agnes, 314

Marx, Karl, 259, 263

Matsch, Franz, 74, 75-76, 78, 94, 280

Mauthner, Fritz, 151

Maximilian, Archduke, 64-65

Mayerling suicides, 21-24, 22n.1, 27-28

Media. *See* Newspapers

Melba, Nellie, 158

Mendelssohn, Felix, 259

Mendieta, Eduardo, 18

Merkel, Reinhard, 149-50, 170

Metternich, Klemens von, 46, 64

Mexico, 64

Meyer, Marie, 47-48

Meynert Clinic, 9

Michaelerplatz, 98, 166; and Café

Griensteidl, 86-87, 98, 166; Loos building, 166; and Old Burgtheater, 77; redesign of, 87, 166; and Rudolf's funeral procession, 28

Mies van der Rohe, Ludwig, 6-7

Milde, Natalie, 193

Miller, J. Hillis, 5n.15

Mises Ludwig von, 8

Moderne Dichtung (Modern Poetry), 40, 104, 250, 268-69

Modernism, Viennese, 1-19; and artistic form, 266-68; and the avant-garde, 8-10, 308; and Bahr, 220, 265-71; and cosmic synthesis, 265-66; and end of cultural blossoming, 304-8; and liberalism, 17-18, 71-72, 71-73, 251; Loos and design in everyday life, 159-65; and other birthplaces of modernism, 3; and postmodernism, 1, 310; and reality, 220-21, 310-11; and religion, 4-8, 14-16, 266-67, 308-15; reuniting romanticism and naturalism, 270-71; scholars' explanations, 17-18; and secularism, 4-8, 5n.15, 16, 309

Modernism and religion, 4-8, 14-16, 266-67, 308-15; and beauty, 266-67, 308, 310; defining religion, 10-14; and method of correlation, 308-9, 310-11; and religious experiences, 12-15; and transcendence, 267, 312-15; yearning for the mystical, 220

Moll, Carl, 112, 287, 288-89

Moore, George, 257

Morton, Frederic, 60

Moser, Koloman, 279-82, 306; and Klimt, 112, 280; and Kunstschau/Wien exhibition, 225; and Secession, 112, 113, 114, 280; *Self-Portrait*, 274; as teacher, 282; and Otto Wagner, 284-85, 286; and *Wiener Werkstätte*, 180, 280-82

Munch, Edvard, 190

Museum für Kunst und Gewerbe (Museum of the Applied Arts), 179

Museum für Kunst und Industrie (Museum for Art and Industry), 75, 162, 279

Museum of Contemporary Art (Chicago), exhibition "Negotiating Rapture," 314

Musil, Robert, 17, 69, 220-21; *Der Mann ohne Eigenschaften (The Man Without Qualities)*, 178, 305

Myrbach, Baron Felician von, 113

Napoleon Bonaparte, 37
Napoleonic Wars, 252
Napoleon III, Emperor, 64, 66
Nationalists, racial, 193-94
Naturalism, 264-65, 270-71
Neue Freie Presse: on election of Lueger, 68; and Herzl, 43-44, 56; on Hummel execution, 125, 126-27; Kraus's vendetta against, 170-73; on Mayerling suicides, 22-24, 27; on New Year (1900), 129; "personals," 51; on Rudolf's funeral procession, 28-29; suicide reports, 61; on superstitiousness in Vienna, 48; on Vienna on cusp of modernism, 26; on Vienna's peculiarities, 44, 54

Neues deutsches Märchenbuch, 91
Neues Wiener Tagblatt, 58, 125-26
Neumann, Friedrich, 60-61
Neuzil, Wally, 233, 235, 236, 237, 291-92
Newman, Barnett, 314
Newspapers: and appetite for words, 150; and coffeehouse culture, 41; German-American, 158-59; on Hummel execution, 125-27; Kraus's vendetta against, 126, 149, 153, 170-73; and mass advertising, 171-72; and Mayerling suicides, 22-24, 27; "personals," 50-51, 171; suicide reports, 60-61; on Vienna's peculiarities, 44, 53-54. See also *Die Fackel* (newspaper); *Neue Freie Presse; Neues Wiener Tagblatt; Die Zeit* (newspaper)

New Woman, 189-90, 193-96. *See also* Feminine divine in fin de siècle Vienna

New Yorker Bannerträger, 158-59
New Yorker Staatszeitung, 158-59
New York Music Critics Association, 159
Nietzsche, Friedrich: artist as "Übermensch," 272; and death of God, 4, 18, 120-21, 241; and Mahler's Third Symphony, 124; rants against women, 190; *The Twilight of the Idols*, 1; and Wagner, 257, 259, 259n.22, 260
Nobelgymnasium Theresianum auf der Wieden (the *Theresianum* gymnasium), 279
Nordau, Max, 63, 205; *Degeneration*, 63

Occult revival, 135-36
Olbricht, Josef, 113, 164, 280, 286
Old Burgtheater, 77
Omens. *See* Signs and omens in fin de siècle Vienna
Osen, Erwin, 233
Otto, Rudolf, 12, 218-19, 244

Palais Stoclet, 209-10
Palmer, Alan, 25
Pappenheim, Bertha, 168
Parades, 54
Partsch, Susanna, 189
Piedmont, 31, 66
Plato, 267
Polgar, Alfred, 30
Polk, James K., 32
Pollack, Michale, 3
Pollak, Theobald, 295
Ponischil, Joseph, 129
Popp, Adelheid, 194
Postal Savings Bank, 285n.5, 285-86
Postmodernism, 1, 310
Prague riots (1897), 68
Prater amusement park, 36, 42-44, 304
Press. *See* Newspapers
Prince of Wales, 25
Prostitution laws, 198-200

Prussia, 5, 6, 31, 66, 88
Psychoanalysis, 167-69, 288
Pulzer, Peter, 67

Raupach, Ernst, "The Miller and His Child," 56
Reality: and Bahr's seeming/being distinction, 262-64, 265; and illusion/cultural confusion, 151, 152; and modernism, 220-21, 310-11; and the Secession, 164; spatial metaphors for, 220-21
Reichel, Oskar, 228
Reinhold, Ernst, 227
Religion. *See* Modernism and religion
Resurrection/Rebirth in fin de siècle Vienna, 94-123; and Klimt, 94-95; Mahler's Second Symphony, 117-23; Secession and the Vienna art world, 111-15; Vienna landmarks and atmosphere, 96-98; and "Young Vienna," 98-111
Revolutions of 1848, 63-64, 66
Revue wagnérienne, 257
Ricoeur, Paul, 12
Riis, Jacob, 36
Ringstrasse: buildings' style, 29-30, 45, 163; construction of, 37-39; landmarks and tourism, 96-97; peculiarities, 44-45; and Wagner's historicist aesthetic, 283-84
Rodin, Auguste, 304
Roessler, Alfred, 231-33, 234-35, 236, 237
Roller, Alfred, 90, 112, 113, 114, 294
Roosevelt, Theodore, Jr., 67
Roosevelt, Theodore, Sr., 67
Roth, Josef, 305
Rückert, Friedrich, 182
Rudolf, Crown Prince, 21-29, 64, 130; on the dying Empire, 70; and father Franz Joseph, 23-24, 52; funeral procession, 28-29; marriage to Stephanie, 23, 25, 52; and Mary Vetsera, 21-22, 27-28; and mother Elizabeth, 25, 52; suicide, 21-24, 65, 129, 219

Rudowsky, Carl, 58-59
Russian Empire, 69

Salten, Felix: and Kraus, 87; and Loos, 164; on Mahler, 116; and Young Vienna, 40, 86, 105, 107
Schaukal, Richard, 166
Scheu, Robert, 159
Schiele, Adolf, 231
Schiele, Edith, 236-37, 292, 306
Schiele, Egon, 189, 230-37, 291-93; artistic style, 82-83, 234-37; death of, 83, 237, 306; and death theme, 82-83; early work, 233-34; and Edith, 236-37, 292; family and early life, 231-33; and Klimt, 82-83; obsession with love, 233-35; scandalous arrest and sentence, 235-36; self-portraits, 234, 236, 274-75; and the uncanny, 230-37; and Wally Neuzil, 233, 235, 236, 237, 291-92
Schiele, Egon, works: *Death and the Girl (Self-Portrait with Walli)*, 83; *The Family*, 291-93; *Johann Harms*, 291; *Marga Boerner*, 291; *Pregnant Woman and Death*, 83
Schiele, Marie Soukup, 231, 232
Schiller, Friedrich, 115
Schimkowitz, Othmar, 286
Schindler, Alma, 287. *See also* Mahler, Alma
Schindler, Emil, 287
Schleiermacher, Friedrich, 12
Schneider, Georg, 136
Schnitzler, Arthur, 144-46, 154, 288, 305; and Altenberg, 176, 276; fictional characters and crisis of language, 173-74, 181; fiction of intimacy and sexuality, 188-89; Jewishness, 84; and Klimt, 83-84; and love/death themes, 83-85, 146; one-act plays, 144-45; and the uncanny, 219-21; and women/the feminine, 188-89; and Young Vienna, 86, 87, 100, 105, 107; youth, 250-51

Schnitzler, Arthur, works: *Anatol* dramas, 84-85; *Liebelei*, 85; *Lieutenant Gustl*, 145; *Das Märchen (A Fairytale)*, 84; *Reigen*, 146; *Die Traumnovelle (Dream Novel)*, 219; *Der Weg ins Freie (The Way of Freedom)*, 181; *Zum grossen Wurstel*, 145

Schoenberg, Arnold, 238-42, 287, 296; early life and early works, 238-39; and external realities, 263; and Mahler, 140, 239, 294; on Mahler's Third Symphony, 140; premiere of Second String Quartet (1910), 15-16, 240; religious themes, 241-42; self-portraits, 239; strange life, 239-40

Schoenberg, Arnold, works: *The Book of the Hanging Gardens*, 239; *Gurrelieder*, 238; "In hellen Träumen hab ich dich oft geschaut" ("In clear dreams I've often seen you"), 238; *Pelléas und Mélisande*, 238; *Pierrot lunaire*, 240-42; *Red Stare*, 239; Second String Quartet, 15-16, 240; *Verklärte Nacht*, 238

Schoenberg, Mathilde Zemlinsky, 238, 239, 273

Schönbrunn Palace, 37

Schönerer, Georg von, 67, 157, 255, 261

Schopenhauer, Arthur, 260, 261; *Die Welt als Wille und Vorstellung (The World as Will and Representation)*, 260

Schorske, Carl: on dying Empire, 71-72; on Kokoschka, 222, 224; on religion and art in Vienna, 14-15; on Schoenberg, 238, 239, 241; on Viennese modernism and death of liberalism, 17-18, 71-72; on Wagner's Postal Savings Bank, 285, 285n.5, 286

Schratt, Katherina, 77

Schreker, Franz, 289

Schröder, Klaus Albrecht, 189, 274-75

Schwarzenbergplatz, 39

Schwarzwald School, 239

Secession, 111-15, 178-81; and earlier artistic secessions, 112; efforts to raise level of art/change art, 112, 115, 179;

journal *Ver Sacrum*, 113-15, 163; *Jugendstil*/Art Nouveau images, 114-15, 179; and Klimt, 112-15, 178-79, 280; Klimt's secession from, 225; and Kokoschka's fairytale, 224; and the Kunstgewerbeschule, 179-80; and the *Künstlerhaus*, 112; and Loos, 163-65; and "modernism," 113; and Moser, 112, 113, 114, 280; name and motto, 113; and reality, 164; rejuvenation/rebirth images, 114-15; and Wagner's architectural designs, 286; and the *Wiener Werkstätte*, 179-81

Secession Building, 113, 164, 280, 286

Secession I exhibition (1898): Klimt's poster, 114, 210

Secession XIV exhibition (1902), 114, 211-12; Klimt's Beethoven Frieze, 211-12; Klinger's Beethoven statue, 211

Self-portraits, 74, 234, 236, 239, 273-75

Semmering district, 289

Seuse Denifle, Heinrich, *Das Geistige Leben (The Spiritual Life)*, 136

Sexuality: Freud on, 191-92; and gender, 202; homosexuality/bisexuality, 202; ideal types/poles, 202-5; Kraus's social criticism on moral hypocrisy, 198-200, 206; and the New Woman, 188-90, 193-96; sexual revolution, 192-93; Weininger's dissertation, 201-5; and women, 203-5. *See also* Feminine divine in fin de siècle Vienna

Seydel, Rudolf, 6

Shapiro, Joseph, 314-15

Shawn, Allen, 240

Signs and omens in fin de siècle Vienna, 55, 59-73, 124-48; cultural crisis of belief and search for meaning, 135-38, 147-48; dreams, 132-40; and Habsburg family, 129-32; Klimt's visions, 140-44; and Mahler, 138-40; occult revival, 135-36; Schnitzler's plays and stories, 144-46; signs of the new century, 128-29; supersti-

tiousness, 47-48, 132. *See also* Uncanny and fin de siècle Vienna
"Sirk," 97
Social-Democratic movement, 252
Sophie, Countess, 52, 130-32
South Kensington Museum (London), 279
Spanish Baroque, 61-62
Specht, Richard, 99
St. Michael's Church, 98
St. Peter's Church, 4, 97-98
St. Stephen's cathedral, 26, 28, 34, 42, 45, 97
Steed, Henry Wickham, 148
Stephanie, Crown Princess, 23, 25, 52
Stifter, Adelbert, 248
Stoclet, Adolphe, 209
Stone, Norman, 3
Strauss, Eduard, *Schleier und Krone* (Veil and Crown), 25
Strauss, Franz, 60
Strauss, Johann, *Myrthenblütenwälzer*, 25
Strauss, Richard, "Also Sprach Zarathustra," 141
Strunz, Franz, 132
Der Sturm, 275
Suicides, 60-61, 305; Crown Prince Rudolf, 21-24, 65, 129, 219; Mayerling, 21-24, 22n.1, 27-28
Superstition: Mahler and Ninth Symphony, 295-96, 300; Viennese beliefs in, 47-48, 132. *See also* Signs and omens in fin de siècle Vienna
Suttner, Bertha von, 194
Swales, Martin, 3
Swinburne, Algernon, 257
Symbolism (movement), 265
Szeps, Moritz, 26, 170, 247
Szeps-Zuckerkandl, Bertha, 246-47, 304

Tchaikovsky, Pyotr, 184
Theresianum gymnasium, 279
Thornhill, John, 5n.15
Tillich, Paul, 18, 304, 308-9, 311-13; on God as the Unconditioned, 311-13;

"kairos," 4, 12, 313; on religion and ultimate concern, 14, 304, 311-13
Tivoli Café, 75
Tolstoy, Leo, 193
Toulmin, Stephen, 3, 151
Trains, 96
Trakl, Georg, 242-45, 290, 305; early life, 242-43; and the Great War, 305; poems, 243-45; strangeness and visions of, 242-43; suicide, 60, 305; and the uncanny, 242-45; "Amen," 244-45; "De profundis," 243-44
Trakl, Grete, 243, 305
Trakl, Tobias, 242
Transcendence, 267, 312-15; and awareness of the Unconditioned, 312-13, 314; negotiating rapture, 314; and religiosity in modern art, 267, 312-15; and symbolic expression/language, 313-14
Trummer, Thomas, 227-28
Tschang Tsi, 297
Tyler, Edward, 10-11

"Übermensch," 272
Uchatius, General Baron Franz von, 60
Uncanny and fin de siècle Vienna, 218-45; and Hofmannsthal, 220; and the Holy, 218-19, 222, 244-45; and Kokoschka, 222-30; Kuntschau 1908, 222, 225-26; Kuntschau 1909, 222, 226-27; and Schiele, 230-37; and Schnitzler, 219-21; and Schoenberg, 238-42; and spatial metaphors for "reality," 220-21; and Trakl, 242-45. *See also* Signs and omens in fin de siècle Vienna
Unconditioned, the, 311-14
University of Czernowitz, 261
University of Graz, 261
University of Vienna: Bahr at, 249, 252, 254-56, 261; redesign of, 39, 73-74, 254-55; student fraternities at, 254-55

Van der Leeuw, Gerardus, 12

Van der Nüll, Eduard, 45, 60

Veith, Gene, 302

Vereinigung Bildender Künstler Osterreichs (the Association of Austrian Artists), 113

Ver Sacrum (Secession journal), 113-15, 163

Very, Françoise, 165

Vetsera, Mary, 21-22, 22n.1, 27-28

Victoria, Queen, 31-32, 259

Vienna, fin de siècle, 21-57; artists' self-images, 245-76; ball season, 39-40; city atmosphere, 41-42, 54-55, 96-98; city borders, 46-47; city bureaucrats, 49; as city of contradictions, 29-30; as city of illusions/multiple realities, 48-57; city peculiarities, 44-47, 52-54; class differences and class rank, 49-50; coffeehouse culture, 40-41; conversion and cosmic optimism, 277-303; costume and dress, 49; cultural crisis of belief/search for meaning, 135-38, 147-48; death aesthetic, 58-93; defining, 8; ethnic heterogeneity, 33-35, 34; the feminine, 187-217; fin de siècle mood, 55-56, 63; geographic size, 35; the Habsburgs, 21-29, 31-33, 52; historic Inner City, 42; history of city growth from medieval times, 36-39; immigration, 33-34, 35-36; landmarks, 38-39, 41-42, 96-98; Landsdale's guide to, 21, 34, 38-39, 41-42, 54-55, 62-63, 96-97; language crisis, 149-86; luxury shopping, 42; neighborhoods, 35-36; obsession with signs and omens, 55, 59-73, 124-48; parades, 54; population growth, 34-35; public/private, 50-51; resurrection/rebirth, 94-123; social rules, 52-53; society, 39-44; suicides, 60-61; superstitiousness, 47-48, 132; time-keeping and public clocks, 44; the uncanny, 218-45; weather, 46, 61. *See also* Habsburgs; Modernism, Viennese; Ringstrasse; "Young Vienna"

Vienna Woods ("Wienerwald"), 61

Viladesau, Richard, 266-67, 308-10

Volkstheater, 153

Von Alt, Rudolf, 112

Waerndorfer, Fritz, 180, 281

Wagner, Otto, 282-87, 306; and *jugendstil*/Art Nouveau, 284, 285, 286; and Moser, 284-85, 286; philosophy of architecture, 283-84

Wagner, Otto, works: *jugendstil* tram station at the Karlskirche, 284; *Kirche am Steinhof*, 286-87; Majolica House, 284-85; *Die moderne Architektur (Modern Architecture)*, 283; Postal Savings Bank, 285-86

Wagner, Richard, 108, 256-61; and Bahr, 256, 259-61; contradictions of, 259; cult of, 256-61; death of, 261; operas, 256, 257-58; on religion and art, 135-36

Wagner, Richard, works: *Judaism in Music*, 259; *Die Kunst und die Revolution (Art and Revolution)*, 260; *Das Kunstwerk der Zukunft (The Art of the Future)*, 260; *Die Meistersinger*, 257; "Religion and Art," 135-36

Wahrmund, Ludwig, 5

Walter, Bruno, 184, 294, 295

Wang Wei, 299

War of 1859, 66

Weather, 46, 61, 129

Webern, Anton, 239, 296

Wedekind, Frank, *Frühlings Erwachen (Spring Awakens)*, 250

Weigel, Hans, 132

Weininger, Otto: suicide of, 60; *Geschlecht und Charakter (Sexuality and Character)*, 201-5

Wells, David, 5n.15

Werfel, Franz, 307

West, Shearer, 63, 135

Weygand, General Maxime, 65

Whistler, James MacNeil, 257

Whitford, Frank: on Klimt, 77, 78-79;

on Kokoschka, 223, 226, 237, 289-90, 306, 306n.4

Wiener Mode (fashion magazine), 194

Wiener Werkstätte (Vienna Workshops), 179-81, 224-25, 280-82

Wiesinger, Albert, 4

Wilde, Oscar, 257, 272

Wilhelm I, Emperor, 26, 128

Wilhelm II, Emperor, 25, 26, 128, 198

Wilson, Edmund, 5n.15

Wilson, Woodrow, 32

Wittgenstein, Ludwig, 60, 149, 170, 243

Wolf, Hugo, 259

Wolff, Eugen, 268-69; *Die jüngste deutsche Literaturströmung und das Prinzip der Moderne (Recent Currents in German Literature and the Principle of the Modern)*, 268-69; "Die Moderne. Zur Revolution und Reformation der Literatur" ("Modernism: On Revolution and Reformation in Literature"), 268

Women. *See* Feminine divine in fin de siècle Vienna; New Woman

World Exposition (1873), 67

World War I (Great War), 237, 250, 305-8

World War II, 305

Wundt, Wilhelm, 58, 59

Yeats, W. B., 257

"Young Vienna," 40, 98-111; Bahr and the café intellectuals, 86-87, 98, 100-101, 154-55; and Café Griensteidl, 40, 86-87, 98, 100, 105, 107, 166; and Hofmannsthal, 99-111; modernist ethic of, 99, 110-11; name for, 99-100; and nervousness, 111

Die Zeit (newspaper), 155, 161-62

Zemlinsky, Alexander von, 238, 287, 294

Zemlinsky Schoenberg, Mathilde, 238, 239, 273

Zentralfriedhof cemetery, 62

Ziolkowski, Theodore, 15

Zohn, Harry, 152

Zola, Emile, 264, 265-66

Zuckerkandl, Bertha, 145, 246-47, 304

Zuckerkandl, Emil, 246

"Zusammenschauen," 108, 109

Zweig, Stefan, 101